The Essence of Teaching Social

Designed for use in elementary and secondary social studies education courses, this book supports the teaching of social studies methods in a range of educational settings. By highlighting long-standing content and principles of social studies education in a concise and direct way, this volume offers the building blocks of a comprehensive course, for use as springboards to the effective presentation of professors' desired course emphases. With sections on foundations, subject areas, and best practices, this text explains the intersection between the "modelling" role of social studies teachers as democratic citizens, social studies fields of study, and strategies implemented in the classroom to encourage students' critical thinking and values formation.

James A. Duplass is Professor of Social Studies Education at the University of South Florida.

The Essence of Teaching Social Studies

Methods for Secondary and Elementary Teacher Candidates

James A. Duplass

Routledge
Taylor & Francis Group

NEW YORK AND LONDON

First published 2021
by Routledge
52 Vanderbilt Avenue, New York, NY 10017

and by Routledge
2 Park Square, Milton Park, Abingdon, Oxon, OX14 4RN

Routledge is an imprint of the Taylor & Francis Group, an informa business

© 2021 Taylor & Francis

Library of Congress Cataloging-in-Publication Data
Names: DuPlass, James A., 1947- author.
Title: The essence of teaching social studies : methods for secondary and elementary teacher candidates James A. DuPlass.
Description: New York, NY : Routledge, 2021. | Includes bibliographical references and index.
Identifiers: LCCN 2020019974 (print) | LCCN 2020019975 (ebook) | ISBN 9780367559144 (hardback) | ISBN 9780367363819 (paperback) | ISBN 9781003095682 (ebook)
Subjects: LCSH: Social sciences–Study and teaching (Secondary)–United States. | Social sciences–Study and teaching (Elementary)–United States. | Social science teachers–Training of–United States.
Classification: LCC H62.5.U5 D86 2021 (print) | LCC H62.5.U5 (ebook) | DDC 300.71/2–dc23
LC record available at https://lccn.loc.gov/2020019974
LC ebook record available at https://lccn.loc.gov/2020019975

ISBN: 978-0-367-55914-4 (hbk)
ISBN: 978-0-367-36381-9 (pbk)
ISBN: 978-1-003-09568-2 (ebk)

Typeset in Times
by Swales & Willis, Exeter, Devon, UK

To

Social Studies Educators

"The Weight of the World is on Your Shoulders."

The image on the paperback cover is of Atlas, who, in Greek mythology, was condemned to hold up the celestial heavens for eternity. A common misconception is that Atlas was forced to carry Earth on his shoulders. But in Greek mythology, the "heavens" are also conceived of a sphere like earth. This mythological story is, however, the origin of the expression "He is carrying the weight of the world on his shoulders."

Teachers of the social studies carry the weight of the world on their shoulders because they are crucial to students who are in the midst of developing the personal and civic identity necessary for the democratic ethos that is essential to the advancement of human potential and society.

Contents

Figures

About the Author

Jimmy Duplass graduated from De La Salle High School in New Orleans and received his degrees from Loyola and Saint Louis Universities. He began his teaching career at the elementary school level in the New Orleans public schools and taught high school while working on his master's degree in counseling. Dr. Duplass has held faculty appointments at Saint Louis University, Loyola, Penn State University, and the University of South Florida. Professor Duplass has taught courses in elementary, middle, and high school social studies methods, social studies reading and basic skills, introduction to technology, philosophical foundations of education, and philosophy of social studies education to undergraduates, master's, and doctoral students.

Dr. Duplass has written seven books, a collection of short stories, over 30 academic articles, and multiple presentations at national and regional conferences. He has received an award for outstanding teaching and a short story, Certificate of Merit from the City of New Orleans, and over $1 million in grants.

Jimmy is married to Anne Heintz Duplass with two children: Chris Duplass, a family physician in the suburbs of Philadelphia, is married to Tina; and Ellie Duplass Tsikalas, a nurse practitioner in a pediatric practice in Madison, Alabama, is married to Manny. "Poppy" has three grandchildren: Liz Duplass, Carly Duplass, and Simon Tsikalas.

Foreword

I am not sure if it is quaint or awkward when telling teacher candidates that I started teaching when the best tools were electric typewriters and mimeograph machines.

The Student Is the Subject

I no longer think of my first job as a teacher at a "black" elementary school in inner-city New Orleans as being the beginning of my career. I now recognize that it started as a YMCA day camp counselor during the summers of high school and college, where I began to understand that teaching was more about the student than the subject. Or better put, when teaching social studies, "The student is the subject!"

My Identity

My identity was certainly shaped by my parents – only one of whom graduated from high school. For both, education for their children was the highest priority. They sacrificed to send all four children to the best schools in New Orleans. Mrs. Erwin, a World War II widow, and Sister Mary Alice were typical of the caring teachers I had in elementary school. As a child, the overly dramatic *Roy Rogers Show* and *Superman* TV series unashamedly encouraged consideration of virtues and *Father Knows Best* portrayed the idyllic family. I read a biography of every president by the end of 8th grade. De La Salle High School led me to Mr. Murphy, the best teacher (social studies, as you might expect) I ever had, and Brother Jeffrey, both of whom cared more about me than I deserved. Discussions in Mr. Murphy's classes, movies such as *Laurence of Arabia* and *Giant*, plays like *The Andersonville Trial*, and books like *To Kill a Mockingbird* and *Profiles in Encourage* compelled me to reflect on democratic ideals and the kind of person I was and wanted to be.

Education

The required philosophy courses taken as an undergraduate introduced me to analytical, systematic thinking and Western Civilization's most impactful intellectuals. All three degrees are from Jesuit universities, which in their unique way placed questions about what kind of person and citizen one should become at the forefront of their curriculum. Jesuits Barry McGannon and Frank Brennan were instrumental in shaping my early career. Mr. Levy, the consummate professional, was my cooperating teacher for the final internship and hired me the next year when he became assistant principal of the high school. My journey from high school social studies teacher through a master's in counseling and doctorate in education and stints as a university faculty member and administrator at Saint Louis, Loyola, Wayne State, Penn State University, and the University of South Florida was circuitous, and nothing if not interesting.

Colleagues

My career as a social studies professor began in earnest when Dr. Barbara Cruz, a Cuban refugee, and I came to USF at the same time. One could not ask for a better, more generous, supportive, and courageous colleague, without whom my work as a professor would never have been realized. The organic synergism of two first-generation college graduates, who had the good fortune to learn the expectations of the academy from outstanding mentors, has led to a wonderful, 30-year friendship and collaboration on program innovation, mentoring of students, teaching, scholarship, publications, and presentations. During our careers, the USF program in social studies education became the largest in the nation. The students' discussions in my doctoral course in philosophy of social studies education were a testing ground for the theory and practices articulated in this book. Our doctoral program has dozens of alumni – wonderful friends and colleagues – sprinkled around the country who proudly count themselves as part of the Cruz, Duplass, and Howard Johnston lineage and professing their own theory and practice of social studies education.

It is hard to imagine a better or more meaningful career than that of a social studies educator in the cradle of democracy.

Acknowledgments

Mrs. Tina Savant Duplass, for her insightful comments and editing of drafts of this book.

The National Council for Social Studies at www.socialstudies.org, for permissions granted.

The Council for Economic Education at www.councilforeconed.org/, for permissions granted.

Educational Theory, Copyright © by John Wiley & Sons, permission granted.

Journal of Philosophy of Education, Copyright © by John Wiley & Sons, permission granted.

Professors' Preface

Of course there's a lot of knowledge in universities: the freshmen bring a little in; the seniors don't take much away, so knowledge sort of accumulates.

A. Lawrence Lowell, President of Harvard,
1909–1923 (Genius Quotes, 2020)

Underlying Concepts of the Book

Dear Colleague:

For multiple reasons, *The Essence of Teaching Social Studies: Methods for Secondary and Elementary Teacher Candidates* is more than just another book about social studies education methods. Our times seem to have succumbed to harsher political rhetoric and greater incivility; an increased atmosphere of disillusionment and cynicism among children and adults; ambient anxiety among the population due to the pace of change, technology, and displacement; uncontrolled access by students to information and unvetted opinions portrayed as facts; unequal access to quality education; and a profession under siege for circumstances largely out of its control. As a consequence, this book not only offers contemporary thinking on curriculum, instruction, and methods of social studies education, but also asks teacher candidates to consider the unique role social studies teachers should embrace.

Unlike other subject fields, where the teacher is most concerned about what a student knows, teachers of social studies are concerned about who students ARE and the kind of person they can BECOME. Social studies teachers should heed the call of Thomas Lickona to intervene and instill more "directly and indirectly, such values as respect, responsibility, trustworthiness, fairness, caring, and civic virtues; and that these values are not merely subjective preferences but that they have objective worth and a claim on our collective conscience" (1993, p. 9). Based on this premise, the following threads are woven through the fabric of the book.

1. **An emphasis on civics education** – thus it is the first methods book to include a comprehensive explanation of the foundations of social studies education. It offers a historically-based definition of a democratic ideology by referencing and synthesizing NCSS position statements, social studies education scholars, and classic philosophy; brings clarity by differentiating between ideology, democratic ideology, political ideology, and political stances and arguing what should be taught, ethically, by teachers of social studies; and makes a robust case for the proposition that a democratic ideology should be the goal of social studies education and

tethering that goal to standards, curriculum, methods, and classroom practices appropriate to elementary and secondary social studies education.

2. **Standards-based education** – is ingrained in K-12 education due to the NCSS C3 Framework, "NCSS Themes," Common Core, state standards, and the recommended standards of the professional organizations of history, geography, economics, and civics. Such standards are vital to achieving the "foundational goals" of social studies and necessary as a stepping stone to the "exalted aims" that requires teachers to consider with their students – "things that matter" (Taylor, 1992, p. 15).

3. **Critical thinking** – by articulating its psychological basis, differentiating between generic and discipline-specific modes of reasoning, critical thinking is put at the forefront of lesson planning. Such a focus recognizes the long-term goal of the social studies to support students as they move forward in their lives in a democratic state, where information must be analyzed and critiqued to become useful knowledge to be acted upon.

4. **Basic skills** – education is a school-wide effort and requires the participation of every teacher of social studies. There are chapters dedicated to literacy, reading, and writing strategies and assessments in social studies.

5. **Social studies teachers must have unique skills** – because social studies knowledge is transformed by each student into the intimate, highly personal "what I think," "what I feel," and "what I should do." For K-12 students to become effective citizens, teachers of the social studies must support students in building the capacities of authenticity, autonomy, efficacy, and agency as part of the process of acquiring the foundational knowledge of social studies and the democratic ideals. The students' formation of a holistic civic and personal identity requires more than teaching; it requires the guiding hand of a social studies teacher willing to act as a philosophical counselor (see Chapter 10).

The Essence of Teaching Social Studies: Methods for Secondary and Elementary Teacher Candidates is based on the following premises.

1. **Compatibility with Course Management Software** (CMS). The CMS should "wrap around" the book to make professors and the adjunct faculty member's work easier. The book is intended for the first, introductory elementary, middle, or high school level initial certification social studies methods course in online, face-to-face (F2F), or hybrid courses. Examples are drawn from grade-appropriate elementary, middle, and high school sources to differentiate the unique characteristics of each.

2. **Flexibility for professors.** Each chapter is a gateway that briefly and concisely "unpacks" (in about only 4000 words) the essential philosophy, theory, policy statements, and best practices of social studies education, thus professors can easily introduce their unique insights and favorite grade-appropriate examples into the CMS depending on the makeup of the class.

3. **Professors' expertise.** The topics will appear more direct and encyclopedic at times because the intent is to create the springboard for a professor's particular area of expertise and preferred examples and analogies.

4. **Accommodation of elementary and secondary education differences.** Elementary teacher candidates typically lack the depth and breadth of declarative and procedural knowledge acquired by secondary social studies education majors in their liberal arts courses. The standards and narrative included in this book provide

a foundation for the modes of reasoning that are typically encapsulated in the social studies academic disciplines and provides links to resources that all teacher candidates can use for background knowledge. Methods are differentiated through examples and resources cited for elementary, middle school, and high school instruction.

5. **Technology integration.** The "*Resources*" at the end of each chapter of links to videos, lesson plans, national organizations, ancillaries, contemporary research papers, position statements, etc., make the best use of the internet in conjunction with a textbook and CMS. Professors can conveniently insert the resources they like into their CMS and students can use them as a resource for creating lesson plans.

6. **Videos for teaching social studies.** Education Week (2018) reports that nearly 60% of college-age students prefer learning through videos, rather than books. As a result, at the end of each chapter there are curated videos that professors can insert into their CMS for candidates to view in online or F2F classes. The videos can replace some of the teacher modeling and explanations traditionally held in F2F classes.

7. **Long shelf life.** Because the chapters are geared to core ideas condensed from historically leading authorities and position papers, the CMS can be stable for multiple semesters.

8. **Encouraging reading of the text by candidates.** The short, less dense, reader-friendly narrative as compared with other textbooks is intended to encourage candidates' "close reading" of the book and to give professors the flexibility to build upon the core ideas in their CMS tasks.

9. **Integration of standards.** The NCSS C3 Framework (NCSS, 2013), NCSS "Themes" (NCSS, 1994/2010), NCSS *Social Studies for Citizens for a Strong and Free Nation* (aka "Democratic Beliefs") (1990), NCSS "Essential Skills" (NCSS, 1989), Common Core, and national history, geography, economics, and civics standards are front and center in the book.

10. **Full use of the internet.** With the exception of the C3 Framework, "Key Word" search terms are provided in each chapter that direct students to more detailed information about items such as the NCSS Themes, Bloom's Taxonomy, Wait Time, etc.

11. **Breadth of topics.** Given that many colleges have eliminated some general education course requirements to meet total credit hour restrictions, there are some topics in the book, such as reading, learning theory, classroom management, etc., that might have been found in other courses required in the past. These sections are written with social studies education in mind.

12. **Accreditation.** The book is written with the Council for the Accreditation of Educator Preparation, state "approved program" status, and NCSS program approval in mind.

Organization of the Book

The book is divided into three parts:

Part 1: Social Studies Education. In response to calls for greater civic understanding, it is the only methods book that situates social studies education in the broader context of a **democratic ideology** and **civic identity**. This is the most theoretical section of the book and takes a distinct humanistic approach to examining the exalted aims of social studies education. It elaborates on civic identity and democratic ideology, how they are acquired and related. It should also motivate teacher candidates to think deeply about their own ideology, political ideology, and ideological stances as a precursor to teaching and modeling a democratic ideology.

Part 2: Schools, Curriculum, and Standards. These chapters emphasize the foundational goals and content of social studies education from the perspective of learned societies, such as the NCSS, the National Council for Geographic Education (NCGE), etc. The importance of the social studies fields of study as the bridge to the exalted aims will be contextualized using NCSS policy statements and the standards and goals of the learned societies.

Part 3: Best Practices in Social Studies Education. This section will focus on pedagogical content knowledge for the social studies by introducing candidates to underlying theories, methods, and best practices most commonly endorsed in social studies education.

Resources and References

At the end of each chapter, a section titled "Resources" is intended to make the best use of the internet in a CMS environment. For professors, these links to resources can be copied to their CMS platform as links to videos, documents, and webpages, or where permitted by copyright law, downloaded and inserted into the CMS modules. For teacher candidates it provides information to better understand a concept or a resource to be used in their teaching or the course.

The online resources are divided into "Videos" and "Documents." According to Rhonda Bradley (2019), "Generation Z" students watch an average of 68 videos across five social media platforms a day! Except in rare instances, all the resources that are cited are in the public domain with no membership fee. The "key words" search terms approach will lead to videos, documents, and website pages that have been curated for relevance and quality. Most of the resources' search terms are sufficiently exact to lead to the specific resource cited, but would also result in additional "hits" of related resources. The key word search term approach is used, rather than URLs, because websites' restructuring is a frequent occurrence, making URL links obsolete. Even with this preventative measure, it is most probably best to download documents and videos or record videos through screen capture software (such as the Camtasia, Flashback Express, etc.) for insertion into modules and labeled with the original URL.

Videos: There are outstanding videos on the internet that demonstrate best practices in K-12 classrooms that professors, traditionally, have tried to explain, model, or demonstrate in the F2F courses. To paraphrase, "A video is worth a thousand words," and the internet has placed them at professors' and teacher candidates' fingertips.

Documents: Search terms will lead to select websites that include additional readings such as position papers, essays, books, articles, or practical resources such as lesson plans and ancillaries.

References: These are from works cited in the chapters. At many universities most of the articles or books cited can be accessed through the university's online library.

CMS Architecture and Textbook Example

The following is a generic illustration of how a professor might envision the integration of this book's chapters into their CMS using *Chapter 22 Lecture* for the illustration.

Overview

The CMS architecture can be based on the sequential, scaffold approach of the book using its table of contents. Based on a hypothetical 16-week semester, one module would cover multiple chapters if all are assigned. The example of *Module 6 Lectures* that follows assumes the course is online, so modifications would be made for a F2F or hybrid version of the course to incorporate class meetings. Viewing of videos on the internet is essential to this example online course because they serve as a substitute for what a professor would demonstrate in an F2F class meeting. Original PowerPoint presentations might be developed by the professor that would be converted to MP3 videos with voice-over replacing some "lectures" formally offered in F2F classes. Each module "home page" follows the same pattern depicted in Figure P1.

Each module has a set day and time once per week by which candidates must have completed all the tasks in the module, take the weekly quiz to assess that the tasks are completed, and upload any assignment that might be due in the module. By having a set day and time, the professor can monitor quizzes, minimize inappropriate sharing of information about quizzes, and set a consistent, definitive due date and time for all assignment submissions.

Sample CMS Module

Figure P1 is the home page of the seven-page lecture module.

M6.1 – M6.7 are clickable links that lead to the sequenced CMS page that has the links to the module's task items.

M6.1 Attention Getter starts with two attention getters, a video, and this quote:

> Direct teaching of the whole class together does not mean a return to the formal chalk and talk approach, with the teacher talking and pupils mainly just listening. Good direct teaching is lively and stimulating. It means that teachers provide clear instruction, use effective questioning techniques, and make good use of pupils' responses.
>
> (Numeracy Task Force, 2004)

A caption "The Best Example of the Worst Lecture" is followed by a link to Ben Stein's "economics" lecture from *Ferris Bueller's Day Off* at www.youtube.com/watch?v=uhiCFdWeQfA.

M6.2 How to do well on the Quiz on Lectures includes key terms and "hints" as to what might appear in the quiz as well as questions candidates should ask themselves while completing the readings and viewing videos.

M6.3 Readings – "Chapter 22 Lecture" from *The Essence of Teaching Social Studies* requires candidates to read the chapter. In some modules, and where permitted by

Module 6 Lectures

M6.1 Attention Getter

M6.2 How to do well on the Quiz on Lectures

M6.3 Readings

Chapter 22 Lecture from *The Essence of Teaching Social Studies*

Jackson, S. (2009). The guide on the stage: In defense of good lecturing in the history classroom. *Social Education*, 6(4), pp. 275-278

M6.4 Five Videos Demonstrating Great Lectures

M6.5 Assignment on Lectures

M6.6 Quiz on Lectures – 20 Questions based on the videos and readings

M6.7 Discussion Board

Figure P1 Lectures Home Page

copyright laws, documents in PDF form are embedded after downloading from the internet. In other cases, directions on how to access the documents through the university library portal or the internet are provided. In this module's page, candidates are required to read Jackson's article, which can be downloaded from www.socialstudies.org/publications/socialeducation/october2009/the_guide_on_stage in addition to the chapter.

M6.4 Five Videos lists the videos (and links) to be watched and a reminder of how to "close" watch instructional videos. These videos, regardless of the proposed grade level, capture the essence of active learning lectures:

M6.5 Assignment on Lectures (Figure P3). Assignments require application of concepts that should have been learned in the tasks in the modules. Each assignment has detailed directions and rubric and a template that appears in a downloadable MSWord document format. MSWord tables in a Word document are used to structure all assignments into one format for ease of grading and to guide candidates in structuring their thinking and presentation of their ideas.

This lecture assignment is the fourth of five assignments that scaffold to two, end-of-semester daily lesson plan culminating assignments: Both lesson plans are "depth" lesson plans (see Chapter 22). The first daily lesson plan assignment requires a PowerPoint and the class detailed notes reflecting the think-aloud and questioning approaches and the second daily lesson plan assignment requires a group annotating activity with a primary source document. The assignments are:

Assignment 1. Define the initial approach to the two depth culminating lesson plans' topics by citing the enduring ideas and/or democratic ideals, foundational

Module 6.4 Five Videos

View each of the videos and take notes on the topics (foundational knowledge), standards achieved, and compelling ideas or democratic ideals. Record the strategies used such as board work, group activities, ancillaries, writing or reading, etc. and the teacher performance, structure of the lesson, teaching talk, questioning, etc. As you view the videos ask yourself how you could adapt some the strategies into your final assignment – depth lesson plans.

1. Learner.org https://archive.learner.org/resources/series166.html.

    Video 9: Explorers in North America - 30 minutes, Fifth-grade

    Video 16: Exploration in Archeology and History – 30 minutes, Sixth-grade

    Video 25: Competing Ideologies – 30 Minutes, High School

2. What Makes a Good Lecture – 5 Minutes
https://www.youtube.com/watch?v=Xuv3yT9XRAA

3. 4 Essential Body Language Tips – 3 Minutes
https://www.youtube.com/watch?v=ZK3jSXYBNak

Figure P2 Lectures Videos Page

Module 6.5 Assignment on Lectures – Upload prior to quiz

Objective: Candidates will simulate planning a direct instruction lesson by synthesizing social studies content from their assigned PDF middle school chapter and the Interactive Lecture Organizations and Modes of Reasoning Lecture Types from Chapter 22 of *The Essence of Teaching Social Studies.*

Directions:

1. Use your assigned PDF chapter as a starting point for content

2. Download Assignment Directions, Examples and Rubric.pdf.

3. Download Lecture Assignment Template.docx and save as last name, first name lecture assignment.docx

4. Complete the template and upload prior to taking the quiz.

Figure P3 Lectures Assignment Page

goals, standards, facts, concepts, and generalizations, lesson plan methods, and sequence using the Inquiry Arc approach.

Assignment 2. Search the internet for resources (ancillaries, images, "off the shelf" exemplary lesson plans that can be integrated into the candidates' plan, etc.) and background content knowledge.

Assignment 3. Refine the initial approach and define the objectives and goals of the lessons in terms of the NCSS Themes, C3 Framework, and candidates' State's standards.

Assignment 4. Apply Interactive Lecture Types and Modes of Reasoning Lectures Types to the assigned topic (students use online K-12 textbook chapters to select their topic).

Assignment 5. Apply Bloom's Hierarchy and questioning strategies to the assigned topic.

Assignment 6. Create Depth Lesson Plan 1.

Assignment 7. Create Depth Lesson Plan 2.

M6.6 Quiz on Lectures is one of 10 quizzes for 16 modules. Quizzes are created based on the tasks in the module. Candidates are informed in the front matter of the CMS that there will be at least one question based on each of the tasks. Quizzes are only 20 minutes in length because there are only 20 true/false or multiple-choice questions. The questions are not intended to be exhaustive or to require higher-order thinking. The intent is to confirm that the teacher candidates have close watched the videos and PowerPoints and completed the readings.

M6.7 Discussion Board is a discussion board for candidates to ask public questions about the content of the module and share thoughts on the modules with other candidates.

Worth Mentioning

A. The choice of references is often based on their recognized, lasting contribution to the field. In other cases, the narrative is a compilation of resources and presented as an accepted or best practice.

B. Unless otherwise stated, the term "teacher" will refer to K-12 teachers of social studies, "student" to K-12 students, and "candidate" to initial certification college students.

C. The male pronoun form is used for readability purposes thus avoiding the "she/he" etc. configuration with the intent for it to be taken as synonymous with "person."

D. Vocabulary used in the textbook, either when first introduced or defined in context, is usually in bold font. This serves the purpose of highlighting terminology that someone new to the profession should consider and as a source for searching the internet for more information about the concept.

Resources

Videos: *(For some video resources, it is best to enter the words below preceded by "video")* *Learner.org:* Home Page | Social Studies in Action a Teaching Practices Library Series (32 videos based on the NCSS Themes); Democracy in America (15 videos); Social Studies in Action a Methodology Workshop K-5 (8 videos); Making

Civics Real a Workshop for Teachers (8 videos); The Constitution that Delicate Balance (13 videos); Story of the Bill of Rights | *TCH (The Teaching Channel)* is a subscription service, effective Spring 2020 but many of the videos may still be found on YouTube by using the title or students could be required to subscribe.

Documents: Engage NY: New York State K-12 Social Studies Resources Toolkit (Over 80, C3 Inquiry Lessons) | C3teachers.org (Over 200 Inquiry Lessons) | *Core Knowledge*: History and Geography (lesson plans).

References

Bradley, R. (2019). *Why generation Z loves YouTube.* Retrieved from https://medium.com/@the_ manifest/why-generation-z-loves-youtube-ec64643bd5b2

Education Week. (2018). *Generation Z prefers learning from YouTube, not books.* Retrieved from blogs.edweek.org/edweek/DigitalEducation/2018/08/generation_z_prefers_learning_from_you tube.html

Genius Quotes. (2020). William Lowell. Retrieved from https://geniusquotes.org/quotes/of-course-theres-a-lot-of-abbott-lawrence-lowell-quote/

Lickona, T. (1993). The return of character education. *Educational Leadership*, *51*(3), 6–11.

NCSS. (1989). In search of a scope and sequence for social studies. *Social Education*, *53*(6), 376–385.

NCSS. (1990). *Social studies for citizens for a strong and free nation.* Social Studies Curriculum Planning Resources. NCSS.

NCSS. (1994/2010). *Expectations of excellence: Curriculum standards for social studies.* Retrieved from www.socialstudies.org/standards/strands

NCSS. (2013). *The college, career, and civic life (C3) framework for social studies state standards: Guidance for enhancing the rigor of K-12 civics, economics, geography, and history.* NCSS.

Taylor, C. (1992). *The ethics of authenticity.* Cambridge, MA: Harvard University Press.

Students' Introduction

Children today are tyrants. They contradict their parents, gobble their food, and tyrannize their teachers.

Socrates, Greek Philosopher,
469–399 BCE (McGowan, R. 2019, cover page)

Welcome!

I hope you are excited about beginning your journey to become a social studies teacher. It is a wonderful and rewarding profession.

In many ways teaching social studies is like songwriters who perform their own music. Song writing is a creative endeavor. Great songs have a meaningful message that resonates with listeners, it stirs the emotions and imagination, and the lyrics and melody are memorable or, even better yet, unforgettable. Great concerts require a passionate artist that pulls the audience in with a planned production, has all the right props and instruments, appears spontaneous, and has a few surprises.

Only you can decide if you want to work hard enough to be Beyoncé, Bruno Mars, Justin Timberlake, or somebody named just Drake and Lady Gaga? I confess, I had to ask my grandchildren for names to make the examples relevant, because my choice would have been Marvin Gaye and the Supremes, and I feared college students buying this book may not know their music.

About the Book

The Essence of Teaching Social Studies: Methods for Secondary and Elementary Teacher Candidates will introduce teacher candidates to the exalted aims, foundational goals, and core strategies for teaching social studies. The word "introduce" is used because, as Socrates said, "I cannot teach you anything, I can only make you think."

The book is designed for elementary, middle, or high school teacher candidates. The book is not intended to be an exhaustive, dense, academic treatise, but a rendition of the essential ideas about social studies education that will help teacher candidates initially conceptualize the kind of teacher they want to be. This book is for candidates who aspire to be great teachers, what the National Council for Social Studies (NCSS, 2013) calls "Ambitious Teachers" of social studies.

An **initial teacher certification** training program has three components: Liberal arts courses in the social studies, education theory and methods courses, and practica including the final internship. But the most decisive factor in the transition to a successful career as a teacher is the teacher candidates themselves. It is the teacher candidates who bring a set of skills and a disposition essential to the profession and make the choice to build on those assets by reflecting on what they are learning. The exalted aims of social studies education (see Part 1) makes teaching of social studies different from teaching the other subject fields because teachers of social studies are interested in more than what students know, but who they will become.

Organization of the Book

The book is divided into three parts:

Part 1: Social Studies Education. This humanistic approach to defining the exalted aims of social studies education is intended to be thought provoking. Part 1 should lead social studies teacher candidates to think deeply about their identity and ideology as a prerequisite to helping K-12 students develop the personal and civic identity necessary for them to thrive and participate in a democratic culture.

Part 2: Schools, Curriculum, and Standards. In these chapters, the foundational goals of social studies education will be examined from the perspective of learned societies, starting with the National Council for Social Studies (NCSS). Standards education is now the driving force of all K-12 teaching and learning and shapes what teachers and teacher candidates think about how and what to teach.

Part 3: Best Practices in Social Studies Education. This section will focus on core pedagogical content knowledge for the social studies by introducing the essential theories and best practices for the most commonly used methods.

Resources and References

At the end of each chapter, there is a list of resources. Except in rare instances, all the resources are in the public domain and do not require a membership or fee. Key word search terms are used rather than URLs because websites restructuring is a frequent occurrence, making the URL obsolete. The resources are intended to provide easy access to online videos and documents that further illuminate the ideas in the chapter. The key word search will lead to videos, documents, and website pages that have been curated for relevance, quality, and authenticity based on topics covered or alluded to in the chapters.

Videos: There are outstanding videos on the internet that model and demonstrate best practices. For best results while using the search terms provided, it is sometimes best to insert "video" in front of search terms.

Documents: These may be readings such as position papers, standards, essays, books, articles, lesson plans, ancillaries for lesson plans, images, etc., that should make the transition from teacher candidate to teacher easier.

References: These are from works cited in the chapter, some of which have URLs for easy access. At many universities, most of the articles or books cited can be accessed through the university's online library portal.

The Terminology of Social Studies Education

Part of becoming a member of a profession is developing a rich vocabulary of terms by which to communicate effectively with others in the profession and express ideas to students and the public. To that end, the first chapter has a list of many of the essential terms of social studies education. Many of those terms, and others, will also appear in the book in bold letters the first time they are used in a substantive way. Previewing these terms and definitions before reading the book will provide improved fluency for reading of the text. Many of the unfamiliar terms can be easily searched on the internet to delve deeper into their significance.

Choosing to be a Teacher

From an early age, individuals begin to imagine themselves in different jobs and careers. There are many variables that affect career preferences and options. Finding a way to the profession that people think they could be "good at" and what would make them happy requires, above all else, an honest and insightful assessment of self. Individuals might have considered being a nurse, but do not like the idea of examining patients. They may want to be a professional basketball player, but if only 5 feet tall, being a jockey is more realistic. The idea of being an engineer may be appealing, but as individuals progress through school it may become apparent that their aptitude for the mathematics needed to be in a technical field is not a strength. Conversely, others may have worked as a day camp counselor and were very good at tactfully managing kids and they recognize the skill is transferrable to teaching. Perhaps it is a love of history or politics that most influences the decision to be a teacher? Or maybe the reason was a social studies teacher who had a profound impact on an individual and "paying it forward" is part of an individual's moral identity.

Praxis

An initial teacher certification program prepares individuals for a profession. That is very different from earning a degree in the liberal arts, like a history major, where a student is only required to demonstrate knowledge of the theory and content of a discipline. **Praxis** is the act of applying theory. As an example, it is one thing to understand, conceptually, the different kinds of active learning lectures (see Chapter 22 Lecture) and the "Arc of Inquiry" (see Chapter 12 Social Studies Education and the NCSS). It is altogether something different to imaginatively plan a compelling active learning lecture based on standards, democratic ideals, foundational knowledge, and sound pedagogy. And, finally, it is an even greater challenge to enact an active learning lecture with 25 rambunctious students in a classroom. Liberal arts courses should provide basic but sufficient background content knowledge to start a teacher candidate's career, but that knowledge will need to be transformed into knowledge appropriate for the K-12 students. This book and the professor of the course will introduce teacher candidates to the theory, standards, and methods used in social studies. But the concern for students, classroom leadership (i.e., classroom management) skills, creativity, organizational skills are dispositional – that is, teacher candidates must bring those attributes with them to the initial teacher certification program and then develop them further.

Dispositions are learned at an early age. By the late teens it is difficult to acquire new ones and can only be acquired by an individual's extraordinary commitment to change cognitively, emotionally, and behaviorally (Combs, 1962; Duplass & Cruz, 2010). College students can acquire new dispositions and behaviors by being immersed in the professional and academic culture of a university and an initial certification program, where striving for excellence, caring, engaged discourse, critical thinking, creativity, impartiality, open-mindedness, and a search for the truth are prized.

Self-Assessment

Teaching is much harder than most teacher candidates think. It may seem easy, but candidates have not seen the time and effort excellent teachers put into preparing for class. Unlike the liberal arts professors whose duty is to only assess students' knowledge, education professors are called upon by States' education departments and accrediting agencies to determine *and* affirm that a candidate has the theory, skills, and disposition to be an ambitious, novice teacher. It is an imperfect assessment that professors in teacher training programs are expected to make, so wise teacher candidates leave no room for error. Assessing significant pedagogical content knowledge and creativity is relatively easy because professors can see it in written lesson plans, assignments, and tests. Determining, in a classroom setting, if characteristics such as caring and commitment to a democratic ideology are present and fixed – particularly when that professor may have a candidate only one time in one course – is much more difficult and imperfect. Some candidates do not exhibit excellence in their courses, but shine in their practica. Others have retained little of the modes of thinking or content from their liberal arts courses and struggle to get the content right or convert it to grade-appropriate knowledge. Most professors have experienced teacher candidates who did wonderful work in their classes but could not enact their knowledge in practica in spite of having an excellent cooperating teacher in the K-12 classroom to guide them. Often inadequate demonstration of the knowledge and disposition to be a teacher is a question of maturity or external circumstances that are complicating the student's life. Some teacher candidates will meet the minimum standards of the program and professors can only hope they will mature into ambitious teachers. Consider the following: Approximately 40% of teacher candidates who pursue undergraduate degrees in education never even enter the classroom; 15.7% of teachers leave their posts every year; and upwards of 50% of teachers will leave the classroom within their first five years of teaching (Ingersoll, 2012). There are many reasons that underlie these statistics, but new teachers often underestimate the extraordinary amount of daily preparation that takes place after school hours and the emotional drain of managing students. Teaching is perhaps the only career where a recent graduate of a college is asked to manage (as an example in the case of a middle or high school teacher) 150 people at the start of their career.

Teacher candidates, no matter how empathetic by temperament or passionate about the social studies, have to be honest with themselves about whether they have the disposition to take on the planning and emotional rigors of the daily challenges of teaching. Teaching can be exceptionally rewarding, it is a noble profession, and at the end, teachers can look back and know that they made a difference in some of their students' lives. An initial teacher certification program is intended to give teacher candidates every opportunity to acquire the characteristics of an ambitious social studies teacher.

What Teacher Candidates Say They Need Help With

The following is a list of activities that novice teachers need help with based on research by Brewster and Railsback (2001):

1. Setting up a classroom for the first time;	6. Developing time management skills;
2. Learning school routines;	7. Understanding policies and procedures;
3. Teaching with less than adequate resources;	8. Motivating students;
4. Where to find supplies;	9. Responding to behavior problems;
5. Involving parents;	10. Developing classroom management skills.

Professional Organizations

The following is a selected list of organizations many of which a teacher candidate might consider joining and attending one of their national, regional, or state conferences. Most provide websites with free resources.

National Council for the Social Studies (also state chapter)	American Historical Association
Association of American Educators	Organization of American Historians
National Education Association	Organization of History Teachers
American Federation of Teachers	The National Council for History Education
National Association for the Education of Young Children	Society for History Education
Council for Exceptional Children	American Association of Geographers
Association for Middle Level Education	The National Council for Geography Teachers
Association for Supervision and Curriculum Development	American Geographical Association
Council for the Accreditation of Educator Preparation	National Geographic Association
National Association of State Directors of Teacher Education and Certification	American Political Science Association
	Center for Civic Education
	American Economic Association
	Council for Economic Education

Resources

Videos: *(For some video resources, it is best to enter the words below preceded by "video.")*

TCH [*The Teaching Channel*]: is a subscription service, effective Spring 2020 but many of the videos may be found on YouTube; The Parent-Teacher Conference; Planning; Differentiating Instruction; Classroom Management; If I had Known; Technology in the Classroom| *YouTube:* 10 Tips for New Teachers; New Teacher Survival Guide Planning; New Teacher Survival Guide Differentiating Instruction.

Documents: *NEA:* What I Wish I Had Known | Survival Kit for New Teacher (400 page MSWord book of tips).

References

Brewster, C., & Railsback, J. (2001). *Supporting beginning teachers: How administrators, teachers, and policymakers can help new teachers succeed.* Portland, OR: Northwest Regional Educational Laboratory. ERIC Document Reproduction Service ED455619.

Combs, A. (1962). *Perceiving, behaving and becoming: A new focus.* ASCD Yearbook. Association for Supervision and Curriculum Development.

Duplass, J., & Cruz, B. (2010). NCATE professional dispositions: What's a social studies education professor to do? *The Social Studies, 101*(4), 141–151.

Ingersoll, R. M. (2012). Beginning teacher induction: What the data tell us: Induction is an education reform whose time has come. *Phi Delta Kappan.* Retrieved from www.edweek.org/ew/art icles/2012/05/16/kappan_ingersoll.h31.html

McGowan, R. (2019). *Children today are tyrants. They contradict their parents, gobble their food, and tyrannize their teachers. Socrates: Humorous notebook.* Independently Published.

NCSS. (2013). Social studies for the next generation: Purposes, practices, and implications of the college, career, and civic Life (C3) framework for social studies state standards: Guidance for enhancing rigor of K-12 civic, economics, geography, and history. Retrieved from www.socialstu dies.org/sites/default/files/2017/Jun/c3-framework-for-social-studies-rev0617.pdf

Numeracy Task Force. (2004). Numercy matters: Final report, implementation of the national numeracy strategy. Retrieved from http://www.dfes.cov.uk/numeracy/contents.shtml

Part 1
Social Studies Education

What we do to our children they will do to our society.

Pliny the Elder, Roman Historian and Philosopher,
23–79 BCE (Bennett, 1992, p. 36)

The democratic ethos of Western civilization evolved from ancient Greece and has been refined based on influences from across the planet. The underpinnings of social studies education can be traced to the lineage of Socrates, Plato, and Aristotle.

Dawson (1922), in his history of the forming of the National Council for the Social Studies (NCSS), foresaw the potential problems of the definition for the term "social studies":

> One thing that stands out in the way of some who would like to support the National Council more freely than they do as yet is its name. The title, "Social Studies" is not fully understood; possibly it is not subject as yet to logical definition ... The term "social studies" was used for lack of a better one, one that would not be so cumbersome as to hamper facile discussions of the elements of this field.
>
> (p. 46)

Seventy years later David Saxe pointed out:

> In a field plagued by a lack of identity, I argue that practitioners and theorists are prevented from articulating viable perceptions of social studies' purpose, theory, and practice because they lack basic understandings of the original historical underpinnings of social studies.
>
> (1992, p. 1)

Part 1 Social Studies Education will examine the idea of a social studies education through a humanistic and education theory lens by integrating historical and contemporary perspectives. It is intended to assist teacher candidates develop a personal, coherent philosophy as to why teaching social studies education is essential, unique, and more challenging than other teaching fields.

NCSS Code of Ethics Principle Four

It is the ethical responsibility of social studies professionals to cultivate and maintain an instructional environment in which the free contest of ideas is prized.

A. Effective social studies instruction necessitates an environment in which social studies professionals and students are free to study, investigate, present, interpret, and discuss relevant facts and ideas. Those engaged in social studies instruction have a responsibility to accept and practice the democratic commitment to open inquiry and to approach controversial issues in a spirit of inquiry rather than advocacy.

B. Social studies professionals have an obligation to exercise and maintain academic freedom in the classroom and to abide by such reasonable considerations as the intent of the course and the age and sophistication of students.

C. The social studies professional should acknowledge the worth and tentativeness of knowledge. He or she should engage in a continuous search for new knowledge, retaining both the right and the obligation as a student scholar to doubt, to inquire freely, and to raise searching questions. The social studies professional has an obligation to distinguish between personal opinion and beliefs that can be supported by verified facts and to impart the knowledge of these differences to his or her students.

D. Social studies professionals have an obligation to establish classroom climates that support student rights to know, to doubt, to inquire freely, to think critically, and to express openly.

NCSS (2016)

A Proposition

The goal of teaching and learning the social studies is to empower students to consider who they are and want to be as authentic human beings and citizens.

Resources

Documents: *Wiley Handbook of Social Studies Research*: A Concise Historiography of the Social Studies; Intellectual History of the Social Studies | *NCSS*: Revised Code of Ethics for the Social Studies Profession.

References

Bennett, W. J. (1992). *The de-valuing of America: The fight for our culture and out children*. Simon and Schuster.

Dawson, E. (1922). The plans of the national council for the social studies. *The Historical Outlook*, *13*(8), 317–321.

NCSS. (2016). *Revised code of ethics for the social studies profession*. Retrieved from www.socialstudies.org/position/ethics

Saxe, D. W. (1992). Framing a theory for social studies foundations. *Review of Educational Research*, *62*(3), 122–127.

1 Definitions and Propositions

Although it may be true that the notion of teaching virtues such as honesty or integrity arouses little controversy, it is also true that vague consensus on the goodness of these virtues conceals a great deal of actual disagreement over their definitions.
Lawrence Kohlberg, American Psychologist, 1927–1987 (Garrod, A., 1992, p. 31)

Definitions

In any field of study and practice, professionals try to carefully define the terms used in their community of practice. To have differences, deficiencies, and nuances of terms is not unusual in applied fields of study, particularly because – as in social studies education – the practice draws on other disciplines. What one professor means by "knowledge," "values," or "active learning" can be slightly or very different from another's. Because this can be confusing for a newcomer to the community of practice, the following definitions are provided as a pre-reading activity to enhance understanding of the concepts and generalizations when encountered in the book. Some definitions are original to this book's author and others are based on the work of select scholars or learned societies.

Academic disciplines – are typically defined as the areas of research and study found in universities.

Arc of Inquiry – is part of the NCSS C3 Framework and is based on constructivist theories. It places a premium on lessons that start with compelling questions or propositions and using active learning "investigations" by which students and teachers, together, pursue answers through the examination of foundational knowledge and democratic ideals.

Active learning – is where students are engaged in the learning process through teacher-created engagements that require students to think critically, such as in problem-solving, decision-making, and values analysis and completing tasks such as writing, creating graphic organizers, etc. This is in contrast to passive learning such as listening to teacher-dominated lectures and activities such as completing fill-in-the-blank worksheets.

Agency – is the capacity of a person to consistently make choices and to act.
  Moral agency – is the ability to make moral judgments as the basis for acting (Barker, 2005).

Authenticity – "whereby each individual is thought to have a unique identity, an original way of being human, to which he or she must be true" to have the Good Life (Taylor, 1992, p. 38).

Autonomy – is the ability to reflect critically on one's principles, decide how to live, consider one's circumstances, and act based on those reflections.

Beliefs – are part of students' identity and ideology. Because individuals have emotional attachments and value beliefs as important to their identity, beliefs are fundamentally different from abstract ideas and are more resistant to change than ideas (Fenstermacher, 1994; Richardson, 1996). When presented with compelling questions and propositions of ideas that matter, students are moved to reflect on their beliefs and identity: They are inspired to reconsider who they are and who they want to be.

C3 Framework – is a curriculum and instruction platform developed by the NCSS that has two parts: A) Grade-level standards for the core social studies subject areas; and B) the Arc of Inquiry, a methodological approach to teaching the social studies based on constructivist theories.

Compelling propositions and questions – based on social studies foundational knowledge, teachers develop questions and propositions that are aimed at the considerations of a democratic ideology. As an example, learning the foundational knowledge of various wars would lead to consideration of the enduring idea of the common attributes of causes of wars. In turn, this would lead to a consideration of a thing that matters – how to decide if a war is just – which leads to examination of at least two democratic beliefs, the right to security and respect for human life.

Caring encounter – entails genuine presence and connectedness between a teacher and student that is initiated by the teacher in order to facilitate the student's formation of a holistic identity and ideology (Buber, 2000; Marcel, 2001/1951). It requires "engrossment," what Noddings defines as "an open, nonselective receptivity to the cared-for" and "where the person being cared for senses the caring's energy is flowing toward him" (Noddings, 1999, 1998, p. 40).

Civics – is not the same as education about government(s), it is teaching and learning for civic competence.

    Civic competence – is "the knowledge, intellectual processes, and democratic dispositions required of students to be active and engaged participants in public life" (NCSS, 2020).

Common Core – is a set of standards created by the National Governors Association that emphasizes basic skills. These standards outline what a student should know and be able to do at the end of each grade level. All but a handful of states have adopted the standards, and those that did not have very similar standards of their own design.

Constructivism – is a widely accepted theory that entails methods of instruction based on a view of learning as a process in which the learner is expected to actively construct knowledge, as opposed to the passive learning approach where a student is viewed as a pitcher to be filled up with knowledge.

    Cognitive constructivism – describes how the individual learner comes to understand and organize knowledge by conceptualizing ideas into schema (Piaget, 1929).

    Social constructivism – emphasizes how meaning and understanding grow out of social encounters with others (Vygotsky, 1978).

Critical thinking – "active, persistent, and careful consideration of any belief or supposed form of knowledge in the light of the grounds that support it, and the further conclusions to which it tends" (Dewey, 1910, p. 6).

Curriculum – is derived from the Latin word meaning race course, as in a race with hurdles an athlete must jump over to get to the finish line. The when and what of teaching has traditionally been referred to as the curriculum, scope and sequence, or framework. The past two decades have also seen the increased use of the word "standards" when referring to curriculum. The how of teaching is usually referred to as pedagogy, approaches, methods, strategies, or instruction.

Democracy and democratic – refers to a (unless stated otherwise) liberal democracy as opposed to the narrower construction of rule by the people. It includes free, multi-candidate elections; universal suffrage; limited government powers through a constitution or set of laws that transcend the government apparatus; the idea of inalienable rights based on equality of persons; and the rule of law. The term "democracy" (small "d") is not to be confused with the "Democrats" or the Democratic Party. Both Republicans and Democrats adhere to a democratic ideology.

Democratic beliefs – for this book's framework, the core democratic beliefs are drawn from the NCSS's *Social Studies for Citizens for a Strong and Free Nation* (1990), which are grouped into four categories: Rights of the Individual, Freedoms of the Individual, Responsibilities of the Individual, and Responsibilities of Government.

Democratic ideals – are the Core Personal Virtues, Democratic Beliefs, and Civic Values as defined in this book (see Figure 2.1).

Democratic ideology – is the product of a disposition to forge an identity based on the democratic ideals.

Efficacy – is individuals' sense of their ability to act; that they can produce desired outcomes. Unless individuals believe this about themselves, they will have little incentive to act (Bandura, 1977).

Enculturation – is more than education or teaching knowledge and skills. It is also the conscious and unconscious process by which individuals acquire the beliefs and ideas, patterns of behavior, and moral code of their societies upon which they will, in part, base their unique identity.

Enduring ideas – are tied to foundational knowledge and are retained long after the associated declarative knowledge is forgotten. As an example, students may learn about the three branches of government by the question, "Why are the three branches important?" This would lead to an investigation of foundational knowledge with students coming to understand the enduring idea of separation of powers and that it is an important safeguard of the right to liberty. Such an enduring idea is tethered to the belief in democratic ideal of a right to freedom. A skill associated with procedural knowledge, such as charting supply and demand in economics, is also an enduring idea.

Exalted aims – of social studies education are aspirations that go beyond the foundational knowledge of social studies education so as to promote a holistic identity and democratic ideology.

Explicit teaching – is the conscious effort by teachers to plan active learning instruction so as to create the grade-appropriate foundational knowledge essential to raising the compelling questions and propositions for students to consider enduring ideas and democratic ideals.

The Good Life – is a life well lived – what Greek philosophers in antiquity called *Eudaimonia* – a sense of well-being that comes from persons knowing they have done the right thing for the right reasons; that one is a decent person (Guignon, 1999).

High-stakes testing – are uniform, standardized, systematic tests used by the States that are typically mandated as part of the accountability framework by the federal government, usually in language arts, mathematics, and science. The tests are used to assess districts, schools, teachers, and students' performance in meeting required standards.

Ideas – are formulated through mental processes based on knowledge, beliefs, and feelings and are part of a person's identity and ideology. Teachers transmit ideas to students in the form of foundational knowledge, enduring ideas, and compelling propositions.

Identity – is individuals' personhood, their unique ways of knowing, being, and acting. It is derived from a unique set of conceptions of ideas, beliefs, and feelings and the identity capacities of agency, authenticity, autonomy, and efficacy. Personal identity gives form to civic identity. Civic and personal identity must be copacetic for a holistic, healthy, and productive identity. As Plato states, "man is not born in the public eye, but he is made there" (Gurley, 1999, p. 360).

    Personal identity – should be "beliefs, attitudes, or feelings that an individual is proud of, is willing to publicly affirm, has been chosen thoughtfully from alternatives without persuasion, and is acted on repeatedly" (Raths, Harmin, & Simon, 1966, p. 28).

    Civic identity – is shaped by the personal identity and understanding of the democratic ideals. It is "a set of beliefs and emotions about oneself as a participant in civic life of a community" (Hart, Richardson, & Wilkenfeld, 2011, p. 773).

Ideology – is how people envision and interpret the world. It is a "world view."

    Political ideology – is "a set of beliefs about the proper order of society and how it can be achieved" (Erikson & Tedin, 2003, p. 64).

    Political ideological stance – comprises the specific policies or programs individuals personally adopt that are based on their ideology and political ideology (Gerring, 1997, 1998).

Knowledge – is both cognizance of ideas, beliefs, and feelings and foundational knowledge.

Foundational knowledge includes:

    Declarative knowledge (also referred to as content, information, and propositional knowledge) – is a record of knowledge that includes, facts, concepts, and generalizations.

    Procedural knowledge – (also referred to as modes of reasoning, executive processes, intellectual processes, disciplinary concepts and tools, and habits of mind) – is the processes used by a community of practice to think about, investigate, organize, and articulate declarative knowledge.

    Basic skills knowledge – includes literacy such as reading, writing, etc., but also the ability to calculate, interpret media, etc.

Moral code – is both a set of rules and expectations promoted by a society and what a person adopts of the external moral code to form a personal ethical code. Moral codes are necessary for social order so that each individual can strive for the Good Life.

Morality – refers to personal conduct in matters of right and wrong that is shaped by knowledge, ideals, intentions, decisions, and actions.

Philosophical counseling – originates from the philosophy community of practice and integrates the theories and strategies of counseling with the methods and ideas of philosophy. Because social studies is, uniquely, a subject field more dedicated to influencing who students become, as opposed to just what they know, it is a practice that requires teachers with a commitment to a democratic ideology and discussion-based strategies. The philosophical counseling approach can be used by social studies teachers to cultivate a holistic personal and civic identity in students.

Social studies – refers to all things having to do with the social studies and social studies education.

The social studies – refers to the subject fields typically thought of as the "core" of history, civics, geography, and economics; the social sciences of anthropology, psychology, and sociology; and the humanities, such as philosophy, art and music history, etc.

Social studies education – is all things having to do with theory and practice related to the teaching and learning of social studies.

Social studies educators – includes social studies teachers and university professors or other scholars who have an interest in social studies education.

Social studies teachers or **teachers of social studies** – are K-12 teachers who teach social studies at the elementary, middle, or high school levels.

Standards-based education – is an accountability strategy that has concise, written descriptions of what students are expected to know and be able to do at a specific stage of their education. Teachers are expected to determine how and what to teach students so they and their students achieve the learning expectations described in the standards.

Students – refers to K-12 students.

Subject areas or **teaching fields** – are the social studies academic disciplines such as history, economics, etc., but different from academic disciplines in that they are the grade-appropriate version as taught at the K-12 level.

Teacher candidates – (i.e., candidates, pre-service teachers, or initial certification candidates) are individuals training to become teachers.

Therapeutic alliance – is the means by which a teacher and student form a relationship to engage with each other to effect a beneficial change in the student (Rogers, 1951). It must begin to be created during the first class meeting and sustained in anticipation of the caring encounter that needs to take place with students for them to consider perfecting their identity and ideology.

Things that matter – should be the focal point of teaching the social studies. The consideration of "things that matter" (Taylor, 1992, p. 15) elevates the classroom experience to the examination of the ideas and beliefs that can be extracted from democratic ideals and foundational knowledge. Things that matter, such "knotty principles as tolerance, impartial justice, the separation of church and state, the need for limits on majority power, or the difference between liberty and license" (Parker, 2005, p. 347), are often presented by teachers as compelling propositions or questions requiring students to consider who they are and what kind of person they want to be (see Chapter 4, "The Essential Identity Questions").

Traditional counseling ("therapy") – as opposed to philosophical counseling, is the therapeutic process delivered by a licensed therapist based on the medical model of diagnosable psychological pathologies.

Understanding – between knowledge and wisdom lies understanding. Teaching the social studies is unique because teachers have a distinct duty, that is to help students understand themselves as human beings and their duties to other human beings, not just know foundational procedural knowledge as in other subject areas.

Values – is a sociological term. Since the 1900s it has been used interchangeably with the term "virtues," creating confusion. As an example, society and students may value good grades, but individual students may lack the virtuous capacity to moderate their behavior to earn good grades. The social studies literature has multiple lists of "civic values" such as justice, liberty, etc., but this book uses the NCSS set of "beliefs" to streamline these kinds of "values." Individuals value certain democratic beliefs, civic values, and virtues.

Civic values – for this book's framework, the core civic values are defined as a disposition or inclination toward critical thinking, engaged discourse, impartiality, open-mindedness, and to search for the truth. It is to be noted that these civic values are politically and ideologically neutral.

Virtue – is a philosophical term for "qualities of the soul," an intrapersonal character trait that brings order to individuals' personal lives while interacting with society (see Plato, 360 BCE).

Personal virtues – for this book's framework the core virtues are defined in the Greek philosophical tradition as the cardinal virtues of courage, justice, moderation, and wisdom. Personal virtues determine what a person chooses to value.

Wisdom – requires understanding based on knowledge derived by reason. It is the capacity to "act at the right times, about the right things, towards the right people, for the right end, and in the right way" (Aristotle, 350 BCE). Since Socrates, wisdom has been thought of as the "super virtue" because it regulates all virtues and vices.

Six Propositions for the Idea of a Social Studies Education

The following propositions are offered for the teacher candidate to consider while developing a personal philosophy about social studies education.

Proposition 1: The social studies are necessary for the development of a holistic personal and civic identity in individuals and the advancement of civilization toward a more humane stance. Nicholas Maxwell (2000) explains the reason why learning social studies matters when he states:

> Two great problems of learning confront humanity: learning about the nature of the universe and our place in it, and learning how to become civilized. The first problem was solved, in essence, in the 17th century, with the creation of modern science. But the second problem has not yet been solved. Solving the first problem without also solving the second puts us in a situation of great danger.
>
> (p. 29)

Proposition 2: Social studies education is intrinsically ideological, but it should not be politicized. Social studies teachers have always struggled with the difference between promoting a democratic ideology and promoting a political stance. The use of the democratic ideology framework in this book (see Figure 4.1) is intended to bring more clarity to the teacher's role and duty.

Proposition 3: Other disciplines are only required to transmit knowledge; social studies education is intended to change the person. Teaching social studies is where students come to grips with who they are and who they want to be as members of a democratic society. Because those decisions involve feelings, beliefs, and ideas, instruction about ideas turns from an academic enterprise to considerations of beliefs about right and wrong – what it is to have the Good Life. The teaching and learning of social studies is a moral activity.

Proposition 4: The social studies classroom should be a safe harbor. The harsh political rhetoric that spills into homes via mass media needs a counter weight. In juxtaposition to the myriad of partisan, hyperbolic, and biased narratives that students are exposed to outside the classroom, the social studies classroom experience should serve as an accommodating space for students to reflect on their identity and things that matter. The classroom experience should emphasize deliberative, civil discourse so that democratic ideals can be fully vetted and practiced.

Proposition 5: Social studies knowledge is inherently ambiguous. Developing a tolerance for ambiguity is necessary for a democracy. In social studies education and a democratic society, it is accepted that more than one interpretation and conclusion can be valid and individuals have a right, and even a duty, to preserve for others the right to their chosen conclusions. The priority for social studies teachers should be to create investigations where students learn to systematically make use of logic and evidence that leads to defensible conclusions about things that matter.

Proposition 6: Social studies education should be liberating because it is intended to create the capacity for wisdom in each person. Becoming liberated frees students to determine, structure, and assert their holistic identity and form a democratic ideology, and thus enjoy the Good Life (Guignon, 1999).

Resources

Videos and documents related to the definitions and propositions will be found within the chapters.

References

Aristotle. (350 BCE). *Nicomachean ethics.* Retrieved from http://classics.mit.edu/Aristotle/nicomachaen.html

Bandura, A. (1977). *Social learning theory.* Alexandria, VA: Prentice-Hall.

Barker, C. (2005). *Cultural studies: Theory and practice.* Sage.

Buber, M. (2000). *I and Thou.* (Trans. R. Smith). New York, NY: Scribner.

Dewey, J. (1910). *How we think.* D.C. Heath. Retrieved from https://archive.org/details/howwethink000838mbp/page/n8

Erikson, R. S., & Tedin, K. L. (2003). *American public opinion* (6th ed.). Longman.

Fenstermacher, G. D. (1994). Chapter 1: The knower and the known: The nature of knowledge in research on teaching. *Review of Research in Education, 20,* 3–56.

Garrod, A. (1992). *Learning for life: Moral education theory and practice.* Praeger.

Gerring, J. (1997). Ideology: A definitional analysis. *Political Research Quarterly, 50*(4), 957–994.

Gerring, J. (1998). *Party ideologies in America, 1828–1996.* Cambridge University Press.

Guignon, C. (1999). *The good life.* Hackett Publishing.

Gurley, J. (1999). Platonic paideia. *Philosophy and Literature, 23*(2), 351–377.

Hart, D., Richardson, C., & Wilkenfeld, B. (2011). Civic identity. In S. J. Schwartz et al. (Eds.), *Handbook of identity theory and research* (pp. 771–787). Springer.

Marcel, G. (2001/1951). *The mystery of being II: Faith and reality* (G. S Fraser, Trans.). St. Augustine Press.

Maxwell, N. (2000). Can humanity learn to become civilized? The crisis of science without civilization. *Journal of Applied Philosophy, 17*(1), 29–44.

NCSS. (2020). *Expectations of excellence: Curriculum standards for social studies.* Author. Retrieved from www.socialstudies.org/standards/introduction

Noddings, N. (1998). Caring. In P. H. Hirst & P. White (Eds.), *Philosophy of education: Major themes in the analytic tradition* (Vol. IV), (pp. 40–50). Routledge.

Noddings, N. (1999). Caring and competence. In G. Griffen (Ed.), *The education of teachers* (pp. 205–220). National Society for the Study of Education.

Parker, W. C. (2005). Teaching against idiocy. *Phi Delta Kappan, 86*(5), 344–351.

Piaget, J. (1929). *The child's conception fo the world*. Harcourt, Brace Jovanovich.

Plato. (360 BCE). *Phaedo*. Retrieved from http://classics.mit.edu/Plato/phaedo.html

Raths, L., Harmin, M., & Simon, S. B. (1966). *Values and teaching*. Charles E. Merrill.

Richardson, V. (1996). The role of attitudes and beliefs in learning to teach. In J. Sikula (Ed.), *Handbook of research on teacher education* (2nd ed., pp. 102–119). Macmillan.

Rogers, C. R. (1951). *Client-centered therapy*. Boston, MA: Houghton Mifflin.

Taylor, C. (1992). *The ethics of authenticity*. Harvard University Press.

Vygotsky, L. S. (1978). *Mind in society: The development of higher psychological processes*. Harvard University Press.

2 The Idea of a Social Studies Education

Why Social Studies now? Because whether you are happy, you are suffering, or you are some combination of both, you cannot do better, intellectually, ethically, and practically speaking, than to come to terms with the question: "What is a well-constituted society – and what is my role in it?"

Amy Gutman, President of the University of Pennsylvania (Gutmann, 2010)

As part of a board conceptual framework to make understanding social studies education more manageable for teacher candidates, social studies education can be separated into two contingent parts: The exalted aims and foundational goals. The exalted aims make teaching social studies unique among the teaching fields because teaching social studies is much more than a teacher transferring knowledge or skills to students. The approach to teaching and ideas within the social studies are intended to be transformational. In the process, students' innate inclinations toward goodness should evolve into personal beliefs grounded in the principles of a democratic ideology that are part of the unique identity that each student will rely on as participants in society and the culture will rely on to sustain the democratic ethos. That evolution, guided by thoughtful teachers who are themselves committed to a democratic ideology, requires what is known in Latin as *"cura personalis"* – care for the whole person.

The Exalted Aims

Steve Thornton uses the term "expansive aims" when he says "Social studies purposes extend beyond whatever personal and academic interest this subject matter generates among students" (2002, p. 178). Duplass (2018) agrees, but refers to these expansive aims as the **"exalted aims"** because those extended "purposes" are aimed at liberating students so each student can envision and mature into the best person and citizen they can be. The disciplines of the social studies are used by humankind in the "quest for certainty" (Dewey, 1988/1929, p. 7) about "things that matter" (Taylor, 1992, p. 15); thus making social studies education unique among the subject fields. The National Council for Social Studies (NCSS) takes a similar tack when it defines the term **"civic competence** – the knowledge, intellectual processes, and democratic dispositions required of students to be active and engaged participants in public life" (NCSS, 2020).

In this chapter this concept will be illuminated by explicating the relationship of identity and "the democratic ideals" in the formation of a student's democratic ideology – a world view that is democratic. E. Doyle McCarthy (1994) points out the reciprocal relationship between ideology and identity when he says:

> Ideologies bestow identities. For what is known and believed and thought are not merely knowledges, beliefs, or thoughts, they are what I know and what I believe and what I think. They inscribe in what I do, who I am – my identity.
>
> (p. 423)

The Good Life

Before social studies had a name, philosophers in ancient Greece proposed the answer as to why the social studies is necessary by coining the term *"eudaimonia,"* the Greek word for living the **Good Life**. *Eudaimonia* means human "flourishing," a deep sense of well-being and contentment with one's self. It requires doing the right things, at the right times, towards the right people, for the right end, and in the right way (Aristotle, 350 BCEa). The Good Life should be the personal quest of humans for both the benefit of the individual and society. In 1961, Carl Rogers updated the same concept with the term **"self-actualization"** and made this observation about the Good Life:

> This process of the Good Life is not, I am convinced, a life for the fainthearted. It involves the stretching and growing of becoming more and more of one's potentialities. It involves the courage to be. It means launching oneself fully into the stream of life.
>
> (p. 196)

Figure 2.1 depicts the relationship of the elements leading to the Good Life that are discussed in the following sections.

From Greek philosophy, the word *telos* is used to describe the intended end or purpose that is intrinsic in an object. For humans it is to fulfill their potential, to self-actualize, to live the Good Life (Aristotle, 350 BCEa, 350 BCEb). For the **cosmos**, the *telos* is also purposeful: It has an intrinsic trajectory toward "the good" in spite of the travesties recorded through the centuries that may suggest otherwise. Further, humans as individuals and acting in concert within the cosmos, move the cosmos to its *telos* of a more enlightened, virtuous world. Humankind's evolution to a more democratic ethos is a landmark on that trajectory. It is more than a form of government; it is "a way of life" (Dewey, 1934). It is the *telos* of social studies education.

A Democratic Ideology Defined

Ideology is how individuals envision and interpret the world; it is an individual's world view. Inexplicably, while the term ideology is used prevalently in the field of political science and philosophy, it is seldom found in the social studies education literature or K-12 social studies textbooks (Duplass, 2018). The term **"democratic"** when referring to a "democratic ideology" does not refer to the American Democratic Party, Democrats, or their political stances. In addition, the term democratic – unless stated otherwise – means **liberal democracy** as opposed to the narrow definition of rule by the people. "Liberal" should not be interpreted to mean a liberal as opposed to a conservative political ideology, as used in American politics. Following the Enlightenment, a "liberal" democracy began to be defined broadly as a nation state that has free, multi-candidate

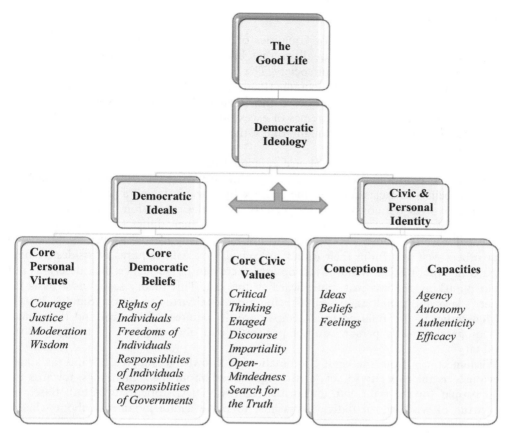

Figure 2.1 Hierarchy of the Good Life

elections; universal suffrage; limited government powers through a constitution or set of laws that transcend the government apparatus; the idea of inalienable rights based on equality of persons; and the rule of law. The following is a definition of a democratic ideology that is used in this book.

> A **democratic ideology** is the product of a disposition to forge a holistic identity based on, at a minimum, the **democratic ideals** of the core **personal virtues** of courage, justice, moderation (temperance), and wisdom; the core **democratic beliefs** in the rights of individuals, freedoms of individuals, responsibility of individuals, and responsibilities of government; and the core **civic values** of critical thinking, engaged discourse, impartiality, open-mindedness, and search for the truth.

Democratic Ideals

The democratic ideals proposed in this book are not exhaustive and subject to preference, but are based on research refined to make a straightforward presentation for teacher candidates (see Duplass, 2018).

Personal Virtues

Virtue is a philosophical term for "qualities of the soul" (see Plato, 360 BCEb). Personal virtues are intrapersonal qualities that bring order to individuals' lives as they propel themselves into the flow of society. The core virtues of wisdom, justice, courage, and moderation originated with Socrates (Plato, 360 BCEb). Aristotle expanded Socrates' four virtues to twelve and proposed the **"theory of the mean,"** explaining that virtues fall in the "mean" of the extremes of excess and deficiency of any virtue (Aristotle, 350 BCEa). Wisdom is best thought of as the super virtue needed to make astute choices between the extremes.

Courage, as an example, is a choice ranging from being rash (excess), courageous (the mean), or cowardly (deficient). Courage can be having the courage by students to state their beliefs in a classroom to the courage by citizens staging a protest.

Justice involves the concept of **just deserts**, as in the expression "you got your just deserts." Those who act well toward others and fulfill their duties to society deserve to be treated well. But those who do not, do not merit being treated as well as those who treat others well and fulfill their duties. A coin, if you will, requires two sides: A one-sided coin cannot exist. Without just deserts, there can be no justice. Just deserts is not about punishing the less just, but rewarding the just. This theory serves as a basis for society's laws and penalties, as well as being a personal virtue to act on (Sandel, 2010).

Moderation is also referred to as temperance. It requires self-control and the regulation of passions so a person can act prudently and obey the laws of the *polis* ("the good city").

Wisdom comes from the right combination of knowledge and reason and, as stated previously, is the capacity to act "at the right times, about the right things, towards the right people, for the right end, and in the right way" (Aristotle, 350 BCEa). Based on the virtue of wisdom, an individual is able to make astute judgments about what is morally right and what action to take.

Democratic Beliefs

The **democratic beliefs** are drawn from the NCSS's *Social Studies for Citizens for a Strong and Free Nation* (1990, pp. 31–32). Each of the listed beliefs are notable because they are politically, ideologically neutral, meaning both conservatives and liberals would likely support them. Further, they promote a democratic ideology over other ideologies because they are stated as universals that all societies should adopt. Each could be defended to students, parents, educators, and communities, even knowing every individual may have a different political ideology and political stance based on the application of each belief.

Civic Values

Values is a sociological term. By the 20th century, the term "values" rather than virtues began to be used and morphed into a noun. To clarify the distinction between values and virtues, consider when someone says an individual has values; what is actually meant is that a person is virtuous. When teachers say they are going to teach values, they are planning to have students consider the democratic ideals and hope students will judge the ideals to be worth valuing and become a belief. There are other lists (see

Rights of the Individual	Freedoms of the Individual
Right to life	Freedom to participate in the political process
Right to liberty	Freedom of worship
Right to dignity	Freedom of thought
Right to security	Freedom of conscience
Right to equality of opportunity	Freedom of assembly
Right to justice	Freedom of inquiry
Right to privacy	Freedom of expression
Right to private ownership of property	
Responsibilities of the Individual	**Responsibilities of Government**
To respect human life	Societies need laws that are accepted by the
To respect the rights of others	majority of the people
To be tolerant	Dissenting minorities are protected
To be honest	Government is elected by the people
To be compassionate	Government respects and protects individual rights
To demonstrate self-control	Government respects and protects individual
To participate in the democratic process	freedoms
To respect the property of others	Government guarantees civil liberties
	Government works for the common good

Figure 2.2 NCSS Democratic Beliefs

Duplass, 2018, pp. 16–17) by multiple authors of "values" such as diligence, kindness, truthfulness, loyalty, willingness to compromise, and beliefs in equality, social justice, etc., most all of which are synonymous with the NCSS's list of democratic beliefs or the democratic ideals.

The core values selected for this framework are influenced by Hunt and Metcalf (1955), who proposed that even if there is not a consensus on the list and meaning of universal, democratic ideals, there must be agreement on "the method of inquiry by which to explore differences in the meaning and the truth of propositions and the justifiability of values" (p. 34). The following core civic values are also politically, ideologically neutral. They are focused on the disposition needed to further an individual's holistic identity and the preservation of the democratic ideological ethos (Sandel, 2010).

Critical thinking is characterized by Dewey as "intellectual integrity, observation, and interest in testing their opinions and beliefs that are characteristic of the scientific attitude" (1934, p. 99). He called for **impartiality, open-mindedness**, and **search for the truth** so students could develop "a quality of mind at once flexible and concentrated in dealing with new material, a certain attitude of mind, a mental openness and eagerness" (1882/1899), p. 51) and an "open-minded preference for conclusions that are properly grounded" (1899/1924, p. 202). Regarding search for the truth, Dewey stated, "There is no belief so settled as not to be exposed to further inquiry" (Dewey, 1998, p. 16). Dewey (1932/1984) recognized that **discourse** about things that matter requires critical thinking and moral reasoning. It is moral reasoning which draws on ideas and beliefs that facilitates the development of the holistic identity and a democratic ideology. Haidt (2013) explains the role of moral reasoning:

Moral reasoning is something we engage in after an automatic process (passion, emotion or, more generally, intuition) has already pointed us toward a judgment or conclusion. We engage in moral reasoning not to figure out what is really true, but to prepare for social interactions in which we might be called upon to justify our judgments to others. It is a distinctive fact about moral judgments that we can't simply point to our own preferences as sufficient justification.

(p. 287)

Civic and Personal Identity

Identity is humankind's way of knowing, being, and acting. **Personal identity** is derived from a set of **conceptions** unique to each individual comprising ideas, beliefs, and feelings, and the **identity capacities** of autonomy, authenticity, efficacy, and agency. Personal identity gives form to an individual's civic identity by individuals becoming aware of and choosing to awaken within themselves the intuitive and intrinsic, but partially veiled, democratic ideals tethered to the *telos* of humanity and the cosmos. Civic and personal identity must be copacetic for a holistic, healthy, and productive identity (Charles Taylor, 1989). While personal identity is intrapersonal, civic identity is interpersonal; it is how ideas and beliefs are projected into the society. Personal identity should be based on the "beliefs, attitudes, or feelings that an individual is proud of, is willing to publicly affirm, has been chosen thoughtfully from alternatives without persuasion, and is acted on repeatedly" (Raths, Harmin, & Simon, 1966, p. 28). **Civic identity** is "a set of beliefs and emotions about oneself as a participant in the civic life of a community" (Hart, Richardson, & Wilkenfeld, 2011, p. 773).

Seneca, the Roman philosopher, described the relationship of the individual to society when he said, "What is required, you see, of any man is that he should be of use to other men – if possible, to many; failing that, to a few; failing that, to those nearest him; failing that, to himself" (Cooper & Procopé, 1995, p. 35). As Plato states, "man is not born in the public eye, but he is made there" (Gurley, 1999, p. 360). It is a democratic society that creates the most supportive context for individuals to develop the holistic identity necessary to achieve the Good Life. It is the pervasiveness of individuals in a society pursing the Good Life that makes it possible for democracy and the *polis* (ancient Greek for the "just city") to thrive.

Conceptions

Based on individuals' formal exposure to the foundational knowledge and the democratic ideals of the social studies, they refine their construct of ideas derived from personal experience about humankind and their place in the cosmos. It is hoped that the democratic ideals evolve into deeply embedded beliefs and feelings about oneself as a participant in the civic life of a community.

Capacities

Every teaching field requires students to learn foundational knowledge. If one accepts the premise that social studies education is not about just what students know, but what a person should and can become, then the following capacities become essential as goals of a social studies education. When teachers of social studies create investigations and discussions of things that matter, the intent is not just to learn foundational knowledge, but to practice the core civic values and reflect on their democratic beliefs and virtues – indeed, it is to have students consider what kind of person they want to be. Such considerations about one's humanity have therapeutic underpinning because students engage their partially developed intrapersonal capacities to explore and express their identity and consider changes when reflecting on things that matter – those "knotty principles such as tolerance, impartial justice, the separation of church and state, the need for limits on majority power, or the difference between liberty and license" (Parker, 2005, p. 347). That process, if viewed through the lens of humanistic psychology and philosophy (see Buber, 2000; Marcel, 2001/1951), is intended to empower students using existing capacities and facilitate the further development of those essential capacities so as to propel the students closer to *eudemonia*.

Agency – is the capacity to make deliberate choices and take actions (Bandura, 2008). **Moral agency** – means the decisions are grounded in concepts of right and wrong and individuals are compelled to take actions based on those judgments because taking the action is the right thing to do (Kant, 1785/1993). It is because human beings are able to govern their own actions that they are also capable and worthy of governing their collective lives, "Democracy is a form of government that presumes a society of moral agents" (Alexander, 2003, p. 378).

Autonomy – is the ability of individuals to reflect critically on their principles, decide how to live, consider their circumstances, and act based on those reflections:

> Autonomy is not the condition of democracy; democracy is the condition of autonomy. Without participating in the common life that defines them and in the decision-making that shapes their social habitat, women and men cannot become individuals. Freedom, justice, equality, and autonomy are all products of common thinking and common living.
>
> (Barber, 1984, p. xv)

Authenticity – "aims at defining and realizing one's own identity as a person" (Guignon, 2006, p. 136). It is based on the principle "whereby each individual is thought to have a unique identity, an original way of being human, to which he or she must be true" to have the Good Life (Taylor, 1992, p. 38). "Authenticity is a personal undertaking insofar as it entails personal integrity and responsibility for self. But it also has a social dimension insofar as it brings with it a sense of belongingness and indebtedness to the wider social context that makes it [authenticity] possible" (Guignon, 1999, p. 163). Autonomy is projected outwardly, "This is who I am and what I stand for," whereas authenticity is directed inwardly, "Do my actions reflect my beliefs?" (Cooke, 1997).

Self-efficacy – makes it possible to choose goals autonomously and achieve them as authentic human beings because individuals have come to believe in themselves, that they can master the difficult challenges to have the Good Life (Bandura, 1982).

Resources

Videos: *CrashCourse:* Government and Politics #35 | *Khan Academy*: Ideology; Mind; Personal Identity; The Good Life Aristotle; The Good Life Kant; The Good Life Plato; Kohlberg Moral Development | *TED Talk*: Michael Sandle The Lost Art of Democratic Debate | *YouTube:* Aristotle and Virtue Theory; Plato on the Cardinal

Virtues; Political Ideology; The Psychology of Authenticity; Rogers in Ten Minutes; Total Philosophy Aristotle's Virtue Ethics; What is the Concept of Autonomy; Why Should We Teach Moral Reasoning Phil Temple.

Documents: *Routledge Handbook of Research in Social Studies Education*: Continuity and Change in Social Studies; Social Justice and the Social Studies) | *Book of Virtues* (classic morality stories and seven videos for K-5) | Constitutional Cases and the Four Cardinal Virtues | Virtuous Minds (book and video) | *ReadWriteThink*: Chasing the Dream: Researching the Meaning of the American Dream.

References

Alexander, H. A. (2003). Moral education and liberal democracy: Spirituality, community, and character in an open society. *Educational Theory, 53*(4), 367–387.

Aristotle. (350 BCEa). *Nicomachean ethics*. Retrieved from http://classics.mit.edu/Aristotle/nicoma chaen.html

Aristotle (350 BCEb). *De Anima*. Retrieved from http://classics.mit.edu/Aristotle/soul.html

Bandura, A. (1982). Self-efficacy mechanism in human agency. *American Psychologist, 37*(2), 122–147.

Bandura, A. (2008). An agentic perspective on positive psychology. Positive psychology: Exploring the best in people. In S. Lopez (Ed.), *Discovering human strengths* (Vol. 1, pp. 167–196). Praeger.

Barber, B. R. (1984). *Strong democracy: Participatory politics for a new age*. University of California Press.

Buber, M. (2000). *I and Thou* (R. Smith, Trans.). Scribner.

Cooke, M. (1997). Authenticity and autonomy: Taylor, Habermas, and the politics of recognition. *Political Theory, 25*(2), 258–288.

Cooper, J. M., & Procopé, J. F. (Ed. & Trans.). (1995). *Seneca: Moral and political essays*. Cambridge University Press.

Dewey, J. (1882/1899). A college course: What should I expect from it? In J. A. Boydston (Ed.), *John Dewey: The early works, 1889–1992* (Vol. 3, pp. 51–55). Southern Illinois Press.

Dewey, J. (1899/1924). Reconstruction in philosophy. In J. A. Boydston (Ed.), *John Dewey: The middle works, 1920* (Vol. 12, pp. 79–201). Southern Illinois University Press.

Dewey, J. (1932/1984). Qualitative thought. In J. A. Boydston (Ed.), *John Dewey: The later works, 1932–1984* (Vol. 5, pp. 242–262). Southern Illinois University Press.

Dewey, J. (1934). *A common faith*. Yale University Press.

Dewey, J. (1938). *Logic: The theory of inquiry*, Henry Holt and Co. Reprinted in J.A. Boydston (Ed.), John Dewey; The later works, 1938 (Vol. 12, pp. 9–30). Southern Illinois Univeristy Press.

Dewey, J. (1988/1929). The quest for certainty. In J. A. Boydston (Ed.), *John Dewey: The later works, 1925–1953* (Vol. 4). Southern Illinois University Press.

Duplass, J. (2018). *The idea of a social studies education. The role of philosophical counseling*. Routledge.

Guignon, C. (1999). *The good life*. Hackett Publishing.

Guignon, C. (2006). *On being authentic*. Routledge.

Gurley, J. (1999). Platonic paideia. *Philosophy and Literature, 23*(2), 351–377.

Gutmann, A. (2010). *Social studies – Then and now*. The Navin Narayan Memorial Lecture, 50th Anniversary Celebration of Social Studies, Harvard University, Retrieved from www.upenn.edu/president/meet-president/Social-Studies-Then-and-Now

Haidt, J. (2013). Moral psychology for the twenty-first century. *Journal of Moral Education, 42*(3), 281–297. Retrieved from: www.tandfonline.com/doi/full/10.1080/03057240.2013.817327?scroll=top&needAccess=true

Hart, D., Richardson, C., & Wilkenfeld, B. (2011). Civic identity. In S. J. Schwartz et al., (Ed.), *Handbook of identity theory and research* (pp. 771–787). Springer.

Hunt, M., & Metcalf, L. (1955). *Teaching high school social studies.* New York: Harper & Row.

Kant, I. (1785/1993). *Grounding for the metaphysics of morals* (3rd ed.) (J. W. Ellington, Trans.). Hackett Publishing.

Marcel, G. (2001/1951). *The Mystery of Being II: Faith and Reality* (G. S Fraser, Trans.). St. Augustine Press.

McCarthy, E. D. (1994). The uncertain future of ideology: Rereading Marx. *Sociological Quarterly, 35*(3), 415–428.

NCSS. (1990). *Social studies for citizens for a strong and free nation.* Social Studies Curriculum Planning Resources, NCSS.

NCSS (2020). *National curriculum standards for social studies: Introduction.* Retrieved from www.socialstudies.org/standards/introduction

Parker, W. C. (2005). Teaching against idiocy. *Phi Delta Kappan, 86*(5), 344–351.

Plato. (360 BCEa). *The republic.* Retrieved from http://classics.mit.edu/Plato/republic.html.

Plato. (360 BCEb). *Phaedo.* Retrieved from http://classics.mit.edu/Plato/phaedo.html.

Raths, L., Harmin, M., & Simon, S. B. (1966). *Values and teaching.* Charles E. Merrill.

Rogers, C. (1961). *On becoming a person: A therapist's view of psychotherapy.* Constable.

Sandel, M. (2010). *The lost art of democratic debate.* TED2020. Retrieved from www.ted.com/talks/michael_sandel_the_lost_art_of_democratic_debate?language=en

Taylor, C. (1989). *Sources of the self: The making of the modern identity.* Harvard University Press.

Taylor, C. (1992). *The ethics of authenticity.* Harvard University Press.

Thornton, S. J. (2002). Does everybody count as human? *Theory & Research in Social Education, 30*(2), 178–189.

3 Perspectives on Being a Teacher of Social Studies

Those who know, do. Those that understand, teach.
Aristotle, Greek Philosopher, 384–322 BCE (Sweet Books, 2019, CP)

A recent graduate was asked what surprised her most upon becoming a teacher. Her answer bears repeating: "I was surprised at how easy it is to get by as a mediocre teacher and how hard the job is if you want to be a really great teacher." While the knowledge about the teaching craft can be learned in books and university classes, an individual can only become a craftsman by practicing the craft. *Praxis* is the Greek word used to describe the practical application of knowledge as opposed to just knowing its theory. S.G. Grant and Jill Gradwell (2010) describe teachers who can practice the craft of teaching as "ambitious" social studies teachers who know:

1. Their subject matter well and see within it the potential to enrich their students' lives;
2. Their students well, which includes the kinds of lives their students lead, how these youngsters think about and perceive the world, and that they are far more capable than they and most others believe them to be; and
3. How to create the necessary space for themselves and their students in environments in which others (e.g., administrators, other teachers) may not appreciate their efforts.

(p. 2)

The following perspectives should be helpful to teacher candidates as they embark on a training program to be a social studies teacher.

Teaching as a Craft

The word "craft" is used because it brings to mind the fine craftsmen of the Renaissance who merged their knowledge and skills with individual imagination and a work ethic that produced the great cathedrals of Europe. The craftsman is described by David Moore (1995) as a person "who knows exactly what she must do, brings the tools she needs, does the work with straightforward competence, and takes pleasure in a job well done" (p. 1).

Teaching as a Profession

Berliner (1994) describes five stages that a teacher can pass through during a career – novice, advanced beginner, competent, proficient, and expert. The ascension through the stages is based largely on ambition and initiative of the teacher candidate through "reflective practice" (Clift, Houston, & Pugach, 1990). **Reflective practice** is "learning through and from experience towards gaining new insights of self and practice" (Finlay, 2008, p. 1). There is significant evidence that teacher candidates are reticent to adopt new practices that are different from how they prefer to learn or were taught, even if their teacher education program promotes reflective practice and research-based practices that are unlike what they experienced or favored as students (Olson, 1993).

Teacher satisfaction is linked to a teacher's sense of control of their craft, leadership by the principal, staff cohesiveness, and collegiality in decision-making. Dissatisfaction is linked to bureaucracy, limited resources, class sizes, discipline problems, and problems beyond the school's control (Polatcan & Cansoy, 2019).

Teaching as a Moral Activity

Almost every action taken by teachers of social studies is a manifestation of their ideology and identity – it expresses a moral perspective. The personal virtues, democratic beliefs, and civic values of social studies teachers, unlike teachers in other subject fields, are of paramount concern because it affects what and how they choose to teach and their moral perspective is on display during the act of teaching. Teachers' credibility is judged by students, in "real time," based on teachers' projection of who they are and what they stand for. If the teacher is underprepared and disorganized, they question the teacher's commitment; if the teacher does not develop a rapport with students, students question how much the teacher cares; if the teacher does not articulate a stance opposed to undemocratic perspectives, the teacher is viewed as inauthentic; and if the teacher is unwilling to honestly navigate with students ideas and beliefs that matter that allow the students to develop their own personal identity and ideology, students will question the teacher's commitment to a democratic ideology. As a consequence, social studies teachers must display a caring disposition while maintaining classroom order and exude the same democratic ideology that they are expected to teach about to their students. Few professions have such a moral calling.

Walter Parker (2005) identifies three principles that should be part of the moral imperative of social studies teachers – two more, altruism and meliorism, are added:

1. "Democracy (rule by the people) is morally superior to autocracy (rule by one person), theocracy (rule by clerics), aristocracy (rule by a permanent upper class), plutocracy (rule by the rich), and the other alternatives, mainly because it better secures liberty, justice, and equality than the others do";
2. "There can be no democracy without democrats [note the small d]. Democratic ways of living together, with the people's differences intact and recognized, are not given by nature; they are created"; and
3. "Engaged citizens do not materialize out of thin air. They do not naturally grasp such knotty principles as tolerance, impartial justice, the separation of church and state, the need for limits on majority power, or the difference between liberty and license" (p. 347).

4. **Altruism** is described by Joseph Adelson (1986) as follows:

> He concentrates neither on himself, nor the subject-matter, nor the discipline, but on the student, saying: "I will help you become what you are". We may recall Michelangelo's approach to sculpture: looking at the raw block of marble, he tried to uncover the statue within it. So does the altruistic teacher regard his unformed student; this type of teacher keeps his achievement and personality secondary; he works to help the student find what is best and most essential.
>
> (p. 114)

5. **Meliorism** is the belief that the specific conditions which exist at one moment, be they comparatively bad or good, may be improved (Dewey, 1899/1924). Meliorism is what Ruetenik (2008) called a "heart-felt belief that human action can mitigate suffering in the world" (p. 498). It is this forward-looking, caring, and hopeful demeanor that says to children and teenagers that whatever their personal or civic identity challenges are or the undesirable circumstances they were born into or created for themselves, there is the Good Life to be had.

Teaching as Enculturation

Students are in the midst of what anthropologists call **enculturation**: The process by which humans acquire their culture. The enculturation of children into a democratic way of life is necessary because the shared democratic ideology is the glue that binds the members of a society, even though members may have different political ideologies and stances. Multicultural, pluralistic, egalitarian, liberal democracies, such as the United States, have designated schools as the organization with a primary responsibility to enculturate its disparate peoples into the flow of the democratic ethos. When teaching social studies, teachers are being asked to mediate between what ideas and beliefs students bring with them to their schools and what a democracy demands (Hedegaard, 2002). Teachers of social studies have, effectively, been asked to replace the elders of preliterate tribes who would explain and model for their next generation the expectations for tribal membership.

Modern democracies assume that parents and teachers are able to articulate what a democratic ideology is, that they themselves practice it, advocate it as something young people should aspire to, and that they can take the educational steps to help young people adopt the ideology. John Childs (1950) explains:

> As we introduce the young to the various aspects of human experience ... we inevitably encourage attitudes and habits of response in and to these affairs. In order to encourage, we must discourage; in order to foster, we must also hinder; in order to emphasize the significant, we must identify the nonsignificant; and finally, in order to select and focus attention on certain subject matters of life, we have to reject and ignore other subject matters.
>
> (p. 6)

Mass media and the internet have changed the landscape of enculturation in the same way the mass production of books led to the dissemination of ideas that revolutionized the West. Marshall McLuhan warned, however, of media's greater impact when he said,

"All media works us over completely. They are so pervasive in their personal, political, economic, aesthetic, psychological, moral, ethical, and social consequences that they leave no part of us untouched, unaffected, unaltered" (McLuhan & Fiore, 1967, p. 26). For all its benefits, mass media and the internet are seen to anesthetize individuals to their own inner consciousness, promulgate un-sifted, undemocratic ideas couched to appeal to self, undemocratic interest, and leads to greater isolation from the larger body politic where their instinctive democratic beliefs have traditionally been reinforced. The social studies classroom is intended to be a unique, safe space for young people to have democratic discussions about democratic ideals with a responsible, nonpartisan "tribal leader."

Teaching as Philosophical Counseling

Nell Noddings makes the case that "Teaching is not just intellectual but is relational so as to engage the purposes and energies of those being taught, teachers must build relationships of care and trust" (1992, p. 196). That care and trust is important for all teaching, but essential to the highly personal feelings and thoughts brought on by considerations of things that matter during social studies instruction. For individuals to reconsider who they are, want to be, and the kind of world they want to help create, the teacher must expect to engage students at a therapeutic level requiring the teacher to act as a philosophical counselor (see Chapter 10).

The Teacher's Ten Roles

The following is a brief delineation of the most common roles that a teacher must assume and every teacher candidate should think deeply about.

1. **Instructor.** Excellent teaching is hard to define, but most people know it when they see it. Great teaching comes from the hard work of planning, innate creativity, openness to different methods, and never being totally satisfied with the way a lesson turned out. With this kind of reflection and diligence, a teacher can turn good instruction into excellent instruction.
2. **Performer.** It cannot be denied that there is a theatrical aspect to instruction. Sometimes individuals mistakenly think they should be comics or they are there to put on a show. Strategic use of humor, use of the staging and props, exaggerating emotions for effect, structuring phrases to catch the learner's attention, and changing voice cadence and volume are crucial to communicating ideas.
3. **Planner.** It would be so simple if teachers only had to plan what they were going to tell the students about the content, like giving a speech. But that would mean teachers do not have to take into consideration the mandated standards, the best instructional practices, or students' age, attention span, interest, readiness, and mood. Teachers cannot plan enough! And planning is not limited to a semester plan and daily class notes and ancillaries. Teachers need to plan their classroom layout, bulletin boards, classroom rules, grading practices, parent notices, etc.
4. **Course manager.** The planning and management roles go hand in hand. An elementary teacher with 25 students and middle or high school teacher with 150 students must manage a series of lessons and documentation of students' progress. Schools may require filings of lesson plans, reports of conferences with parents, detailed

record keeping of grades, standards achieved, attendance, referrals, etc. Grading of papers, exams, and portfolios can be overwhelming unless structured to minimize the effort.

5. **Stakeholder/change agent.** The duty of teachers extends beyond their classes and students. Participation in national, state, school district, school, and department undertakings and extracurricular activities require their attention and participation.

6. **Advisor/mentor.** In this role, students (and parents) will seek teachers' counsel on matters related to students' general well-being. This kind of continuous and often spontaneous interactions with students and parents requires thoughtfulness, caring, and judgment: It is crucial to the kind of human connection that allows social studies teachers to have success in their role a teacher.

7. **Coach/moderator.** Providing "out-of-class" opportunities for students has evolved into an essential part of schools. Most agree that the additional financial compensation for a teacher to coach or serve as a moderator is rarely worth the time commitment financially and is seldom the motivation for taking on such assignments. Teachers may have extensive experience in sports or activities like acting or debating and it may be one of the motivations for becoming a teacher. Choosing to be a coach or moderator has the advantage of students getting to know teachers outside the classroom in a less formal light and has a positive effect on the classroom climate.

8. **Colleague.** Teachers may make lifelong friends in their workplace that will include janitorial staff, secretaries, security offices, librarians, counselors, administrators, and fellow teachers. A new teacher's goal should be to "fit in" and get a "lay of the land," appreciate the wise advice that will be offered, and not be reticent to ask for advice and resources from colleagues. As a new teacher, the best way to do that is to become a good listener, to work at "winning friends and influencing people" (see *Resources*).

9. **Scholar and lifelong learner.** A university degree does not mean a teacher stops learning. Even though the social studies' content does not change rapidly at the K-12 level, how to make it usable and teach it in new ways continuously evolves. Few predicted how the digital age and the standards movement would change the teaching craft. Consider a master's degree as a formalized way of keeping up with practices. Join a regional or national professional organization (refer to *Students' Introduction*), which usually comes with a journal subscription. Attend regional and national conferences.

10. **Classroom manager.** New teachers may have great ideas on how to teach and can love their assigned courses, but managing students' behaviors must be the first priority. Teachers who fail to take charge will not get to teach the subject matter that they so dearly love or try out the great ideas on how to teach it. New teachers are at a disadvantage compared with second-year and experienced teachers, because they will not have a "reputation" that precedes them. As a result, students will "push boundaries" of classroom behavior and decorum. One of the most important tasks for new teachers is to make sure students understand who has to be in charge and to convey that message with a demeanor that does not provoke resistance or animosity. A teacher's demeanor and communication style from the first minutes of the first class set the tone. A classroom, while it can be enjoyable and everyone can have a good laugh from time to time, is a place where serious work gets done by serious-minded people.

Resources

Videos: *ABC News:* What Makes Great Teachers | *PBS:* Altruism | *TCH:* (is a subscription service, effective Spring 2020, but many of the videos may be found on YouTube); New Teacher Survival Guide; Parent-Teacher Conference; Planning; Classroom Management | *YouTube:* The Medium is the Message | How to Win Friends and Influence People by Dale Carnegie Animated Book.

Documents: *Routledge Handbook of Research in Social Studies Education*: The Education of Social Studies Teachers; The Professional Development of Social Studies Teachers | *Wiley Handbook of Social Studies Research*: Becoming an Expert Teacher | *NEA:* Management Tips for New Teachers; What I Wish I Had Known | *The Power Moves*: How to Win Friends and Influence People.

References

Adelson, J. (1986). *Inventing adolescence: The political psychology of everyday schooling.* Piscataway, NJ: Transaction Publishers.

Berliner, D. C. (1994). Teacher expertise. In B. Moon & A. S. Mayes (Eds.), *Teaching and learning in the secondary school.* (pp. 20–26). Routledge/The Open University.

Childs, J. L. (1950). *Education and morals.* Appleton-Century-Crofts.

Clift, R. T., Houston, W. R., & Pugach, M. C. (Eds.). (1990). *Encouraging reflective practice in education: An analysis of issues and programs.* Teachers College Press.

Dewey, J. (1899/1924). Reconstruction in philosophy. In J. A. Boydston (Ed.), *John Dewey: The middle works, 1920* (Vol. 12, pp. 79–201). Southern Illinois University Press.

Finlay, L. (2008). *Reflecting on "reflective practice".* PBPL paper 52. England: The Open University. Retrieved from www.open.ac.uk/opencetl/sites/www.open.ac.uk.opencetl/files/files/ecms/web-content/Finlay-(2008)-Reflecting-on-reflective-practice-PBPL-paper-52.pdf

Grant, S. G., & Gradwell, J. (Eds.). (2010). *Teaching history with big ideas: Cases of ambitious teachers.* Rowman & Littlefield Education.

Hedegaard, M. (2002). *Learning and child development.* Aarhus University Press.

McLuhan, M., & Fiore, Q. (1967). *The medium is the massage.* Random House.

Moore, D. (1995). *Remarks on receiving the MAA's 1994 Award for Distinguished College or University Teaching of Mathematics.* San Francisco, CA, January 1995. MAA Focus 15 (1995) Number 2, 5–8. Retrieved from www.stat.purdue.edu/~dsmoore/articles/Craft.pdf

Noddings, N. (1992). *The challenge to care in schools.* Teachers College Press.

Olson, M. R. (1993). *Knowing what counts in teacher education.* Paper presented at the Canadian Association of Teacher Educators, Canadian Society of Studies in Education, Ottawa, CA.

Parker, W. C. (2005). Teaching against idiocy. *Phi Delta Kappan, 86*(5), 344–351.

Polatcan, M., & Cansoy, R. (2019). Examining studies on the factors predicting teachers' job satisfaction: A systematic review. *International Online Journal of Education and Teaching (IOJET), 6*(1), 116–134. Retrieved from www.iojet.org/index.php/IOJET/article/view/477

Ruetenik, T. L. (2008). Meliorism. In J. Lachs & R. Talisse (Eds.), *Encyclopedia of American philosophy* (pp. 498–501). Routledge.

Sweet Books. (2019). *Those who know, do. Those that understand, teach.* Independently Published.

4 Ideology

The unexamined life is not worth living.
> Socrates, Greek Philosopher and Counselor, 470–399 BCE (Plato, 399 BCE)

It is often overlooked, but asking the fundamental question of "What is my goal in teaching my students?" is central to deciding the what, when, and how of teaching. For non-social studies teachers, it is sufficient to ask, "At the end of the year, what do I want my students to KNOW?" For social studies teachers, that question would be deficient; they have a more exalted and complicated question: "At the end of the year, what do I want my students to have considered that they should BELIEVE in?"

Finding that single term that scholars, practitioners, and learned societies are able to agree upon as to what students should believe in has proven to be elusive (Duplass, 2018; Vinson, 1998). In this chapter, a justification will be made for the use of the term "**democratic ideology**." The choice of the term and the definition is certainly worthy of academic debate. In its defense, it has the advantage of concisely answering the question, the term is used extensively in philosophical and political science discourse, encompasses and condenses many widely accepted lengthy renditions found in the social studies education literature, is neither ideologically conservative nor liberal, and elegantly fits with the emphasis of the NCSS on civics education (NCSS, 2020).

Ideology, Political Ideology, and Political Ideological Stances

In Chapter 2, a democratic ideology was defined as composed of the democratic ideals of personal virtues, democratic beliefs, and civic values that is reflected in an individual's civic and personal identity. This paradigm helps not only define the difference between a democratic ideology and undemocratic ideologies, but also encompasses the range of political ideologies that are democratic and the core civic values required to examine differences. By this archetype, social studies teachers should be better positioned to teach and model the democratic ideals that students should come to believe in with less concern about claims of bias, partiality, or indoctrination. However, to fully explicate this idea of a democratic ideology, the following differences between ideology, political ideology, and political stances and their relationship to a personal and civic identity are proposed.

Figure 4.1 depicts the relationship of identity to a political stance.

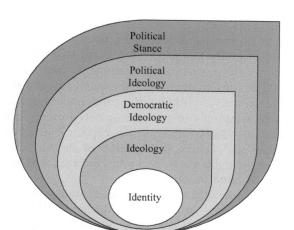

Figure 4.1 Identity to Political Stance

Based on individuals' identity, they project an ideology.

Ideology is how each person interprets and envisions the world; it is an individual's world view. Through enculturation, democratic societies promote the democratic ideals and encourage the identity necessary for individuals and society to thrive.

A **political ideology** is a "set of beliefs about the proper order of society and how it can be achieved" (Gerring, 1997, 1998). In the US, political ideology is often envisioned on a simplistic scale from liberal to conservative.

A **political ideological stance** comprises the policies or programs individuals personally support based on their political ideology (Gerring, 1997, 1998).

As an example, there were different political ideologies at work through the centuries that resulted in different political stances as to who should be eligible to vote in the United States. This should not be taken to mean that the people in their time and place did not hold a democratic ideology (see "Histories Hazards" in Chapter 13); rather, that the teleology of the cosmos toward a more humane global community is working and dissenting individuals' peaceful acquiescence reflects an evolving, global commitment to an increasingly more democratic way of life.

Students bring to the social studies classroom their preexisting identity and ideology from their homes, communities, and experienced mass media. It appears that most students come to the classroom door with the basic concepts of democratic ideals as part of their identity. Often democratic and undemocratic notions have been adopted imperceptibly as part of the flow of living, without the benefit of reflection and reason. Teachers of social studies are called upon to alter that trajectory by insisting that students' ideology, political ideology, and ideological stances be based on reason. The examination of factual examples of ideological stances and concepts of political ideology with a teacher of social studies leads to internalization of concepts by students in what becomes an essential part of their identity. For a democratic ideology and an authentic holistic identity, ideology through political stances must be consistent, selected freely, and justified by logic.

Based on the code of ethics of the profession (NCSS, 2016, see Part I), it would be unthinkable for teachers to promote an undemocratic ideology or political stance. They are, however, expected to investigate all ideologies, because their students may not have, as of yet, considered alternatives that must be rejected when placed under the microscope of reason. Teachers are not to dissuade students from their chosen democratic stances, but they should compel students to witness and practice the art of democratic thinking. The unfortunate, naïve, unthoughtful, and undemocratic assertions of students are best viewed as symptoms of an inadequately formed identity and a lack of understanding of democratic ideals. The remedy is explicit instruction geared to individuals clarifying their ideas and beliefs; illumination of the virtues, democratic beliefs, and civic values of the democratic ideals; and a teacher that students perceive as caring and a role model of a democratic ideology.

By using this ideology framework, teachers of social studies can avoid being "impaled on the horns of an indoctrination – or – neutrality dilemma" (Hand, 2014, p. 531). Hand uses the term "tenets" as equivalent to democratic ideals and argues for three pedagogies that promote a democratic ideology, but not a political ideological stance:

One, "robustly justified" essential, admirable moral tenets should be taught in two ways. Teachers should first aim to have children subscribe to them through "praise and admonition, example and modelling, habituation and training" and second, aim to have children see the good and compelling reasons for the tenets.

Two, admirable moral tenants should be taught by nondirective moral inquiry that focuses on the possible justifications. The teacher should not attempt to persuade children to take any one political stance that might flow from the moral tenet, but help them clarify their reasoning so that identity, ideology, political ideology, and political stances are consistent.

Three, there are some moral standards that are straightforwardly unjustified, such as racism, and to which teachers must take a stand. However, even "These standards should be subject to critical scrutiny in the classroom with a view to bringing out the inadequacy of their supporting arguments" (Hand, 2014, pp. 530–531).

It is noteworthy that these strategies are contingent on extensive discourse in classrooms. Regrettably, time dedicated to social studies (much less discussion about things that matter) in elementary schools has dramatically declined and when social studies is taught at any K-12 level, there is little time dedicated to discussing enduring ideas or democratic ideals (Kahne, Rodriguez, Smith, & Thiede, 2000; Nystrand, Gamoran, & Carbonara, 1998; O'Connor, Heafner, & Groce, 2007).

The Essential Identity Questions

The following "**essential identity questions**" are intended to set the "tone" so the year-long social studies lessons can focus on things that matter. Envision these questions on poster paper permanently placed on the classroom wall and discussed in depth during the first days and weeks of class and then referred to during discussions of things that matter.

The first question is a sufficient starting point for the foundational goals of social studies education. The second question requires a judgment about ideas and beliefs, the current state of affairs in the world, and the alternative political ideological stances. The third question transitions to the exalted aims by requiring an individual judgment based on personal virtues and democratic beliefs by positing the concept of duty – an obligation to something greater than one's self. The last two questions are tied to the exalted aims by having

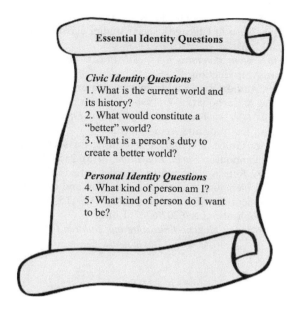

Figure 4.2 Classroom Scroll of the Essential Identity Questions

students reflect on their identity. Throughout a discussion brought on by the questions, the civic values would be insisted upon by the teacher. By repeatedly drawing students' attention to the essential identity questions during lessons, teachers are promoting students' understanding of themselves as human beings and their duties to others.

Resources

Videos: *CrashCourse:* Government and Politics #35; Political Ideology | *Kahn Academy:* Political Ideology and Economics; Ideologies of Political Parties in the United States; Ideology and Social Policy | *TED Talk:* Jonathan Haidt The Moral Roots of Liberals and Conservatives.

Documents: *Routledge Handbook of Research in Social Studies Education:* Knowing and Doing in Democratic Citizenship Education | *PBS:* Take the Political Party Quiz to Find Out Where You Fit | *TEXAS CTE:* Lesson Plan Political Ideology | What is Ideology John Levi Martin.

References

Duplass, J. (2018). *The idea of a social studies education. The role of philosophical counseling.* Routledge.

Gerring, J. (1997). Ideology: A definitional analysis. *Political Research Quarterly, 50*(4), 957–994.

Gerring, J. (1998). *Party ideologies in America, 1828–1996.* Cambridge University Press.

Hand, M. (2014). Towards a theory of moral education. *Journal of Philosophy of Education, 48*(4), 519–532.

Kahne, J., Rodriguez, M., Smith, B., & Thiede, K. (2000). Developing citizens for democracy? Assessing opportunities to learn in Chicago's social studies classrooms. *Theory and Research in Social Education, 28*(3), 311–338.

NCSS. (2020). *National curriculum standards for social studies: Introduction.* Retrieved from www.socialstudies.org/standards/introduction.

NEA. (1975). *Code of ethics.* Author. Retrieved from www.nea.org/home/30442.htm

Nystrand, M., Gamoran, A., & Carbonara, W. (1998). *Towards an ecology of learning: The case of classroom discourse and its effects on writing in high school English and social studies.* National Research Center on English Learning and Achievement.

O'Connor, K., Heafner, T., & Groce, E. (2007). Advocating for social studies: Documenting the decline and doing something about it. *Social Education, 71*(5), 255–260.

Plato. (399 BCE). *The apology.* Retrieved from http://classics.mit.edu/Plato/apology.html

Vinson, K. D. (1998). The problematics of character education and civic virtue: A critical response to the NCSS position statement. *Social Education, 62*(2), 112–115. Retrieved from www.socialstudies.org/sites/default/files/publications/se/6202/620211.html

Westheimer, J. (2015). *What kind of citizen? Educating our children for the common good.* Teachers College Press.

5 Wisdom and Knowledge

Goodness without knowledge is blind; knowledge without goodness is dangerous.
Inscription above the entry to Phillips Exeter Academy
(Phillips Exeter Academy, 2020)

The above inscription captures the primary reason why this book emphasizes the relationship between exalted aims and foundational goals. Terms like knowledge, ideas, and beliefs have different nuanced meanings in philosophy, psychology, social studies education, and everyday use. As Jack Nelson points out, "Definitions of knowledge are the product of history and ideology, and this is nowhere truer than in the social sciences and social studies" (2001, p. 21).

Wisdom

Social studies education inherited four pivotal assumptions from Greek philosophy:

1. Knowledge is not an end in itself, but a pathway to wisdom.
2. Knowledge can be taught, but is no guarantee of wisdom.
3. Wisdom is the capacity to "act at the right times, about the right things, towards the right people, for the right end, and in the right way" (Aristotle, 350 BCE).
4. Teachers can help students understand themselves and their duties to others, thus increasing the likelihood students will be wise in their personal and civic endeavors.

Socrates makes a distinction between "opinion," "true opinion," and "knowledge" (Plato, 360 BCEb). **Opinions** are, at best, educated guesses that may be correct or incorrect. **True opinions** are guesses that happen to end up being correct – "they proved to be true." But true opinion is as unreliable as opinions for decision-making because they are still a guess. **Knowledge** differs from opinion and true opinion because it has been justified by the "calculation of reason" and defended by *logos*, a cogent, logical account of why an observation is true (Vlastos & Graham, 1996). Socrates' "calculation of reason" requires not only reasoning what is the wise thing to believe in or do, but also having reasoned why the alternatives are not wise. It is today's "critical thinking."

Part of the human endeavor is for people to help each other acquire and understand knowledge and share their reasoning so that all individuals can become wiser. Knowledge is both interpersonal, that is, it is exchanged between teachers and students, as an example, and intrapersonal, in that it is a conceptualization unique to an individual. Social studies teachers provide the knowledge *and* assist students with reasoning to achieve what Aristotle refers to as "**practical wisdom**" – the capacity to "deliberate well on what is the Good Life in general" (350 BCE). The process begins with foundational knowledge, but the Good Life is contingent on the capacity of individuals to understand themselves and their duty to others. Robert Nozick puts wisdom in a contemporary context: "Wisdom is what you need in order to live well and cope with the central problems of living and avoid the dangers in the predicaments human beings find themselves in" (1989, p. 267).

Foundational Knowledge

Knowledge as the basis for the hoped-for wisdom begins in the informal day-to-day experience of living and then turns to the more structured, accumulated knowledge found in the academic disciplines, the **foundational knowledge**. The NCSS standards for teacher preparation (NCSS, 2018) anticipate that "teacher candidates must understand how the disciplines – civics, economics, geography, and history, and the social/behavioral sciences – create knowledge through disciplinary inquiry to inform action in civic life" (p. 13). Ambitious social studies teachers "push beyond teaching isolated disciplinary content and toward teaching integrated concepts, facts, and tools that can be used for social studies inquiry to foster civic competence" (p. 15). To move beyond foundational knowledge to the exalted aims, the teacher must have the insight and inclination to look for the opportunities to reveal the enduring ideas and compelling principles that are laced within the foundational knowledge.

Foundational knowledge can be categorized as follows.

Declarative Knowledge

Declarative knowledge (sometimes referred to as **content**, **information**, and **propositional knowledge**) has its origins in *epistêmê*, which is usually translated as "knowing what." For example, a person knows what a cake is, what its ingredients are, what it looks like – that it is not a pie or a cookie. The National Center for History Standards (1996; and see Part 2), as an example, divides its standards into "U.S. History Content Standards" (declarative knowledge) and "Historical Thinking Standards" (procedural knowledge). An example of content standards for grades K-4 would be "The causes and nature of various movements of large groups of people into and within the United States, now and long ago," and for grade 5–12 is "How political, religious, and social institutions emerged in the English colonies." Declarative knowledge can be divided into facts, concepts, and generalizations.

Facts are **definitive information**. They are unequivocal and undisputed. Facts are typically used as evidence to support a concept. As examples, Trump, Xi Jinping, and Obrador are facts that share an attribute, the concept of a "head of state." Facts tend not to be remembered long term unless they are part of a concept or generalization or tethered to the affective domain. As an example, to an American, "July 4" is rich with attached affective domain connotations such as patriotism, liberty, parades, hotdogs, and warm weather. The cognitive fact of the date and emotional attachment create a cultural bond with other Americans. An Australian or Ethiopian would not share with an American any of these cultural associations or emotional attachments to the date July 4. This is an example of what E.D. Hirsch (1987) refers to as "**cultural literacy**," in which he argues such cognitive and affective knowledge is necessary to the cohesion required for peoples to maintain democratic societies.

Concepts are mental labels, abstractions such as congress, head of state, longitude and latitude, etc. The facts that are examples of these concepts could be the 101st Congress, Boris Johnson, or 29.9511 N, 90.0715 W. Concepts can be conceptualized horizontally and vertically. As an example, heads of state can be subdivided into concepts such as presidents, prime ministers, chancellors, etc., which in turn can be subdivided into people (facts) who held the office. These are **definitive concepts** because they can be justified as universal, demonstrably true with facts or sub-concepts that represent the concept. Most of the democratic beliefs (refer to Chapter 2) are **indefinite concepts** because they are subject to multiple interpretations.

Generalizations are inferences or conclusions that may or may not be true. They are opinions and express relationships between and among facts and concepts. Telling students a non-fact-based generalization such as "President Johnson was a great president" has a very different learning objective than a fact-based statement such as "President Johnson signed more civil rights legislation than any other president." The former reflects the teacher's personal conclusion, the latter is evidence-based and defers a judgment to the students. With generalizations, teachers should expect to join students in providing evidence in the form of concepts and facts while modeling critical thinking.

Procedural Knowledge

Dewey (1916/2004) made the distinction between a **"record of knowledge"** (declarative knowledge) and "knowledge" (both declarative and procedural knowledge). In history, for example, to know the dates of important battles in the Civil War is a record of knowledge, but also being able to explain how the chronology and outcomes of each influenced the outcome of the war is Dewey's "knowledge." **Procedural knowledge** is knowing *how* to make sense of declarative knowledge and create understanding.

Generic procedural knowledge is critical thinking (see Chapter 8).

Social studies procedural knowledge is often referred to as **modes of reasoning, executive processes, intellectual processes, disciplinary concepts** and **tools**, and **habits of mind**. The procedural knowledge of a discipline is developed by the community of practice to make sense of its declarative knowledge (Resnick & Klopfer, 1989). By analogy, if declarative knowledge is the cake's ingredients, then procedural knowledge is the directions and skills to make the cake. As an example, the NCSS C3 Framework (see Chapter 12) offers an example of procedural knowledge for middle grades under the heading "Processes the Learner Will be Able to Do" – "identify sound reasoning, assumptions, misconceptions, and bias in sources, evidence, and arguments used in presenting issues and positions." Note there is no declarative knowledge in the statement. Both the NCSS Themes (1994) and the NCSS C3 Framework (2013) are structured as procedural knowledge to be used across all the social studies' subject areas. In addition to the emphasis on procedural knowledge by the NCSS, the core disciplines learned societies for history, geography, economics, and civics have also stressed the explicit teaching of procedural knowledge (see Part 2).

Basic Skills Knowledge (i.e., "Literacy")

The awareness that some Americans do not have the skills required to thrive in contemporary society has led to an emphasis on a "back-to-basics" approach in which reading, writing, and numeracy skills are emphasized. Social studies teachers, in addition to teaching to the foundational goals and exalted aims of social studies, are expected to integrate the development and practice of basic skills into social studies as part of school-wide efforts to upgrade the abilities of Americans (see Chapters 27, 28, and 29).

Ideas, Beliefs, and Universals

As a way of thinking about social studies knowledge, the following formulation might be helpful.

Ideas

Ideas are formulated through intrapersonal mental processes based on knowledge, beliefs, and feelings. Ideas can be formed out of watching television, a response to an event such as a student being bullied, learning in a classroom, or an original thought, such as when Charles Darwin conceptualized "evolution." For the purposes of teaching and learning, an idea can be transmitted such as hearing about the American Revolution from a teacher, reading a book or internet page, etc. Facts, concepts, and generalizations are typically communicated as parts of a superseding idea. Once communicated, students then re-conceptualize the idea and its components and the idea becomes a formulation that is unique to the student. Hopefully that re-conceptualization closely matches the teacher's more expert, objective version. Children's versions of ideas are not as well formed as adults due to incomplete or less sophisticated information, maturation, and mental acuity, but that does not necessarily make their ideas incorrect: These are often referred to as "naïve" or "simplistic" ideas. **Enduring ideas** are meant to have a more lasting intrapersonal presence within the student. As an example, longitude and latitude are concepts, but that longitude and latitude can be used to find a fixed location on earth and that it can be used to navigate are ideas that are, hopefully, enduring.

Compelling propositions are formed out of ideas and communicated to students – not as fact – but for their consideration as a candidate for the status of a belief. Such propositions are constructed to consider things that matter which engage the students' ideas about the democratic ideals and their identity. As an example, asking students to consider the idea of patriotism based on the well-known quote, "My country, right or wrong; if right, to be kept right; and if wrong, to be set right," would be a compelling proposition. Every student, unlike the idea of longitude and latitude, is entitled to their unique conception of the idea of patriotism based on the democratic ideals.

Beliefs

Beliefs are fundamentally different from the ideas. Because individuals have emotional attachments to beliefs, they value beliefs as important to their identity and therefore beliefs are more resistant to change than ideas (Fenstermacher, 1994; Richardson, 1996). When presented with compelling questions and propositions of ideas that matter, students are moved to reflect on their existing beliefs and identity: They are inspired to reconsider who they are and who they want to be. As examples, people may have an idea of the responsibility to be honest or the right to liberty, but they must elect to accept as true the underlying moral principle for it to be a belief. Individuals can hold a belief in the right to dignity, but think or act prejudicially, thus creating an intrapersonal conflict between what they know to be morally correct (a belief) and how they act. Beliefs can have little basis in knowledge. As an example, knowledge should lead individuals to the idea and then belief that one "race" is not superior to another, but individuals can choose to hold the belief anyway. Giving up a belief can be emotionally draining, but it is made easier if teachers can provide a bridge from an idea to a potential belief by leading discussions of competing ideas and creating the caring encounter (see Chapter 9 and 10) whereby students are supported in navigating emotions, ideas, and beliefs.

Universals

Is there a universal idea of right and wrong, meaning it is unchanging and absolute over time and space? As an example, is it wrong to steal under any circumstances? The philosophical area of study known as "the problem of universals" has significant implications for social studies education's exalted aims (see Alleman & Brophy, 2010; Byrd, 2012). If there is not a universal idea of what is right or wrong, if everything is subjective, then stealing, cheating, etc., would not be thought of as morally impermissible. What ideas, then, can a teacher reliably promote as warranted to be held as beliefs, if they are all relative; if there are no universals?

In his **Theory of Forms**, Plato (360 BCEb) argues that there are universals. He makes the case that human beings are naturally flawed because – unlike beings – *human* beings must filter all ideas and perceptions through an imperfect prism, the senses, and thus are not capable of consistently knowing the universal of, as an example, right or wrong. Refined over the years by other philosophers, this theory of forms accounts for why people can believe there is "A" justice in the cosmos, but different individuals and cultures at different times have different conceptions of what justice is. Immanuel Kant (1785/1993) emphasized that the moral, virtuous life is grounded in these external universals. Even though individuals do not know for sure these universals exist – they choose to believe in them, prescribe them to themselves, act on them, and expect others to act reciprocally.

Personal and Public Knowledge

Knowledge, once conceptualized as an idea or belief, becomes personal.

Personal Knowledge

In the social studies classroom, learning about foundational knowledge of the three branches of government is not that different from learning about the solar system. In contrast, knowledge for the exalted aims, because it takes on the form of beliefs, is an intimate and impassioned process. Of particular importance to the exalted aims is the misconception that reason must be dispassionate. Dewey (1976/1983) believes passion is necessary to call individuals to take action and that reason should account for passions during consideration of an idea or belief and course of action.

The concept of personal knowledge can benefit from taking liberties with what Bertrand Russell called "**knowledge by acquaintance**" (1912). For example, if individuals have personally tasted a cake, they have experienced knowledge by acquaintance. Compared with entering the mathematics classroom, where students likely know nothing of algebra, students enter the social studies classroom having experienced the positive and negative application of the democratic ideals, personal virtues, and civic values in their lives. Caring, authenticity, courage, selflessness, decency, open-mindedness, friendship, liberty, rule of law, etc., are experienced by acquaintance, giving students first-hand knowledge. The line dividing the world students live in and the social studies classroom is more seamless than in other disciplines and carries with it emotional underpinning not found in other subject fields.

Conversely, a second kind of personal knowledge might be called **knowledge by description** and flows in the opposite direction of knowledge by acquaintance. Teachers introduce the social studies topics and use the foundational knowledge to examine ideas that matter not experienced or contemplated by students. For the best results the connections to life should be explicit and visceral by arousing students' curiosity and passions (Plato, 360 BCEa). The dialogue about ideas that matter offers students the knowledge by description that prepares them for the world outside the classroom.

Public Knowledge

The experience of social studies education is also unique because that private, intimate, personal knowledge must become public knowledge as an essential communal obligation in a democracy (Oliver & Shaver, 1966). Continuing the earlier analogy, public knowledge requires that individuals must reveal what kind of cake they prefer and that perhaps they do not like the kind of cake someone else likes. The classroom discussions reveal who people are (their identity and ideology), who they want to be (their aspirations), and what kind of world they want to live in (their belief in the idea of the *polis*). Participation in the discussions requires that students have the courage to reveal their beliefs, the willingness to engage in thoughtful dialogue, and a disposition to reconsider their existing identity and ideology. Dewey insists:

> To cooperate by giving differences a chance to show themselves because of the belief that the expression of difference is not only a right of the other persons but is a means of enriching your own life experience, is inherent in the democratic personal way of life.
>
> (1925/1953, p. 228)

The risk of students revealing more about themselves than they are comfortable with can be emotionally daunting and is a formidable deterrent to participation in the social studies classroom. This reticence can be overcome by establishing a **therapeutic alliance** (Rogers, 1951) and **caring encounter** (Noddings, 1998), just as therapists do in group therapy (Yalom & Leszcz, 2005; and see Chapter 10).

Resources

Videos: *Kahn Academy*: Theory of Knowledge, Kant, Theory of Knowledge | *YouTube*: Aristotle on Wisdom; Hirsch and Cultural Literacy on McNeil/Lehrer News Hour; Plato on the Forms; Wisdom; Problem of Universals | *TEDEd*: Plato's Allegory of the Cave.

Documents: *Stanford Encyclopedia of Philosophy*: Knowledge by Acquaintance vs. Description; *Theaetetus* (Plato's theory of knowledge); Wisdom.

References

Alleman, J., & Brophy, J. (2010). Cultural universals. In M. E. McGuire & B. Cole (Eds.), *Making a difference: Revitalizing elementary social studies* (pp. 11–24). NCSS.

Aristotle. (350 BCE). *Nicomachean ethics*. Retrieved from http://classics.mit.edu/Aristotle/nicomachaen.html

Byrd, D. (2012). Social studies education as a moral activity: Teaching towards a just society. *Educational Philosophy and Theory, 44*(10), 1073–1079.

Dewey, J. (1916/2004). *Democracy and education*. Dover.

Dewey, J. (1925/1953). Ethics. In J. A. Boydston (Ed.), *John Dewey: The later works, 1932* (Vol. 7). Southern Illinois University Press.

Dewey, J. (1976/1983). The school and society. In J. A. Boydston (Ed.), *John Dewey: The middle works, 1899–1924* (Vol. 1). Southern Illinois University Press.

Fenstermacher, G. D. (1994). Chapter 1: The knower and the known: The nature of knowledge in research on teaching. *Review of Research in Education, 20*, 3–56.

Hirsch, E. D. (1987). *Cultural literacy: What every American needs to know*. Houghton Mifflin.

Kant, I. (1785/1993). *Grounding for the metaphysics of morals* (3rd ed., J. W. Ellington, Trans.). Hackett Publishing.

National Center for History Standards. (1996). *National standards for history*. Retrieved from https://phi.history.ucla.edu/nchs/history-standards/

NCSS. (1994). *Expectations of excellence: Curriculum standards for social studies*. NCSS. Retrieved from www.socialstudies.org/standards/introduction

NCSS. (2013). *The college, career, and civic life (C3) framework for social studies state standards: Guidance for enhancing the rigor of K-12 civics, economics, geography, and history*. NCSS. Retrieved from www.socialstudies.org/sites/default/files/c3/C3-Framework-for-Social-Studies.pdf

NCSS (2018). *National standards for the preparation of social studies teachers*. NCSS. Retrieved from www.socialstudies.org/sites/default/files/media/2017/Nov/ncss_teacher_standards_2017-rev9-6-17.pdf

Nelson, J. L. (2001). *Defining social studies*. Retrieved from www.researchgate.net/publication/265660266_DEFINING_SOCIAL_STUDIES

Noddings, N. (1998). Caring. In P. H. Hirst & P. White (Eds.), *Philosophy of education: Major themes in the analytic tradition* (Vol. IV, pp. 40–50). Routledge.

Nozick, R. (1989). What is wisdom and why do philosophers love it so? In J. Kekes (Ed.), *The examined life* (pp. 267–278). Bucknell University Press.

Oliver, D., & Shaver, J. (1966). *Teaching public issues in the high school*. Houghton Mifflin.

Phillips Exeter Academy. (2020). Retrieved from www.exeter.edu/about-us/academy-mission

Plato. (360 BCEa). *Crito*. Retrieved from http://classics.mit.edu/Plato/crito.html

Plato. (360 BCEb). *The republic*. Retrieved from http://classics.mit.edu/Plato/republic.html

Resnick, L. B., & Klopfer, L. E. (1989). Toward the thinking curriculum: Current cognitive research. In *Association for supervision and curriculum development yearbook*.

Richardson, V. (1996). The role of attitudes and beliefs in learning to teach. In J. Sikula (Ed.), *Handbook of research on teacher education* (2nd ed., pp. 102–119). Macmillan.

Rogers, C. R. (1951). *Client-centered therapy*. Boston, MA: Houghton Mifflin.

Russell, B. (1912). *The problems of philosophy*. Retrieved from www.gutenberg.org/files/5827/5827-h/5827-h.htm

Vlastos, G., & Graham, D. W. (1996). *Studies in Greek philosophy: Socrates, Plato, and their tradition* (Vol. II). Princeton University Press.

Yalom, I. D., & Leszcz, M. (2005). *Theory and practice of group psychotherapy*. Basic Books.

6 Psychology of Learning

To know psychology, therefore, is absolutely no guarantee that we shall be good teachers. To advance to that result, we must have an additional endowment altogether, a happy tact and ingenuity to tell us what definite things to say and do when the pupil is before us.
William James, American Philosopher and Psychologist, 1842–1910 (Philips, 2014, p. 433)

The history of the philosophy and psychology of learning can offer teacher candidates a rich array of theories upon which they could base their classroom practices. The theory and research of learning these last 50 years has moved toward **constructivist learning theory** (Cuban, 1993) based on the works of such notables as Piaget (Piaget & Cook, 1952), Vygotsky (1978), Keating (1979), and Gardner (1983). The shift was away from viewing students more like pitchers that teachers poured information into, to teachers creating experiences that require students to be actively engaged in constructing knowledge.

Plato and Aristotle originally articulated the idea that our mind structures the information we receive through our senses into conceptualizations of facts, concepts, generalizations, ideas, and beliefs. As an example, individuals can touch a tree, observe a tree, and read about a tree and the mind of the person constructs a concept of a tree. Unlike a tree, concepts such as poverty or the virtue courage are intangible objects, but humankind has developed concepts of these based on perceptions of historical and current human activity. The cosmos seems ordered, even if actually not, because humans have constructed an idea of it in their minds. Individuals choose to believe in the idea of an ordered cosmos because it is intellectually and emotionally reassuring.

Constructivism

Consider the case of a newborn baby who is at home in his crib. He has little understanding of who he is, his humanity, immediate circumstances, or surroundings. His senses are only partially developed and so he experiences the sensations of uncontrollable noises coming from the physical entity of his being (his body); a sense of comfort from something (a liquid) that periodically flows into an unimagined opening (his mouth); and images, sounds, and touch on the skin are confusing sensations, none of which he is capable of conceptualizing. The infant is in a state of **disequilibrium**, an unsettling emotional and cognitive imbalance between what is encountered and understood. It becomes the driving force to learn, to construct a conceptualization of his experience so he can have greater control of his self and surroundings. This leads him to use reason to form **schema** – organized mental representations of knowledge in the mind. As an example, the graphical representation in Chapter 2's

Figure 2.1, Hierarchy of the Good Life, is the author's attempt to communicate the schema of the components of a democratic ideology.

After repeated interactions, the child begins conceptualizing sensations, images, language, and emotions into networks of ideas and beliefs based on patterns (Palmer, 1997; Schwab, 1978). When the father comes into the room with a different movement, voice, sound, etc., from the mother, the child feels compelled due to disequilibrium, to alter the unnamed "schema box" of mother and create a new box to make sense of his experiences. Eventually a third box of "parents" is created as part of the ongoing restructuring of schema into a hierarchy with "parents" subdivided into "mother" and "father" boxes underneath. As language is acquired, the child places labels on the boxes to improve the organization, modify the boxes' content, and communicate his schema. Each time the child has a new experience, there is **disequilibrium** driving the child to seek a new equilibrium by either **assimilation** of the experience into existing schema or **accommodation** by altering the schema structure themselves. This is, effectively, the constructivist version of learning.

The process of creating schema separate from firsthand experience also starts at an early age through mass media and books being read to toddlers. These experiences prepare children to encounter "scientific concepts" (the term used by Vygotsky is not limited to science) during formal education. School shifts learning toward knowledge by description and requires students be in the "**zone of proximal development**" **(ZPD)** (Vygotsky, 1978). To be in the ZPD, the learner must have sufficient reasoning and pre-existing schema so that the parent or teacher can create the bridge from what is not conceptualized or not conceptualized accurately to the more grade-appropriate conceptualization. This is, essentially, the constructivist framework of teaching.

With the advent of the digital age, media "teaches" serendipitously and often unknowingly to the learner but typically lacks the traditional adult supervision or, at least, immediate access to an adult to bring insight to what is being learned. The power of learning by media stems from the medium blurring the once sharp distinction between learning by description or learning by acquaintance.

Sharing metacognition, creating graphic organizers, using analogies and metaphors, and providing multiple examples in a dialogue are best practices for teaching based on constructivist leaning theory. As an example of the power of metaphors and analogies to create the bridge from what students do not know to what the teacher wants them to understand, the following dialogue uses an analogy for a democratic ideal with a controversial topic. In a first-grade classroom, a student introduces his uncle, who is his "VIP guest" shortly after the 9/11 attacks and says: "I asked my uncle to come because he is a Muslim." The first comment from a well-intentioned student is: "My dad says Muslims killed people with a plane and that they are bad," referring to the 9/11 World Trade Center attack. This dialogue follows:

VIP GUEST: "Does everyone have cousins?"

CHILDREN: "Yes."

VIP GUEST: "Have any of your cousins done something bad?"

ONE CHILD: "Yes, my cousin took some cake when he was not supposed to and blamed it on me."

VIP GUEST: "Because that one cousin did something bad, is everyone in your family bad?" (paraphrased from the Showtime TV series *Sleeper Cell* (Voris, 2005–06).

Cognition and Caring

Aristotle, in the "**Three Proofs**" (350 BCE), defined three qualities a student must see in the teacher for learning to occur: **Ethos** – meaning the teacher has good intentions – the students' best interest is the priority; **empathy** – the teacher understands the problem from the learner's perspective, and has the desire to help the individual student; and **competence** – the teacher has greater expertise.

Nell Noddings (1984) emphasizes that learning is "relational" and defines what the teacher must do on an intimate level for learning to occur. She states, "If I care about students I must do two things: I must make the problem my own, receive it intellectually, immerse myself in it; I must also bring the students into proximity, receive such students personally" (1984, p. 113) and "not simply be a textbook like source from which the student may or may not learn" (Noddings, 1984, p. 70). She adds:

> The child wants to attain competence in his own world of experience. He needs the cooperative guidance of a fully caring adult to accomplish this. The one caring, as teacher, then has two major tasks: to stretch the student's world by presenting an effective selection of that world with which she had contact with, and to work cooperatively with the student in his struggle to achieve competence in that world.
>
> (p. 178)

The reason why caring is important to the conceptualization process is because disequilibrium caused in an effort to achieve competence creates two problems for the student: the problem itself and the problem of the emotional distress associated with the problem. As Aristotle (350 BCE) points out, you feel your thoughts and think your feelings. Peck (1997) explains how the "terrible twos" are emblematic emotional distress felt through life that accompanies coming to grips with changing behavior due to the realities of living. The role of the parent is to comfort the child while the child struggles through both problems. It is the relationship of caring witnessed by the child that suggests what it is to be more human and leads the child to the self-control and accommodating himself to the reality of life.

In social studies education (see Chapter 8 "Problem-Solving") as an example, figuring out why it is colder in Chicago than Juneau is the problem itself that is created by a teacher for the student. The emotional distress stems from having to "work" at thinking critically while delaying the gratification from other activities that the student perceives as more enjoyable. In social studies education during consideration of things that matter such as poverty, however, there is the additional distress of students having to come to grips with who they are as authentic and autonomous persons. As a result, for social studies instruction for the exalted aims to be successful, teachers of social studies need to take on the attributes of a philosophical counselor and create the **therapeutic alliance** (Rogers, 1951) and **caring encounter** (Noddings, 1998) characterized by genuine presence and connectedness between a teacher and student (Buber, 2000).

Cognition and SSE Foundational Goals

Definite information is typically limited to the facts and concepts in foundational knowledge such as dates, places, events, etc., just like the other disciplines. As an example, it is not unreasonable to expect students to be well-versed by the end of high school about

US presidents, what the country and culture was like at the time of their administrations, and the nation's accomplishments and failures that are attributed to each president. **Indefinite information** is where there is no right or wrong answers. It requires personal judgments because there are conflicting facts, ambiguous definitions, and evidence. Indefinite information presents the opportunity for teachers to frame lessons around enduring ideas, such as what weight in the ranking of presidents should be given to John F. Kennedy's expansion into the Vietnam War and handling of the Cuban missile crises; Nixon's end to the Vietnam War; and Clinton's balancing of the budget? If the teacher emphasizes the modes of reasoning of the social studies and critical thinking while developing that lesson, the students would create schema of declarative information but also the procedural knowledge schema that can be applied going forward as they independently evaluate any presidential administration. Following the methodology of the Arc of Inquiry approach (see Chapter 12), a lesson on ranking the presidents would first emphasize developing criteria (such as legislation passed, wars started or ended, economic challenges, character issues, etc.) that could be universally applied to the ranking question and having students investigating the definite and indefinite information and applying the criteria and the democratic ideals.

Cognition, Emotions, and SSE Exalted Aims

The exalted aims require teachers to go beyond foundational knowledge and raise compelling questions such as, "Should a president's character be considered in the ranking?" If yes, how much weight should be given to John F. Kennedy's extramarital activities, Nixon's authorization of a crime, and Clinton's perjury in the ranking of presidents? By explicit instruction, the question is elevated to a universal; it is a question about what makes a person admirable or "good." This becomes a therapeutic engagement because students organically contextualize the question in terms of self: "How would I judge myself to be a good person?" For these exalted aims questions, students must draw on their capacities and beliefs, thus crossing the line from an exclusively academic consideration to a reflection on "self." Having students synthesize the definite and indefinite information and share their beliefs, ideas, and reasoning during discussions exposes a range of complex schema about how to think about multifaceted criteria, emotional attachments (to presidents' personas), what is admirable, etc., thus forcing students to reconsider their identity and ideology. Consider that most historians rank John F. Kennedy quite low, 35th out of 45 presidents. However, in a Gallup Poll of the public he was ranked 4th (Gallup, 2011; National Rankings of Presidents, 2011).

Through the dialogue in the classroom of multiple voices, the goal is for students to adjust their schema and thus their personal and civic identities so they are more democratic and congruent, thus the student is in equilibrium. The complicating factor in this rendition of how students form schema and identity is the accounting for emotions brought on by the intrapersonal challenges to a student's existing identity. The complex issue of abortion, as an example, and "how you *feel* about it" needs to be reconciled with "how you *think* about it" in light of the ideals of a democratic society. The intrapersonal tension between ideas and the feelings tethered to the ideas and the intrapersonal tension between autonomy and duty to the *polis* give rise to emotions that can adversely affect the critical thinking process. Emotions can lead to acting without reason or skew conceptualizations toward defective conclusions that become part of the schema. Conversely, it is emotions that give rise to the passions to pursue the democratic ideals. Consider Dewey's analysis:

> The conclusion is not that the emotional, passionate phase of action can be or should be eliminated on behalf of a bloodless reason. More "passions," not fewer, is the answer. To check the influence of hate there must be sympathy, while to rationalize sympathy there are needed emotions of curiosity, caution, respect for the freedom of others – dispositions which evoke objects which balance those called up by sympathy and prevent its degeneration into maudlin sentiment and meddling interference. Rationality, once more is not a force to evoke against impulse and habit. It is the attainment of a working harmony among diverse desires.
>
> (Dewey, 1976/1983, p. 136)

Conceptualizations, Identity, and Ideology

Individuals create a **narrative** of their lives out of the complex schema of emotions, ideas, beliefs, and experiences (Epston, 1989; Epston & White, 1992; White, 1995). It is a closely held internalized voice, like a movie of individuals' lives from their perspective, and is constantly referenced to determine who they are and who they might become (Carr, 1998). This narrative becomes a moral map that is always being compared with their cultural moral heritage and individuals immediately around them (Guignon, 1993). By students examining their own internal narrative, they are forced into uncertainty about the adequacy of their existing identity (Achenbach, 1995). Erikson referred to this as an "identity crisis" (1993) and pointed out how it came to shape Martin Luther's personal and civic identity, resulting in one of the most significant revolutions in Western Civilization. When teachers of social studies explicitly elevate discussions to ideas that matter, students are purposely put into what is analogous to an identity crisis where they reference their narrative and come to recognize the insufficiencies of their reasoning and existing schema. As emotionally and cognitively challenging as it may be, it is necessary for the welfare of students (and society) to consider and re-conceptualize their identity and ideology on the way to more advanced thinking about their political ideology and stances. The teacher must try to understand the students as the students see themselves in their narrative and view instruction as the process by which the student can revise the inadequate or unsatisfactory parts of their narratives based on the democratic ideals. Cheyne and Tarulli (1999) note that the Socratic Method is one of the dominant strategies of discourse to achieve this end. **Socratic Method** and **talk therapy** from the philosophical counseling community of practice become almost indistinguishable in the classroom because they share the same goals and characteristics – through critical examination and reference to moral and ethical ideals that permeate society, and like those defined in the democratic ideals, the students will come to re-conceptualize their identity and ideology (Schuster, 1991). With the new conceptualization, the students are liberated and empowered to write their future narrative with autonomy and authenticity and become the person and citizen needed to sustain a democratic society (Bruner, 1986, 1991).

Resources

Videos: *Learner.org:* The Learning Classroom – Theory into Practice; Discovering Psychology Updated Edition [26 videos] | *Kahn Academy*: Piaget | *YouTube:* Constructivist Approaches; Vygotsky; Erikson's Stages of Identity Formation; Aristotle's Three Proofs.

Documents: *Handbook of Research in Social Studies Education*: Social Constructivism and Student Learning | *NCSS:* Principles for Learning | Jean Piaget Society | History Alive! Six Powerful Constructivist Strategies.

References

Achenbach, G. B. (1995). Philosophy, philosophical practice, and psychotherapy. In R. Lahav & M. da Venza Tillmanns (Eds.), *Essays on philosophical counseling* (pp. 61–74). Press of America.

Aristotle. (350 BCE). *Rhetoric*. Retrieved from http://classics.mit.edu/Aristotle/rhetoric.html.

Bruner, J. (1986). *Actual minds, possible worlds*. Harvard University Press.

Bruner, J. (1991). The narrative construction of reality. *Critical Inquiry, 18,* 1–21.

Buber, M. (2000). *I and Thou*. (Trans. R. Smith). Scribner.

Carr, A. (1998). Michael White's narrative therapy. *Contemporary Family Therapy, 20*(4), 485–503.

Cheyne, J. A., & Tarulli, D. (1999). Dialogue, difference and voice in the zone of proximal development. *Theory & Psychology, 9*(1), 5–28.

Cuban, L. (1993). *How teachers taught: Constancy and change in American classrooms, 1890–1990*. Teachers College Press.

Dewey, J. (1976/1983). The school and society. In J. A. Boydston (Ed.), *John Dewey: The middle works, 1899–1924* (Vol. 1). Southern Illinois University Press.

Epston, D. (1989). *Collected papers*. Dulwich Centre Publications.

Epston, D., & White, M. (1992). *Experience, contradiction, narrative and imagination*. Dulwich Centre Publications.

Erikson, E. H. (1993). *Young man Luther: A study in psychoanalysis and history*. W.W. Norton & Company.

Gallup. (2011). *Americans say Reagan is the greatest U.S. president*. Retrieved from https://news.gallup.com/poll/146183/americans-say-reagan-greatest-president.aspx.

Gardner, H. (1983). *Frames of mind: The theory of multiple intelligences*. Basic Books.

Guignon, C. (1993). Authenticity, moral values and psychotherapy. In C. Guignon (Ed.), *The Cambridge companion to Heidegger* (pp. 262–293). Cambridge University Press.

Keating, D. (1979). Adolescent thinking. In J. Adelson (Ed.), *Handbook of adolescent psychology* (pp. 211–246). Wiley.

National Rankings of Presidents. (2011). In *Wikipedia*. Retrieved from https://en.wikipedia.org/wiki/Historical_rankings_of_presidents_of_the_United_States.

Noddings, N. (1984). *Caring: A feminine approach to ethics and moral education*. University of California Press.

Noddings, N. (1998). Caring. In P. H. Hirst & P. White (Eds.), *Philosophy of education: Major themes in the analytic tradition* (Vol. IV, pp. 40–50). Routledge.

Palmer, P. J. (1997). *The courage to teach: Exploring the inner landscape of a teacher's life*. Jossey-Bass.

Peck, M. S. (1997). *The road less traveled*. Simon & Schuster.

Philips, D. C. (2014). *Encyclopedia of educational theory and philosophy*. Sage.

Piaget, J., & Cook, M. T. (1952). *The origins of intelligence in children*. International University Press.

Rogers, C. R. (1951). *Client-centered therapy*. Houghton Mifflin.

Schuster, S. C. (1991). Philosophical counselling. *Journal of Applied Philosophy, 8*(2), 219–223.

Schwab, J. J. (1978). Eros and education: A discussion of one aspect of discussion. In I. Westbury & N. J. Wilkof (Eds.), *Science, curriculum, and liberal education: Selected essays* (pp. 105–132). University of Chicago Press.

Voris, C. (2005–06). *Sleeper cell*. Showtime.

Vygotsky, L. S. (1978). *Mind in society: The development of higher psychological processes*. Harvard University Press.

White, M. (1995). *Re-authoring lives*. Dulwich Centre Publications.

7 Concept Formation, Examples, Analogies, and Graphic Organizers

We teach a lot of concepts poorly over many years. In the Asian systems they teach you very few concepts very well over a few years.

Bill Gates, Entrepreneur and Philanthropist, 1955–present (Riley, 2011)

Whether it is lecturing, questioning, modeling, debriefing, or discussion directed toward foundational knowledge or democratic ideals, teachers are creating a bridge to the students from what the teacher has decided is important for the students to know, consider, and understand.

Concepts in the Broadest Sense

In prior chapters, fine distinctions were made between the foundational knowledge of facts, concepts, generalizations, and ideas and beliefs, values, and virtues. However, in the broadest sense, all of these are often referred to as concepts. While more nuanced than presented here, the consideration of foundational knowledge during instruction is typically referred to as **concept formation** or **concept attainment**. Whereas, consideration of things that matter inherently is typically referred to as **values analysis, values inculcation**, or **values formation** (see Chapters 9 and 10). Both use the deductive and inductive reasoning capacities that make the human species unique. Since both teacher and student have this reasoning capacity, learning occurs when the teacher creates experiences that demonstrate reasoning and require students to use theirs. Lessons created to require critical thinking about concepts create the bridge from a new concept to an intrapersonal conceptualization.

Foundational Knowledge Concepts

When using the concept formation strategy, teachers envision a set of definitions and a mental map of the concepts that is grade-appropriate. In social studies, there are multiple ways of organizing mental maps that are reflected in graphic organizers such as hierarchies, temporally (with chronologies), cause and effect, problem–solution, etc. Figure 7.1, Earth Concept Hierarchy, is offered as a partially completed elementary school level representation of a definite information mental map to demonstrate the characteristics of concept formation with foundational knowledge. Graphic organizers are mirror images of teachers' and students' mental maps, with the teacher's representation depicting the best thinking of the community of practice that is grade-appropriate.

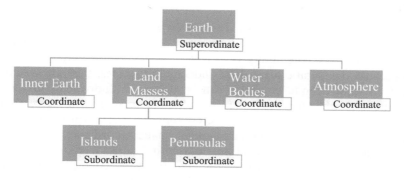

Figure 7.1 Earth Concept Hierarchy

During the lesson planning process, teachers conceptualize their mental maps that they intend to communicate to their students or have students conceptualize.

Depicted in this concept map are four coordinates (equalities) that are also subordinates of the superordinate (earth) and two subordinate samples of land masses that are coordinates of each other. Concept maps of things that matter, because they deal with indefinite information are not as unequivocal as Figure 7.1, can have multiple versions based on an individuals' beliefs, and all versions could be accurate in their own way.

The Components of Concept Formation

Concept maps are constructed based on two operating principles.

Critical attributes. The critical attributes strategy leads to a definition. It is where the teacher structures the lesson to focus on the essential elements of a concept so that students do not form inaccurate or less than adequate concepts. As an example, the three critical attributes of a peninsula that are appropriate for lower elementary students could be a body of (1) land (2) surrounded by water (3) on three sides. The attributes, during instruction, should be reinforced with images and examples and nonexamples (Tennyson, Youngers, & Suebsonthi, 1983). **Comparable entities** is a powerful method to facilitate understanding the critical attributes because it allows students to compare the critical attributes about two similar entities at one time. For example, comparing and contrasting critical attributes of peninsulas vs. islands or the criteria to be US senator vs. US representative.

Conceptual relationships. The above definitional process sets the stage for the conceptual relationships. Like most concepts, islands and peninsulas should not be learned in a vacuum; they are parts of a larger concept and idea. Students learning how to visualize concepts and depict them is a skill and a form of procedural knowledge.

Definitions and concept representations range in complexity based on the age of the students. The absence of cells does not necessarily make a representation inaccurate, but grade-appropriate.

Democratic Ideals Concepts

Woven into the fabric of social studies' foundation knowledge are the democratic ideals that are subject to judgment and conceptualized as intrapersonal beliefs. Unlike foundational knowledge, the community of practice cannot legitimately define the critical attributes because democratic ideals have indefinite attributes, they are beliefs that are conditioned on what definite attributes can be discerned. Individuals may collectively agree on some applicable attributes and examples, but reasonably disagree about others offered to "prove" the concept. Unlike the concept "islands," which has undisputable, definite, critical attributes, examples, and superordinate, subordinate, or coordinate relationships, the democratic beliefs of "right to security" and "freedom of assembly," as examples, are concepts that could have different but valid concept maps imagined by individuals due to different levels of knowledge and preferred ideological stances. As a result, concept formation for the democratic ideals is achieved through logic, argument, and consensus, but rarely is perfected to the state of definite information. Racism (vs. equality) would be logically argued to be outside the boundary of a democratic ideology. But even in the case of racism, there can be a lack of agreement on what are or are not racist acts because intent and knowledge would be a consideration. Laws forbidding protest (vs. freedom of assembly) may or may not be outside the boundary of a democratic ideology when balanced against the right to security, thus "peaceful" vs. "violent" protest needs to be defined. Because it is a given that the end product, the concept inherent in a democratic belief, will vary by person, the emphasis is on the process of trying to arrive at the most logical understanding of concept so as to understand why one person believes in one concept map and another person believes in another.

Reasoning and Discovery Learning

Students can acquire concepts through **direct instruction**, lecture as an example, or by **indirect instruction**, where teachers structure lessons so that students construct the conceptualization and the teacher confirms the conceptualization based on the thinking of the community of practice. In both cases, the teachers may use prototypes, analogies, images, models, examples/nonexamples during **teacher talk** (Adams & Engelmann, 1996; Tennyson & Cocchiarella, 1986; also see Chapter 21).

The concept formation process can be organized as an active or passive process as well as a deductive or inductive experience. The following simplistic example of foundational knowledge using land forms should illuminate the pedagogical practice for both foundational knowledge and democratic ideals.

Active Learning Approaches

These two examples of active learning are frequently referred to in the literature as **discovery learning**. Research indicates that these kinds of active learning strategies are significantly more effective than lecture, but not as efficient.

Inductive reasoning is the process of drawing conclusions from observations (see Figure 7.2). It is a more open-ended process in which ideas are explored.

Figure 7.2 Inductive Reasoning

1. Using foundational knowledge, the inductive approach starts with pictures of islands and peninsulas. Students might be divided into groups and asked to analyze (observe) the pictures to see if they can place them into categories based on similarities that form a pattern.
2. When they have grouped the islands in one stack and the peninsulas in another stack, students would be asked to develop a "hypothesis" that would include a definition of the critical attributes of stack X and stack Y.
3. Each group might present their theory of a definition and the teacher would probe their thinking by asking questions or showing more pictures.
4. A debriefing would include confirming the definition, reinforcing that X is an island – a body of land surrounded by water, and Y is a peninsula – a body of land surrounded by water on three sides.
5. Students would record the definition that they discovered.

Deductive reasoning is the process of applying a generalization to an illustration (see Figure 7.3). It is focused on proving a theory rather than discovering a theory.

1. The teacher writes the definitions of *island* and *peninsula* on the board (theory).
2. Students are given pictures and asked to apply the definition to the illustrations (hypothesis).
3. After they have placed the islands in one stack and the peninsulas in another stack, students would be expected to justify their decisions (observations).
4. A debriefing would include reinforcing the concept (confirmation).
5. Students would record the definition.

Both strategies can be applied to foundational knowledge and democratic ideals. In both deductive and inductive strategies, the teacher is promoting a precise formulation of the concepts by having students identify its critical attributes. Both inductive and deductive strategies shift the burden to the students to do the thinking, use their observation skills, predict, and justify. It is active learning because students construct knowledge, rather than the teacher explaining the concept as in a lecture.

A large part of the art of teaching, and one of the great challenges, is converting sophisticated ideas inherent in things that matter into grade-appropriate knowledge. As an example, freedom of assembly is a bedrock of democracy. Having students ferret out the critical attributes and comparable entities using examples such as the Boston Tea Party, the New York draft riots of 1853, 1960 civil rights protest in Montgomery,

Figure 7.3 Deductive Reasoning

Boston school bussing riots of 1974, the 1969 New York Stonewall "riots" and Ku Klux Klan assemblies requires students to consider freedom of assembly as a universal regardless, even if challenging to their personal beliefs.

Passive Learning Approach

The very nature of inductive reasoning makes it difficult to imagine a passive inductive learning approach. However, passive deductive reasoning approaches are used in direct instruction in spite of the shortcomings and can be made much more "active" by extensive use of questions as part of a lecture. It does not shift the burden to the students to discover the critical attributes, but it requires them to be actively thinking as multiple questions are spread around to members of the class.

1. The teacher gives the definitions of *islands* and *peninsulas*.
2. Students record the definitions.
3. The teacher shows pictures of examples, asks questions, and students confirm the application.
4. Students memorize the definitions.
5. Students are tested.

Another passive deductive approach is the extensive use of worksheets, which too often use the simplistic "find-and-record strategy" in conjunction with the textbook. Unlike graphic organizers, such worksheets do not require students to construct or reconstruct knowledge; therefore, little reasoning is required of the students. Find-and-record worksheets can be useful strategies for creating a baseline of information as summaries of homework reading assignments, but completing a graphic organizer is more effective because it requires critical thinking.

Examples in Concept Formation

In preparation for instruction, teachers need to plan the examples that illuminate, if not prove and disprove, the concepts they will be teaching by working out the critical attributes and including them in their teacher talk (Ali, 1981; also see Chapter 21). Research indicates that presenting positive and negative examples is better than just positive (confirming) or just negative (non-confirming) examples. Positive examples should have every attribute of the concept, whereas negative examples should have some of the attributes and others should have none of the attributes. Positive examples should be presented first and approximately four examples seems to be optimal. Lessons should be constructed so that students participate *with* the teacher in examining the critical attributes.

Alford and Griffin (2019) point out how easy it is for teachers to create students' misconceptions. They reported that an elementary teacher taught a lesson on Martin Luther, the German theologian. In a short quiz, every student answered every question incorrectly because they used their knowledge of Dr. Martin Luther King Jr. In a second class, the teacher began the lesson by asking how many students knew who Martin Luther King Jr. was. All the students raised their hands. The teacher then asked, does anyone know how his parents gave him his name and explained the connection. He then taught the exact same lesson, and every student got all the answers correct.

Analogies in Concept Formation

When given multiple examples, students can identify through reason the critical attributes, that is an elm tree, oak tree, etc., are examples of the idea of a tree. When given an analogy, "boy is to girl as rooster is to hen," there is a one-to-one relationship established between an existing concept that students know and to an unknown concept. Analogies are among the most powerful ways of creating that conduit to a new idea, but must start with something the student knows (Readence, et al. 1986). Analogies are effective because they create a form of tension between the known and unknown (Thompson, 1986) and that creates the disequilibrium that compels students to conceptualize abstractions.

Analogies are most frequently thought of as based in verbal or written words, but models, simulations, literature, media (film, music, etc.) are, in a larger sense, metaphors for ideas. Analogies of this kind tend to appeal to the affective domain to convey the idea. The scenes of soldiers landing on D-Day in the film *Saving Private Ryan* is an analogy as to what combat is like without having to experience it and, by all accounts, successfully tapped into the viewers' emotions. Expressions like, "I was a morsel for a monarch" from Shakespeare's *Antony and Cleopatra* and John Dean's, of Watergate fame, "There is a cancer growing on the Presidency," also appeal to our emotions.

General communication is so frequently laced with analogies that analogies are taken for granted. However, good teaching requires careful construction of analogies and metaphors by teachers. Teacher-created analogies are invented while developing lesson plans as part of the script of teacher talk.

Similes are explicit comparisons of two unlike things, usually using *like* or *as*: "The financial crises is like an economic Pearl Harbor." This kind of comparison draws direct connections from one idea to another. For example, when using the term *prime minister* for the first time, a teacher can quickly and efficiently create a bridge to the new concept by saying, "It is like the president of the United States." The teacher's analogy can be further developed with additional examples and by dissecting the attributes that are the same and those that are different depending on the age of the students.

Metaphors are implied comparisons of two unlike things in which *like* and *as* are not typically used, such as, "She was a morsel for a monarch." Metaphors are more complex and subtler than similes. Figurative language can be more powerful triggers to long-term memory of concepts because they are constructed to engage emotions. They may also require more analysis. President Theodore Roosevelt's statement, "Walk softly but carry a big stick," expresses a complex set of ideas about America's position on the world stage. If a teacher says, "I came to a fork in the road," some young students will want to know if the teacher leaned down to pick up the fork unless the teacher clarifies the meaning.

Analogical Construction

Ortony and his associates (1984, 1978) define analogies as having a *vehicle*, a *topic*, and the *matching characteristics*. Figure 7.4 depicts a topic, topic characters, a story, a vehicle, and vehicle characters. Constructing the analogy includes framing the idea in relation to a vehicle and selecting its components. Teachers should plan analogies to ensure that the vehicles and characters have appropriate and as accurate a parallel construction as

Topic	Vehicle
Story Analogue: The Civil War is like two brothers fighting	
America in 1860	Family
Topic Characters	*Vehicle Characters*
Civil War	An Argument
North	One brother
South	Another brother

Figure 7.4 Parallel Construction: Civil War

possible. This is known as **framing** the analogy. By their nature, analogies are imperfect, but even the examination of the imperfection can be an important part of a lesson.

Pitfalls of Analogies

Social studies teachers must be acutely aware that it is exceptionally difficult to frame an analogy that is free of bias. Because analogies are so powerful, they can be used to overtly or covertly mislead or misinform people or steer students toward an ideological stance. The metaphor about Cleopatra cited above is sympathetic to her, and the President Roosevelt quote places America in a very positive light to US citizens, but not necessarily other countries.

Analogies are efficient and powerful, but culture and age differences can also limit their effectiveness (Readence, Baldwin, & Rickelmanm, 1983; Tierney, 1991). In a social studies class, the teacher asked if anyone knew who Lewis and Clark were. A middle school student whose first language was not English and was relatively new to the US said that he was Superman and she was his girlfriend in the *Lois and Clark* TV series. I recently relied on my childhood experiences and referred to my students as the "peanut gallery," but because all of them were born well after the *Howdy Doody* TV show had left the air, they did not know what to make of it.

Graphic Organizers in Concept Formation

With direct instruction, as an example, a graphical image (such as Figure 7.1) is often used to depict for the students what the concepts are and how their mental map should be organized. It then serves as a baseline of information to which the teacher adds examples and analogies, has a discussion, and then, perhaps, an application or practice. The teacher often uses the "**reveal method**," where the teacher pauses and reveals parts of the graphic image as questions are asked of students along with examples and analogies supplied by the teacher as talking points. In indirect instruction, teachers often do not share their visualization with students but create an instructional sequence that forces the students to collectively or individually create what they think the concepts and their relationships are and then the teacher debriefs the students to ensure all students have formed the appropriate schema. In reading, converting the concepts found in paragraph form into a graphical image produces both a baseline of information and a mental map.

Resources

Videos: *Minnesota Center for Social Studies Videos for Teachers* (multiple videos such as concept-based learning, primary documents, etc.) | *YouTube:* Concept Formation Lessons; Concept Formation Egypt; How to Teach a Concept Attainment Lesson | Jerome Bruner on Discovery Learning.

Documents: *Teachinghistory.org*: Concept Formation | *Edb.gov.hk* Graphic Organizers (103 pages of graphic organizers).

References

Adams, G., & Engelmann, S. (1996). *Research on direct instruction: Twenty years beyond DISTAR.* Educational Achievement Systems.

Alford, K., & Griffin, T. (2019). *Unleashing the power of examples.* Retrieved from www.facultyfocus.com/articles/effective-teaching-strategies/unleashing-the-power-of-examples/.

Ali, M. A. (1981). The use of positive and negative examples during instruction: Some important issues related to the design and development of instructional materials. *Journal of Instructional Development, 5*(1), 2–7.

Ortony, A. (1984). Understand figurative language. In P. D. Pearson (Ed.), *Handbook of reading research* (pp. 453–470). Longman.

Ortony, A., Reynolds, R. F., & Arter, J. A. (1978). Metaphor: Theoretical and empirical research. *Psychology Bulletin, 85*(5), 919–943.

Readence, J. E.; others. (1986). Direct instruction in processing metaphors. *Journal of Reading Behavior, 18*, 325–340.

Readence, J. E., Baldwin, R., & Rickelmanm, R. J. (1983). Work knowledge and metaphorical interpretation. *Research in Teaching English, 17*, 349–358.

Riley, N. P. (2011). Was the $5 billion worth it? *Wall Street Journal.* Retrieved from www.wsj.com/articles/SB10001424053111903554904576461571362279948

Tennyson, R., & Cocchiarella, M. (1986). An empirically based instructional design theory for teaching concepts. *Review of Educational Research, 56*, 40–71.

Tennyson, R. D., Youngers, J., & Suebsonthi, P. (1983). Concept learning by children using instructional presentation forms for prototype formation and classification-skill development. *Journal of Educational Psychology, 75*(2), 280–291.

Thompson, S. J. (1986). Teaching metaphoric language; An instructional strategy. *Journal of Reading, 30*, 105–109.

Tierney, D. S. (1991). The social studies teacher as analogist. *Social Science Record, 28*, 53–57.

8 Critical Thinking and the NCSS C3 Framework

Spoon feeding in the long run teaches us nothing but the shape of the spoon.
E.M. Forster, Novelist, 1879–1970

Richard Paul (2020) refers to what he disapprovingly calls "mother robin" teaching, where teachers think their job is to "mentally chew up everything for our student so we can put it into their intellectual beaks to swallow." Based on the body of research and theories on constructivism and character formation, the best practices have moved away from the mother robin approach to an emphasis on active learning and critical thinking strategies. A landmark in the movement was the development of **Bloom's Taxonomy of Educational Objectives** (see Anderson & Krathwohl, 2001; and Chapter 25). In 2013, the NCSS adopted *College, Career, and Civic Life C3 Framework for Social Studies State Standards* (NCSS, 2013, should be downloaded). This "**Framework**" consists of two parts: One, a set of K-12, grade-level standards for the social studies (see Chapters 12–17); and two, the "**Arc of Inquiry**" (see Chapter 12), a teaching-learning methodology based on constructivism that is intended to "build critical thinking, problem-solving, and participatory skills to become engaged citizens" (NCSS, 2020).

With the Arc approach, teachers no longer think of themselves as the "sage on the stage." Ambitious teachers shift their thinking during planning from what they will tell students, to creating lessons that require students to "do the work" of figuring out what they need to know, what is important, what is accurate, what is the compelling belief or enduring idea that they should consider or know. This "restructuring" of lesson plans for critical thinking for teacher candidates is often a challenge because it is different from the mother robin experience that perhaps teacher candidates were too frequently exposed to while they were students. The Arc's starting point typically begins with a compelling question as a prompt to begin the critical thinking process, such as: "Was the American Revolution justified?"

The Goal of Critical Thinking

Critical thinking becomes systematized when social studies teachers purposely create lessons that require students to think critically through active learning experiences or by teachers modeling critical thinking through "**think alouds**" (see Chapter 26). Such lessons begin with questions that the teacher and students discuss, such as:

What precise question are we trying to answer?
What information do we need to answer the question?
What conclusions seem justified in light of the facts?
Is there another way to look at the question?
What are some related questions we need to consider?
The Foundation for Critical Thinking (2020a)

Critical Thinking Defined

Critical thinking is self-disciplined, self-monitored, and aimed at problem-solving and decision-making. It is layered upon the process of basic reasoning. When students are thinking critically, they tend to use words like "since," "thus," "because," "given," etc. John Dewey (1910) warned against teachers presenting "ready-made knowledge" and referred to critical thinking as "reflective thinking" and defined it as "active, persistent and careful consideration of any belief or supposed form of knowledge in the light of the grounds that support it, and the further conclusions to which it tends" (p. 6).

Critical thinking is not only the mental tool used to properly illuminate the information extracted from the social studies, but it is intrapersonal in the sense that it exposes for examination intrapersonal flaws in logic, biases, naïve theories, and insufficient understanding of the democratic ideals. Richard Paul (2020) points to the personal benefit of critical thinking when he says, "Imagine the satisfaction of looking through the inventory of one's beliefs and finding that many of them were consciously, deliberately, and painstakingly chosen for their accuracy, their depth, their clarity, their consistency – in other words, their legitimate merit!" (1995, p. ii).

Edward Glaser (1941) defines critical thinking as involving three things:

1. An attitude of being disposed to consider in a thoughtful way the problems and subjects that come within the range of one's experiences;
2. Knowledge of the methods of logical inquiry and reasoning; and
3. Some skill in applying those methods.

Critical thinking generally requires the ability to:

A. Recognize problems,
B. Find workable means for meeting those problems,
C. Gather and marshal pertinent information,
D. Recognize unstated assumptions and values,
E. Comprehend and use language with accuracy, clarity, and discrimination, and interpret data,
F. Appraise evidence and evaluate arguments,
G. Recognize the existence (or non-existence) of logical relationships between propositions,
H. Draw warranted conclusions and generalizations,
I. Put to test the conclusions and generalizations at which one arrives,
J. Reconstruct one's patterns of beliefs on the basis of wider experience, and
K. Render accurate judgments about specific things and qualities in everyday life.

(pp. 5–6)

Foundational Knowledge and Problem-Solving

The approach to critical thinking lessons in the realm of foundational knowledge tends to follow the path of **problem-solving** that has too frequently been viewed as the exclusive province of the sciences. Such problem-solving does not involve decision-making (see next section) about compelling propositions, although decisions are being made.

The Five Steps in Problem-Solving (with geography example)

There are many variations of the steps in problem-solving. The following example is based on Beyer (1988) and Kalsounis (1987) and is envisioned as an upper elementary grade lesson example.

1. **Become aware of the problem:** The teacher introduces a topic such as "Why is Juneau, Alaska, on average, warmer than Chicago, Illinois in December?" and points out the locations of each on a world map. Intuitively, given the visual imagery of the map showing latitudes, one would expect Juneau to be colder.
2. **Gather data:** Students discuss what declarative knowledge is needed to solve the problem and are given packets of information or they are directed to online resources to include maps, latitude, longitude, climate, weather, water currents, winds, etc.
3. **Form hypotheses:** Students are placed in groups to form questions about the possible categories of determinants of temperatures. Are water bodies, landforms, wind, etc., possible determinants, and what attribute of those determinants might be the most significant causes that allow an answer to the question?
4. **Test the hypotheses by analyzing, evaluating, and interpreting data:** Students examine the information and apply the concepts to test the hypotheses derived from the questions they formulated.
5. **Reach a conclusion:** Students collaborate on the most logical answers and support their findings and conclusions during a debriefing led by the teacher.

To assist the students in how to think critically, the lesson would be guided by a handout such as Figure 8.1. After the students have worked in groups, teachers would use a "whole class" debriefing approach by calling on groups to provide the determinants and attributes while filling in on a whiteboard display that is identical to the Figure 8.1 handout. In this example, modeling a deliberate, systematic thinking process by the teacher cannot be overemphasized. Further, while soliciting answers from

Determinants	Chicago	Juneau
Topography		
Fixed Location Latitude		
Fixed Location Longitude		
Wind Currents		
Water Bodies/Water Currents		
Elevation		
???		

Figure 8.1 Climate Example

students, teachers would use prepared **talking points** (see Chapters 19 and 20) and share their critical thinking metacognition through the **think-aloud approach** (see Chapter 26). To state the obvious, any two cities could be used because the lesson is not about Juneau or Chicago. They happen to be two cities that create a paradox that makes the problem interesting by creating curiosity.

By this kind of critical thinking investigation, students create concepts and schema about climate, land formations, wind currents, water bodies, longitude, and latitude, etc., but – of equal or greater importance – they acquire the schema about the procedure of structuring an investigation. It is those critical thinking schemata that are transferable to the examination of other social studies content. The same emphasis on critical thinking and questions should be used for decision-making about things that matter.

Democratic Ideals and Decision-Making

Critical thinking for exalted aims requires systematic decision-making and starts with the introduction of a problem by the teacher. In contrast to problem-solving, **decision-making** typically involves indefinite information, reflection on ideology, political ideology and stances, and choosing between alternative solutions about things that matter.

Eight Steps in the Decision-Making Process

Naylor and Diem (1987) have identified eight steps in decision-making. Note that step 2 includes the five steps in problem-solving. A lesson on homelessness for middle school students illustrates the process. The teacher introduces the topic of the homeless with images of homeless people. Through the **"setup" lecture**, the teacher covers steps 1 and 2. Packets of information are distributed to pairs of students, who conduct an investigation of the declarative information made up of documents on statistics, causes, government programs, the role of nonprofits, compelling narratives, etc. Following this, a debriefing starts at step 3.

1. **Recognize the situation as one in which a decision needs to be made:** Should people in a country like the US be homeless? What are the causes? Who should solve the problem (city, state, national government)? Etc.
2. **Clarify the problem:** Follow the problem-solving steps.
3. **Identify relevant values:** In groups, students discuss their ideas *and* feelings about people who are homeless and the causes of homelessness.
4. **Indicate the desired outcome (goal):** Have the students collaborate in their groups to decide on what would be reasonable goals for a democratic society that has a homeless population.
5. **Propose and consider a range of potential alternatives:** Expect the groups to come up with solutions such as developing low-income housing, raising taxes, providing jobs, creating orphanages, government subsidies to nonprofits, etc.
6. **Project the likely consequences for each alternative (both positive and negative):** Expect the groups to systematically identify advantages and disadvantages of each proposed solution and possible unintended consequences.
7. **Choose the best alternative, or rank the alternatives based on analysis of projected outcomes of each solution and consistency with the stated goal:** Have the students attempt to forge a consensus in their groups.

8. **Apply the decision and assess the consequences:** Have each group report their decision and then, during the debriefing, the teacher probes for missing determinants and attributes. Teachers make the lesson "real" when students who propose higher taxes, as an example, are asked what they are willing to give up because their families will have less money.

On the surface, it appears students are examining a public policy. But from an identity development perspective, students are being asked to answer the questions "What kind of person am I?" and "What kind of society do I want?" Teachers may find they have homeless students and students who have relatives or acquaintances who are homeless. In the free flow of ideas, biases may be revealed that are unavoidably emotionally painful. The mediation of feelings, ideas, and beliefs by students requires teachers who see their role as caring for students grappling with feelings of empathy and balancing those feelings with beliefs in justice and injustice. It can be emotionally taxing for teachers to probe students' ideas, feelings, and beliefs, but that is what is needed for the kind of authentic self-reflection by students to advance their ideology and political ideology and stances. The solution is not for teachers to avoid such topics because they are uncomfortable or to impose their political ideology and stance through direct instruction: But for teachers to intensively prepare themselves to create grade-appropriate lessons and the caring encounter necessary to help the student through intrapersonal conflicts (see Chapters 9 and 10). As important as any societal problem may be, the schema of deliberate decision-making employed within the entanglements of emotions that can be carried forward is the primary learning goal.

Key Principles for Teaching Critical Thinking

In addition to the above practices, the following key principles should be kept in mind as teachers emphasize critical thinking:

1. **Remodel lessons for critical thinking.** The Foundation for Critical Thinking (2020b) and C3 Literacy Collaborative (see *Documents*) provide explanations and examples on how to "remodel" typical lessons so they explicitly focus on teaching critical thinking.
2. **Metacognition** is "thinking about thinking," the internal, mental control process we use to direct our thinking process. Students need to be exposed to the metacognition of critical thinking by someone more expert in the social studies than they are (Ennis, 2020/2015). Bandura calls metacognition "one of the most powerful means of transmitting values, attitudes, and patterns of thought and behavior" (1979, p. 47).
3. **Metacognitive modeling** requires teachers to teach by "**think-aloud**." As teachers critically think during investigations, they verbally share their thoughts, step-by-step. Modeling of metacognition by teachers is essential to the students adopting the strategy as a disposition toward all learning.
4. **Explicit teaching.** Teachers need to make think-alouds part of their planning. Students need to be alerted by teachers that they will be sharing their way of thinking before they start to teach so that students focus on the process as well as the content (Vijaya Kumari & Jinto, 2014).
5. **Framing the problem.** For about six months during the spring and summer of 2019, the Democrats and Republicans could not agree as to whether there was an

immigration crisis on the US–Mexico border, much less agree on the causes, fault, or solutions. This is typical of the problem of "**framing**." Framing the problem may be influenced based on political ideology, differences in expertise, mass media reports, etc. The prism through which each side sees the problem is, arguably, tainted by partisanship, which has the effect of minimizing the civic values of open-mindedness, search for the truth, impartiality, and engaged discourse. Such partisanship may be a reality in the political arena, but teachers, when entering into an investigation or discussion with students, need to frame any issue as a question or proposition as objectively as possible. As a prerequisite, teachers must research the problem, think deeply about the issue, and weed out their own political ideological preferences.

6. **Give students the license** to articulate their metacognition by creating a caring, non-judgmental environment (Tanner, 2012).

Resources

Videos: *Learner.org:* The Learning Classroom Theory into Practice (13 videos) | *Kahn Academy*: Fundamentals Introduction to Critical Thinking | *Smithsonian.com*: Overview of the College, Career, and Civic Life Framework | *YouTube:* Inquiry Arc Social Studies.

Documents: *Wiley Handbook of Social Studies Research*: Disciplined Inquiry in Social Studies Classrooms; Children's Learning and Understanding in Their Social World | *Foundation for Critical Thinking:* K-12 Instruction Strategies and Samples | *NCSS*: C3 Framework for Social Studies PDF; Completing the Inquiry Arc Exploring Dimension 4 of the C3 Framework; C3 Framework Arc of Inquiry | *C3 Literacy Collaborative*: C3 Teachers Join the Inquiry Revolution (lesson plans) | *Critical Thinking in a World of Accelerating Change and Complexity.*

References

Anderson, L. W., & Krathwohl, D. (2001). *A taxonomy for learning, teaching, and assessing: A revision of Bloom's taxonomy of educational objectives.* New York: Longman.

Bandura, A. (1979). *Social learning theory.* Englewood Cliffs, NJ: Prentice Hall.

Beyer, B. K. (1988). *Developing a thinking skills program.* Boston, MA: Allyn & Bacon.

Dewey, J. (1910). *How we think.* Boston: D.C. Heath. Retrieved from https://archive.org/details/how wethink000838mbp/page/n8.

Ennis, R. (2020/2015). The nature of critical thinking: Outlines of general critical thinking dispositions and abilities. Retrieved from http://criticalthinking.net/wp-content/uploads/2018/01/The-Nature-of-Critical-Thinking.pdf.

Foundation for Critical Thinking. (2020a, n.p.). *About critical thinking.* Retrieved from www.criti calthinking.org//.

Foundation for Critical Thinking, (2020b, n.p.). *K-12 instruction strategies & samples.* Retrieved from www.criticalthinking.org/pages/k-12-instruction-strategies-amp-samples/613.

Glaser, E. (1941). *An experiment in the development of critical thinking.* New York: Teacher's College, Columbia University.

Kalsounis, T. (1987). *Teaching social studies in the elementary school: The basics for citizenship* (2nd ed.). Englewood Cliffs, NJ: Prentice-Hall.

Naylor, D., & Diem, R. (1987). *Elementary and middle school social studies.* New York: Random House.

NCSS. (2013). *Social studies for the next generation: Purposes, practices, and implications of the college, career, and civic Life (C3) framework for social studies state standards: Guidance for enhancing rigor of K-12 civic, economics, geography, and history.* Silver Spring, MD: Author. Retrieved from www.socialstudies.org/sites/default/files/2017/Jun/c3-framework-for-social-studies-rev0617.pdf

NCSS. (2020). *The college, career, and civic life (C3) framework for social studies state standards: Guidance for enhancing the rigor of K-12 civics, economics, geography, and history.* Silver Spring, MD: Author. Retrieved from www.socialstudies.org/c3

Paul, R. (2020). *Critical thinking: How to prepare students for a rapidly changing world.* The Foundation for Critical Thinking, (1995). Retrieved from www.criticalthinking.org/pages/the-art-of-redesigning-instruction/520.

Tanner, K. D. (2012). Promoting student metacognition. *CBE—Life Sciences Education, 11,* 113–120. Retrieved from www.lifescied.org/doi/full/10.1187/cbe.12-03-0033

Vijaya Kumari, S. N., & Jinto, M. (2014). Effectiveness of KWL metacognitive strategy on achievement in social science and metacognitive ability in relation to cognitive styles. *International Journal of Educational Research and Technology, 5*(1), 92–98.

9   Morality and Modernity

Democracy is a form of government that presumes a society of moral agents.
Hanna Alexander, Professor of Philosophy, University of Haifa
(Alexander, 2003, p. 378)

Morality

Morality refers to an individual's own principles regarding right and wrong. It is the outward manifestation of a person's ideas and beliefs.

The Greeks in antiquity and the Founders of the United States' sense of morality came from an amalgamation of religious and philosophical traditions. In philosophical terms, people become what they contemplate and act morally due to the drive to perfection, their intrinsic *telos* (Aristotle, 350 BCE; Plato, 380 BCE). Because people are social beings, their perfection depends on the well-being of others and this is a reason why individuals should care about others and help them seek perfection as well. In theological terms, the "Good" or perfection is the divine, god, the omega, etc. Many students rely on their inherited religious beliefs as a basis for their personal morality. This is an important part of students' identity and is appropriately a part of any discussion of things that matter. While it is paramount that teachers do not promote one religion over another, it is also often necessary (and appropriate) for teachers to rely on their students for information about morality that stems from their religions. Strauss (1983) points out that religion and secular notions of morality are not in conflict but that "Western man became what he is through the coming together of biblical faith and Greek thought. In order to understand our-selves and to illuminate our trackless way into the future, we must understand Jerusalem and Athens" (p. 147). Jeffrey Hart (2001) elaborates on this idea when he argues that the Athens/philosophy/reason secular view of the world and the Jerusalem/scripture/faith view of the world have created a unique tension that has propelled Western Civilization to its status as the most significant force of liberty and equality in the history of humankind. Social studies in the US has built on this tradition as it incorporates multicultural and global education perspectives.

In the Middle Ages, morality was conceived as a form of obedience to the sovereign and church. The Enlightenment brought forth the idea that morality is based in individual autonomy and self-governance of the people (Handler, 1986). By the end of the 18th century, the movement of society to egalitarianism led to the belief that individuals are equally able to live together in a morality of self-governance. All of us, in this view, have an equal ability to see for ourselves, what morality calls for, and are in principle equally able to move ourselves to act accordingly.

(Schneewind, 1998, p. 4)

The modern democratic societies in the West provide context for individuals to thrive and new liberties to advance as movements (MacIntyre, 2007). Hanna Alexander (2003) offered the following perspective:

The political success (of the West) entails the creation of modern liberal democracies that enable people who hold conflicting conceptions of the good to live in a common civil society ... This capacity to influence (within reasonable limits) one's own destiny in such a way that is neither a function of previous causes nor a matter of chance, but a matter of choice, intent, and purpose, lies at the very heart of the democratic ethos. It is because human beings are agents able to govern their own actions that they are also capable and worthy of governing their collective lives. Democracy is a form of government that presumes a society of moral agents, and the first task of liberalism is to protect democratic citizens' capacity to exercise their agency.

(pp. 367, 377)

Modernity

An individual's democratic ideology and identity are forged within democratic societies, where democratic beliefs are prized and practiced (Taylor, 1989, 1992). But with the agency to be autonomous and authentic comes unanticipated stresses on the human psyche as individuals face the new challenge of balancing that independence with obligations to the democratic societies that make it possible. Mass communication competing with parents and schools as the primary source of information, speed of technological change, social media that encourages self-promotion, evolving family structures, limited amounts of meaningful work, excessive consumerism, schools that become "work factories," unstable neighborhoods, economic inequalities, and dispassionate and bureaucratic institutions create what is referred to as "ambient" fear (Hubbard, 2003; Massumi, 1993): It produces greater anxiety, alienation, selfishness, narcissism, and depression than is thought to have existed in the past (Kanfer, 1979). In *Bowling Alone: The Collapse and Revival of American Community* (2000), Robert Putnam points out that starting in the 1950s, Americans began to gradually withdraw from churches, political parties, civic organizations, and recreational associations. Even family dinners have dropped by 43% and having friends over has dropped by 35%. He argues that these behaviors have "impoverished our lives and communities" and left more decisions to politicians and the powerful.

Narcissistic personality traits, which correlate with less empathy and concern for others, have increased over the last four generations of students (Stewart & Bernhardt, 2010; Twenge & Foster, 2010). David Brooks, in his book *The Road to Character* (2016), points out that in 1950, 12% of high school students told the Gallup organization that they considered themselves "very important," but by 2005 that figure had risen to 80%. The consequence of societal forces in modernity is, as Morris Eagle (1984) believes, children and teenagers who suffer from "a lack of sustaining interests, goals, ideals, and values ... stable ideologies ... an atmosphere of disillusionment and cynicism in the surrounding society" (pp. 72–73). Erik Erikson (1950) makes the same argument when he says today's student agonizes more than past generations about "the problem of what he should believe in and who he should – or, indeed, might – be or become" (p. 279). Thomas Lickona (1991, 1999) believes that due to modernity, teachers must intervene and instill more "directly and indirectly, such values as respect, responsibility, trustworthiness, fairness, caring, and civic virtues; and that these values are not merely subjective preferences but that they have objective worth and a claim on our collective conscience" (1993, p. 9).

Morality and Duties

Brian Barry (1973) believes that in a liberal democracy, every individual

> must take his stand on the proposition that some ways of life, some types of character are more admirable than others ... He must hold that societies ought to be organized in such a way as to produce the largest possible proportion of people with an admirable type of character and the best possible chance to act in accordance with it.
>
> (p. 126)

Children and teenagers, more than ever, need to rely on adults to provide the direction in which to develop their ideology in tandem with their identity (Marcia, 1980). Michael Boylan (2011) argues that all adults have "protective duties" to all children, not just their own. Thus schools, and social studies education in particular, are effectively the result of the modern nation state's decision to formally interject itself into the developmental process of children because it has a stake in the moral quality of society as a whole. Amitai Etzioni (2011) emphasizes this point when he says:

> Making a child is a moral act. It obligates the community to the parents. But it also obligates the parents to the community. For we all live with the consequences of children who are not brought up properly, whether bad economic conditions or self-centered parents are to blame.
>
> (p. 8)

The two following approaches by Nell Noddings (1984; 2002; 2003) and Alasdair MacIntyre (2007) provide a valuable insight for social studies teachers about the process of identity formation for a democratic ideology.

Morality through Caring

In contemporary social studies literature there are calls, as examples, for greater emphasis on social justice, LGBTQ rights, multicultural education, global education, etc. But the shortcomings of society that serve as the impetus for these calls to action might be summed up in the idea of a lack of **caring**. If a caring disposition is developed and thrives in children and teenagers, caring can become an essential part of their identity and they will be less inclined to acts of incivility, injustice, intolerance, and discrimination as they become more active participants in the flow of the democratic ethos.

Sherman (1989) believes learning to care requires more than the child's observations of other actors, lessons about caring, or children's literature about caring, but it requires caregivers (parents and teachers) to participate in the emotions of the child or teenager being cared for. Nel Noddings (1984) asserts, "It is that longing for caring – to be in that special relation – that provides the motivation for us to be moral" (pp. 4–5).

Noddings (1984, 2002) brings an analysis of moral formation that is focused on individual identity. She believes that moral actions flow spontaneously from deep-seated dispositions that are revealed in relationships to other people: It is tied to the intimate relationship of those "cared-for" and those "caring-for." The teacher's nurturing and the sense of well-being that students feel by being cared-for have a greater impact on moral development than abstract ethical codes or lists of virtues, as important as those may be.

Ethical caring is a moral duty that compels teachers to enter into a caring relationship with their students because they decided to be a teacher (Noddings, 1984). Teachers practice ethical caring because they have a "special responsibility for the enhancement of the ethical ideal" (p. 178). Personal memories of caring and the experience of being cared for serve as, at least, subliminal moral ideals. Because the experiences resonate with a person's innate drive to the Good Life, individuals feel a duty to act ethically, to truly care for others. Children and teenagers who sense they are cared for by parents and teachers grow up to be "the best self," persons who in turn practice natural and ethical caring (pp. 80–81).

Social studies topics geared to things that matter are intended to compel students into contemplations of right and wrong. Teachers acting as philosophical counselors exercise their duty as ethical caregivers. Teachers do not only share their ideas about how to think about moral questions; they empathize with students as the student suffers through the moral decision-making that leads to an identity that makes democracy possible.

Morality through Practice

Alasdair MacIntyre, in *After Virtue* (2007), offers a unique insight into the conceptualization of morality as a cultural phenomenon, as compared with Professor Noddings' relational identity formation approach. Morality requires what he calls "practice" (p. 193). In modernity, this occurs in families, work, schools, religious institutions, organizations, etc., and importantly, a democratic society.

Personal Practice

To explain how a person comes to understand the morality of being in a democratic state, MacIntyre uses the metaphor of teaching a child to play chess, a "practice." Chess is inherently competitive, requires skill, and is not a game of chance. To entice a child into playing an unfamiliar game like chess, a person might initially need to offer an inducement such as candy. This, MacIntyre refers to as an **external good**; it is an **extrinsic motivator**. While external goods may have the potential to motivate the child to begin to play, it may also motivate the child to win, by any means – even cheating. By playing the game over time, however, the child will come to appreciate the techniques of chess, the self-discipline he has acquired to learn the practice of the game, his own mental acuity, and he shifts his thinking to becoming a better chess player for its own sake. MacIntyre refers to this as **internal goods**; it is an **intrinsic motivator**. The internal goods mean all the good things that come from engaging in the hard work of the practice such as a sense of satisfaction, social bonding, delayed gratification, excellence in performance, self-worth, i.e., the kinds of things that build agency, authenticity, autonomy, and efficacy. Cheating no longer becomes an option, as that would mean losing because the child recognizes that cheating to win denies him the satisfaction of having developed the skills and *eudaimonia* that can come only from the internal goods.

The only way to obtain the internal goods is to actually play chess (not observing or reading about it) and do so virtuously by abiding by the rules, not gloating, accepting defeats, praising others' efforts, etc. The child develops respect and admiration for other players because they take the time (the care) to teach him the rules and tactics, encourage him, answer questions, and objectively evaluate his play. In competing, the child and his opponents develop each other's skills collaboratively while competing. Each can recognize and value those skills in the other and hence the child values and admires the other person.

A practice "requires standards of excellence and obedience to the rules as well as the achievements of good" (MacIntyre, 2007, p. 190). As a newcomer to the practice, the child must subordinate himself to the practice, accept the rules as rules in order to play. He accepts those who play better than he does as the authorities because he does not have their experience and cannot just decide that he is a grand master because those standards have become universals that predate his decision to join the game. The rules of the past are binding on the present and can be changed, but only with the consent of the community of players in the practice and only if consistent with the universals that form the essence of the game. As the child gains experience, he too will have a say over the standards of excellence and possible changes to the rules.

At the core of any practice are the internal goods and these are universals. Morality within practices may be culturally-based just as different games have evolved in different cultures, but what is universal is the internal goods, expectations for excellence, and the process of coming to know what is moral, what it is to be virtuous. MacIntyre (2007) says, "The virtues are precisely those qualities the possession of which will enable an individual to achieve *eudaimonia* [the Good Life] and the lack of which will frustrate his movement toward that *telos*" (p. 148).

Civic Practice

Charles Taylor makes the connection between personal identity and civic identity when he explains that individual moral identity can be forged, "Only against a backdrop of things that matter ... only if I exist in a world in which history, or the duties of citizenship, or the call of God, or something else of this order ... matters crucially" (1992, p. 15). As novices in society, children and teenagers do not have the knowledge and experience to evaluate themselves in the practice of a democratic ideology. Thus, teachers of social studies have the duty to introduce them to the practice of democracy. Morality is learned by "practicing" the democratic ideology, which is unavoidably carried out in juxtaposition to the others who sense, if not know, its internal goods. Individuals are not practicing a democratic ideology if they are only following the rules or laws – the external goods – of a democratic state. If they practice, earnestly – for the internal goods – it becomes dispositional, "which will not only sustain practices and enable us to achieve the goods internal to practices, but which will sustain us in the relevant kind of quest for the good," by enabling us to overcome the harms, dangers, temptations and distractions which we encounter, and which will furnish us with increasing self-knowledge and increasing knowledge of "the good" (MacIntyre, 2007, p. 219).

Social studies classrooms should be thought of as a place of practice that society has created so as to formally enculturate maturing members of society into the practice of a liberal democracy. If taken in this context, the social studies classroom would not meet its societal mandate if it is just a place for passing on foundational knowledge. The awakening of the student's morality based on the democratic ideals and identity formation is made possible by the skill of teachers acting as philosophical counselors who have, themselves, experienced the practice of a democratic ideology (Maritain, 1943). The end result is the liberation of the student.

Resources

Videos: *Learner.org:* Ethics in American (I & II) | *TED Talk:* Moral Roots of Liberals and Conservatives Jonathan Haidt; Moral Issues | *YouTube*: Road to Character with David Brooks; Virtue Ethics Return of Virtue in Later 20th Century American Philosophy; Alasdair Macintyre; Ethics Unwrapped.

Documents: *Wiley Handbook of Social Studies Research*: Media and Social Studies Education | *Khan Academy:* Kohlberg Moral Development | *NCSS:* Study about Religions in the Social Studies Curriculum | *ReadWriteThink:* Living the Dream; 100 Acts of Kindness | *Sage Publications:* The Psychology of Morality Personality and Social Psychology Review | *Simply Psychology:* Kohlberg's Stages of Moral Development.

References

Alexander, H. A. (2003). Moral education and liberal democracy: Spirituality, community, and character in an open society. *Educational Theory, 53*(4), 367–387.

Aristotle. (350 BCE). *Nicomachean ethics*. Retrieved from http://classics.mit.edu/Aristotle/nicomachaen.html.

Barry, B. (1973). *The liberal theory of justice*. Clarendon Press.

Boylan, M. (2011). Duties to children. In M. Boylan (Ed.), *The morality and global justice reader* (pp. 385–403). Westview Press.

Brooks, D. (2016). *The road to character*. Random House.

Eagle, M. N. (1984). *Recent developments in psychoanalysis: A critical evaluation*. McGraw-Hill.

Erikson, E. H. (1950). *Childhood and society*. Norton.

Etzioni, A. (2011). *The parenting deficit*. Demos Publishing.

Handler, R. (1986). Authenticity. *Anthropology Today, 2*(1), 2–4.

Hart, J. (2001). *Toward the revival of higher education*. Yale University Press.

Hubbard, P. (2003). Fear and loathing at the multiplex: Everyday anxiety in the post-industrial city. *Capital & Class, 27*(2), 51–75.

Kanfer, F. H. (1979). Personal control, social control, and altruism: Can society survive the age of individualism? *American Psychologist, 34*(3), 231–239.

Lickona, T. (1991). *Educating for character*. Bantam.

Lickona, T. (1993). The return of character education. *Educational Leadership, 51*(3), 6–11.

Lickona, T. (1999). Character education: Seven crucial issues. *Action in Teacher Education, 20*(4), 77–84.

MacIntyre, A. (2007). *After virtue*. University of Notre Dame Press.

Marcia, J. E. (1980). Identity in Adolescence. In J. Adelson (Ed.), *Handbook of adolescent psychology* (pp. 159–187). Wiley.

Maritain, J. (1943). *Education at the crossroads.* Yale University Press.

Massumi, B. (Ed.). (1993). *The politics of everyday fear.* University of Minnesota Press.

Noddings, N. (1984). *Caring: A feminine approach to ethics and moral education.* University of California Press.

Noddings, N. (2002). *Educating moral people: A caring alternative to character education.* Teachers College Press.

Noddings, N. (2003). *Happiness and education.* Cambridge University Press.

Plato. (380 BCE). *Ion.* Retrieved from http://classics.mit.edu/Plato/ion.html.

Putnam, R. (2000). *Bowling alone: The collapse and revival of American community.* Simon & Schuster.

Putnam. (2020). *Bowling alone: The collapse and revival of American community.* Retrieved from http://bowlingalone.com/.

Schneewind, J. B. (1998). *The invention of autonomy: A history of modern moral philosophy.* Cambridge University Press.

Sherman, N. (1989). *The fabric of character: Aristotle's theory of virtue.* Clarendon Press.

Stewart, K. D., & Bernhardt, P. C. (2010). Comparing millennials to pre-1987 students and with one another. *North American Journal of Psychology, 12,* 579–602.

Strauss, L. (1983). Jerusalem and Athens: Some preliminary reflections. In T. I. Pangle (Ed.), *Studies in platonic political philosophy* (pp. 147–171). University of Chicago Press.

Taylor, C. (1989). *Sources of the self: The making of the modern identity.* Harvard University Press.

Taylor, C. (1992). *The ethics of authenticity.* Harvard University Press.

Twenge, J. M., & Foster, J. D. (2010). Birth cohort increases in narcissistic personality traits among American college students, 1982–2009. *Social Psychological & Personality Science, 1,* 99–106.

10 Character Education and Philosophical Counseling

Plato not Prozac!
Lou Marinoff, Professor of Philosophy, the City College of New York (Marinoff, 1999, CP)

Socrates, by today's standards, would be considered a social studies teacher. He explicitly counseled students about things that matter, exemplified by his statement, "the unexamined life is not worth living." He understood his role was to help his students come to understand who they were and who they might become. Today's teacher of social studies must also recognize that a holistic approach to the examination of feelings, beliefs, and ideas is needed to help students form an ideology to live by. Charles Guignon (1993) provides an important insight into the unique duty that is inherent in teaching social studies:

> A central part of what goes on in helping people in the modern world will consist in addressing questions about what constitutes the Good Life and how we can be at home in the world. And these are clearly moral questions in the broad sense, where "morality" includes not just questions about right actions, but "questions about how I am going to live my life" – questions "which touch on the issue of what kind of life is worth living ... or of what constitutes a rich, meaningful life – as against one concerned with secondary matters or trivia."
>
> (p. 270, quoting Taylor, 1989, p. 14)

Character Education

Social studies educators use the terms **character education**, **values education**, and **moral education** when describing the pedagogy and topics used to teach about things that matter. Stanley (2005) points out that "In the United States, schooling is generally understood as an integral component of a democratic society" (p. 282). As a result, ideas of patriotism, nationalism, and democratic ideals have been part of (social studies) education since the Europeans first arrived on the North American east coast (Stanley & Nelson, 1994). Initially it took the form of moral education steeped in bible-based Christian orthodoxy and it was thought to be inseparable from matters of politics and social welfare (McClellan, 1999). The publication of the *McGuffey Reader* in 1836 (Bohning, 1986) is emblematic of a shift to a more nondenominational, secular approach to character education befitting a state-sponsored, nonsectarian education. The *McGuffey Reader* included moral lessons in adventure stories, poems, and fables, such as "The Greedy Girl" and "The Honest Boy and the Thief."

No discussion, today, of character education would be complete without consideration of the work of Lawrence Kohlberg (1969). Kohlberg's analysis evolved out of Jean Piaget's concepts of cognitive development. The focus of Kohlberg's work is on how individuals at different stages of life *think* – not on how they feel – about ethical issues. As an example, Kohlberg's ground-breaking research has demonstrated that most children aged ten and younger believe that rules are fixed and absolute. They think that rules are handed down by adults or by God and cannot be changed. As children mature, they understand that it is permissible to change rules: Rules become guidelines. If children are nurtured, they will eventually begin to autonomously formulate ideas and beliefs of right and wrong that reflects the democratic ideals of their society. Those ideas and beliefs are developed within a context of social norms, ideology, and identity. All things being equal, children and adults are inclined to conceptualize what is morally "good." Kohlberg's research and findings are widely accepted but there is some criticism that it may have a degree of cultural and gender bias (Gilligan, 1982; Shweder, 1982).

Value inculcation and **value analysis** are two ways that educators promote character formation. When teachers of social studies say they are going to teach values, they are planning to teach the democratic ideals so students can form a holistic identity. They hope students will judge the ideals to be worth valuing, thus becoming the beliefs by which students will be virtuous. This classroom process of sharing and listening to perspectives of others is the platform for students to build the capacities of autonomy, authenticity, agency, and efficacy.

Ambitious teachers develop lessons that draw the democratic ideals out of the rich topics in foundational knowledge, but they – particularly at the lower elementary grades – prepare stand-alone character education lessons that explicitly aim to analyze and/or promote the democratic ideals. Morally compelling literary works and moral dilemmas are valuable sources for teaching character formation and should be considered part of humanities in social studies education. Most trade books recommended by the NCSS (2020) are based in moral dilemmas or promote democratic ideals: They encourage the development of identity capacities, just as the *McGuffey Reader* did in the 19th century.

Values Inculcation Approach

Values inculcation is more explicit than the value analysis approach. As examples, reciting the Pledge of Allegiance and singing the national anthem; a field trip to a World War II exhibit; and raising funds to support the homeless are intended to promote democratic ideals. Literature can be integrated into social studies topics that endorse a particular democratic ideal or facilitate identity capacity at any grade level. The story of the three little pigs, when part of a social studies curriculum, is intended to promote the virtue of wisdom, not for children to learn about plot, protagonist, etc. *The Gift of the Magi* by O. Henry (1905) is a poignant short story of personal sacrifice about the working poor set at the turn of the century. Instead of provoking debate about the right thing to do as in the values analysis approach, such stories provide a narrative intended to inspire virtuous acts. *The Book of Virtues: A Treasury of Great Moral Stories* by William J. Bennett (1996) is a collection of stories, such as "The Bishop's Tale" from *Les Misérables*, that are used in social studies education for both the values analysis and inculcation approaches. Middle and high school teachers can use a short story such as *Desiree's Baby*, a Civil War period story, to create a lesson focused on racism and women's liberation (see Duplass & Cruz, 2009).

Values Analysis Approach

The values analysis approach tends to use case studies structured around **moral dilemmas** in which students must consider principles of right and wrong. Examples include the *Heinz dilemma, the overcrowded lifeboat, Sophie's Choice,* and *the trolley problem* (see *Resources*). During the debriefing, students hear different perspectives, reflect on inadequacies of their own thinking and perspective taking, and are motivated to formulate and articulate moral positions while the teacher contextualizes the dialogue within the framework of the democratic ideals. The students adopt more sophisticated conceptions of how to think about such moral choices based on the ideas expressed by fellow students or the teacher. A landmark study by Blatt and Kohlberg (1975) demonstrated that students who participated in teacher-led case studies of moral dilemmas improved their moral reasoning.

The Heightened Need for Philosophical Counseling

Modernity is considered to have heightened the challenges students are experiencing in forming a holistic identity and democratic ideology (Eagle, 1984) – arguably the most fundamental reason for character education and social studies education. Wittgenstein (2010) describes this heightened state as the emotional "disquiet" that arises from the intellectual problems of how to live one's life due to "a lack of sustaining interests, goals, ideals and values … stable ideologies … an atmosphere of disillusionment and cynicism in the surrounding society" (Eagle, 1984, p. 73) This cognitive and emotional disquiet if not examined impedes students' development but it does not rise to the level of a diagnosable pathology where a typical medically or psychologically trained therapist's intervention would be needed.

The term "**philosophical counseling**" has been appropriated from the field of philosophy to define the part of social studies education where students are led by a teacher to explicitly consider things that matter (Duplass, 2018). The engagement requires more of a teacher than other subject fields that are only interested in what students know. It demands more of students by compelling them to consider "questions about how I am going to live my life" – questions "which touch on the issue of what kind of life is worth living … or of what constitutes a rich, meaningful life" (Taylor, 1989, p. 14). As Lou Marinoff (2004) points out, philosophical counseling is "therapy for the sane," that it is not "traditional" group therapy, but intends to help ordinary individuals deal "with the problems of living" (Szasz, 1960, p. 114). It is teachers of social studies who are positioned to shoulder the significant burden of helping students "achieve an accurate, defensible, action-guiding, and truth-oriented self-understanding" (Jopling, 1996, p. 304).

Philosophical Counseling for the Social Studies Classroom

A dichotomous distinction between education and therapy is not especially helpful … because such a sharp distinction implies a cognition-emotion split, as if education deals only with the cognitions and therapy only with the emotions – neither of which is true, because cognitions and emotions are thoroughly intertwined in both endeavors.

(Doherty, 1995, p. 353)

Because all education is relational, but in particular character education, success is heavily reliant on the disposition of the teacher and the engagement with students on an intimate level like that of a counselor.

The basic dynamics of any therapy starts with a client's discontent due to inability to analyze the problem itself to bring it to a satisfactory conclusion and cope with the emotional problem associated with the problem itself. Through talk therapy, the former is resolved cognitively and through the cathartic experience that is inherent to talk therapy, the emotional disquiet is reduced. Unlike a therapist where the client brings in matters of concern, the social studies teacher has a set of topics to explore with students that compel students into cognitive uncertainty about their ideas and beliefs, a state of disequilibrium. The emotional problem tethered to the topic may produce passions in the group discussion, but do not typically rise to the level found in individual or group therapy.

Oliver and Shaver (1966) point out that "When a student 'joins an issue' he is often relating fundamental components of his own personality (e.g., beliefs, attitudes) to a public decision-making situation" (p. 167). As an example, from a discussion about food stamps and poverty, a student might share "I was in line at the register and someone was using food stamps for junk food." This reveals that the student has already initially judged the action to be morally questionable, but also reveals an openness to other opinions. When students begin to voice such perspectives, they are contextualizing a civic concern in the form of a personal identity proposition. Given that the student has had the courage to make the personal knowledge public, the teacher should recognize that the student is conflicted by the tension between empathy and justice. The student's aspiration to bring greater understanding to his ideas, beliefs, and feelings become the thing that matters; economic or sociological nuances of the food stamp subsidies is foundational knowledge and will change over time: Identity questions last forever. The student has revealed his own initial conceptualization of what is the appropriate personal virtue (spending money only on nutritious food when money is scarce) and what should be a civic duty (anyone receiving food stamps should restrain themselves or be restrained from spending money on non-nutritious food). In this example, the strategy for a social studies teacher acting as a philosophical counselor is to elevate the dialogue so as to engage the student's intrapersonal concern by allowing all the students to share and contrast how they think *and* feel about the issue of balancing the concepts of justice, just deserts, and empathy in an intellectually and emotionally honest way.

Philosophical Counseling Strategies

Philosophical counseling begins with the social studies teacher embracing the idea that "The student is infinitely more important than the subject" (Nodding, 1984, p. 20). It requires "The special gift of the teacher to receive the student, to look at the subject matter with him. Her commitment is to him, the cared-for, and he is – through this commitment – set to pursue his legitimate projects" (Noddings, 1984, p. 177).

The process of philosophical counseling looks much like the decision-making process referred to in Chapters 7 and 8.

1. The examination of client's arguments and justifications;
2. The clarification, analysis, and definition of important terms and concepts;

3. The exposure and examination of underlying assumptions and logical implications;
4. The exposure of conflicts and inconsistencies; and
5. The exploration of traditional philosophical theories and their significance for client issues (American Society for Philosophy, Counseling, and Psychotherapy, ASPCP, 2014, p. 1).

It is *philosophical* counseling because it systematically examines ideas and beliefs of a moral nature and draws on the vast, well-reasoned perspectives from philosophy's ideas on morality as points of reference. Even teachers without a rich experience in college philosophy courses would be surprised at how being immersed in a democratic ideology, liberal arts college courses, and pluralistic school systems with knowledgeable teachers has prepared them for this undertaking. Two books, however, that could assist with background knowledge that makes clear the therapeutic attributes of Western philosophy are Alain de Botton's short book *The Consolations of Philosophy* (2000) and the accompanying PBS video series (see *Resources*) and Charles Guignon's (1999) *The Good Life*.

It is philosophical *counseling* because it is the social studies where things that matter bring forward students' deeply held beliefs and feelings about who they are, who they can become, and who they want to be. Public sharing of students' beliefs and feelings reveals the limitations of each student's identity capacities and the intrapersonal conflict the students would like to resolve, just as a client would in individual or group therapy sessions. The introspection about self requires a more developmental relationship between teacher and students than in other subject fields – one more like that of a therapist to a client. Helping students to new insights about their beliefs and feelings in a classroom environment is more than teaching; it requires a caring encounter.

The Caring Encounter

The **caring encounter** necessitates that the teacher is "not simply a textbook like source from which the student may or may not learn" (Noddings, 1984, p. 70). It requires "**engrossment**," what Noddings defines as "an open, nonselective receptivity to the cared-for" [the student] (1998, p. 40) and where the person being cared for senses the one caring's energy is flowing toward him (Noddings, 1999). It is the interpersonal attachment to the teacher that makes change by the student possible. Noddings (1984, 1992) describes the engagement this way:

> When a teacher asks a question in class and a student responds, she receives not just the "response" but the student. What he says matters, whether it is right or wrong, and she probes gently for clarification, interpretation, contribution. She is not seeking the answer but the involvement of the cared-for.
>
> (Noddings, 1984, p. 176)

> If I care about students, I must do two things: I must make the problem my own, receive it intellectually, immerse myself in it; I must also bring the students into proximity, receive such students personally.
>
> (Noddings, 1984, p. 113)

Talk Therapy

Talk therapy is a descendent of the Socratic method and adapted by the counseling community. Whether in group therapy or the classroom, it concentrates on self-exploration. The teacher guides the students through discussions with an eye to minimizing anxieties and frustrations so that students can explore their beliefs and feelings. The objectives are to:

1. Alleviate confusion and disquiet;
2. Explore everyone's opinions, intuitions, emotions, ideas, and beliefs;
3. Test their validity and coherence;
4. Better understand the issues causing disequilibrium;
5. Know one's self better; and
6. Establish a new perspective.

(Modified from Lewis, 1983; Pietrofesa, Hoffman, & Splete, 1984)

Enacting Philosophical Counseling

Lou Marinoff (1999) provides an outline of his client-based philosophical counseling approach, which can be helpful to the application of philosophical counseling in the classroom setting. He employs the acronym PEACE. It parallels the more widely known social studies "values clarification" pedagogical model (Raths, Harmin, & Simon, 1978). The following example of PEACE using a high school level social studies topic describes what the teacher wants the students to do.

PEACE

P, identify your problem – In a classroom setting, the teacher introduces and contextualizes a social studies topic, such as the Stonewall riots. Students complete an investigation and would be asked to consider what NCSS Democratic Beliefs are in question (refer to Figure 2.2).

E, express your emotions constructively – Students are solicited for comments with questions about the events, encouraged to express their feelings about the events based on the essential identity questions (refer to Figure 4.2).

A, analyze your options – Students are asked to reflect on their personal virtues, democratic beliefs, and feelings by focusing on the essential identity questions by the question, "Would you support the LGBTQ community by marching with protestors?"

C, contemplate a philosophy that helps you choose and live with your best option – During the exchange among students, introduce from the philosophy of Immanuel Kant, "What is the basis upon which I could deny others rights and privileges that I would want for myself?"

E, reach a new equilibrium – Students integrate the emotional part of the problem by having systematically processed any ambiguities in reasoning, have formed knowledge as opposed to opinion or true opinion, and have considered the democratic beliefs.

Positive Outcomes

There are a number of "curative factors" that stem from group therapeutic engagements. Individuals:

1. Realize others have similar concerns, thus know they are "not alone";
2. Tend to gravitate to positive narratives shared by the teacher and students;
3. Experience altruism by sharing with others;
4. Learn and practice conversational skills;
5. Model productive behaviors;
6. Express feelings and thus experience the benefits of catharsis; and
7. Observe others who accept responsibility for their own identity's strengths and deficits. (modified from Yalom & Leszcz, 2005)

Philosophical Counselor and Teacher Disposition

The National Council for the Accreditation of Teacher Education (NCATE/CAEP) calls for teacher educators to create programs that instill "caring, fairness, honesty, and responsibility" in its teacher candidates (NCATE, 2007). Effective counselors tend to be described by their clients in much the same way, being "understanding and accepting, empathic, warm, and supportive" (Lambert & Barley, 2002, p. 26). Social studies teachers must have a greater "emotional understanding" of themselves than other teachers if they are to guide students in their self-examination (Denzin, 1984). Combs (1962) describes the effective social studies teacher as having a disposition toward empathy; a caring, positive view of others; a positive view of self; authenticity; and a purposeful vision. McCroskey (1992) and Thomas, Richmond, and McCroskey (1994) identified three factors necessary for students to perceive the teacher as caring:

Empathy is the ability to identify with another's situation or feelings;
Understanding is the ability to comprehend another person's ideas, feelings, and needs; and
Responsiveness involves having sensitivity toward others by being sympathetic, compassionate, sincere, and friendly.

Social studies teachers' own adherence to a democratic ideology needs to be reflected in the pedagogy and knowledge they select to teach – it must be modeled in the classroom. As Kristjánsson (2006) explains:

> It suffices to say that there exists a reasonably wide consensus outside, no less than inside, the circles of character education that the professional role of the teacher cannot be clearly disentangled from the moral qualities of the person who occupies the role, that at every working moment the teacher is indirectly, through conduct and attitude, sending out a moral message. Thus, a good teacher is also a certain kind of person.
>
> (p. 38)

Best Practices for Philosophical Counseling in the Classroom

Gleaned from multiple authors, the teacher as philosophical counselor:

1. Adopts a demeanor as consultant, clarifier, and questioner. Even in cases where philosophy has provided substantial answers that the teacher is aware of, the philosophical counselor presents them as ideas for consideration and allows the students to grapple with alternatives;

2. Phrases open-ended questions during the "academic" analysis that are directed at feelings, such as "How did you *feel* about the situation?";
3. Makes sure the questions are nonjudgmental questions, such as "Can you elaborate?" rather than "Why did you say that?" which can imply a judgment;
4. Matches the mood of the student – if the student seems sad or enthusiastic, respond with the same affect;
5. Diplomatically de-escalates the overdramatic stance by clarifying in less emotive tones and language that often typifies children's and adolescents' more hyperbolic, exaggerated manner;
6. Is an active, nonjudgmental listener, which requires being hypersensitive to the language, tone, and nonverbal gestures surrounding students' statements by listening and reading body language, more than speaking;
7. Encourages students to think-aloud as a way to share their thought process;
8. Articulates connections whereby students recognize similarities in perspectives and appreciate observations more in tune with a democratic ideology;
9. Initiates blocking, where teachers keep unfocused or more assertive students from disrupting the class by redirecting them to prevent them from monopolizing conversations;
10. Seeks clarifications, rather than questioning students' articulated facts and adds new facts;
11. Draws analogies and provides examples so as to compare factual situations and raise them to a conceptual level;
12. Identifies competing values, democratic beliefs, and virtues;
13. Shares his own thinking process when introducing alternative perspectives drawn from philosophy;
14. Abstracts general concepts from concrete examples that students can use in developing their identity and democratic ideology;
15. Uses "bracketing" whereby the teacher is constantly checking his own identity and ideological stances so as not to indoctrinate the ones being cared for;
16. Summarizes, in which students become aware of what has occurred in the engagement and how the class's perspectives have evolved to a more well-conceived, well-considered ideological stance and identity.

Resources

Videos: *The Atlantic:* The Heinz Dilemma | Lou Marinoff on the Power of Philosophy | *YouTube:* Antti Mattila Concepts for Philosophical Counseling; *The Gift of the Magi*; Alain de Botton's *The Consolations of Philosophy* (6 videos); Book of Virtues; Former FBI Agent Explains How to Read Body Language; Kohlberg Moral Development.

Documents: *Routledge Handbook of Research in Social Studies Education*; International Political Socialization Research | *ASCD*: The Return of Character Education | 11 Principles of Effective Character Education | *Goodcharacter*: The Daily Dilemma (for elementary level educators) | Moral Dilemmas.

Two readings of value for someone new to counseling would be Frederick Thorne's (1948) article *Principles of Directive Counseling* and M. Scott Peck's (1997) best seller, *The Road Less Traveled*.

References

American Society for Philosophy, Counseling, and Psychotherapy (ASPCP). (2014). Standards of practice. Retrieved from http://npcassoc.org/documents/governance/.

Bennett, W. J. (1996). *Book of virtues: A treasury of great moral stories.* Touchstone Books.

Blatt, M., & Kohlberg, L. (1975). The effects of classroom moral discussion upon children's level of moral judgment. *Journal of Moral Education, 4,* 129–161.

Bohning, G. (1986). The McGuffey eclectic readers: 1836–1986. *The Reading Teacher, 40*(3), 263–269.

Combs, A. (1962). *Perceiving behaving and becoming: A new focus.* ASCD Yearbook 127. Association for Supervision and Curriculum Development.

de Botton, A. (2000). *The consolations of philosophy.* Penguin Books.

Denzin, N. K. (1984). *On understanding emotion.* Jossey-Bass.

Doherty, W. J. (1995). Boundaries between parent and family education and family therapy: The levels of family involvement model. *Family Relations, 44*(4), 353–358.

Duplass, J. (2018). *The idea of a social studies education. The role of philosophical counseling.* Routledge.

Duplass, J., & Cruz, B. (2009). Making sense of 'race' in the history classroom: A literary approach. *The History Teacher, 42*(4), 426–440.

Eagle, M. N. (1984). *Recent developments in psychoanalysis: A critical evaluation.* McGraw-Hill.

Gilligan, C. (1982). *In a different voice: Psychological theory and women's development.* Harvard University Press.

Guignon, C. (1993). Authenticity, moral values and psychotherapy. In C. Guignon (Ed.), *The Cambridge companion to Heidegger* (pp. 262–293). Cambridge University Press.

Guignon, C. (1999). *The good life.* Hackett Publishing.

Henry, O. (1905). *The gift of the Magi.* Retrieved from www.gutenberg.org/files/7256/7256-h/7256-h.htm.

Jopling, D. A. (1996). Philosophical counselling, truth and self-interpretation. *Journal of Applied Philosophy, 13*(3), 297–310.

Kohlberg, L. (1969). Stage and sequence: The cognitive-developmental approach to socialization. In D. A. Goslin & M. Rand (Eds.), *Handbook of socialization theory and research* (pp. 347–480).

Kristjánsson, K. (2006). Emulation and the use of role models in moral education. *Journal of Moral Education, 35*(1), 37–49. Retrieved from www.tandfonline.com/doi/full/10.1080/03057240500495278.

Lambert, M. J., & Barley, D. E. (2002). Psychotherapy relationships that work: therapist contributions and responsiveness to patient needs. In J. C. Norcross (Ed.), *Psychotherapy relationships that work* (pp. 17–32). Oxford University Press.

Lambert, M. J., & Ogles, B. M. (2004). The efficacy and effectiveness of psychotherapy. In A. E. Bergin & S. L. Garfield (Eds.), *Handbook of psychotherapy and behavior change* (4th ed., pp. 139–193). Wiley.

Lewis, D. (1983). *Philosophical papers* (Vol. 1). New York: Oxford University Press.

Marinoff, L. (1999). *Plato, not Prozac! Applying eternal wisdom to everyday problems.* HarperCollins.

Marinoff, L. (2004). *Therapy for the sane: How philosophy can change your life.* Bloomsbury.

McClellan, B. E. (1999). *Moral education in America: Schools and the shaping of character from colonial times to the present.* Teachers College Press.

McCroskey, J. C. (1992). *An introduction to communication in the classroom.* Burgess International Group.

NCATE. (2007). *NCATE issues call for action: Defines professional dispositions as used in teacher education.* NCATE. Retrieved from www.ncate.org/public/102407.asp?ch=148.

NCSS. (2020). *NCSS notable trade books.* Retrieved from www.socialstudies.org/publications/notables.

Noddings, N. (1984). *Caring: A feminine approach to ethics and moral education.* University of California Press.

Noddings, N. (1992). *The challenge to care in schools.* Teachers College Press.

Noddings, N. (1998). Caring. In P. H. Hirst & P. White (Eds.), *Philosophy of education: Major themes in the analytic traction* (Vol. IV). (pp. 40–50). Routledge.

Noddings, N. (1999). Caring and competence. In G. Griffen (Ed.), *The education of teachers* (pp. 205–220). National Society for the Study of Education.

Oliver, D., & Shaver, J. (1966). *Teaching public issues in the high school.* Houghton Mifflin.

Peck, M. S. (1997). *The road less traveled.* Simon & Schuster.

Pietrofesa, J. J., Hoffman, A. J., & Splete, H. H. (1984). *Counseling: An introduction.* Mifflin Harcourt.

Raths, L. E., Harmin, M., & Simon, S. B. (1978). *Values and teaching* (2nd ed.). Merrill.

Shweder, R. (1982). Beyond self-constructing knowledge: The study of culture and morality. *Merrill- Palmer Quarterly, 28,* 41–69.

Stanley, W. B. (2005). Social studies and the social order: Transmission or transformation? *Social Education, 69*(9), 282–286.

Stanley, W. B., & Nelson, J. L. (1994). The foundations of social education in historical context. In R. Martusewicz & W. Reynolds (Eds.), *Inside/out: Contemporary critical perspectives in education* (pp. 266–284). St. Martin's.

Szasz, T. S. (1960). The myth of mental illness. *American Psychologist, 15*(2), 113.

Taylor, C. (1989). *Sources of the self: The making of the modern identity.* Harvard University Press.

Thomas, C. E., Richmond, V. P., & McCroskey, J. C. (1994). The association between immediacy and socio-communicative style. *Communication Research Reports, 11,* 107–115.

Thorne, F. C. (1948). Principles of directive counseling and psychotherapy. *American Psychologist, 3*(5), 160.

Wittgenstein, L. (2010). *Philosophical investigations.* John Wiley & Sons.

Yalom, I. D., & Leszcz, M. (2005). *Theory and practice of group psychotherapy.* Basic Books.

Part 2

Schools, Curriculum, and Standards

Teachers can teach any topic effectively in some intellectually honest form to any child at any stage of development.

Jerome Bruner, Professor, Harvard and Oxford Universities (Bruner, 1960, p. 33)

Schools

In 2019, there were about 35,000 private schools and 98,000 public schools in the US. There are approximately 13,600 school districts for a population of K-12 students of 51 million in public schools. Through consolidations, the number of school districts has declined by 83% in 50 years. The average elementary school size is about 450 students, middle school 574, and high school 854. The class sizes for elementary school classrooms is about 22, middle school 26, and high school 24. There are about 3.2 million teachers (Education Week, 2019).

Curriculum

The when and what of teaching has traditionally been referred to as the **Curriculum, Scope** and **Sequence**, or **Framework**. The past two decades has also seen the increased use of the term **Standards** to define the curriculum.

Standards-Based Education

Standards-based education is an accountability strategy that has concise, written descriptions of what students are expected to know and be able to do at a specific stage of their education. Teachers are expected to determine how and what topics to teach students so their students achieve the benchmarks described in the standards. Mandated standards are required if adopted by a state. Learned societies' standards are rarely adopted by a state, but are used by teachers to consider the how and what to teach.

C3 Framework

In the next eight chapters, the standards of the learned societies for civics, history, economics, geography, and social sciences and the NCSS **C3 Framework** (see NCSS, 2013, *College, Career, and Civic Life C3 Framework for Social Studies State Standards*) will play a prominent role in revealing what should be emphasized in planning and teaching the social studies. The *C3 Framework* PDF brochure should be downloaded (see *References*).

Comparative Testing

The National Assessment of Educational Progress (NAEP, 2020) is the "Nation's Report Card." In social studies, it measures civics, geography, economics, and US history at the 8th grade level. The Program for International Assessment (**PISA**, see Schleicher, 2018) is the international report card that tests 15-year-old students in approximately 70 countries. The US stands 25th in the combined scores of sciences, mathematics, and reading with China as number 1, Canada 8th, Finland 10th, Turkey 40th, and Chile 46th.

Resources

Videos: *Study. Com* (a for-profit, fee-based resource) offers a 30-day free trial. It has full courses in history and social sciences through high-quality video lessons of ten minutes or less. As an example, search for *study.com geography*, which has 22 courses with well over 1000 individual, visually rich, and grade-appropriate lessons using voice over and visuals.

Documents: *NAEP:* History, Economics, Geography, or Civics | *NCES:* Annual Reports; International Comparisons | *NCSS:* Curriculum Guidelines for Social Studies Teaching and Learning | *PISA*: Rankings | *Pew*: U.S. Stands in Middle of the Pack.

References

Bruner, J. S. (1960). *The process of education*. Harvard University Press.

Education Week. (2019). *Education statistics: Facts about American schools*. Retrieved from www.edweek.org/ew/issues/education-statistics/index.html.

NAEP. (2020). *Assessments*. Retrieved from https://nces.ed.gov/nationsreportcard/assessments/.

NCSS. (2013). *Social studies for the next generation: Purposes, practices, and implications of the college, career, and civic Life (C3) framework for social studies state standards: Guidance for enhancing rigor of K-12 civic, economics, geography, and history*. Retrieved from www.socialstudies.org/sites/default/files/2017/Jun/c3-framework-for-social-studies-rev0617.pdf.

Schleicher, A. PISA. (2018). *PISA: Insights and interpretations*. Retrieved from www.oecd.org/pisa/PISA%202018%20Insights%20and%20Interpretations%20FINAL%20PDF.pdf.

11 Curriculum and Standards

Compared to home life, schools are like village squares, cities, crossroads, meeting places, community centers, marketplaces. When aimed at democratic ends and supported by the proper democratic conditions, the interaction in schools can help children enter the social consciousness of puberty and develop the habits of thinking and caring necessary for public life.

Walter Parker, Professor of Education, University of Washington (Parker, 2003. p. 78)

What Do Students Want from Their Schools?

Although the following reports focus on high school students, it is reasonable to apply the information to students at every grade level. In a national 1997 survey of over 1300 high school students (Education Week, 1997), teenagers were asked what they wanted from their schools. Three of the most compelling observations are:

1. Order – teachers were cited for lax instruction and unenforced rules;
2. Higher expectations – teachers expected too little and they (the students) would work harder if more was required; and
3. Moral inspiration – teachers needed to promote virtues like hard work and honesty.

In the 2017 report by the Thomas Fordham Institute, 83–95% of high school students report being motivated to apply themselves in school by thinking deeply, listening carefully, and completing assignments. Most students report experiencing active learning where they ask themselves questions and have to figure things out. ESchool News (2020) reports the five things students say they want are:

1. Real-world applications and relevancy;
2. More choices of what courses to take;
3. Innovative teaching to eliminate boredom;
4. Teachers who respect and care for them; and
5. More interactive technology.

Meeting the needs of students takes on the form of innovations and movements that have led to changes in schools that effect the teaching of social studies.

Schools

Elementary Schools

Common Core Standards (National Governors Association, 2010) and "**high stakes testing**" have led to a "narrowing of the curriculum" at the elementary school level, resulting in a significant decline in the time elementary school teachers are allocating to social studies education (Boyle-Baise et al., 2008). Even when elementary school teachers are teaching social studies, researchers have found that its main purpose is to teach literacy (Pace, 2011) or it is "social studies light" such as the "holiday curriculum" where tribute is briefly made to historical figures or events.

Curriculum integration with language arts has been promoted as a strategy to "save" social studies at the elementary school level. However, in most cases the social studies foundational knowledge to be learned seems to be left unattended to, leading to Levstik's critique, "Hoping for students to understand social studies in any meaningful way simply by literacy happenstance cannot be supported by current research" (2008, p. 57). Based on Bruner's (1977) theory of a **spiral curriculum**, the enduring ideas and compelling propositions of the social studies must be taught at every grade level so when the topics are revisited in higher grade levels, students have the schema to make sense of the new or deeper meanings being investigated. Social studies foundational knowledge can be used to achieve many of the Common Core reading and writing standards for elementary education. In addition, there is a rich history of children's trade books that can be effectively used when teaching about things that matter because literature also amplifies the human experience.

However, trade books offer only **narrative text**, not the **informational text** (see Chapters 27 and 28) needed by students to acquire the vocabulary or grade-appropriate concepts as building blocks for future years of social studies learning. Children must be taught how to read social studies informational text as a pathway to absorb the structure of the academic discipline as presented in text, such as how facts, arguments, and conclusions are presented, to look for bias, how to interpret images, maps, graphs, political cartoons, etc.

Middle Schools

The "middle school movement" began in the 1960s because many educators believed that junior high schools of grades 7–9 were little more than watered-down high schools with a lack of commitment to the "tweenager." Moving sixth grade to a "middle school" and ninth grade to high school was the most noticeable change. But more significant changes were envisioned in this new philosophy of a unique school culture, organization, and curriculum delivered by teachers committed to this age group. Teachers would be attentive to the attributes of this developmental stage, such as heightened focus on peer acceptance, intense curiosity, idealism, interest in exploring values, physical awkwardness, and inclinations to over-dramatization and test authority.

Teams vs. Departments

Unlike the high school departmental structure, where teachers are grouped into a social studies department, middle schools are to be planned around multidiscipline teams of teachers. A team would be made up of teachers from each core subject area (mathematics, social studies, science, and literacy) who would teach a "pod" of students. The team would share a planning period with two essential goals: (1) to share information about students so they can coordinate efforts to advance every student's academic and personal development; and (2) to plan interdisciplinary lessons that cross the subject areas' lines so learning is integrative. Teams have been shown to reduce discipline problems, improve attendance, decrease failure rates, and increase teachers' sense of accomplishment (Dickinson & Erb, 1997).

Exploratory Courses

Exploratory courses are electives such as calligraphy, robotics, theater, Mandarin. These courses allow students to investigate interests, develop new skills, and cultivate talents that they and their parents feel are important. Teachers volunteer to create such courses which provide a creative outlet for teachers outside their typical subject area course assignment.

Block Scheduling

Rather than the six, 50-minute class periods, **block** scheduling has four blocks of 85 to 100 minutes. Approximately 30% of the nation's schools have adopted some form of longer class periods (Rettig, 2020). Block scheduling has the advantages of less disruption due to fewer classroom changes and facilitates use of time-intensive strategies such as group activities, discussions, investigations, and differentiated instruction.

High Schools

Tracking and Ability Grouping

Tracking is widely used in both middle and high schools. **Tracking** involves grouping students into paths like vocational, general, and college prep, and within college prep, electives such as honors and Advance Placement (AP) courses based on prior academic success and/or testing. There is concern that it ends up being discriminatory based on "race," lowers expectations, and creates esteem issues for low achievers. Conversely, advocates argue that homogeneous classes are necessary for the best education of individual students at either end of the low- and high-achieving student spectrum.

Electives

Elective were introduced in the 1960s. Additionally, at both middle and high schools, online courses, magnet schools, and charter schools have become options in most states.

Curriculum and Standards

The when and what of teaching has traditionally been referred to as the **curriculum**. The **formal curriculum** often provides a sequence of topics by grade level that is explicitly detailed as part of a state's standards. The **enacted curriculum** is what students experience in the day-to-day interactions with their teacher.

Unlike many nations, the United States does not have a nationally mandated curriculum or standards. In the Constitution, the Founders reserved such matters to the individual states. However, in response in part to the landmark study and recommendations of *A Nation at Risk: The Imperative for Educational Reform* (National Commission on Excellence in Education, 1983), Presidents Clinton's "Goals 2000," Bush's "No Child Left Behind (NCLB)," Obama's "Race to the Top," Common Core, standardization of textbooks, and mandates tied to federal funding, there is a *de facto* national curriculum.

The term "**high-stakes testing**" reflects the fact that the stakes are high because the standardized tests can adversely affect federal funding and are used to assess and grade schools, teachers, and students. Testing is mandated as part of the accountability framework by the federal government in language arts, mathematics, and science, but not social studies. However, every state requires students to complete coursework in civics or social studies in order to graduate from high school. The amount of required social studies coursework varies by state. Seventeen states include civics in their accountability framework (Education Commission of the States, 2016).

States create their high-stakes tests based on their formal curriculum. Standardized, systematic testing (online or paper-based) is considered the only practical way to collect comparative statistical data of student performance needed for policy decisions. Good policy says such testing should never be used as the sole assessment of an individual student, but it is a helpful tool for teachers and parents to know how their students and children are doing, comparatively.

Social studies foundational knowledge can be assessed like other subject areas. A state might test to determine if students know the concept of freedom of speech, but whether students believe in it and would act on it consistently through their lifetime is unmeasurable. Considering the nature of social studies democratic ideals and students' identity capacities and feelings, it would be hard to argue that any traditional test could measure if students value the tenets of a democratic ideology. Ultimately, the only "test" of social studies instruction rests in the kind of persons and citizens students are throughout their lifetimes.

An unintended consequence of high-stakes testing in social studies education is that it adversely affects the therapeutic alliance and caring encounter needed for consideration of the things that matter: "Stress from accountability and absolutes has begun to cause teachers to see their students not as people in need of their services, but as soon-to-be released test scores that ultimately will decide their [the teachers'] futures," (Vogler & Virtue, 2017, p. 56).

There are only two sets of mandated standards, Common Core and a state's standards. The NCSS and learned societies standards are more appropriately considered guides to states and teachers as to what should be taught. The NCSS and other learned societies documents on curriculum and methods, in almost all cases, preceded and influenced the Common Core and states' standards. Many learned societies' standards have been revised subsequently to become more aligned with Common Cores and states' content standards.

Common Core

The "**Common Core**," to dispel a myth, was not created by the federal government, but by the National Governors Association to provide a voluntary curriculum for reading, writing, and mathematics for states to consider. It does not address which social studies content is to be offered or at what grade level; it is focused on basic skills. Forty-two of the states have adopted the Common Core Standards with most of the other eight

Part 1 Sample of Common Core Standard Grade 3				
Grade level	Column 1 Reading for Informational Text	Column 2 Writing	Column 3 Speaking & Listening	Column 4 Language
Third (pp. 12–28)	**Key Ideas and Details:** 1. Ask and answer questions to demonstrate understanding of a text, referring explicitly to the text as the basis for answers. **Craft and Structure:** 4. Determine the meaning of general academic and domain-specific words and phrases in a text relevant to a grade 3 topic or subject area. **Integration of Knowledge and Ideas:** 7. Use information gained from illustrations (e.g., maps, photographs) and the words in a text to demonstrate understanding of the text (e.g., where, when, why, and how key events occur). **Range of Reading and Level of Text Complexity**: 10. By the end of the year, read and comprehend informational texts, including history/ social studies, science, and technical texts, at the high end of the grades 2–3 text complexity band independently and proficiently.	**Test Types and Purposes:** 1. Write opinion pieces on topics or texts, supporting a point of view with reasons. **Production and Distribution of Writing:** 4. With guidance and support from adults, produce writing in which the development and organization are appropriate to task and purpose. (Grade-specific expectations for writing types are defined in standards 1–3 above.) **Research to Build and Present Knowledge** 7. Conduct short research projects that build knowledge about a topic. **Range of Writing:** 10. Write routinely over extended time frames (time for research, reflection, and revision) and shorter time frames (a single sitting or a day or two) for a range of discipline-specific tasks, purposes, and audiences.	**Comprehension and Collaboration:** 1. Engage effectively in a range of collaborative discussions (one-on-one, in groups, and teacher-led) with diverse partners on grade 3 topics and texts, building on others' ideas and expressing their own clearly. **Presentation of Knowledge and Ideas:** 4. Report on a topic or text, tell a story, or recount an experience with appropriate facts and relevant, descriptive details, speaking clearly at an understandable pace.	**Conventions of Standard English:** 1. Demonstrate command of the conventions of standard English grammar and usage when writing or speaking. **Knowledge of Language** 3. Use knowledge of language and its conventions when writing, speaking, reading, or listening. **Vocabulary Acquisition and Use:** 4. Determine or clarify the meaning of unknown and multiple-meaning words and phrases based on grade 3 reading and content, choosing flexibly from a range of strategies.

Figure 11.1 Sample of Common Core Standards

Part 2 Standards for Literacy in History/Social Studies, Science, and Technical Subjects Grades 6–12		
9–10 Reading (pp. 60–66)	Key Ideas and Details	1. Cite specific textual evidence to support analysis of primary and secondary sources, attending to such features as the date and origin of the information.
	Craft and Structure	4. Determine the meaning of words and phrases as they are used in a text, including vocabulary describing political, social, or economic aspects of history/social studies.
	Integration of Knowledge and Ideas	7. Integrate quantitative or technical analysis (e.g., charts, research data) with qualitative analysis in print or digital text.
	Range of Reading and Level of Text Complexity	10. By the end of grade 10, read and comprehend science/technical texts in the grades 9–10 text complexity band independently and proficiently.
Writing	Text Types and Purposes	1. Write arguments focused on *discipline-specific content.*
	Production and Distribution of Writing	Produce clear and coherent writing in which the development, organization, and style are appropriate to task, purpose, and audience.

Figure 11.1 (Cont.)

having adopted a similar set of standards that accomplish many of the same goals at the same grade levels. Arguably, the Common Core, standards-based education, and accountability movement have led to the most sweeping changes in the formal and enacted curriculum in a century.

Common Core and state standards are written so as to produce outcomes that are measurable. This level of specificity was new to education when it was introduced. Previously, teachers had broad discretion in decisions of what to teach and were heavily influenced by the textbooks they were given. Most national textbook publishers shape their textbooks based on ideas from learned societies, Common Core, and the standards that are common to the most populated states because authoring textbooks for each state is not cost-effective.

Figure 11.1 is a sample of the Common Core Standards (see National Governors Association, 2010, to download a copy of the 66-page PDF). In Part 1, third grade was arbitrarily selected as representative of the way the standards are defined for the K-5 grade levels. The **standard** appears in bold and then a **benchmark** preceded with a number. The numbers are not sequential because this is only an example: For *Key Ideas and Details* in column one, there are actually three benchmarks and that is why *Craft and Structure* starts with the number 4. Part 2 is a sample drawn from grades 6–12's standards for literacy in social studies. For both parts, the benchmarks would be used by a teacher when planning social studies lessons. Note that the standards do not specify the declarative knowledge to be used in achieving the standards; that is left to states' curriculum or teachers.

State Standards in Social Studies

In Figure 11.2 examples of three states' standards are presented. A standard from the four core subject fields and four grade levels are provided to illustrate how standards are typically presented by states. The standard appears first and then the first of what could be multiple benchmarks (in italics) appear second. These formal curriculum requirements rarely explicitly detail the learning of the democratic ideals, but focus on the foundational and procedural knowledge and thus effectively presume the teacher elevates the learning to the consideration of the democratic ideals implicit in the content. It is the enacted curriculum where the teacher lifts the foundational knowledge to consideration of things that matter. Note that most benchmarks would be measurable in a high-stakes test.

Grade Level	California	Florida	Minnesota
Civics – Lower Elementary	**Standard** 2.3 Students explain governmental institutions and practices in the United States and other countries. *Benchmark 1. Explain how the United States and other countries make laws, carry out laws, determine whether laws have been violated, and punish wrongdoers.*	**Standard** 3: Structure and Functions of Government *Benchmark SS.2.C.3.1 Identify the Constitution as the document which establishes the structure, function, powers, and limits of American government.*	**Standard** 7. The primary purposes of rules and laws within the United States constitutional government are to protect individual rights, promote the general welfare and provide order. *Benchmark 1.1.4.7.1 Identify characteristics of effective rules; participate in a process to establish rules. For example: Characteristics of effective rules – fair, understandable, enforceable, connected to goals.*
Geography – Upper Elementary	**Standard** 4.1 Students demonstrate an understanding of the physical and human geographic features that define places and regions in California. *Benchmark 1. Explain and use the coordinate grid system of latitude and longitude to determine the absolute locations of places in California and on Earth.*	**Standard** 1: The World in Spatial Terms *Benchmark SS.4.G.1.1 Identify physical features of Florida.*	**Standard** 1. People use geographic representations and geospatial technologies to acquire, process and report information within a spatial context *Benchmark 4.3.1.1.1 Create and use various kinds of maps, including overlaying thematic maps, of places in the United States, and also Canada or Mexico; incorporate the "TODALS" map basics,*

Figure 11.2 Examples of State Standards

			as well as points, lines and colored areas to display spatial information. For example: "TODALS" map basics – title, orientation, date, author, legend/key, and scale. Spatial information – cities, roads, boundaries, bodies of water, regions.
History (American) – Middle or High School, depending on the State	**Standard** 8.1 Students understand the major events preceding the founding of the nation and relate their significance to the development of American constitutional democracy. **Benchmark** *1. Describe the relationship between the moral and political ideas of the Great Awakening and the development of revolutionary fervor.*	**Standard** 3: Demonstrate an understanding of the causes, course, and consequences of the American Revolution and the founding principles of our nation. **Benchmark** *SS.8.A.3.1 Explain the consequences of the French and Indian War in British policies for the American colonies from 1763–1774.*	**Standard** 17. The divergence of colonial interests from those of England led to an independence movement that resulted in the American Revolution and the foundation of a new nation based on the ideals of self-government and liberty. (Revolution and a New Nation: 1754–1800) **Benchmark** *9.4.4.17.2 Analyze the American revolutionaries' justifications, principles and ideals as expressed in the Declaration of Independence; identify the sources of these principles and ideals and their impact on subsequent revolutions in Europe, the Caribbean, and Latin America. (Revolution and a New Nation: 1754 – 1800)*
Economics – Middle or High School, depending on the State	**Standard** 12.6 Students analyze issues of international trade and explain how the U.S. economy affects, and is affected by, economic forces beyond the United States' borders. **Benchmark** *1. Identify the gains in consumption and production efficiency from trade, with emphasis on the main products and changing*	**Standard** 3: Understand the fundamental concepts and interrelationships of the United States economy in the international marketplace. **Benchmark** *SS.912. E.3.1 Demonstrate the impact of inflation on world economies.*	**Standard** 12. International trade, exchange rates and international institutions affect individuals, organizations, and governments throughout the world. **Benchmark** *9.2.5.12.1 Apply the principles of absolute and comparative advantage to explain the increase in world production due to*

Figure 11.2 (Cont.)

	geographic patterns of twentieth-century trade among countries in the Western Hemisphere.		*specialization and trade; identify the groups that benefit and lose with free-trade treaties, trading blocs and trade barriers.* *For example: Dropping United States restrictions on the importation of sugar would benefit sugar consumers through lower prices, but hurt sugar beet farmers; however, the net economic benefit for the United States would be positive. Role of the World Trade Organization.*

Figure 11.2 (Cont.)

Resources

Videos: *Corestandards:* Learn About the Common Core in 3 minutes | *PBS*: Common Core Video Series | *YouTube:* Teaching to High Stakes Test.

Documents: *Wiley Handbook of Research of Social Studies Research*: The Problem of Knowing What Students Know; Knowing and Doing in Democratic Citizenship Education | *ASCD*: Common Core Myths and Facts | *NCSS:* Notable Trade Books; *Social Studies and the Young Learner* | *Association of Middle Level Education:* This we Believe | *Thomas Fordham Institute*: What Teens Want from Their Schools.

References

Boyle-Baise, M., Hsu, M., Johnson, S., Serriere, S., & Stewart, D. (2008). Putting reading first: Teaching social studies in elementary classrooms." *Theory & Research in Social Education*, *36*(3), 233–255.

Bruner, J. (1977). *The process of education*. Harvard University Press.

California Department of Education. (2000). *California history-social sciences content standards for public schools*. Retrieved from www.cde.ca.gov/be/st/ss/documents/histsocscistnd.pdf.

Dickinson, S.T., & Erb, T. E. (1997). *We gain more than we give: Teaming in middle schools*. Routlege Falmer.

Education Commission of the States. (2016). *50 state comparison: Civic education policies*. Retrieved from www.ecs.org/citizenship-education-policies/.

Education Week. (1997). *Survey reveals teens yearn for high standards*. Retrieved from www.edweek.org/ew/articles/1997/02/12/20public.h16.html.

ESchool News. (2020). *Five things students say they want from education*. Retrieved from www.eschoolnews.com/2011/07/28/five-things-students-say-they-want-from-education/3/?all.

Florida Department of Education. (2008). *Florida social studies sunshine state standards.* Retrieved from www.google.com/search?q=next+generation+sunshine+state+standards+social+stu dies&rlz=1C1GCEU_enUS820US821&oq=sunshine+state+social+stuidesstandards&aqs=chro me.2.69i57j0l5.23499j0j4&sourceid=chrome¡UTF-8.

Levstik, L. (2008). What happens in social studies classrooms? Research on K-12 social studies practices. In L. Levstik & C. Tyson (Eds.). *Handbook of research in social studies education* (pp. 50–62). Routledge.

Minnesota Department of Education. (2011). *Minnesota K-12 academic standards in social studies.* Retrieved from https://education.mn.gov/MDE/dse/stds/soc/.

National Commission on Excellence in Education. (1983). *A nation at risk: The imperative for educational reform.* Department of Education.

National Governors Association. (2010). *Common core state standards initiative.* Retrieved from www.corestandards.org/read-the-standards/.

Pace, J. L. (2011). The complex and unequal impact of high stakes accountability on untested social studies. *Theory & Research in Social Education, 39*(1),32–60.

Parker, W. C. (2003). *Teaching democracy; Unity and diversity in public life.* Teachers College Press.

Rettig, M. (2020). *The effects of block scheduling.* AASA. Retrieved from www.aasa.org/SchoolAd ministratorArticle.aspx?id=14852

Vogler, K., & Virtue, D. (2017). Social studies in the era of standards and high-stakes testing. *The Social Studies, 98*(2),54–58.

12 Social Studies Education and the NCSS

If you are not part of the solution, you are part of the problem.
Eldridge Clever, Author and Leader of the Black Panthers,
1935–1998 (Goodreads, 2020)

The National Council for the Social Studies (NCSS) was formed in 1921 as a professional organization ("learned society") for educators interested in K-12 social studies education. NCSS serves as the primary advocate for social studies education with the public, federal government, and states. Teacher candidates can join the state chapter and the national organization, attend its national and state conferences, and take an active role in formulating policy positions and advocacy for social studies education.

The NCSS, Exalted Aims, and Foundational Goals

The NCSS (1994) officially defines social studies as:

> The integrated study of the social sciences and humanities to promote civic competence. Within the school program, social studies provides coordinated, systematic study drawing upon such disciplines as anthropology, archaeology, economics, geography, history, law, philosophy, political science, psychology, religion, and sociology, as well as appropriate content from the humanities, mathematics, and natural sciences. The primary purpose of social studies is to help young people make informed and reasoned decisions for the public good as citizens of a culturally diverse, democratic society in an interdependent world.

Since its founding, the NCSS has adopted a number of influential position papers that articulate positions on curriculum and issues such as academic freedom, civic learning, etc. (see NCSS, 2020a). The NCSS has four position papers, in particular, that should guide teacher candidates' thinking about what and how they teach.

NCSS Democratic Beliefs

As discussed in Chapter 2, The Idea of a Social Studies Education, the NCSS (1990) defined the following set of "**Democratic Beliefs**" (see Figure 12.1). Combined with the personal virtues and civic values also presented in Chapter 2, they represent the democratic ideals that should be promoted by teachers of social studies. It is suggested that these banners be permanently displayed on the wall of a classroom.

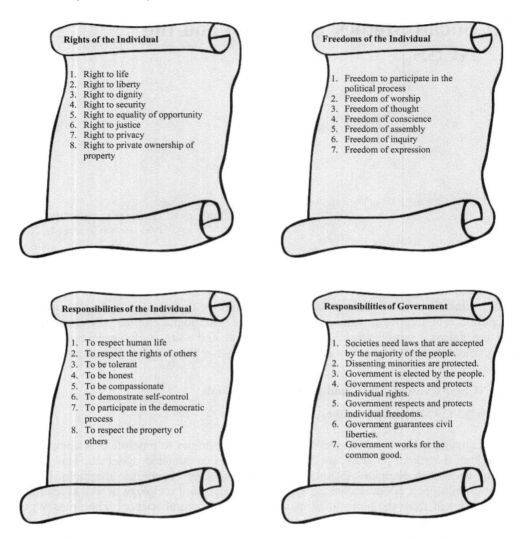

Figure 12.1 Classroom Scrolls of the NCSS Democratic Beliefs

At the lower elementary level, a lesson could be designed to explicitly tease out one or more of the responsibilities of the individual by using a "story-based" textbook chapter such as "Why Do Governments and Citizens Need Each Other?" (see Figure 17.1) so as to elevate the lesson to things that matters. At the middle and high school level, the declarative knowledge in textbooks are structured in the pattern of the academic discipline (temporally or conceptually), where teachers would explicitly make the connection to a belief. However. each right, freedom, and responsibility would be worthy of an investigation, in and of itself. So, rather than starting lesson planning with a topic such as the American Revolution and teasing out the related underlying beliefs, a teacher could reverse the process, creating a lesson on each belief with questions and examples drawn from history, geography, economics, civics, and the social sciences or humanities.

NCSS Essential Skills of a Social Studies Education

Published in 1989, *The Essential Skills of Social Studies Education* detailed a list of three categories of skills that should be modeled and taught by teachers of social studies. The two in Figure 12.2, "Organizing & Using Information" and "Interpersonal Relationships & Social Participations" are directed at procedural knowledge, the core civic values, and civic participation skills. The third, "Acquiring Information Skills," is enumerated in Chapter 28, Reading Social Studies and Vocabulary. The language used in Figure 12.2 can be valuable in precisely stating a teacher's objectives.

In the haze of social studies' voluminous content, what is often lost is that teachers need to explicitly plan lessons where teachers model how to carry out these skills and students practice the skills using the social studies declarative content (see Chapter 26).

Organizing and Using Information	
A. Thinking Skills	
1. Classify Information • Identify relevant factual material • Sense relationship among items of factual information • Group data in categories according to appropriate criteria • Place in proper sequence: – order of occurrence – order of importance • Place data in tabular form: charts, graphs, and illustrations	*2. Interpret Information* • State relationships between categories of information • Note cause-and-effect relationships • Draw inferences from factual material • Predict likely outcomes based on factual information • Recognize the value dimension of interpreting factual material • Recognize instances in which more than one interpretation of factual material is valid
3. Analyze Information • Form a simple organization of key ideas related to a topic • Separate a topic into major components according to appropriate criteria • Examine critically relationships between and among elements of a topic • Detect bias in data presented in various forms: graphics, tabular, visual, print • Compare and contrast credibility of differing accounts of the same event	*4. Summarize Information* • Extract significant ideas from supporting illustrative details • Combine critical concepts into a statement of conclusions based on information • Restate major ideas of a complex topic in concise form • Form opinion based on critical examination of relevant information • State hypotheses for further study
5. Synthesize Information • Propose a new plan of operation, create a new system, or devise a futuristic scheme based on available information • Reinterpret events in terms of what might have happened, and show the likely effects on subsequent events • Present visually (chart, graph, diagram, model, etc.) information extracted from print • Prepare a research paper that requires a creative solution to a problem • Communicate orally and in writing	*6. Evaluate Information* • Determine whether or not the information is pertinent to the topic • Estimate the adequacy of the information • Test the validity of the information, using such criteria as source, objectivity, technical correctness, and currency

Figure 12.2 Essential Organizing, Thinking, Interpersonal, and Participation Skills

B. Decision-Making Skills	C. Metacognitive Skills
• Identify a situation in which a decision is required • Secure needed factual information relevant to making the decision • Recognize the values implicit in the situation and the issues that flow from them • Identify alternative courses of action and predict likely consequences of each • Make decision based on the data obtained • Take action to implement the decision	• Select an appropriate strategy to solve a problem • Self-monitor one's thinking process
Interpersonal Relationships and Social Participations	
A. Personal Skills	**B. Group Interaction Skills**
• Express personal convictions • Communicate own beliefs, feelings, and convictions • Adjust own behavior to fit the dynamics of various groups and situations • Recognize the mutual relationship between human beings in satisfying one another's needs	• Contribute to the development of a supportive climate in groups • Participate in making rules and guidelines for group life • Serve as a leader or follower • Assist in setting goals for the group • Participate in delegating duties, organizing, planning, making decisions, and taking action in group settings • Participate in persuading, compromising, debating, and negotiating in the resolution of conflicts and differences
C. Social and Political Participation Skills	
• Keep informed on issues that affect society • Identify situations in which social actions are required • Work individually or with others to decide on an appropriate course of action • Work to influence those in positions of social power to strive for extensions of freedom, social justice, and human rights • Accept and fulfill social responsibilities associated with citizenship in a free society	

Figure 12.2 (Cont.)

The NCSS "Themes"

In 1994, and revised in 2010, the NCSS (1994/2010) published *Expectations of Excellence: Curriculum Standards for Social Studies*, the ten "**Themes**." The 1994, 187-page PDF version of the book is available at no cost and should be downloaded and used as a reference when lesson planning (see *References* Schneider, *Expectations for Excellence*). These standards are a particularly valuable resource for examples of how teachers can focus on procedural knowledge and compelling ideas.

I. Culture The study of culture and cultural diversity.	VI. Power, Authority, and Governance The study of how people create, interact with, and change structures of power.
II. Time, Continuity, and Change The study of the past and its legacy	VII. Production, Distribution, and Consumption The study of how people organize for the production, distribution, and consumption of goods and services.
III. People, Places, and Environments The study of people, places, and environments.	VIII. Science, Technology, and Society The study of relationships among science, technology, and society.
IV. Individual Development and Identity The study of individual development and identity.	IX. Global Connections The study of global connections and interdependence.
V. Individuals, Groups, and Institutions, The study of interactions among individuals, groups, and institutions.	X. Civic Ideals and Practices, The study of the ideals, principles, and practices of citizenship in a democratic republic.

Figure 12.3 The Ten NCSS Themes

Both editions of the Themes include exemplary lesson plan ideas for elementary, middle, and high school grade levels for each theme. In the 2010 edition, each theme is organized into the four categories as depicted below. Figure 12.4 is representative of the kind of advice given for each theme at each grade.

One of the most valuable resources on the internet for teaching social studies are videos and lesson plans based on the Themes. Created by the Annenberg Foundation (2020a) at the website *learner.org*, there are 32 videos organized by K-5, middle, and high school levels that show exemplary, creative teachers engaging students. An excellent example from 2nd grade is the video "#4 China through Mapping." Ms. Norton's creativity borders on genius with hands-on, multiple active learning activities that achieve the themes of culture; time, continuity, and change; people, places, and environments; and global connections. Another excellent and creative lesson is "#16 Explorations in Archeology and History." Ms. Larsen with her 6th-grade students explores family histories leading to artifacts as part of investigating the tools of archeology and anthropology and achieves the themes culture and time, continuity, and change.

The NCSS C3 Framework

In 2013, in part in response to the standards movement, the NCSS adopted *College, Career, and Civic Life C3 Framework for Social Studies State Standards* (NCSS, 2013), the "C3 Framework." The document has two parts: (A) set of standards by grade level that is compatible with Common Core; and (B) a recommended method of teaching named the "Inquiry Arc." Its purpose is to provide guidance to states as to their decisions on standards and teachers on best practices. The Framework should be downloaded as a PDF booklet (see reference NCSS, 2013):

Purposes:
Basic freedoms, rights, and the institutions and practices that support shared democratic principles are foundations of a democratic republic. Civic ideals developed over centuries. In some instances, civic practices and their consequences are becoming more congruent with ideals, while in other cases the gap is wide and calls for continued civic action by individuals and groups to sustain and improve the society. Learning how to apply informed civic action to more fully realize civic ideals is of major importance for the health of individuals, groups, and the nation.

Questions for Exploration	Knowledge the Learner will Understand:	Processes the Learner will be able to do:	Products Learners Demonstrate Understanding by:
• What are civic ideals and practices? • What documents support civic ideals and practices in a democratic republic? • How does one become informed about civic issues? • How can students participate in meaningful civic action?	• the origins and continuing influence of key ideals of a democratic republic, such as individual human dignity, liberty, justice, equality, individual rights, majority and minority rights, the common good, and the rule of law; • key documents and excerpts from key sources that define and support democratic ideals and practices. (e.g., Declaration of Independence, U.S. Constitution, Gettysburg Address, etc.); • The origins and function of major institutions and practices developed to support democratic ideals and practices; • key issues past and present involving democratic ideals and practices, as well as perspectives of various stakeholders in proposing possible outcomes; • the rights and responsibilities of citizenship and the practices involved in exercising citizenship (e.g., voting, serving on a jury, expressing views on issues, collaborating with others to take civic action); and	• identify and describe the role of citizen in various forms of government past and present; • analyze and evaluate the effectiveness of various forms of civic action influencing public policy decisions that address the realization of the ideals of a democratic republic; • build background through research, make decisions and solve problems as they locate, research, analyze, organize, synthesize, evaluate, and apply information about selected civic issues (past and present) in key primary and secondary sources; • identify sound reasoning, assumptions, misconceptions, and bias in sources, evidence, and arguments used in presenting issues and positions; • identify, seek, describe, and evaluate multiple points of view surrounding issues–noting the strengths, weaknesses, and the consequences associated with holding each position; • evaluate the significance of public opinion and positions of	• articulating an informed personal position on a civic issue based on reasoned arguments resulting from consulting multiple sources; • practicing forms of civil, civic discussion and participation consistent with the ideals of citizens in a democratic republic; • sharing policy positions in such forms as position statements, editorials, or political cartoons; • using a variety of media to report findings from surveys, debates, petitions; and • writing a plan of action in collaboration with others on an issue of public concern, after carefully weighing possible options for the most effective citizen action.

Figure 12.4 Theme X: Civic Ideals and Practices – Middle Grades

| | • the importance of becoming informed in order to make positive civic contributions | policymakers in influencing public policy development and decision-making;
• evaluate the degree to which public policies and citizen behaviors reflect or foster the stated ideals of a democratic republican form of government; and
• participate in persuading, compromising, debating, and negotiating in the resolution of conflicts and differences. | |

Figure 12.4 (Cont.)

The C3 Framework is centered on an Inquiry Arc – a set of interlocking and mutually supportive ideas that frame the ways students learn social studies content. By focusing on inquiry, the framework emphasizes the disciplinary concepts and practices that support students as they develop the capacity to know, analyze, explain, and argue about interdisciplinary challenges in our social world.

(p. 6)

On page 12 of the Framework, the authors provide four "**Dimensions**" of the Inquiry Arc (Figure 12.5). A significant impetus for the Framework is to "build critical thinking, problem-solving, and participatory skills to become engaged citizens" (NCSS, 2020b). Much of the information that follows and that appears in the following chapters is excerpted from the C3 Framework booklet.

Dimension 1: Developing Questions and Planning Inquiries

Dimension 1 anticipates that teachers move their planning away from "what I plan to tell the students" to "what questions do I want students to learn to ask" and

Dimension 1: Developing Questions and Planning Inquiries	Dimension 2: Applying Disciplinary Tools and Concepts	Dimension 3: Evaluating Sources and Using Evidence	Dimension 4: Communicating Conclusions and Taking Informed Action
Developing Questions and Planning Inquiries	Civics	Gathering and Evaluating Sources	Communicating and Critiquing Conclusions
	Economics		
	Geography	Developing Claims and Using Evidence	Taking Informed Action
	History		

Figure 12.5 NCSS C3 Framework Dimensions

organizing the resources for students to conduct "investigations." As Nosich (2001) points out, "critical thinking begins with asking questions, [and] trying to answer those questions by reasoning them out" (p. 5).

The website *Engage NY: New York State K-12 Social Studies Resource Toolkit* (2020a) has free, detailed, high-quality lesson plans by grade level and topics developed using the C3 Framework standards and the Inquiry Arc. As two examples, the lesson "Rules" is designed for 2nd grade (Engage NY, 2020b) and starts with the question, "Do we have to have rules?" and a lesson at the high school level on the "Treaty of Versailles" (Engage NY, 2020c) is based on the compelling question, "Can peace lead to war?" Social studies teacher candidates need all the free resources they can accumulate. It would be worthwhile to download every PDF of every lesson for the grades a teacher plans to teach as part of a library of resources.

Dimension 2: Applying Disciplinary Tools and Concepts

The C3 Framework focuses on the unique ways each academic discipline structures its procedural and declarative knowledge and how teachers can restructure the sophisticated modes of reason into useable, grade-appropriate knowledge. What is termed here as "disciplinary tools and concepts" are the same as mode of reasoning, procedural knowledge, executive processes, and intellectual processes and will be developed in the following chapters.

Dimension 3: Evaluating Sources and Using Evidence

Students should use various technologies and skills to find information and to express their responses to compelling questions through well-reasoned explanations and evidence-based arguments. Through the rigorous analysis of sources and application of information from those sources, students should craft the evidence-based claims that will form the basis for their judgments that inform their ideology and identity. This includes:

Gathering and Evaluating Sources is where students are asked to work with the sources that they gather and/or are provided for them. It is important for students to use print sources of primary type documents as a complement and alternative to the textbook.

Developing Claims and Using Evidence is where students learn to develop claims using evidence and argumentation based on the source-to-evidence relationship emphasizing the development of claims and counterclaims and the purposeful selection of evidence in support of those claims and counterclaims.

Dimension 4: Communicating Conclusions and Taking Informed Action

The process of learning in the social studies classroom should be directed at developing students' capacity to effectively communicate their ideology and political ideological stances. Opportunities to practice the learned civic values, democratic ideals, and personal virtues are an essential part of social studies education.

Communicating and Critiquing Conclusions is where students formalize their arguments and explanations. This should come after having worked independently and collaboratively through the development of questions, the application of disciplinary knowledge and concepts, and the gathering of sources and use of evidence and information.

Graphic organizers and products such as essays, reports, and multimedia presentations offer students opportunities to represent their ideas in a variety of forms and communicate their conclusions to a range of audiences. Students' primary audiences will likely be their teachers and classmates, but even young children benefit from opportunities to share their conclusions with audiences outside their classroom doors.

Taking Informed Action is where students learn that civic action should be grounded in and informed by the inquiries using the modes of reasoning of the disciplines and cross-disciplinary approaches. In that way, action is then a purposeful, informed, and reflective experience.

The Framework provides indicators for each dimension. **Indicators** are similar to benchmarks and objectives. They are a way to more precisely explain what teachers should teach and students should know or do by the end of specific grade levels. The Framework's tables of indicators in the PDF brochure can be very helpful to gauge instruction to be grade-appropriate. Figure 12.6 is one example drawn from Dimension 4.

BY THE END OF GRADE 2	BY THE END OF GRADE 5	BY THE END OF GRADE 8	BY THE END OF GRADE 12
Individually and with others, students use writing, visualizing and speaking to			
D4.1.K-2. Construct an argument with reasons.	**D4.1.3-5.** Construct arguments using claims and evidence from multiple sources.	**D4.1.6-8.** Construct arguments using claims and evidence from multiple sources, while acknowledging the strengths and limitations of the arguments.	**D4.1.9-12.** Construct arguments using precise and knowledgeable claims, with evidence from multiple sources, while acknowledging counterclaims and evidentiary weaknesses.

Figure 12.6 Communicating Conclusions Example

Resources

Videos: *Learner.org:* Home Page or Series Social Studies in Action a Teaching Practices Library K-12 Series (32 videos based on the NCSS Themes); Democracy in America (15 videos); Social Studies in Action a Methodology Workshop K-5 (8 videos); Making Civics Real a Workshop for Teachers (8 videos); The Constitution that Delicate Balance (13 videos); Story of the Bill of Rights | *Smithsonian:* C3 Framework.

Documents: *Core Knowledge* (among the most detailed and cross-disciplinary lesson plans on the internet) | *Engage NY:* New York State K-12 Social Studies Resources Toolkit (over 80, C3 Inquiry Lessons) | *C3teachers.org* (over 200 Inquiry Lessons) | NCSS: C3 Framework for Social Studies PDF; Schneider *Expectations for Excellence* (PDF); Completing the Inquiry Arc; A Vision of Powerful Teaching and Learning in the Social Studies; *Social Studies and the Young Learner; Social Education; Middle Level Learning; Theory and Research* [journals].

References

Annenberg. (2020a). *Social studies in action: A teaching practices library, K-12.* Retrieved from www.learner.org/series/social-studies-in-action-a-teaching-practices-library-k-12/

Engage NY. (2020a). *New York state K-12 social studies resource toolkit.* Retrieved from www.engageny.org/resource/new-york-state-k-12-social-studies-resource-toolkit.

Engage NY. (2020b). *Rules.* Retrieved from www.c3teachers.org/wp-content/uploads/2015/09/New York_K_Rules.pdf

Engage NY. (2020c). *Can peace lead to war.* Retrieved from www.c3teachers.org/wp-content/uploads/2015/10/NewYork_10_Versailles.pdf.

Goodreads. (2020). *Eldredge Cleaver.* Retrieved from www.goodreads.com/quotes/21458-if-you-are-not-a-part-of-the-solution-you.

NCSS. (1989). In search of a scope and sequence for social studies. *Social Education, 53*(6), 376–385.

NCSS. (1990). *Social studies for citizens for a strong and free nation.* Social Studies Curriculum Planning Resources. Author.

NCSS. (1994). *Expectations of excellence: Curriculum standards for social studies.* NCSS. Retrieved from www.socialstudies.org/standards/execsummary.

NCSS. (1994/2010): *Expectations of excellence: Curriculum standards for social studies.* Washington, DC. Retrieved from www.socialstudies.org/standards/strands.

NCSS. (2013). *Social studies for the next generation: Purposes, practices, and implications of the college, career, and civic Life (C3) framework for social studies state standards: Guidance for enhancing rigor of K-12 civic, economics, geography, and history.* NCSS. Retrieved from www.socialstudies.org/sites/default/files/2017/Jun/c3-framework-for-social-studies-rev0617.pdf.

NCSS. (2020a). NCSS position statements. Retrieved from www.socialstudies.org/positions.

NCSS. (2020b). *The college, career, and civic life (C3) framework for social studies state standards: Guidance for enhancing the rigor of K-12 civics, economics, geography, and history.* NCSS. Retrieved from www.socialstudies.org/c3.

Nosich, G. (2001). *Learning to think things through: A guide to critical thinking in the curriculum.* Prentice Hall.

Schneider, D., et al. (1994). *Expectations of excellence: Curriculum standards for social studies.* Bulletin 89. NCSS. ERIC ED378131. Retrieved from https://files.eric.ed.gov/fulltext/ED378131.pdf.

13 Civics Education

The stakes ... are too high for government to be a spectator sport.
Barbara Jordan, U.S. Representative, 1936–1996 (Quoteswise, 2020)

Civic Education

Civics can be a single course, but considering the thesis presented in Part 1 of this book, civic education is the thread running through all the social studies.

Aristotle (350 BCE) recognized that the nation state was more than just a regulator of behavior through laws, but that a democratic government was also the guardian of the community's moral code. Dewey (1938/1978) pointed out that the modern democratic state requires personal freedom and personal freedom depends on social stability, which then requires a relinquishing of some freedoms to the judgment of representative government. Thus, there is a perpetual tension between individuals' ideas of morality that are necessary for fulfillment of their identity and the morality demanded by the *polis* for societal stability. The tensions stem from the nature and imperfections of humankind itself. Individuals come into the world with different innate capacities and begin their lives at different starting points by the happenstance of birth. The opportunities made possible by the goodwill of the more fortunate members of a democracy are intended to help mitigate the inequities. The remedies include government programs and laws that promote equality of opportunity, redistribution of wealth policies, philanthropy, and volunteerism: All of which depend on trust in the electorate and government. Of concern, in 1964, "77% of the American people said they trusted the government to do the right thing all the time or almost all the time. Today, it's 17%" (Wehner, 2019, quoting George Will).

The Founders feared centralized government and chose a governance system that they hoped would be un-intrusive and perpetuate goodwill. Alexis de Tocqueville (1835/2020), as a result of his tour of America in the early 1830s, believed American democracy was unique because when there was a problem, ordinary people banned together – organically – without government involvement to address problems. Neighbor helping neighbor, religious institutions, and secular nonprofit, philanthropic, charitable, and fraternal organizations have been a hallmark of American society since its beginning.

The common misstatements, such as "The government gives me food stamps" or "The small business administration gives me a low-interest loan for my business," distort and hamper communal attachments because they depersonalize the actual events they describe. The following more precise statements create a different sensibility and understanding of the transaction between citizens: "My neighbor makes it possible for me to have food stamps," or "My neighbor makes it possible for me to get a low-interest loan for my business." Government bureaucracies, by serving as an intermediary, inherently depersonalize the transaction and veil the goodwill of neighbors needed in a civil society.

John F. Kennedy's (1961) "Ask not what your country can do for you, ask what you can do for your country" echoes that tradition identified by de Tocqueville. William Galston (1991) believes there has been too little attention paid to self-restraint – where the citizen should resist the temptation to rely too much on the government. Galston argues that to maintain a liberal democracy, a person must: (a) ask only for the services that his government can afford; (b) be willing to pay for the services he asks for; and (c) agree to painful fiscal responsibility measures when necessary. In this sense, the first obligation of members of a democracy is to ask more of themselves regardless of their circumstances. The practice for this civic duty starts with children entering school, where they are obligated to take advantage of their free public education, both as a duty to themselves and their fellow citizens. Social studies teachers should call students to this civic duty so as to establish the beginning of a democratic ideology.

The Moral Imperative for Parents and Teachers

Children have traditionally (and should) relied heavily on their families for their first ideas about a democratic way of life and what temperament and skills are needed for effective participation in a democratic state (Hess & Torney, 1967/2009). Kristjánsson (2006) sounds a caution due to modernity when he says young people:

> Are in urgent need of role models at their impressionable age and that the moral quality of such models has deteriorated as of late. Instead of looking to their parents and grandparents, charismatic leaders from history and literature, and renowned paragons of moral virtue as their guiding lights, it is argued that the attention of the young is nowadays held in a firm grip by the mass media, which depict a society in moral decline. Thus, drug-snorting pop idols and rumbustious sport stars have allegedly taken over as the leading role models of our age.
>
> (p. 39)

Brian Barry (1973) believes that in a liberal democracy,

> man must take his stand on the proposition that some ways of life, some types of character are more admirable than others ... He must hold that societies ought to be organized in such a way as to produce the largest possible proportion of people with an admirable type of character and the best possible chance to act in accordance with it.
>
> (p. 126)

Sherman (1989) contends this requires more than the child's observations of other actors, but requires caregivers to participate in the emotions of the child being cared for. Parents and teachers listening deeply to children recognize the child's need for moral imperatives and manufacture opportunities for children to practice moral actions. Nurturing parents and teachers of social studies do more than explain to children how to think about moral questions; they must empathize with children through the suffering of moral decision-making and action for the idea of personal and civic duty to habituate.

Four Vital Concepts of a Democratic State

In addition to the democratic ideals outlined previously, the citizens' understanding and support for the following four concepts are necessary for a democratic nation to thrive.

1. **Patriotism** is love of and devotion to one's country. Most nations promote it through such public affirmations as singing their national anthem before athletic events, monuments to soldiers and leaders, etc. Democracies advocate patriotism as a belief that should be based on reasoned choices – not "blind" patriotism. Two individuals can hold different political ideological positions, but both can be patriotic. Regrettably, people are sometimes accused of being unpatriotic if they hold unpopular, but still democratic, political ideological views and stances. In less democratic societies, patriotism and civil dissent are seen as contradictory and blind patriotism is promoted as a higher goal than deliberate, thoughtful decision-making. US students, in the early grades in particular, are given the opportunity to express pride in their country by reciting the Pledge of Allegiance, singing patriotic songs, dramatizing events like the signing of the Declaration of Independence, learning of courageous deeds of patriots, and learning about and celebrating national holidays.

2. **Social criticism** is tied to the democratic belief of free speech and a free press. In some nations, voicing an opinion that is contrary to the prevailing view or critical of the powerful or privileged can result in imprisonment or execution. The fear of retaliation undermines the free discourse of ideas that allows for the advancement of democratic ethos across the globe. In a democracy, individuals can be both patriotic and a social critic: In fact, it can be argued that social criticism is an obligation of every citizen so as to push forward the *telos* of a more humane world. Social criticism should be promoted as an essential component of patriotism. Learning the art of social criticism begins with students learning to pursue investigations as called for in the Arc of Inquiry so that their criticisms are grounded in foundational knowledge, democratic ideals, and critical thinking.

3. **Social activism** should be premised on the analysis that takes place during social criticism. It is also essential to a democratic state and students should be given opportunities to act on their beliefs. A clean-up day at the school, in a park or playground could be taken on by the class, but only if a rationale based in duty is a prerequisite to the activity. After students have a thorough grounding in an issue or public policy, students can be given an opportunity to decide what political ideological stances they wish to take and write to a legislator proposing changes to laws. In the high school years it can lead to students being activists in their communities. History lessons on how social activism has changed the US for the better are a crucial part of promoting virtues and democratic beliefs.

4. **Civil disobedience** requires individuals not only knowing the right thing to do and doing it, but also a willingness to suffer the consequences of their beliefs and actions for the good of society. It requires the virtue of courage. The signers of the Declaration of Independence were, on the whole, members of the privileged class, and their decision to lead a rebellion against their motherland was considered treason in Britain. Not only could they have lost their earthly possessions; they also could have lost their very lives. Muhammad Ali was prohibited from boxing for three years, lost millions of dollars, ran the risk of never being allowed to box again, and going to jail because he refused induction into the army during the Vietnam War on religious grounds. Learning about such individuals such as Rosa Parks, Gandhi, Oskar Schindler, etc., leads students to consider who they are and who they ought to be (refer to Figure 4.2, The Essential Identity Questions)

The NCSS Themes and the C3 Civics Dimensions

There are five particularly relevant NCSS Themes that provide important insights into the breadth and depth of civics: Individual Development and Identity; Individuals, Groups, and Institutions; Power, Authority, and Governance; Global Connections; and Civic Ideals and Practices.

As explained in Chapter 12, in Dimension 2: Applying Disciplinary Concepts and Tools of the C3 Framework, the NCSS defines the grade-level "**pathways**" for the four core subject areas of civics, history, geography, and economics by employing the term "**indicators**" as comparable to benchmarks.

In the C3 Framework for the civics pathway, the authors state, "Students need the intellectual power to recognize societal problems; ask good questions and develop robust investigations into them; consider possible solutions and consequences; separate evidence-based claims from parochial opinions; and communicate and act upon what they learn" (NCSS, 2013, p. 6). Civics is divided into the following three pathways and the indicators for each by grade level.

Civic and Political Institutions

In order to act responsibly and effectively, citizens must understand the important institutions of their society and the principles that these institutions are intended to reflect. That requires mastery of a body of knowledge about law, politics, and government.

Processes, Rules, and Laws

Civics is the discipline of the social studies most directly concerned with the processes and rules by which groups of people make decisions, govern themselves, and address public problems. People address problems at all scales, from a classroom to the agreements among nations. Public policies are among the tools that governments use to address public problems. Students must learn how various rules, processes, laws, and policies actually work, which requires factual understanding of political systems and is the focus of this section.

BY THE END OF GRADE 2	BY THE END OF GRADE 5	BY THE END OF GRADE 8	BY THE END OF GRADE 12
INDIVIDUALLY AND WITH OTHERS, STUDENTS...			
D2.Civ.1.K-2. Describe roles and responsibilities of people in authority.	**D2.Civ.1.3-5.** Distinguish the responsibilities and powers of government officials at various levels and branches of government and in different times and places.	**D2.Civ.1.6-8.** Distinguish the powers and responsibilities of citizens, political parties, interest groups, and the media in a variety of governmental and nongovernmental contexts.	**D2.Civ.1.9-12.** Distinguish the powers and responsibilities of local, state, tribal, national, and international civic and political institutions.
D2.Civ.2.K-2. Explain how all people, not just official leaders, play important roles in a community.	**D2.Civ.2.3-5.** Explain how a democracy relies on people's responsible participation, and draw implications for how individuals should participate.	**D2.Civ.2.6-8.** Explain specific roles played by citizens (such as voters, jurors, taxpayers, members of the armed forces, petitioners, protesters, and office-holders).	**D2.Civ.2.9-12.** Analyze the role of citizens in the U.S. political system, with attention to various theories of democracy, changes in Americans' participation over time, and alternative models from other countries, past and present.
D2.Civ.3.K-2. Explain the need for and purposes of rules in various settings inside and outside of school.	**D2.Civ.3.3-5.** Examine the origins and purposes of rules, laws, and key U.S. constitutional provisions.	**D2.Civ.3.6-8.** Examine the origins, purposes, and impact of constitutions, laws, treaties, and international agreements.	**D2.Civ.3.9-12.** Analyze the impact of constitutions, laws, treaties, and international agreements on the maintenance of national and international order.
D2.Civ.4.K-2. *Begins in grades 3–5*	**D2.Civ.4.3-5.** Explain how groups of people make rules to create responsibilities and protect freedoms.	**D2.Civ.4.6-8.** Explain the powers and limits of the three branches of government, public officials, and bureaucracies at different levels in the United States and in other countries.	**D2.Civ.4.9-12.** Explain how the U.S. Constitution establishes a system of government that has powers, responsibilities, and limits that have changed over time and that are still contested.
D2.Civ.5.K-2. Explain what governments are and some of their functions.	**D2.Civ.5.3-5.** Explain the origins, functions, and structure of different systems of government, including those created by the U.S. and state constitutions.	**D2.Civ.5.6-8.** Explain the origins, functions, and structure of government with reference to the U.S. Constitution, state constitutions, and selected other systems of government.	**D2.Civ.5.9-12.** Evaluate citizens' and institutions' effectiveness in addressing social and political problems at the local, state, tribal, national, and/or international level.

Figure 13.1 Civics and Political Institutions

D2.Civ.6.K-2. Describe how communities work to accomplish common tasks, establish responsibilities, and fulfill roles of authority.	**D2.Civ.6.3-5.** Describe ways in which people benefit from and are challenged by working together, including through government, workplaces, voluntary organizations, and families.	**D2.Civ.6.6-8.** Describe the roles of political, civil, and economic organizations in shaping people's lives.	**D2.Civ.6.9-12.** Critique relationships among governments, civil societies, and economic markets.

Figure 13.1 (Cont.)

BY THE END OF GRADE 2	BY THE END OF GRADE 5	BY THE END OF GRADE 8	BY THE END OF GRADE 12
INDIVIDUALLY AND WITH OTHERS, STUDENTS...			
D2.Civ.11.K-2. Explain how people can work together to make decisions in the classroom.	**D2.Civ.11.3-5.** Compare procedures for making decisions in a variety of settings, including classroom, school, government, and/or society.	**D2.Civ.11.6-8.** Differentiate among procedures for making decisions in the classroom, school, civil society, and local, state, and national government in terms of how civic purposes are intended.	**D2.Civ.11.9-12.** Evaluate multiple procedures for making governmental decisions at the local, state, national, and international levels in terms of the civic purposes achieved.
D2.Civ.12.K-2. Identify and explain how rules function in public (classroom and school) settings.	**D2.Civ.12.3-5.** Explain how rules and laws change society and how people change rules and laws.	**D2.Civ.12.6-8.** Assess specific rules and laws (both actual and proposed) as means of addressing public problems.	**D2.Civ.12.9-12.** Analyze how people use and challenge local, state, national, and international laws to address a variety of public issues.
Begins in grades 3–5	**D2.Civ.13.3-5.** Explain how policies are developed to address public problems.	**D2.Civ.13.6-8.** Analyze the purposes, implementation, and consequences of public policies in multiple settings.	**D2.Civ.13.9-12.** Evaluate public policies in terms of intended and unintended outcomes, and related consequences.
D2.Civ.14.K-2. Describe how people have tried to improve their communities over time.	**D2.Civ.14.3-5.** Illustrate historical and contemporary means of changing society.	**D2.Civ.14.6-8.** Compare historical and contemporary means of changing societies, and promoting the common good.	**D2.Civ.14.9-12.** Analyze historical, contemporary, and emerging means of changing societies, promoting the common good, and protecting rights.

Figure 13.2 Process, Rules, and Laws

Participation and Deliberation: Applying Civic Virtues and Democratic Principles

This book's division of personal virtues, democratic ideals, and civic values are aggregated by the C3 Framework into the language of "virtues" and "democratic principles" used below. This category calls for the promotion of a democratic ideology by teachers and therefore is most directly tied to the exalted aims.

BY THE END OF GRADE 2	BY THE END OF GRADE 5	BY THE END OF GRADE 8	BY THE END OF GRADE 12
INDIVIDUALLY AND WITH OTHERS, STUDENTS...			
D2.Civ.7.K-2. Apply civic virtues when participating in school settings.	**D2.Civ.7.3-5.** Apply civic virtues and democratic principles in school settings.	**D2.Civ.7.6-8.** Apply civic virtues and democratic principles in school and community settings.	**D2.Civ.7.9-12.** Apply civic virtues and democratic principles when working with others.
D2.Civ.8.K-2. Describe democratic principles such as equality, fairness, and respect for legitimate authority and rules.	**D2.Civ.8.3-5.** Identify core civic virtues and democratic principles that guide government, society, and communities.	**D2.Civ.8.6-8.** Analyze ideas and principles contained in the founding documents of the United States, and explain how they influence the social and political system.	**D2.Civ.8.9-12.** Evaluate social and political systems in different contexts, times, and places, that promote civic virtues and enact democratic principles.
D2.Civ.9.K-2. Follow agreed-upon rules for discussions while responding attentively to others when addressing ideas and making decisions as a group.	**D2.Civ.9.3-5.** Use deliberative processes when making decisions or reaching judgments as a group.	**D2.Civ.9.6-8.** Compare deliberative processes used by a wide variety of groups in various settings.	**D2.Civ.9.9-12.** Use appropriate deliberative processes in multiple settings.
D2.Civ.10.K-2. Compare their own point of view with others' perspectives.	**D2.Civ.10.3-5.** Identify the beliefs, experiences, perspectives, and values that underlie their own and others' points of view about civic issues.	**D2.Civ.10.6-8.** Explain the relevance of personal interests and perspectives, civic virtues, and democratic principles when people address issues and problems in government and civil society.	**D2.Civ.10.9-12.** Analyze the impact and the appropriate roles of personal interests and perspectives on the application of civic virtues, democratic principles, constitutional rights, and human rights.

Figure 13.3 Participation and Deliberation: Applying Civic Virtues and Democratic Principles

Learned Societies and Standards

The Center for Civic Education published the *National Standards for Civic and Government* (2014), which can be retrieved at the website cited in the *References*. The Center framed the content standards as essential questions that students should be able to answer by the end of K–4, 5–8, and 9–12 grade levels. Each grade level has primary and sub-primary questions. Below are the primary questions by grade level. At the website, the clickable primary questions lead to an elaboration of each concept that can serve as the impetus for a grade-appropriate lesson.

K-4 Content Standards

I. What is Government and What Should It Do?
II. What are the Basic Values and Principles of American Democracy?
III. How Does the Government Established by the Constitution Embody the Purposes, Values, and Principles of American Democracy?
IV. What is the Relationship of the United States to Other Nations and to World Affairs?
V. What are the Roles of the Citizen in American Democracy?

5-8 Content Standards

I. What are Civic Life, Politics, and Government?
II. What are the Foundations of the American Political System?
III. How Does the Government Established by the Constitution Embody the Purposes, Values, and Principles of American Democracy?
IV. What is the Relationship of the United States to Other Nations and to World Affairs?
V. What are the Roles of the Citizen in American Democracy?

9-12 Content Standards

I. What are Civic Life, Politics, and Government?
II. What are the Foundations of the American Political System?
III. How Does the Government Established by the Constitution Embody the Purposes, Values, and Principles of American Democracy?
IV. What is the Relationship of the United States to Other Nations and to World Affairs?
V. What are the Roles of the Citizen in American Democracy?

Resources

Videos: *C3LC*: Webinars | *Learner.org:* Home Page; Social Studies in Action a teaching practices library series (32 videos based on the NCSS): Themes Creating Effective Citizens; [Elementary] Leaders Community and Citizens; Caring for the Community; State Government and the Role of the Citizen; Making a Difference Through Giving; [Middle] Landmark Supreme Court Cases; [High School] Public Opinion; Competing Ideologies; The Individual in Society | *Learner.org:* Democracy in America (15 videos); Social Studies in Action a Methodology Workshop K-5 (8 videos); Making Civics Real a Workshop for Teachers (8 videos); The Constitution that Delicate Balance (13 videos); Story of the Bill of Rights | *Center for Civic Education:* Video Gallery | *ICivics*: Games | *PBS Digital Studies*: Crash Course in Government | *Study.com*: Social Science Courses | *TCH or YouTube*: Deep Dive Educating for Democracy; Get into Character Develop Empathy Through Drama; Illustrating Democracy Art Brings Words to Life; Making the Declaration of Independence Come Alive; Structured Academic Controversy (SAC) | *WatchNowLearn.org* Social Studies | *PBS*: Newshour Government-Civics | *YouTube*: Civics; Teaching the Declaration of Independence as a Breakup Letter.

Documents: *Routledge Handbook of Research in Social Studies Education*: Diversity and Citizenship Education; Historical, Theoretical, and Philosophical Issues; Global Education | *Wiley Handbook of Social Studies Research*: Global Education | Controversial Issues and Democratic Discourse | *Avalon Project* (primary documents related to civics) | *BCcampus* (Open textbooks political science) | *C3teachers.org* (22 inquiry lessons)| *CivicsRenewalNetwork* (over 1000 lesson plans) | *Consource* lesson plans | *CivicED* lesson plans | *CrashCourse* Government | *Library of Congress:* American Memory | *National Constitution Center* lesson plans and videos | *NEA* civics education | *NCSS*: Schneider *Expectations for Excellence* (NCSS Themes); Revitalizing Civic Learning in Our Schools; Why Vote? 5th Graders Informed Action | C3 Framework for Social Studies PDF; Completing the Inquiry Arc; *Social Studies and the Young Learner; Social Education; Middle Level Learning; Theory and Research* (Journals) | | *NEH Edsitement* lesson plans | 100 Milestone Documents | *ReadWriteThink:* "America the Beautiful;" Analyzing Famous Speeches as Arguments; Censorship in the Classroom: Understanding Controversial Issues; Developing Citizenship Through Rhetorical Analysis; Exploring and Writing About the Constitution; Fighting Injustice by Studying Lessons of the Past; Freedom of Speech and Automatic Language: Examining the Pledge of Allegiance; Myth and Truth: Independence Day; Myth and Truth: The "First Thanksgiving"; Myth and Truth: The Gettysburg Address; Proverbs: At Home and Around the World; Storytelling in the Social Studies Classroom; Using Music and Art to Develop Vocabulary; Vote for Me! Developing, Writing, and Evaluating Persuasive Speeches; Voting! What's It All About?; What Are My Rights? | United States Constitution for Kids | What So Proudly We Hail (lesson plans and videos).

References

Aristotle. (350 BCEc). *The politics.* Retrieved from http://classics.mit.edu/Aristotle/politics.html.

Barry, B. (1973). *The liberal theory of justice.* Clarendon Press.

Center for Civic Education. (2014). *National standards for civic and government.* Retrieved from www.civiced.org/standards.

de Tocqueville, A. (1835/2020). *Democracy in America.* Retrieved from www.gutenberg.org/files/815/815-h/815-h.htm#link2H_4_0001.

Dewey, J. (1938/1978). Experience and education. In J. A. Boydston & J. Dewey (Eds..), *The later works.* 1938 (Vol. 12). Southern Illinois University Press.

Galston, W. A. (1991). *Liberal purposes: Goods, virtues, and diversity in the liberal state.* Cambridge University Press.

Hess, R. D., & Torney, J. V. (1967/2009). *The development of political attitudes in children.* Transaction Publishers.

Kennedy, J. F. (1961). *Inaugural address.* Retrieved from www.jfklibrary.org/Research/Research-Aids/Ready-Reference/JFK-Quotations/Inaugural-Address.aspx.

Kristjánsson, K. (2006). Emulation and the use of role models in moral education. *Journal of Moral Education, 35*(1), 37–49. www.tandfonline.com/doi/full/10.1080/03057240500495278

NCSS. (2013). *Social studies for the next generation: Purposes, practices, and implications of the college, career, and civic Life (C3) framework for social studies state standards: Guidance for enhancing rigor of K-12 civic, economics, geography, and history.* NCSS. Retrieved from www.socialstudies.org/sites/default/files/2017/Jun/c3-framework-for-social-studies-rev0617.pdf

Quoteswise. (2020). *Barbara Jordon.* Retrieved from www.quoteswise.com/barbara-jordan-quotes.html.

Sherman, N. (1989). *The fabric of character: Aristotle's theory of virtue.* Clarendon Press.

Wehner, P. (2019). George Will changes his mind – But stays true to his convictions. *The Atlantic.* www.theatlantic.com/ideas/archive/2019/07/what-makes-a-true-conservative/594889/.

14 History Education

Those who cannot remember the past are condemned to repeat it.
George Santayana, Philosopher and Cultural Critic, 1863–1953
(Santayana, 1905 Vol. 1, p. 284)

Academic History

"History" is the Greek word for inquiry. Herodotus (484–425 BCE) is credited with authoring the earliest form of **academic history**. Earlier "histories" such as the exploits of Odysseus were in verse form with the intention to promote the virtues and beliefs prized by Greek culture. Such stories today are considered **folklore**, such as stories of Paul Bunyan, George Washington and the cherry tree, the midnight ride of Paul Revere, and Betsy Ross as maker of the first American flag. **Historical fiction** such as *To Kill a Mockingbird*, *Les Misérables*, or the musical *Hamilton*, whether a book, theatrical production, or film, serve as gateways for students to enter the flow of democratic ideals. Distinct from folklore and historical fiction is **popular history**, biographies, and stories, which are often written because they promote democratic ideals, such as John F. Kennedy's *Profiles in Courage*, a biography of Harriet Tubman, or *Twenty-five Yards of War: The Extraordinary Courage of Ordinary Men in World War II* by Ronald Drez. These different genres blur the lines between academic history and fictionalized history and students need to become aware of the differences.

Academic history, such as found in textbooks and history books, is, for the most part, filled with foundational knowledge. The authors of academic histories strive to objectively distinguish between facts and interpretations in their narratives and base conclusions on evidence so that readers can decide whether to agree or disagree. History, even academic history, is never totally objective. Because students are inclined to trust in the authenticity and objectivity of textbooks (and the internet) and the truthfulness of teachers, students will tend to absorb history without understanding that they need to interpret authors' or teachers' conclusions and draw their own logical conclusions from the evidence.

Mass media, changes in ethical standards in journalism, blurred lines between TV commentators and reporters, and polarization in politics make trusting what appear to be authoritative and objective sources more challenging. Healthy skepticism needs to be emphasized to students at the outset when teaching history.

The study of history involves two key components:
One, "it rests on knowledge of facts, dates, names, places, events, and ideas," and two,

> true historical understanding requires students to engage in historical thinking: to raise questions and to marshal solid evidence in support of their answers; to go

beyond the facts presented in their textbooks and examine the historical record for themselves; to consult documents, journals, diaries, artifacts, historic sites, works of art, quantitative data, and other evidence from the past, and to do so imaginatively – taking into account the historical context in which these records were created and comparing the multiple points of view of those on the scene at the time.

(National Center for History in the Schools, 1996)

The following are seven hazards of historical thinking that should be demonstrated and explained to students.

Seven Hazards of History

If not considered, the following limit individuals' ability to interpret historical works:

1. **Inference and bias determination** is the ability to read critically and with skepticism. Due to space limitations alone, authors must be selective about what is included and what is left out. If an elementary textbook has Andrew Jackson's victory in the Battle of New Orleans but leaves out the Trail of Tears, the question to be considered is, is it bias or based solely on the economics of the number of textbook pages? Textbooks may be factually correct, but reflect subtle or overt bias in the choices of words that are used: It is the Yom Kippur war in Israel and the Ramadan war in Arab countries. Bias in textbooks may exist – without malice, subtly, or purposefully – and questions about inference and bias should be part of investigations in students' early education.
2. **Multiple valid interpretations** requires recognition that there can be more than one valid justified opinion based on the same evidence. Individuals, even when in disagreement with others, need to practice open-mindedness, impartiality, tolerance for ambiguity, and critical thinking, and the democratic beliefs of tolerance and freedom of thought, conscience, and expression.
3. **Present-mindedness** is the distortion of reading the present into the past. Eugene Goodheart (2011) argues that moral judgments about the past must consider what he terms "the horizon of possibility." The abolition of slavery was not on the horizon for Plato and Aristotle, but Hitler's acts of genocide were judged to be within his horizon and thus morally corrupt.
4. **Lack of proportionality** is a bias that stems from failure to interpret objectively. It takes the form of thinking the events of today are unique and more impactful than events in the past were on people in their time and place. It is due to being in the midst of the events that are impacting us in our time and place.
5. **Empathy** is the capacity to enter the minds, the thoughts *and* feeling, of people in the past. The reader must develop the imagination based on "common humanity" to put themselves in the circumstance of the people of the time period (Little, 1983).
6. **Overgeneralization** is the product of intellectual laziness or bias. Historian Joan Hoff Wilson (1976) states in an American history textbook that "the American Revolution produced no significant benefits for American women" (p. 387). This language reflects her conclusion based on the facts she garnered, but begs the question: To what degree was the conclusion influenced by the ideological prism she used? Another historian could come to a different conclusion because there is considerable evidence that the beliefs of the Founders regarding women's rights were advanced for their time in comparison with other societies. Votes were taken by all-

male legislatures so that women had the right to inherit; property could be subdivided to provide for inheritance to the female spouse instead of estates required to be left only to the first-born male (Salmon, 1986); and women gained the right to initiate divorce (Basch, 1995).

7. **Confirmation bias** causes individuals to, subliminally, give more credence to ideas that support their existing beliefs and **disconfirmation bias** leads them to give more energy to finding arguments to disprove ideas that contradict their current beliefs. To overcome this bias, students must develop insight into their identity's limitations and commit to impartiality.

Major Interpretations of History

There are a number of fundamental ways in which history can be interpreted. The following are the most prevalent when encountering historical texts:

1. **Great figures** emphasizes the impact of individuals on history. The approach is frequently attributed to Plutarch (45–125 CE), who chronicled the lives of well-known Romans and the roles they played in Roman history.
2. **Great challenges** focuses on the rise and fall of great civilizations based on their responses to new ideas, technology, etc. Western Roman civilization and the Eastern Byzantine response to Christianity are examples of this interpretation. British historian Arnold Toynbee (1889–1975) is credited with developing this perspective.
3. **Irresistible forces** proposes that ideas can become movements that eventually overcome prevailing institutions. The civil rights movement of the 1960s and the Muslim sweep of the Arab world are examples. Herbert Spencer (1820–1895) applied Darwin's theory of evolution to societies, showing how they evolved through internal and external conflict. He theorized that the groups and societies that adapt the best lead in the advancement of humankind as a whole.
4. **Dialectical determinism** proposes that old ideas (thesis) will be countered by new ideas and movements (antithesis), and that out of the conflict will come new ideas that are a synthesis. Karl Marx (1818–1893) cast dialectical materialism, proposing that history is primarily a struggle between economic classes.
5. **Geographical determinism** emphasizes the role of geography in history. The effect of climate, natural resources, and being bordered by two oceans on the prosperity and the role of the United States as a world leader cannot be overstated. The African continent's lack of natural harbors and navigable rivers compared with the Americas partially accounts for differences in the development of the two continents. England's development as a sea power is due in large measure to being an island. Frederick Jackson Turner's (1861–1932) "frontier thesis" pegged the two centuries of westward expansion as to why the American democratic ethos was so different from Europe. Free land on the frontier had prevented large estates and had provided an opportunity for whole families to evolve into a large middle class.

The NCSS Themes and C3 History Dimension

The Theme specifically focused on history is Time, Continuity, and Change, but woven through all of history are the other nine Themes.

In the C3 Framework, the authors posit these two crucial concepts:

Historical thinking requires understanding and evaluating change and continuity over time, and making appropriate use of historical evidence in answering questions and developing arguments about the past. It involves going beyond simply asking, "What happened when?" to evaluating why and how events occurred and developments unfolded; and

Historical inquiry involves acquiring knowledge about significant events, developments, individuals, groups, documents, places, and ideas to support investigations about the past. Acquiring relevant knowledge requires assembling information from a wide variety of sources in an integrative process.

(NCSS, 2013, p. 45)

History, like the **pathways** for economics, civics, and geography, is divided into the following four pathways, subdivided by grade level, with multiple **indicators** for each grade level.

Change, Continuity, and Context

Historical thinking requires understanding and evaluating change and continuity over time, and making appropriate use of historical evidence in answering questions and developing arguments about the past as a way to develop students' personal and civic identity. Understanding the interrelation of patterns of change requires bringing together political, economic, intellectual, social, cultural, and other factors so that events, individuals, groups, and developments can be evaluated as a whole so as to assess their significance.

Perspectives

Historical understanding requires recognizing a multiplicity of points of view in the past, which makes it important to seek out a range of sources on any historical question and recognizing that perspectives change over time.

BY THE END OF GRADE 2	BY THE END OF GRADE 5	BY THE END OF GRADE 8	BY THE END OF GRADE 12
INDIVIDUALLY AND WITH OTHERS, STUDENTS…			
D2.His.1.K-2. Create a chronological sequence of multiple events.	**D2.His.1.3-5.** Create and use a chronological sequence of related events to compare developments that happened at the same time.	**D2.His.1.6-8.** Analyze connections among events and developments in broader historical contexts.	**D2.His.1.9-12.** Evaluate how historical events and developments were shaped by unique circumstances of time and place as well as broader historical contexts.
D2.His.2.K-2. Compare life in the past to life today.	**D2.His.2.3-5.** Compare life in specific historical time periods to life today.	**D2.His.2.6-8.** Classify series of historical events and developments as examples of change and/or continuity.	**D2.His.2.9-12.** Analyze change and continuity in historical eras.

Figure 14.1 Change, Continuity, and Context

BY THE END OF GRADE 2	BY THE END OF GRADE 5	BY THE END OF GRADE 8	BY THE END OF GRADE 12
D2.His.3.K-2. Generate questions about individuals and groups who have shaped a significant historical change.	**D2.His.3.3-5.** Generate questions about individuals and groups who have shaped significant historical changes and continuities.	**D2.His.3.6-8.** Use questions generated about individuals and groups to analyze why they, and the developments they shaped, are seen as historically significant.	**D2.His.3.9-12.** Use questions generated about individuals and groups to assess how the significance of their actions changes over time and is shaped

Figure 14.1 (Cont.)

BY THE END OF GRADE 2	BY THE END OF GRADE 5	BY THE END OF GRADE 8	BY THE END OF GRADE 12
INDIVIDUALLY AND WITH OTHERS, STUDENTS…			
D2.His.4.K-2. Compare perspectives of people in the past to those of people in the present.	**D2.His.4.3-5.** Explain why individuals and groups during the same historical period differed in their perspectives.	**D2.His.4.6-8.** Analyze multiple factors that influenced the perspectives of people during different historical eras.	**D2.His.4.9-12.** Analyze complex and interacting factors that influenced the perspectives of people during different historical eras.
Begins in grades 3–5	**D2.His.5.3-5.** Explain connections among historical contexts and people's perspectives at the time.	**D2.His.5.6-8.** Explain how and why perspectives of people have changed over time.	**D2.His.5.9-12.** Analyze how historical contexts shaped and continue to shape people's perspectives.
D2.His.6.K-2. Compare different accounts of the same historical event.	**D2.His.6.3-5.** Describe how people's perspectives shaped the historical sources they created.	**D2.His.6.6-8.** Analyze how people's perspectives influenced what information is available in the historical sources they created.	**D2.His.6.9-12.** Analyze the ways in which the perspectives of those writing history shaped the history that they produced.
Begins in grades 9–12	*Begins in grades 9–12*	*Begins in grades 9–12*	**D2.His.7.9-12.** Explain how the perspectives of people in the present shape interpretations of the past.
Begins in grades 9–12	*Begins in grades 9–12*	*Begins in grades 9–12*	**D2.His.8.9-12.** Analyze how current interpretations of the past are limited by the extent to which available historical sources represent perspectives of people at the time.

Figure 14.2 Perspectives

Historical Sources and Evidence

Historical inquiry is based on materials left from the past that can be analyzed and evaluated so they become evidence in the creation of conclusions.

BY THE END OF GRADE 2	BY THE END OF GRADE 5	BY THE END OF GRADE 8	BY THE END OF GRADE 12
INDIVIDUALLY AND WITH OTHERS, STUDENTS...			
D2.His.9.K-2. Identify different kinds of historical sources.	**D2.His.9.3-5.** Summarize how different kinds of historical sources are used to explain events in the past.	**D2.His.9.6-8.** Classify the kinds of historical sources used in a secondary interpretation.	**D2.His.9.9-12.** Analyze the relationship between historical sources and the secondary interpretations made from them.
D2.His.10.K-2. Explain how historical sources can be used to study the past.	**D2.His.10.3-5.** Compare information provided by different historical sources about the past.	**D2.His.10.6-8.** Detect possible limitations in the historical record based on evidence collected from different kinds of historical sources.	**D2.His.10.9-12.** Detect possible limitations in various kinds of historical evidence and differing secondary interpretations.
D2.His.11.K-2. Identify the maker, date, and place of origin for a historical source from information within the source itself.	**D2.His.11.3-5.** Infer the intended audience and purpose of a historical source from information within the source itself.	**D2.His.11.6-8.** Use other historical sources to infer a plausible maker, date, place of origin, and intended audience for historical sources where this information is not easily identified.	**D2.His.11.9-12.** Critique the usefulness of historical sources for a specific historical inquiry based on their maker, date, place of origin, intended audience, and purpose.
D2.His.12.K-2. Generate questions about a particular historical source as it relates to a particular historical event or development.	**D2.His.12.3-5.** Generate questions about multiple historical sources and their relationships to particular historical events and developments.	**D2.His.12.6-8.** Use questions generated about multiple historical sources to identify further areas of inquiry and additional sources.	**D2.His.12.9-12.** Use questions generated about multiple historical sources to pursue further inquiry and investigate additional sources.
Begins at grade 3–5	**D2.His.13.3-5.** Use information about a historical source, including the maker, date, place of origin, intended audience, and purpose to judge the extent to which the source is useful for studying a particular topic.	**D2.His.13.6-8.** Evaluate the relevancy and utility of a historical source based on information such as maker, date, place of origin, intended audience, and purpose.	**D2.His.13.9-12.** Critique the appropriateness of the historical sources used in a secondary interpretation

Figure 14.3 Historical Sources and Evidence

Causation and Argumentation

Historical thinking involves using evidence and reasoning to draw conclusions about probable causes and effects, recognizing that these are multiple and complex.

BY THE END OF GRADE 2	BY THE END OF GRADE 5	BY THE END OF GRADE 8	BY THE END OF GRADE 12
INDIVIDUALLY AND WITH OTHERS, STUDENTS…			
D2.His.14.K-2. Generate possible reasons for an event or development in the past.	**D2.His.14.3-5.** Explain probable causes and effects of events and developments.	**D2.His.14.6-8.** Explain multiple causes and effects of events and developments in the past.	**D2.His.14.9-12.** Analyze multiple and complex causes and effects of events in the past.
Begins in grades 6–8	*Begins in grades 6–8*	**D2.His.15.6-8.** Evaluate the relative influence of various causes of events and developments in the past.	**D2.His.15.9-12.** Distinguish between long-term causes and triggering events in developing a historical argument.
D2.His.16.K-2. Select which reasons might be more likely than others to explain a historical event or development.	**D2.His.16.3-5.** Use evidence to develop a claim about the past.	**D2.His.16.6-8.** Organize applicable evidence into a coherent argument about the past.	**D2.His.16.9-12.** Integrate evidence from multiple relevant historical sources and interpretations into a reasoned argument about the past.
Begins in grades 3–5	**D2.His.17.3-5.** Summarize the central claim in a secondary work of history.	**D2.His.17.6-8.** Compare the central arguments in secondary works of history on related topics in multiple media.	**D2.His.17.9-12.** Critique the central arguments in secondary works of history on related topics in multiple media in terms of their historical accuracy.

Figure 14.4 Causation and Argumentation

Learned Societies and Standards

The *National Standards for History in Schools*, the "History Standards" (National Center for History in the Schools, 1996), predates the C3 Framework. It has standards for both content and historical thinking. Teaching of history is uniquely tied to the reading of narratives in textbooks and documents and learning to evaluate their meaning (see Chapters 27 and 28). The historical thinking skills in the History Standards are organized into five categories.

History Thinking Standards

1.   Chronological Thinking;
2.   Historical Comprehension;
3.   Historical Analysis and Interpretations;
4.   Historical Research Capabilities;
5.   Historical Issues – Analysis and Decision Making.

At the website (see *Resources*) there are detailed explanations of the critical thinking/procedural knowledge skills that are expected to be taught for each of the five standards. As one example, under "Historical Comprehension," for one of the nine abilities, it states:

> **Appreciate historical perspectives** – the ability (a) describing the past on its own terms, through the eyes and experiences of those who were there, as revealed through their literature, diaries, letters, debates, arts, artifacts, and the like; (b) considering the historical context in which the event unfolded – the values, outlook, options, and contingencies of that time and place; and (c) avoiding "present-mindedness," judging the past solely in terms of present-day norms and values.

The Content Standards

The Content Standards are organized by Grades K-4, World history, and US history. The following are examples from each.

K-4 History Content Standards (has four topics)

Topic 1: Living and Working Together in Families and Communities, Now and Long Ago
   Standard 1: (is divided into 1A and 1B, the following is one example for 1A)
   Family life now and in the recent past; family life in various places long ago.
   Standard 1A: (has five abilities in total, A through E). The following is one example. The student understands family life now and in the recent past; family life in various places long ago. Therefore, the student is able to:

> Investigate a family history for at least two generations, identifying various members and their connections in order to construct a timeline. (Teachers should help students understand that families are people from whom they receive love and support. Understanding that many students are raised in nontraditional family structures–i.e., single-parent families, foster homes, guardians raising children–teachers must be sensitive and protect family privacy.

World History Content Standards (has nine eras)

Era 1: The beginnings of Human Society Giving Shape to World History (has two Standards)
   Standard 1: The biological and cultural processes that gave rise to the earliest human communities (has 1A and 1B).
   Standard 1A: The student understands early hominid development in Africa, therefore the student is able to (has three abilities by grade levels 5–12, 7–12, and 9–12).

Grade 5–12 Infer from archaeological evidence the characteristics of early African hunter-gatherer communities, including tool kits, shelter, diet, and use of fire.

U.S. History Content Standards (has ten eras)

Era 1: Three Worlds Meet (Beginnings to 1620) (has two Standards)
Standard 1: Comparative characteristics of societies in the Americas, Western Europe, and Western Africa that increasingly interacted after 1450.
Standard 1A: The student understands the patterns of change in indigenous societies in the Americas up to the Columbus voyages (has four abilities by grade level 5–12, 7–12, and 9–12).
Grade 5–12: Draw upon data provided by archaeologists and geologists to explain the origins and migration from Asia to the Americas and contrast them with Native Americans' own beliefs concerning their origins in the Americas.

Resources

Videos: *Learner.org*: Social Studies in Action a Teaching Practices Library [elementary]; Historical Change; Explorers in North America; Using Primary Sources [middle school]; Explorations in Archeology & History; Exploring Geography through African History; The Amistad Case [high school]; Public Opinion & the Vietnam War | *Learner.org*: Democracy in America (15 videos); Social Studies in Action a Methodology Workshop K-5 (8 videos); Making Civics Real a Workshop for Teachers (8 videos); The Constitution that Delicate Balance (13 videos) | Story of the Bill of Rights | *BBC* A History of the World in 100 objects | *CrashCourse:* World History; U.S. History; Big History | *History.org* What is Historical Thinking | *Minnesota History Education:* videos for teachers | *Study.com:* History | *TCH*: Reading Like a Historian; Making the French Revolution Meaningful; Social Studies the Kindergarten Experience; Theater Boxes; Historical Detective; Exploring the World of Ancient Civilizations; Inquiry Based Teaching Discussing Nonfiction; Slavery in America Building Background Knowledge; Farming in the Gilded Age a Simulation; Inquiry-based Teaching Powerful Ideas; Peer Teaching (the Civil War); 3 Rs: Revolution, Reaction and Reform | *YouTube*: SHED Reading Like an Historian; What is Historical Thinking; The Problem of History; KS2 History Teaching Chronology.

Documents: Handbook of Research in Social Studies Education: Research on Students' Ideas About History | *American History Association:* Teaching & Learning (A gateway website) | *Annenberg Learner*: Primary Sources Workshop in American History (8 workshops with lesson plans) | *Avalon Project:* primary documents | *BBC bitesize history* [lower elementary grades appropriate videos and documents] | *BCcampus:* open textbooks (US History and World History) | *C3teachers.org:* Inquiry (over 200 C3 inquiry lessons) | *Core Knowledge:* history and geography extensively detailed lesson plans | *This Day in History* | *History Channel:* history classroom | *The History Teacher* (journal) | *Engage NY:* New York State K-12 Social Studies Resources Toolkit [5, K-4, 16, 5–8 & 20, 9–12 grades Inquiry Arc lesson plans] | *Library of Congress:* American Memory | *Hyperhistory* timeline | *National Achieves* History main page | *Library of Congress Teachers* (A gateway website) | *Smithsonian* archives | *Stanford History Education Group:* Reading like an Historian | *Teaching history.org* (videos, lesson plans, history content, and documents) | *World History Archives* | *Readwritethink:* Creating

Family Timelines: Graphing Family Memories and Significant Events; Great American Inventors: Using Nonfiction to Learn About Technology Inventions; Packing the Pilgrim's Trunk: Personalizing History in the Elementary Classroom; Strategic Reading and Writing: Summarizing Antislavery Biographies | *University of Oklahoma:* Exploring U.S. History (a gateway website).

References

Basch, N. (1995). From the bonds of empire to the bonds of matrimony. In D. T. Konig (Ed.), *Devising liberty: Preserving and creating freedom in the new American republic.* (pp. 217–242). Stanford University Press.

Goodheart, E. (2011). On *present-mindedness in the writing of history.* 1st of the Month.org. Retrieved from www.firstofthemonth.org/archives/2011/02/on_presentminde.html.

Little, V. (1983). What is historical imagination. *Teaching History, 36,* 27–32. Retrieved from www.jstor.org/stable/43254801

National Center for History in the Schools. (1996). National standards for history. Retrieved from https://phi.history.ucla.edu/nchs/history-standards/.

NCSS (2013). *Social studies for the next generation: Purposes, practices, and implications of the college, career, and civic Life (C3) framework for social studies state standards: Guidance for enhancing rigor of K-12 civic, economics, geography, and history.* Silver Spring, MD: NCSS. Retrieved from https://www.socialstudies.org/sites/default/files/2017/Jun/c3-framework-for-social-studies-rev0617.pdf

Salmon, M. (1986). *Women and the law of property in early America.* University of North Carolina Press.

Santayana, G. (1905) Reason in common sense. Retrieved from www.gutenberg.org/ebooks/15000.

Wilson, J. H. (1976). The illusion of change. In A. F. Young (Ed.), *The American revolution: Explorations in the history of American radicalism.* (pp. 383–445). Northern Illinois University Press.

15 Economics Education

Economics is the study of money and why it is good.
Woody Allen, Comedian and Playwright, 1935–present (Brockway, 1995, p. 10)

The field of economics appears in Greek political philosophy as a question of ethics, that is, "What is a just price?" That moral question persists today and in many forms in modern society, ranging from questions of poverty to sharing of finite resources on the planet. Economics has also evolved into a complex discipline that relies heavily on students' ability to apply quantitative skills for personal and civic decision-making about personal finance and government policies.

Much of economics since Adam Smith's landmark book, *An Inquiry into the Nature and Causes of the Wealth of Nations* (1776), has focused on a debate about the appropriate role of government in regulation, ownership, and distribution of resources; the best or optimal economic approach to providing adequate opportunity for human potential to be realized; and ensuring sufficient redistribution of wealth to minimize class struggles. The movements from 18th-century mercantilism to laissez-faire policies, John Stuart Mill's proposals for taxation and worker education, and Karl Marx's call for an international workers' revolution are examples of approaches to scarcity and redistribution of wealth.

In *General Theory of Employment, Interest, and Money* (1936/2007), John Maynard Keynes was the first economist to explain the complex cycles of recession, inflation, and unemployment. Keynes proposed an important but limited role for government in the world economy to avert economic problems. The American free enterprise system promotes private ownership of property and production based on consumer demand. The American economy is not a pure free enterprise system; it promotes redistribution of wealth through free public education, graduated tax rates, and government-subsidized housing, medicine, and food. Such activities tend to be characterized as government assistance. The common misstatements such as "The government gives me food stamps" or "The small business administration gives me a low-interest loan for my business" distort and hamper communal attachments because they depersonalize the actual events they describe. It is more precise to say, "My neighbor makes it possible for me to have food stamps," or "My neighbor makes it possible for me to get a low-interest loan for my business." Government bureaucracies, by serving as an intermediary, depersonalize the transaction and veil the goodwill of neighbors needed in a civil society.

The NCSS Themes and the C3 Economics Dimensions

The Theme specifically focused on economics is production, distribution, and consumption, but economics is intertwined with all ten of the NCSS Themes.

In the C3 Framework for the civics pathway, the authors state, "Effective economic decision-making requires that students have a keen understanding of the ways in which individuals, businesses, governments, and societies make decisions to allocate human capital, physical capital, and natural resources among alternative uses" (NCSS, 2013, p. 35). The C3 Framework for economics is divided into the following four pathways.

Economic Decision-Making

People make decisions about how to use scarce resources to maximize the well-being of individuals and society. Alternative ways to use the resources are investigated in terms of their advantages and disadvantages and the incentives that motivate people.

Exchange and Markets

People voluntarily exchange goods and services when both parties expect to gain as a result of the trade. Markets exist to facilitate the exchange of goods and services. When buyers and sellers interact in well-functioning, competitive markets, prices are determined that reflect the relative scarcity of the goods and services in the market. The principles of markets apply to markets for goods and services, labor, credit, foreign exchange, and others. Comparison of benefits and costs helps identify the circumstances under which government action in markets is in the best interest of society and when it is not.

BY THE END OF GRADE 2	BY THE END OF GRADE 5	BY THE END OF GRADE 8	BY THE END OF GRADE 12
INDIVIDUALLY AND WITH OTHERS, STUDENTS...			
D2.Eco.1.K-2. Explain how scarcity necessitates decision making.	**D2.Eco.1.3-5.** Compare the benefits and costs of individual choices.	**D2.Eco.1.6-8.** Explain how economic decisions affect the well-being of individuals, businesses, and society.	**D2.Eco.1.9-12.** Analyze how incentives influence choices that may result in policies with a range of costs and benefits for different groups.
D2.Eco.2.K-2. Identify the benefits and costs of making various personal decisions.	**D2.Eco.2.3-5.** Identify positive and negative incentives that influence the decisions people make.	**D2.Eco.2.6-8.** Evaluate alternative approaches or solutions to current economic issues in terms of benefits and costs for different groups and society as a whole.	**D2.Eco.2.9-12.** Use marginal benefits and marginal costs to construct an argument for or against an approach or solution to an economic issue.

Figure 15.1 Economic Decision-Making

BY THE END OF GRADE 2	BY THE END OF GRADE 5	BY THE END OF GRADE 8	BY THE END OF GRADE 12
INDIVIDUALLY AND WITH OTHERS, STUDENTS...			
D2.Eco.3.K-2. Describe the skills and knowledge required to produce certain goods and services.	**D2.Eco.3.3-5.** Identify examples of the variety of resources (human capital, physical capital, and natural resources) that are used to produce goods and services.	**D2.Eco.3.6-8.** Explain the roles of buyers and sellers in product, labor, and financial markets.	**D2.Eco.3.9-12.** Analyze the ways in which incentives influence what is produced and distributed in a market system.
D2.Eco.4.K-2. Describe the goods and services that people in the local community produce and those that are produced in other communities.	**D2.Eco.4.3-5.** Explain why individuals and businesses specialize and trade.	**D2.Eco.4.6-8.** Describe the role of competition in the determination of prices and wages in a market economy.	**D2.Eco.4.9-12.** Evaluate the extent to which competition among sellers and among buyers exists in specific markets.
D2.Eco.5.K-2. Identify prices of products in a local market.	**D2.Eco.5.3-5.** Explain the role of money in making exchange easier.	**D2.Eco.5.6-8.** Explain ways in which money facilitates exchange by reducing transactional costs.	**D2.Eco.5.9-12.** Describe the consequences of competition in specific markets.
D2.Eco.6.K-2. Explain how people earn income.	**D2.Eco.6.3-5.** Explain the relationship between investment in human capital, productivity, and future incomes.	**D2.Eco.6.6-8.** Explain how changes in supply and demand cause changes in prices and quantities of goods and services, labor, credit, and foreign currencies.	**D2.Eco.6.9-12.** Generate possible explanations for a government role in markets when market inefficiencies exist.
D2.Eco.7.K-2. Describe examples of costs of production.	**D2.Eco.7.3-5.** Explain how profits influence sellers in markets.	**D2.Eco.7.6-8.** Analyze the role of innovation and entrepreneurship in a market economy.	**D2.Eco.7.9-12.** Use benefits and costs to evaluate the effectiveness of government policies to improve market outcomes.
Begins in grades 3-5	**D2.Eco.8.3-5.** Identify examples of external benefits and costs.	**D2.Eco.8.6-8.** Explain how external benefits and costs influence market outcomes.	**D2.Eco.8.9-12.** Describe the possible consequences, both intended and unintended, of government policies to improve market outcomes.
D2.Eco.9.K-2. Describe the role of banks in an economy.	**D2.Eco.9.3-5.** Describe the role of other financial institutions in an economy.	**D2.Eco.9.6-8.** Describe the roles of institutions such as corporations, non-profits, and labor unions in a market economy.	**D2.Eco.9.9-12.** Describe the roles of institutions such as clearly defined property rights and the rule of law in a market economy.

Figure 15.2 Exchange and Markets

The National Economy

Changes in the amounts and qualities of human capital, physical capital, and natural resources influence economic conditions and standards of living. Monetary and fiscal policies are often designed and used in attempts to moderate fluctuations and encourage growth. Policies changing the growth in the money supply and overall levels of spending in the economy are aimed at reducing inflationary or deflationary pressures; increasing employment or decreasing unemployment levels; and increasing economic growth over time.

The Global Economy

Economic globalization occurs with cross-border movement of goods, services, technology, information, and human, physical, and financial capital. While trade provides

BY THE END OF GRADE 2	BY THE END OF GRADE 5	BY THE END OF GRADE 8	BY THE END OF GRADE 12
INDIVIDUALLY AND WITH OTHERS, STUDENTS…			
D2.Eco.10.K-2. Explain why people save.	**D2.Eco.10.3-5.** Explain what interest rates are.	**D2.Eco.10.6-8.** Explain the influence of changes in interest rates on borrowing and investing.	**D2.Eco.10.9-12.** Use current data to explain the influence of changes in spending, production, and the money supply on various economic conditions.
Begins in grades 3–5	**D2.Eco.11.3-5.** Explain the meaning of inflation, deflation, and unemployment.	**D2.Eco.11.6-8.** Use appropriate data to evaluate the state of employment, unemployment, inflation, total production, income, and economic growth in the economy.	**D2.Eco.11.9-12.** Use economic indicators to analyze the current and future state of the economy.
D2.Eco.12.K-2. Describe examples of the goods and services that governments provide.	**D2.Eco.12.3-5.** Explain the ways in which the government pays for the goods and services it provides.	**D2.Eco.12.6-8.** Explain how inflation, deflation, and unemployment affect different groups.	**D2.Eco.12.9-12.** Evaluate the selection of monetary and fiscal policies in a variety of economic conditions.
D2.Eco.13.K-2. Describe examples of capital goods and human capital.	**D2.Eco.13.3-5.** Describe ways people can increase productivity by using improved capital goods and improving their human capital.	**D2.Eco.13.6-8.** Explain why standards of living increase as productivity improves.	**D2.Eco.13.9-12.** Explain why advancements in technology and investments in capital goods and human capital increase economic growth and standards of living.

Figure 15.3 The National Economy

significant benefits, it is not without costs. Comparing those benefits and costs is essential in evaluating policies to influence trade among individuals and businesses in different countries.

Learned Societies and Standards

The Council for Economic Education (NCEE) has published two documents that are valuable to a deep understanding of economics needed by teachers: The *National Standards for Financial Literacy* (2003) and the *Voluntary National Content Standards in Economics* (2nd edition, 2010). Each comes with standards and benchmarks organized at grades 4, 8, and 12. At no cost, PDF documents of these standards with details and an elaboration of benchmarks can be downloaded from the website. The following summaries are provided for a basic explanation of what constitutes financial literacy by grade level. At the website, there are multiple, creative, compressive lesson plans for each standard at each grade level (see *References*).

The national economic standards (Figure 15.6) have more detailed and numerous benchmarks than the financial literacy standards. PDF documents of the standards and an elaboration of the benchmarks can be downloaded from the website as well as multiple lesson plans on how to teach to each standard and benchmark (see *Resources*).

BY THE END OF GRADE 2	BY THE END OF GRADE 5	BY THE END OF GRADE 8	BY THE END OF GRADE 12
INDIVIDUALLY AND WITH OTHERS, STUDENTS...			
D2.Eco.14.K-2. Describe why people in one country trade goods and services with people in other countries.	**D2.Eco.14.3-5.** Explain how trade leads to increasing economic inter-dependence among nations.	**D2.Eco.14.6-8.** Explain barriers to trade and how those barriers influence trade among nations.	**D2.Eco.14.9-12.** Analyze the role of comparative advantage in international trade of goods and services.
D2.Eco.15.K-2. Describe products that are produced abroad and sold domestically and products that are produced domestically and sold abroad.	**D2.Eco.15.3-5.** Explain the effects of increasing economic interdependence on different groups within participating nations.	**D2.Eco.15.6-8.** Explain the benefits and the costs of trade policies to individuals, businesses, and society.	**D2.Eco.15.9-12.** Explain how current globalization trends and policies affect economic growth, labor markets, rights of citizens, the environment, and resource and income distribution in different nations.

Figure 15.4 The Global Economy

Standard	By 4th Grade	By 8th Grade	By End of 12th Grade
1. Earning Income. This standard focuses on income earned or received by people	Different types of jobs as well as different forms of income earned or received.	Benefits and costs of increasing income through the acquisition of education and skills.	Types of income and taxes, highlights bene-fit-cost decisions related to jobs and careers, and introduces labor markets
II. Buying Goods and Services.	Scarcity, choice, and opportunity cost. Factors that influence spending choices, such as advertising, peer pressure, and spending choices of others, are analyzed. Attention is given to comparing the costs and benefits of spending decisions. The basics of budgeting and planning are introduced	Continued	Consumer's decision using economic ideas such as satisfaction, determinants of demand, costs of information search, choice of product durability and other features, and the role of government and other institutions in providing information for consumers.
III. Saving.	How people save money, where people can save money, and why people save money, as well as the concept of interest.	The role that financial institutions, the role of markets in determining interest rates and the mathematics of saving	Real versus nominal interest rates, present versus future value, financial regulators, the factors determining the value of a person's savings over time, automatic savings plans, "rainy-day" funds, and saving for retirement.
IV. Using Credit.	Credit and the cost of using credit namely, the obligation to repay what is borrowed plus interest Students should recognize that a reputation for repaying loans contributes to a person's ability to obtain loans in the future.	Why people use credit, the sources of credit, why interest rates vary across borrowers, and the reasons for using credit to invest in education and durable goods. Students should be able to make basic calculations related to borrowing, including principal and interest payments as well as compound interest	Behaviors that contribute to strong credit reports and scores. Consumer protection laws as they apply to credit and credit card use are also covered.
V. Financial Investing.	Investment means using resources to expand an individual's or business's abilities to produce in the future.	The variety of possible financial investments and be able to calculate rates of return.	Relevance of and to calculate real and after-tax rates of return
VI. Protecting and Insuring.	Financial risk and learn that individuals can reduce that risk by altering their behavior to reduce the likelihood and size of a loss	Risk associated with identity theft.	Health, property/casualty, disability, and life insurance products.

Figure 15.5 The National Standards for Financial Literacy

Standards	Students will Understand that:	Students will be able to:
1. Scarcity	Productive resources are limited. Therefore, people can not have all the goods and services they want; as a result, they must choose some things and give up others.	Identify what they gain and what they give up when they make choices.
2. Decision Making	Effective decision making requires comparing the additional costs of alternatives with the additional benefits. Many choices involve doing a little more or a little less of something: few choices are "all or nothing" decisions.	Make effective decisions as consumers, producers, savers, investors, and citizens.
3. Allocation	Different methods can be used to allocate goods and services. People acting individually or collectively must choose which methods to use to allocate different kinds of goods and services.	Evaluate different methods of allocating goods and services, by comparing the benefits to the costs of each method.
4. Incentives	People usually respond predictably to positive and negative incentives.	Identify incentives that affect people's behavior and explain how incentives affect their own behavior.
5. Trade	Voluntary exchange occurs only when all participating parties expect to gain. This is true for trade among individuals or organizations within a nation, and among individuals or organizations in different nations.	Negotiate exchanges and identify the gains to themselves and others. Compare the benefits and costs of policies that alter trade barriers between nations, such as tariffs and quotas.
6. Specialization	When individuals, regions, and nations specialize in what they can produce at the lowest cost and then trade with others, both production and consumption increase.	Explain how they can benefit themselves and others by developing special skills and strengths.
7. Markets and Prices	A market exists when buyers and sellers interact. This interaction determines market prices and thereby allocates scarce goods and services.	Identify markets in which they have participated as a buyer and as a seller and describe how the interaction of all buyers and sellers influences prices. Also, predict how prices change when there is either a shortage or surplus of the product available.
8. Role of Prices	Prices send signals and provide incentives to buyers and sellers. When supply or demand changes, market prices adjust, affecting incentives.	Predict how changes in factors such as consumers' tastes or producers' technology affect prices

Figure 15.6 The Voluntary National Content Standards in Economics

9. Competition and Market Structure	Competition among sellers usually lowers costs and prices, and encourages producers to produce what consumers are willing and able to buy. Competition among buyers increases prices and allocates goods and services to those people who are willing and able to pay the most for them.	Explain how changes in the level of competition in different markets can affect price and output levels.
10. Institutions	Institutions evolve and are created to help individuals and groups accomplish their goals. Banks, labor unions, markets, corporations, legal systems, and not-for-profit organizations are examples of important institutions. A different kind of institution, clearly defined and enforced property rights, is essential to a market economy.	Describe the roles of various economic institutions and explain the importance of property rights in a market economy.
11. Money and Inflation	Money makes it easier to trade, borrow, save, invest, and compare the value of goods and services. The amount of money in the economy affects the overall price level. Inflation is an increase in the overall price level that reduces the value of money	Explain how their lives would be more difficult in a world with no money, or in a world where money sharply lost its value.
12. Interest Rates	Interest rates, adjusted for inflation, rise and fall to balance the amount saved with the amount borrowed, which affects the allocation of scarce resources between present and future uses.	Explain situations in which they pay or receive interest, and explain how they would react to changes in interest rates if they were making or receiving interest payments.
13. Income	Income for most people is determined by the market value of the productive resources they sell. What workers earn primarily depends on the market value of what they produce.	Predict future earnings based on their current plans for education, training, and career options.
14. Entrepreneurship	Entrepreneurs take on the calculated risk of starting new businesses, either by embarking on new ventures similar to existing ones or by introducing new innovations. Entrepreneurial innovation is an important source of economic growth.	Identify the risks and potential returns to entrepreneurship, as well as the skills necessary to engage in it. Understand the importance of entrepreneurship and innovation to economic growth, and how public policies affect incentives for and, consequently, the success of entrepreneurship in the United States.

Figure 15.6 (Cont.)

15. Economic Growth	Investment in factories, machinery, new technology, and in the health, education, and training of people stimulates economic growth and can raise future standards of living.	Predict the consequences of investment decisions made by individuals, businesses, and governments.
16. Role of Government and Market Failure	There is an economic role for government in a market economy whenever the benefits of a government policy outweigh its costs. Governments often provide for national defense, address environmental concerns, define and protect property rights, and attempt to make markets more competitive. Most government policies also have direct or indirect effects on people's incomes	Identify and evaluate the benefits and costs of alternative public policies, and assess who enjoys the benefits and who bears the costs.
17. Government Failure	Costs of government policies sometimes exceed benefits. This may occur because of incentives facing voters, government officials, and government employees, because of actions by special interest groups that can impose costs on the general public, or because social goals other than economic efficiency are being pursued.	Identify some public policies that may cost more than the benefits they generate, and assess who enjoys the benefits and who bears the costs. Explain why the policies exist.
18. Economic Fluctuations	Unemployment imposes costs on individuals and the overall economy. Inflation, both expected and unexpected, also imposes costs on individuals and the overall economy. Unemployment increases during recessions and decreases during recoveries.	Make informed decisions by anticipating the consequences of inflation and unemployment.
19. Unemployment and Inflation	Unemployment imposes costs on individuals and the overall economy. Inflation, both expected and unexpected, also imposes costs on individuals and the overall economy. Unemployment increases during recessions and decreases during recoveries.	Make informed decisions by anticipating the consequences of inflation and unemployment.
20. Fiscal and Monetary Policy	Federal government budgetary policy and the Federal Reserve System's monetary policy influence the overall levels of employment, output, and prices.	Anticipate the impact of federal government and Federal Reserve System macroeconomic policy decisions on themselves and others.

Figure 15.6 (Cont.)

Resources

Videos: *Learner.org*: Economics U$A: 21st Century Edition (30 videos); Social Studies in Action a Teaching Practices Library Series [elementary]; Making Bread Together [middle school]; Population and Resource Distribution [high school]; Economic Dilemmas and Solutions | *CrashCourse:* Economics | *Kahn Academy:* Economics & Finance | *Study.com:* Social Science Courses | *Wetheeconomy* (24 comical videos that explain economics).

Documents: *Routledge Handbook of Research in Social Studies Education*: Recent Research on the Teaching and Learning of Pre-collegiate Economics | *Annenberg Learner* Workshop: The Economics Classroom (8 video workshops with lesson plans) | *C3teachers.org* Inquiry [28 economics inquiry lessons] | *Econedlink Resources*: (over 900 excellent lesson plans, videos, and activities) | *FDIC* teacher online resource center (lesson plans, videos, and simulations) | Capitalism.org | *Federal Reserve* home page | *Federal Reserve Bank of Philadelphia* lesson plans for teachers; The American Currency Exhibit | *Journal of Economics Education* | *Journal of Economics Teaching* | *Practical Money Skills* (lesson plans and interactive activities) | *McMaster University* Archive for the History of Economic Thought | *ReadWriteThink:* Finding Fabulous Financial Literacy Vocabulary With Fancy Nancy| Stock Market Game | *USmint for Kids* | United States Mint for Kids (9 videos, games, etc.).

References

Brockway, G. P. (1995). *The end of economic man*. W. W. Norton & Company.
Keynes, J. M. (1936/2007). *General theory of employment, interest, and money*. Macmillan.
NCSS. (2013). *Social studies for the next generation: Purposes, practices, and implications of the college, career, and civic Life (C3) framework for social studies state standards: Guidance for enhancing rigor of K-12 civic, economics, geography, and history*. Silver Spring, MD: NCSS. Retrieved from https://www.socialstudies.org/sites/default/files/2017/Jun/c3-framework-for-social-studies-rev0617.pdf
Smith, A. (1776). *An inquiry into the nature and causes of the wealth of nations*. Retrieved from www.gutenberg.org/ebooks/3300.
The Council for Economic Education. (2003). *National standards for financial literacy*. Retrieved from www.councilforeconed.org/resource/national-standards-for-financial-literacy/#sthash.6qXZoxOf.dpbs. Copyright © 2013 Council for Economic Education, permission granted.
The Council for Economic Education. (2010). *Voluntary national content standards in economics* (2nd ed.). Retrieved from www.councilforeconed.org/resource/voluntary-national-content-standards-in-economics/#sthash.J2Ecams1.dpbs. Copyright © 2010 Council for Economic Education.

16 Geography Education

War is God's way of teaching us geography.
Paul Rodriguez, Comedian, 1955–present (Christon, 1987, p. 7)

Maps are so central to geography that they are often the first thing to come to mind when someone thinks of geography. Regrettably, for many students the drudgery of memorizing facts about states or countries also comes to mind when geography is mentioned. One only needs to visit the National Geographic website to quickly move on from this limited appreciation of geography and to see how it can affect students' understanding of the world.

The Five Geography Themes

In 1984, the Joint Committee on Geographic Education's publication, *Guidelines for Geographic Education*, was a landmark report in the national reform movement in geography education. The most enduring contribution of the Guidelines has been the articulation of the **Five Themes of Geography**. The Five Themes of Geography (see Boehm & Peterson, 1994 for an in-depth explanation) is an organizing scheme for how teachers can structure lessons. The Themes are organized around the following concepts:

Location refers to the absolute location, usually determined by use of latitude and longitude coordinates, of places and people on Earth. Location also refers to relative location determined by associating a particular place with other places (near to, for example, or a short drive from). Before any geographic analysis or higher-order thinking can take place, it is essential to know the location of the place one is trying to understand.

Place refers to the describable physical and human characteristics of places. All places on Earth have distinctive tangible and intangible characteristics that give them meaning and character and distinguish them from other places. Using observation and description, the themes of location and place set the stage for further geographic analysis.

Human–environment interaction refers to how people interact with particular places. All places on Earth have advantages and disadvantages for human settlement. This theme encourages the study of the modification and transformation of environments by human and physical causes and the effects of physical features on the lives of people.

Movement refers to people interacting with each other on Earth. Humans occupy places unevenly on Earth, but they interact with each other through the transportation of commodities and through travel, trade, information flows, and political events. This theme also concentrates on the patterns of human migration and the movement of ideas from one place to another.

Regions are a basic unit of geography study. A region is an area that displays a coherent unity in terms of specific criteria, such as a governmental unit, a language group, or a landform type. Regions are human constructs, and they can be mapped and analyzed.

The NCSS Themes and the C3 Geography Dimensions

The NCSS Themes most aligned with the breadth of geography are culture, people, places, and environments and global connections. Geography education at the elementary education level often starts by using the school, neighborhood, and the city where children live to begin teaching the geography concepts. A scavenger hunt in school so students learn how to read and follow a map and birds-eye view of the school's floor plan can be used to expose students to reading a map. At the middle and high school level, the geography themes often emerge as stand-alone geography chapters in history textbooks or are laced through topics in history courses where location becomes a key part of the story. Technology applications via the internet such as Google Earth create more options for what and how to teach geography.

In the geography pathways of the C3 Framework, the authors state

> Geographic reasoning rests on deep knowledge of Earth's physical and human features, including the locations of places and regions, the distribution of landforms and water bodies, and historic changes in political boundaries, economic activities, and cultures. Geographic reasoning requires using spatial and environmental perspectives, skills in asking and answering questions, and being able to apply geographic representations including maps, imagery, and geospatial technologies.
>
> (NCSS, 2013, p. 40)

Geography is divided into the following four pathways.

Geographic Representations: Spatial Views of the World

Creating maps and using geospatial technologies requires a process of answering geographic questions by gathering relevant information; organizing and analyzing the information; and using effective means to communicate the findings. Once a map or other representation is created, it prompts new questions concerning the locations, spaces, and patterns portrayed. Creating maps and other geographical representations is an essential part of seeking new geographic knowledge that is personally and socially useful and that can be applied in making decisions and solving problems.

Human–Environment Interaction: Place, Regions, and Culture

Human–environment interactions are essential aspects of human life in all societies and they occur at local-to-global scales. Culture influences the locations and the types of interactions that occur.

BY THE END OF GRADE 2	BY THE END OF GRADE 5	BY THE END OF GRADE 8	BY THE END OF GRADE 12
INDIVIDUALLY AND WITH OTHERS, STUDENTS...			
D2.Geo.1.K-2. Construct maps, graphs, and other representations of familiar places.	D2.Geo.1.3–5. Construct maps and other graphic representations of both familiar and unfamiliar places.	D2.Geo.1.6–8. Construct maps to represent and explain the spatial patterns of cultural and environmental characteristics.	D2.Geo.1.9–12. Use geospatial and related technologies to create maps to display and explain the spatial patterns of cultural and environmental characteristics.
D2.Geo.2.K-2. Use maps, graphs, photographs, and other representations to describe places and the relationships and interactions that shape them.	D2.Geo.2.3–5. Use maps, satellite images, photographs, and other representations to explain relationships between the locations of places and regions and their environmental characteristics.	D2.Geo.2.6–8. Use maps, satellite images, photographs, and other representations to explain relationships between the locations of places and regions, and changes in their environmental characteristics.	D2.Geo.2.9–12. Use maps, satellite images, photographs, and other representations to explain relationships between the locations of places and regions and their political, cultural, and economic dynamics.
D2.Geo.3.K-2. Use maps, globes, and other simple geographic models to identify cultural and environmental characteristics of places.	D2.Geo.3.3–5. Use maps of different scales to describe the locations of cultural and environmental characteristics.	D2.Geo.3.6–8. Use paper-based and electronic mapping and graphing techniques to represent and analyze spatial patterns of different environmental and cultural characteristics.	D2.Geo.3.9–12. Use geographic data to analyze variations in the spatial patterns of cultural and environmental characteristics at multiple scales.

Figure 16.1 Geographic Representations: Spatial Views of the World

BY THE END OF GRADE 2	BY THE END OF GRADE 5	BY THE END OF GRADE 8	BY THE END OF GRADE 12
INDIVIDUALLY AND WITH OTHERS, STUDENTS...			
D2.Geo.4.K-2. Explain how weather, climate, and other environmental characteristics affect people's lives in a place or region.	D2.Geo.4.3–5. Explain how culture influences the way people modify and adapt to their environments.	D2.Geo.4.6–8. Explain how cultural patterns and economic decisions influence environments and the daily lives of people in both nearby and distant places.	D2.Geo.4.9–12. Analyze relationships and interactions within and between human and physical systems to explain reciprocal influences that occur among them.

Figure 16.2 Human–Environment Interaction: Place, Regions, and Culture

D2.Geo.5.K-2. Describe how human activities affect the cultural and environmental characteristics of places or regions.	**D2.Geo.5.3–5.** Explain how the cultural and environmental characteristics of places change over time.	**D2.Geo.5.6–8.** Analyze the combinations of cultural and environmental characteristics that make places both similar to and different from other places.	**D2.Geo.5.9–12.** Evaluate how political and economic decisions throughout time have influenced cultural and environmental characteristics of various places and regions.
D2.Geo.6.K-2. Identify some cultural and environmental characteristics of specific places.	**D2.Geo.6.3–5.** Describe how environmental and cultural characteristics influence population distribution in specific places or regions.	**D2.Geo.6.6–8.** Explain how the physical and human characteristics of places and regions are connected to human identities and cultures.	**D2.Geo.6.9–12.** Evaluate the impact of human settlement activities on the environmental and cultural characteristics of specific places and regions.

Figure 16.2 (Cont.)

BY THE END OF GRADE 2	BY THE END OF GRADE 5	BY THE END OF GRADE 8	BY THE END OF GRADE 12
INDIVIDUALLY AND WITH OTHERS, STUDENTS...			
D2.Geo.7.K-2. Explain why and how people, goods, and ideas move from place to place.	**D2.Geo.7.3–5.** Explain how cultural and environmental characteristics affect the distribution and movement of people, goods, and ideas.	**D2.Geo.7.6–8.** Explain how changes in transportation and communication technology influence the spatial connections among human settlements and affect the diffusion of ideas and cultural practices.	**D2.Geo.7.9–12.** Analyze the reciprocal nature of how historical events and the spatial diffusion of ideas, technologies, and cultural practices have influenced migration patterns and the distribution of human population.
D2.Geo.8.K-2. Compare how people in different types of communities use local and distant environments to meet their daily needs.	**D2.Geo.8.3–5.** Explain how human settlements and movements relate to the locations and use of various natural resources.	**D2.Geo.8.6–8.** Analyze how relationships between humans and environments extend or contract spatial patterns of settlement and movement.	**D2.Geo.8.9–12.** Evaluate the impact of economic activities and political decisions on spatial patterns within and among urban, suburban, and rural regions.
D2.Geo.9.K-2. Describe the connections between the physical environment of a place and the economic activities found there.	**D2.Geo.9.3–5.** Analyze the effects of catastrophic environmental and technological events on human settlements and migration.	**D2.Geo.9.6–8.** Evaluate the influences of long-term human-induced environmental change on spatial patterns of conflict and cooperation.	**D2.Geo.9.9–12.** Evaluate the influence of long-term climate variability on human migration and settlement patterns, resource use, and land uses at local-to-global scales.

Figure 16.3 Human Population: Spatial Patterns and Movements

Human Population: Spatial Patterns and Movements

The size, composition, expansion, distribution, and movement of human populations are fundamental, ongoing features on Earth's surface. Past, present, and future conditions on Earth's surface cannot be fully understood without asking and answering questions about the spatial patterns of human population.

Global Interconnections: Changing Spatial Patterns

Global interconnections occur in both human and physical systems. Earth is a set of interconnected ecosystems of which humans are an influential part. Humans have spread across the planet, along with their cultural practices, artifacts, languages, diseases, and other attributes. All of these interconnections create complex spatial patterns at multiple scales (regions such as the Mississippi river delta to small ecosystems such as a pond adjacent to a school) that continue to change over time.

BY THE END OF GRADE 2	BY THE END OF GRADE 5	BY THE END OF GRADE 8	BY THE END OF GRADE 12
INDIVIDUALLY AND WITH OTHERS, STUDENTS...			
D2.Geo.10.K-2. Describe changes in the physical and cultural characteristics of various world regions.	D2.Geo.10.3–5. Explain why environmental characteristics vary among different world regions.	D2.Geo.10.6–8. Analyze the ways in which cultural and environmental characteristics vary among various regions of the world.	D2.Geo.10.9–12. Evaluate how changes in the environmental and cultural characteristics of a place or region influence spatial patterns of trade and land use.
D2.Geo.11.K-2. Explain how the consumption of products connects people to distant places.	D2.Geo.11.3–5. Describe how the spatial patterns of economic activities in a place change over time because of interactions with nearby and distant places.	D2.Geo.11.6–8. Explain how the relationship between the environmental characteristics of places and production of goods influences the spatial patterns of world trade.	D2.Geo.11.9–12. Evaluate how economic globalization and the expanding use of scarce resources contribute to conflict and cooperation within and among countries.
D2.Geo.12.K-2. Identify ways that a catastrophic disaster may affect people living in a place.	D2.Geo.12.3–5. Explain how natural and human-made catastrophic events in one place affect people living in other places.	D2.Geo.12.6–8. Explain how global changes in population distribution patterns affect changes in land use in particular places.	D2.Geo.12.9–12. Evaluate the consequences of human-made and natural catastrophes on global trade, politics, and human migration.

Figure 16.4 Global Interconnections: Changing Spatial Patterns

Learned Societies and Standards

In 1994, and revised in 2012, the National Council for Geographic Education (NCGE, 1994/2012) published *Geography for Life: National Geography Standards*. The goal was to set standards where students would "do" geography. It established the 18 standards listed below. One of the best ways to understand the standards in depth is to visit the National Geographic website and search for "national geography standards." At the website, the standards are organized with benchmarks by 4th, 8th, and 12th grades. In addition, at National Geographic's "Classroom Resources," teacher candidates can sort by grade level the most extensive set of lesson plans and ancillaries for geography education found on the internet.

The 18 National Geography Standards

The World in Spatial Terms

Standard 1: How to use maps and other geographic representations, tools, and technologies to acquire, process, and report information.
Standard 2: How to use mental maps to organize information about people, places, and environments.
Standard 3: How to analyze the spatial organization of people, places, and environments on Earth's surface.

Places and Regions

Standard 4: The physical and human characteristics of places.
Standard 5: That people create regions to interpret Earth's complexity.
Standard 6: How culture and experience influence people's perception of places and regions.

Physical Systems

Standard 7: The physical processes that shape the patterns of Earth's surface.
Standard 8: The characteristics and spatial distribution of ecosystems on Earth's surface.

Human Systems

Standard 9: The characteristics, distribution, and migration of human populations on Earth's surface.
Standard 10: The characteristics, distributions, and complexity of Earth's cultural mosaics.
Standard 11: The patterns and networks of economic interdependence on Earth's surface.

Standard 12: The process, patterns, and functions of human settlement.
Standard 13: How forces of cooperation and conflict among people influence the division and control of Earth's surface.

Environment and Society

Standard 14: How human actions modify the physical environment.
Standard 15: How physical systems affect human systems.
Standard 16: The changes that occur in the meaning, use, distribution, and importance of resources.

The Uses of Geography

Standard 17: How to apply geography to interpret the past.
Standard 18: To apply geography to interpret the present and plan for the future.

Resources

Videos: *Learner.org:* Social Studies in Action a Teaching Practices Library Series [elementary]; China Through Mapping; Celebration of Light; California Missions [middle school]; Exploring Geography Through African History; Population & Resource Distribution [high school]; The Middle East Conflict; Migration from Latin America | *National Geographic:* (The most extensive geography lesson plans and videos on the internet) | *Smithsonian:* Learning Lab Collections | *Study.com:* Geography | *TCH or YouTube:* Document-Based Questions Warm & Cool feedback; Exploring Emigration Maps & Migration; Geography with a Sensory Approach; History of the Earth | *YouTube:* 101 Videos National Geographic.

Documents: Handbook of Research in Social Studies Education (Research on K-12 Geography Education) | *C3teachers.org:* Inquiry (27 Geography Inquiry lessons) | *CIA* Fact Book | Council for Geographic Education | *David Rumsey:* Map Collection | *The Geography Teacher* [journal] | *Library of Congress:* Digital Map Collection; Geography & Map Reading Room | *National Geographic:* Education | *National map.gov* | *Perry-Castañeda Library* Map Collection | *ReadWriteThink:* Travel Brochures; Highlighting the Setting of a Story | U.S. Geography Lesson Plans and Resources | *USGS.gov:* National Atlas | U.S. Census Data | World Geography Educational Resources and Lesson plans.

References

Boehm, R. C., & Peterson, J. F. (1994). An elaboration of the fundamental themes in geography. *Social Education*, 58(4), 211–218. Retrieved from www.socialstudies.org/sites/default/files/publications/se/5804/580402.html

Christon, L. (1987). Comic relief: An HBO tradition: Comedians weave laughter into plea for homeless at amphitheatre. *Los Angeles Times*, Nov. 16, p.7.

National Council for Geographic Education. (1987). *Geographic education national implementation project: K-6 geography: Themes, key ideas, and learning opportunities.* Western Illinois University.

National Council for Geographic Education. (1994). *Geography for life: National geography standards.* NCGE.

National Council for Geographic Education. (1994/2012). *Life: National geography standards.* Revised 2012. NCGE. Retrieved from http://ncge.org/geography-for-life.

NCSS. (2013). *Social studies for the next generation: Purposes, practices, and implications of the college, career, and civic Life (C3) framework for social studies state standards: Guidance for enhancing rigor of K-12 civic, economics, geography, and history.* Silver Spring, MD: NCSS. Retrieved from https://www.socialstudies.org/sites/default/files/2017/Jun/c3-framework-for-social-studies-rev0617.pdf

17 Elementary Grades Social Studies and the Social Sciences

The greatest sign of success for a teacher is to be able to say, "The children are now working as if I did not exist."
Maria Montessori, Italian Physician and Educator, 1870–1952 (Cummings, 2000, p. 2)

The C3 Framework focuses its attention on the core social studies teaching fields of history, geography, economics, and civics (NCSS, 2013). In the appendix of the C3 booklet and aimed at high school level courses (see later in this chapter), the NCSS also provides guidance on three social sciences courses: anthropology, psychology, and sociology. These three social sciences are most closely associated with the NCSS Themes (2013), Culture, Individual, Development and Identity, and Individuals, Groups, and Institutions. The following are just two ideas where integration with the humanities such as art (historical paintings or art projects), music (patriotic or period songs), and language arts (trade books and literature) is possible.

The third grade C3 Framework lesson plan "Symbols" (see EngageNY, 2020) could easily be integrated with drawing, writing, and poetry. The Core Knowledge "Colossal Structures & Sculptures" unit plan (see Core Knowledge, 2020b) is six, one-hour lessons focused on visual arts from the Pantheon to Mt. Rushmore.

At the secondary level, *The History Teacher* journal has a lesson plan using the short story, "Desiree's Baby" that could be integrated into an American history lesson or current events lesson on racism (see Duplass & Cruz, 2009). At CarolinaK12, teachers have created a comprehensive, 47-page lesson "The Vietnam War and Protest Music" where students examine music of the 1960s as part of studying the Vietnam period.

(see CarolinaK12, 2020)

Elementary Grades Content Sequence

Typically, there is one social studies textbook at each grade in elementary education, as opposed to separate textbooks for each subject area as there are at the secondary level. Because each state's standards vary from the nationally produced textbooks, elementary teachers often have to improvise by finding content and lesson plans on the internet. The NCSS provides resources for elementary school teachers through a journal, *Social Studies & The Young Learner* (2020b). At the website cited in the reference, there are numerous, excellent elementary-level social studies lesson plans in each edition of the journal. These can be accessed without membership in the NCSS. As examples, the following lesson plans appear in the following edition:

January/February 2016, "The Climate is A-Changin': Teaching Civic Competence for
    a Sustainable Climate;"
January/February 2017, "Cultivating Civic Life through Studying Current Events;"
March/April 2018, "Handouts for Studying Street Traffic;"
January/February 2019, "Remembering the Ladies: Connect to Local Women's History
    using Story Telling."

In addition, a panel of social studies educators have selected and published a listing of the best social studies trade books since the year 2000 (see NCSS, 2020a). Having the school library invest in a collection of trade books or having the PTA donate a collection for a teacher's classroom would create multiple opportunities to integrate reading and social studies.

Expanding Communities

Figure 17.1 has the headings/topics from textbooks for two elementary curriculums by two publishers. McGraw-Hill (2020a), in the first column, is heavily influenced by the **expanding communities** approach developed in the 1940s by Paul Hanna (1965). Hanna also promoted an integrated thematic approach which might be thought of as a forerunner of the NCSS Themes. This expanding community's approach is based on the theory that social studies should start with what students know and has dominated elementary education since it was articulated. It has been characterized as a series of concentric circles with the student at the center and progressing outward from what children are most familiar with: themselves, then family, school, neighborhood, state, nation, and the international community. In the first column, the second row of the first-grade topics is "Why do people work?" The teacher's edition can be viewed at the Amazon website (see reference, McGraw-Hill, 2020b). It is noteworthy that the teacher's edition incorporates guidance for an elementary education version of the Arc of Inquiry framework.

The Core Knowledge social studies curriculum (2020a) appears in the second column of Figure 17.1. E.D. Hirsch (1987, 2016)) introduced the concept of **core knowledge** and **cultural literacy** as an alternative to Hanna's expanding communities' curriculum sequence. Core knowledge could be argued to be more focused on endowing students with a shared cultural heritage through knowledge of the humanities, history, and geography. At the Core Knowledge website (NCSS, 2020b) there are hundreds of some of the most detailed and extensive, free, downloadable PDF lesson plans. As examples, under "Language Conventions" is a lesson "Name that Virtue," which is directly aimed at democratic ideals, and under "History and Geography" there are 27 lesson plans with one example, "The American Revolution and Its Heroes" aiming at both foundational knowledge and democratic ideals. Such lessons, while pegged to the core knowledge sequence, can be moved up or down a grade level, modified, and easily be restructured into the Arc of Inquiry framework. Elementary teachers will find this website particularly helpful because it also has high-quality lessons on science, mathematics, art, music, and language arts.

Grade Level	McGraw-Hill Topics	Core Knowledge Topics
K	How Do People Learn and Work Together? Where Do We Live? What Does It Mean to Be an American? How Has Our World Changed? Why Do People Have Jobs?	Let's Explore Our World! Native Americans Exploring and Moving to America The Mount Rushmore Presidents
First	What Are the Rights and Responsibilities of Citizens? How Can We Describe Where We Live? How Do We Celebrate Our Country? How Does the Past Shape Our Lives? Why Do People Work?	Continents, Countries, and Maps Mesopotamia Ancient Egypt Three World Religions Early Civilizations of the Americas The Culture of Mexico Early Explorers and Settlers From Colonies to Independence Exploring the West
Second	Why Is It Important to Learn About the Past? How Does Geography Help Us Understand Our World? How Do We Get What We Want and Need? Why Do We Need Government? How Can People Make a Difference in Our World?	Ancient India Ancient China The Culture of Japan Ancient Greece Geography of the Americas Making the Constitution The War of 1812 Americans Move West The Civil War Immigration and Citizenship Civil Rights Leaders
Third	Why Does It Matter Where We Live? What Is Our Relationship to Our Environment? What Makes a Community Unique? How Does the Past Impact the Present? Why Do Governments and Citizens Need Each Other? How Do People in a Community Meet Their Wants and Needs?	World Rivers Ancient Rome The Vikings The Earliest Americans Exploration of North America The Thirteen Colonies
Fourth	How Does America Use Its Strengths and Face Its Challenges? Why Have People Moved to and From the Northeast? How Has the Southeast Changed Over Time? How Does the Midwest Reflect the Spirit of America? How Does the Southwest Reflect Its Diverse Past and Unique Environment? What Draws People to the West?	Exploring Maps and World Mountains Medieval Europe Early Islamic Civilizations and African Kingdoms Dynasties of China The American Revolution The United States Constitution Early Presidents and Social Reformers

Figure 17.1 Elementary Curriculum Sequences and Textbook

Fifth	How Were the Lives of Native Peoples Influenced by Where They Lived? What Happened When Diverse Cultures Crossed Paths? What Is the Impact of People Settling in a New Place? Why Would a Nation Want to Become Independent? What Does the Revolutionary Era Tell Us About Our Nation Today? How Does the Constitution Help Us Understand What It Means to Be an American? What Do the Early Years of the United States Reveal About the Character of the Nation? What Was the Effect of the Civil War on U. S. Society?	World Lakes Maya, Aztec, and Inca Civilizations The Age of Exploration From the Renaissance to England's Golden Age (includes The Reformation) Czars and Shoguns: Early Russia and Feudal Japan The Geography of the United States Westward Expansion Before the The Civil War Native Americans and Westward Expansion: Cultures and Conflicts

Figure 17.1 (Cont.)

In an elementary classroom, social studies is just one subject competing for time with the other subject fields. As depicted above, the topics in elementary textbooks are not ordered temporally as in a textbook for a history course or tiered conceptually as in most of the other social studies subject fields as they are for middle and high school textbooks. The topic, "Why Do People Work?" is, at its core, an economics lesson about human capital and income. But it is also a platform for the concepts from the sociology of the family and could be raised to the exalted aims by examining the duty of citizens to work as opposed to relying on their neighbors for assistance. Such topical approaches at the lower elementary school level are typical and require the teacher to tease out the social studies concepts because they are not explicitly stated. The *Econedlink* (refer to Chapter 15) provides background knowledge and excellent lesson plans about work. To integrate a Common Core standard, a writing activity from the *Read-WriteThink* website could be modified to add a writing assignment.

Secondary Social Sciences

The following is the C3 Framework for anthropology, psychology, and sociology. Its pathways provide insights for teaching these social sciences, regardless of grade level.

Anthropology and the C3 Framework

Anthropology is the study of human beings, past and present, in societies around the world. A central anthropological insight is the notion of cultural *relativism* – that no cultural group is inherently "superior" or "inferior" to any other, and that all human behaviors are understandable in their cultural context, even if humans may ultimately aspire to certain universal standards (see AAA, 2001).

Concept 1. What It Means to be Human: Unity and Diversity: The students	
Understand patterns of human physical variability and the evidence for arguing that humans cannot be sorted into distinct biological races	Use anthropological concepts and practice to reflect on representations of "otherness" and consider critically students' own cultural assumptions.
Develop through comparison awareness of human unity and cultural diversity, and of the connections among peoples from around the world.	Apply anthropological concepts and theories to the study of contemporary social change, conflict, and other important local, national, and international problems.
Understand the reasons for and development of human and societal endeavors, such as small-scale societies and civilizations, across time and place.	

Concept 2. Methods and Ethics of Inquiry: The students	
Identify and critically assess the opportunities to use anthropological knowledge in a variety of work settings and in everyday experience, as well as issues of description and representation in anthropology.	Identify and critically assess ethical issues that arise in the practice of anthropological research, including issues of informed consent.
Develop an understanding of the methods by which anthropologists collect data on cultural patterns and processes, and of ways of interpreting and presenting these data in writing and other media.	Under the guidance of teachers, design, undertake, and report on personal research on an anthropological topic of interest, such as a limited ethnographic study of a local culture or a visit to an archaeological dig.

Concept 3. Becoming a Person: Processes, Practices, and Consequences: The students	
Understand the variety of gendered, racialized, or other identities individuals take on over the life course, and identify the social and cultural processes through which those identities are constructed.	Understand how one's local actions can have global consequences, and how global patterns and processes can affect seemingly unrelated local actions.
Apply anthropological concepts of boundaries to the analysis of current ethnic, racial, or religious conflicts in the world or in a local setting.	Become critically aware of ethnocentrism, its manifestations, and consequences in a world that is progressively interconnected.
Understand and appreciate cultural and social difference, and how human diversity is produced and shaped by local, national, regional, and global patterns.	Apply anthropological concepts to current global issues such as migrations across national borders or environmental degradation.

Concept 4. Global and Local: Societies, Environments, and Globalization: The students	
Understand and appreciate cultural and social difference, and how human diversity is produced and shaped by local, national, regional, and global patterns.	Become critically aware of ethnocentrism, its manifestations, and consequences in a world that is progressively interconnected.
Understand how one's local actions can have global consequences, and how global patterns and processes can affect seemingly unrelated local actions.	Apply anthropological concepts to current global issues such as migrations across national borders or environmental degradation.

Figure 17.2 The Four Standards for Anthropology

Psychology and the C3 Framework

Psychology contributes to the understanding of human development, emotion and motivation, cognition, learning processes, perceptual systems, and sociocultural interactions, and promotes improvement in health and well-being. Psychological literacy of self and others is a foundation for civic engagement and is necessary for citizens to make informed decisions about their daily lives (see APA, 2011)

Psychological Perspectives and Methods of Inquiry: The students	
D2.Psy.1.9-12. Demonstrate a basic understanding of the scientific methods that are at the core of psychology	**D2.Psy.5.9-12.** Explain how the validity and reliability of observations and measurements relate to data analysis.
D2.Psy.2.9-12. Investigate human behavior from biological, cognitive, behavioral, and sociocultural perspectives.	**D2.Psy.6.9-12.** Collect and analyze data designed to answer a psychological question using basic descriptive and inferential statistics.
D2.Psy.3.9-12. Discuss theories, methodologies, and empirical findings necessary to plan, conduct, and especially interpret research results.	**D2.Psy.7.9-12.** Explore multicultural and global perspectives that recognize how diversity is important to explaining human behavior.
D2.Psy.4.9-12. Adhere to and consider the impact of American Psychological Association and federal guidelines for the ethical treatment of human and nonhuman research participants.	
Influences on Thought and Behavior: The students	
D2.Psy.8.9-12. Explain the complexities of human thought and behavior, as well as the factors related to the individual differences among people.	**D2.Psy.11.9-12.** Identify the role psychological science can play in helping us understand differences in individual cognitive and physical abilities.
D2.Psy.9.9-12. Describe biological, psychological, and sociocultural factors that influence individuals' cognition, perception, and behavior.	**D2.Psy.12.9-12.** Explain how social, cultural, gender, and economic factors influence behavior and human interactions in societies around the world.
D2.Psy.10.9-12. Explain the interaction of biology and experience (i.e., nature and nurture) and its influence on behavior.	
Critical Thinking: Themes, Sources, and Evidence: The students	
D2.Psy.13.9-12. Explain common themes across the field of psychological science, including ethical issues, diversity, developmental issues, and concerns about health and wellbeing.	**D2.Psy.16.9-12.** Use critical thinking skills to become better consumers of psychological knowledge.
D2.Psy.14.9-12. Use information from different psychological sources to generate research questions.	**D2.Psy.17.9-12.** Acknowledge the interconnectedness of knowledge in the discipline of psychology.
D2.Psy.15.9-12. Use existing evidence and formulate conclusions about psychological phenomena.	

Figure 17.3 The Four Standards for Psychology

Applications of Psychological Knowledge: The students	
D2.Psy.18.9-12. Apply psychological knowledge to their daily lives.	**D2.Psy.21.9-12.** Discuss ways in which the applications of psychological science can address domestic and global issues.
D2.Psy.19.9-12. Apply the major theoretical approaches in psychology to educational, emotional, political, ethical, motivational, organizational, personal, and social issues.	**D2.Psy.22.9-12.** Use psychological knowledge to promote healthy lifestyle choices.
D2.Psy.20.9-12. Suggest psychologically based ethical solutions to actual problems including, but not limited to, those encountered in education, business and industry, and the environment.	**D2.Psy.23.9-12.** Apply psychological knowledge to civic engagement.

Figure 17.3 (Cont.)

Sociology and the C3 Framework

Sociology is the study of social life, social change, and the social causes and consequences of human behavior. Since all human behavior is social, the subject matter of sociology ranges from the intimate family to the hostile mob; from organized crime to religious traditions; and from the divisions of race, gender, and social class to the shared beliefs of a common culture (see ASA, 2009).

Resources

Videos: *Learner.org*: Social Studies in Action a Teaching Practices Library Series; [elementary] Caring for the Community; Celebrations of Light; Understanding Stereotypes; [middle] Explorations in Archeology and History; [high school] Migration From Latin America; Gender-Based Distinctions; Unity and Diversity; Discovering psychology [26 high school level videos] | *CrashCourse:* Sociology; psychology, anthropology | *Kahn Academy*: Intro to Anthropology | *National Geographic*: Anthropology | *NOVA* teachers | *TCH or YouTube*: Creating Family Flags | *TedEd:* anthropology; sociology; psychology | *YouTube:* Anthropology & the Study of Humanity.

Documents: *Routledge Handbook of Research in Social Studies Education*: Early Elementary Social Studies | *Wiley Handbook of Social Studies Research* (Children's Learning and Understanding in Their Social World) | *BCcampus*: Open Textbooks (anthropology, psychology, and sociology) | *Core Knowledge* (among the most detailed and cross-disciplinary level lesson plans on the internet) | *NYSUT:* Social Studies – Instructional Strategies & Resources (a Pre-K–Grade 6 272-page PDF of concrete strategies and topics) | Paul Hanna and Expanding Communities PDF |Teaching Anthropology | Teaching Psychology | Teaching Sociology | *ReadWriteThink:* (more than 500 excellent elementary education lesson plans that integrate social studies, reading, and writing).

The Sociological Perspective and Methods of Inquiry: The students	
D2.Soc.1.9-12. Explain the sociological perspective and how it differs from other social sciences.	**D2.Soc.4.9-12.** Illustrate how sociological analysis can provide useful data-based information for decision making.
D2.Soc.2.9-12. Define social context in terms of the external forces that shape human behavior.	**D2.Soc.5.9-12.** Give examples of the strengths and weaknesses of four main methods of sociological research: surveys, experiments, observations, and content analysis.
D2.Soc.3.9-12. Identify how social context influences individuals.	
Social Structure: Culture, Institutions, and Society: The students	
D2.Soc.6.9-12. Identify the major components of culture.	**D2.Soc.9.9-12.** Explain the role of social institutions in society.
D2.Soc.7.9-12. Cite examples of how culture influences the individuals in it.	**D2.Soc.10.9-12.** Analyze how social structures and cultures change.
D2.Soc.8.9-12. Identify important social institutions in society.	
Social Relationships: Self, Groups, and Socialization: The students	
D2.Soc.11.9-12. Analyze the influence of the primary agents of socialization and why they are influential.	**D2.Soc.13.9-12.** Identify characteristics of groups, as well as the effects groups have on individuals and society, and the effects of individuals and societies on groups.
D2.Soc.12.9-12. Explain the social construction of self and groups.	**D2.Soc.14.9-12.** Explain how in-group and out-group membership influences the life chances of individuals and shapes societal norms and values.
Stratification and Inequality: The students	
D2.Soc.15.9-12. Identify common patterns of social inequality.	**D2.Soc.17.9-12.** Analyze why the distribution of power and inequalities can result in conflict.
D2.Soc.16.9-12. Interpret the effects of inequality on groups and individuals.	**D2.Soc.18.9-12.** Propose and evaluate alternative responses to inequality.

Figure 17.4 The Four Standards for Sociology

References

American Anthropology Association (AAA). (2001). *Why should anthropology be integrated in schools?* Statement by the Anthropology Education Committee. Anthropology Education Committee. Retrieved from www.aaanet.org/committees/commissions/aec/why.htm.

American Psychological Association (APA). (2011). *National standards for high school psychology curricula.* Retrieved from www.apa.org/education/k12/national-standards.aspx.

American Sociological Association (ASA). (2009). *21st century careers with an undergraduate degree in sociology.* ASA. Retrieved from www.uh.edu/class/sociology/undergraduate/careers/21st_century_careers.pdf.

CarolinaK12. (2020). *The Vietnam War and protest music.* Retrieved from https://civics.sites.unc.edu/files/2012/05/VietnamWarProtestMusic1.pdf.

Core Knowledge. (2020a). *Curriculum.* Retrieved from www.coreknowledge.org/curriculum/.

Core Knowledge. (2020b). *First grade lesson plans.* Retrieved from www.coreknowledge.org/commu nity/teacher-workroom/teacher-created-lesson-plans/first-grade-lesson-plans/.

Cummings, C. (2000). *Winning strategies for classroom management.* ASCD.

Duplass, J., & Cruz, B. (2009). Making sense of "race" in the history classroom: A literary approach. *The History Teacher, 42*(4), 426–440. Retrieved from www.jstor.org/stable/40543494? seq=1#page_scan_tab_contents

Engaging, N. Y. (2020). *Symbols.* Retrieved from www.c3teachers.org/wp-content/uploads/2015/09/ NewYork_2_Symbols.pdf.

Hanna, P. R. (1965). *Design for a social studies program: Focus on the social studies.* NEA, Department of Elementary School Principals.

Hirsch, E. D. (1987). *Cultural literacy: What every American needs to know.* Houghton Mifflin.

Hirsch, E. D. (2016). *Why Knowledge Matters.* Harvard Education Press.

McGraw-Hill. (2020a). *Impact social studies.* www.mheducation.com/prek-12/program/microsites/ MKTSP-AAS02M0/resources/content-by-grade.html.

McGraw-Hill. (2020b). Our place in the world "Chapter 5: Why do people work?" Retrieved from https://s3.amazonaws.com/ecommerce-prod.mheducation.com/unitas/school/explore/sites/ impact-social-studies/flipbook/te_microsite_sampler_grade_1_impact/index.html.

NCSS. (2010). *Expectations of excellence: Curriculum standards for social studies.* Retrieved from www.socialstudies.org/standards/strands.

NCSS. (2013). *Social studies for the next generation: Purposes, practices, and implications of the college, career, and civic Life (C3) framework for social studies state standards: Guidance for enhancing rigor of K-12 civic, economics, geography, and history.* NCSS. Retrieved from www. socialstudies.org/sites/default/files/2017/Jun/c3-framework-for-social-studies-rev0617.pdf.

NCSS. (2020a). *Notable trade books.* Retrieved from www.socialstudies.org/publications/notables.

NCSS. (2020b). *Social studies and the young learner.* Retrieved from www.socialstudies.org/publica tions/ssyl/ssyl_online.

18 Current Events and Controversial Issues

Children have never been very good at listening to their elders, but they have never failed to imitate them.
James Baldwin, Novelist, Playwright, and Activist, 1924–1987 (Goodreads, 2020)

Teaching current events as compared with "traditional" content and the prospect of examining controversial issues often raise apprehension among teachers (Johnston & Johnston, 1979). Selection of which problems (events or issues) to engage in with students is, for the most part, a teacher's decision made during lesson planning. However, in many cases, a student may spontaneously raise a question or make a connection to a controversy during a lesson – creating a "teachable moment." The teacher should take advantage of the opportunity. However, there is nothing wrong – and indeed it may be prudent if a teacher does not feel prepared – with saying, "Let me have a day or two to think through how we can best discuss this" and returning in the next day or two with a well-thought-out plan. The C3 Framework's emphasis on framing questions and structured investigations is an ideal vehicle to prepare students for the all-important discussion of things that matter (refer to Chapter 10 on philosophical counseling and see Chapter 24). The teacher promotes a democratic ideology, but not a particular political ideological stance.

Current Events and Foundational Goals

There are topics, such as the benefits and disadvantages of the Electoral College vs. popular vote, that could be planned as a lesson or it could arise serendipitously because the ten-year census or a presidential election is in the news. This would likely fall into the foundational goals arena and include a discussion of the pros and cons. It could create interest, particularly if imaginatively orchestrated with scenarios, having students figure out if and why the electoral college incentivizes candidates to campaign more in the most populated states, examples of past presidential elections, and an interactive map. However, and although it engages democratic beliefs, it is not as likely to generate the kind of passion found in topics such as gun control or racial profiling. These two examples are more controversial and are "hot" (Dewey, 1960, p. 112) topics because they force students to weigh democratic beliefs that are in conflict, give rise to passions, have consequences that have personal ramifications, and require consideration of revisions to beliefs about closely held political ideology and positions.

Controversy and Exalted Aims

Discussions of controversial issues that stem from current events or otherwise are essential because they are about things that matter. Johnston and Johnston (1979) remind teachers that from the students' perspective, the conflict generated by controversies is not just a disagreement among students in the classroom (and perhaps with the teacher), but there is intrapersonal conflict of emotions, ideas, and beliefs that is the source of students' dissonance and leads students to resolve the conflict by seeking new information and reexamination of their identity. By listening to the teacher's and other students' perspectives, respect – if not empathy for others as persons as well as their ideas and beliefs – is created even if the political stances are different. Discussions about things that matter "is central to cognitive development, moral reasoning, self-esteem, social intelligence, and cooperation" (Johnston & Johnston, 1979, p. 54).

Teacher Opinions

It would be disingenuous and hurt a teacher's credibility if teachers were to pretend to their students that they do not have an ideological position and political ideological stance on a current event or controversial issue under discussion. Furthermore, teachers would be abandoning their duty to provide the moral leadership to bend the Arc of Inquiry toward a democratic ideology.

In Thomas Kelly's classic work of 1986, he described four perspectives before settling on "committed impartiality" as the teacher's best approach to teaching controversial topics.

Exclusive neutrality: Stems from concerns about teachers and schools taking political ideology and political stances and argues that the only way to avoid promoting a preference is to not discuss current events at all.

Exclusive partiality: Is indoctrination through a deliberate or inadvertent suppression of competing political ideology or stances and/or covert or overt promotion of the teacher's privileged ideological position.

Neutral impartiality: Calls for teachers to be silent about their personal political ideology and stance and attempt to do their very best at moderating an impartial, objective investigation and discussion.

Committed impartiality: Requires, (A) teachers express their views on controversial issues so that students know from the outset where a teacher stands so as to empower students to make judgments about the teacher's fair treatment of the subject, and (B) conduct discussion where all competing perspectives are voiced.

Exclusive neutrality and exclusive partiality run contrary to the development of a civic and personal identity of the students, the exalted aims of social studies education, and the mission of schools in a democratic society. However, neutral impartiality is necessary at times in leading discussions about controversial topics, particularly when teaching elementary school-aged students. The reasoning for this position is based on the following, as the story goes: An elementary school teacher mentioned on Friday to the first-grade class that his favorite color was red; on Monday every student wore red. Teachers would still use committed impartiality at the elementary level, but only after students have initially grappled with the issue. By middle and high school, students' greater autonomy are believed to make students more likely to assert their views even if the teacher's personal political ideological stance is different from their own. For this reason, committed impartiality is preferable, whenever grade-appropriate.

The following two examples of controversial issues are intended to illuminate the subtleties and complexities of discussing current and controversial events.

Racism

There would not likely be an explicit state standard to teach about and against such topics as racism or any undemocratic "isms." Although, a statement on professionalism expecting teachers to support the democratic belief in equality would be aimed at the same end. The teacher's ideology and disposition are intended to thwart what Noddings and Brooks (2017) refer to as "educated despair," a sense of futility that might encumber students when they are considering a controversial issue such as racism. A social studies teacher committed to the democratic ideals should want to help mitigate prejudice as a pernicious, worldwide problem based on the belief that racism is an obstacle to a more humane society and the Good Life. The teacher's disposition should be toward meliorism, the democratic ideological belief that the world can be a better place and that students have a duty to work toward that end. Teachers are expected to have a more enlightened perspective on the teleology of the cosmos than their students, more direct experience taking up the challenge of trying to live the Good Life, and a more sophisticated understanding of the social studies that would inform them about topics such as "race" and how best to think and teach about it. As an example, "race" appears early in humankind's history in the Bible in the story of Noah and later took on the appearance of being scientifically sound in the 1700s. The American Anthropological Association (1998) states that "race" should be put in quotation marks because, as a social and biological construct, there is no definitive, legitimate way to define it.

Children are not "color blind" and observe skin color and physical differences in others at an early age, but do so with curiosity, not prejudice. Differences observed in "races" become negative conceptions only when demeaning labels are placed upon them. From human development theory, we know that in seeking identity, some children (and adults) resort to negative labels based on "race" because of shortcomings in their own identity. Children may adopt such views due to their limited autonomy and unfortunate exposure to undemocratic ideology. Racism should not come from a teacher, and when encountered in a classroom, the teacher must lead a discussion that points out the deficiencies in the undemocratic proposition.

At the elementary school level, teachers frequently use children's books that question racial stereotypes and caricatures in an effort to inoculate children from adopting racist views and to bolster an identity for minorities that is not based on "race" but achievement. Ambitious teachers explore cultures and ancestry as a way to embrace and celebrate differences and to further autonomy and authenticity in their students. By upper elementary and middle school, teachers should explore institutional and historical racism, stereotypes, and caricatures. Investigations can proceed through high school by looking for racial bias and caricatures in textbooks, TV shows, commercials, social media, etc. By middle and high school, students can participate in investigations into legal and legislative approaches to combat racism employed in democratic societies. Teachers are morally obligated to promote a democratic ideology and political ideology that says to students there is no such thing as "race," only racism. Teachers are equally obligated not to promote any particular political ideological stance they might privilege as to how to mitigate the effects of racism.

In this case, assume a teacher appears to be of "white" European ancestry, a likely relatively privileged position that brought a freedom from the harshness experienced by some minorities in American society. Teaching about American history will bring forward the concepts of "race" and racism. How teachers have treated minority students in class and affirmations of meliorism will be crucial to their success in having students consider potentially racist ideas and beliefs because it assists in creating the therapeutic alliance needed to counsel students to new beliefs. In all likelihood, the teacher will have the occasion to say something such as, "We have come a long way" or "We have come a long way and have a long way to go" or "We have a long way to go." The harshness of the climate of political correctness in America creates an environment where every articulated phrase of a teacher can come under unforgiving scrutiny and taken as an offense. The prism through which students will view each of those phrases will be based on their unique personal and civic identity and the level of trust teachers have created in their classroom. Some may feel the first statement suggests that the teacher thinks enough has been done. The third might suggest that the teacher thinks too little has been done. The second statement might suggest that the teacher is being "balanced," while some may feel the teacher is just pandering, being "politically correct" to avoid leaning to one belief or the other. An honest discussion with students about these three phrases, the adverse effects of the coarseness of politics on classroom conversations and civil discourse, and negative presumptions of others' good character and intentions would be a valuable lesson in and of itself and would achieve an exalted aim.

Even in the cases of students who express a racist or insensitive idea, they deserve and need a teacher who projects the caring disposition necessary to command the students' attention for the possibility of change to take place in the students' identity. Viewing such a statement from a philosophical counseling position leads to recognizing the statement as symptomatic of a flaw in the student's identity and reasoning. Through a dialogue involving all students, the teacher asks questions, provides conflicting examples, and draws analogies that compel students to reconsider their beliefs. Teachers must also turn their attention to offended students, reassure them by publicly recognizing the pain suffered by such unfortunate statements, and encourage the goodwill of all to learn from the interaction.

The instructional practices identified above are preferable to "preaching" because it allows students to reason themselves into a more democratic belief. Proselytizing approaches are not lasting because they are a form of coercion by an authority figure. Students have to reason their way into a new belief; philosophical counselors create the sense of caring that allows students to give themselves permission to change their way of thinking and beliefs.

Columbus Day

Depending on people's political ideological prism, Christopher Columbus and the celebration of his "discovery" of America is a history of death, destruction, slavery, and genocide, or it is a navigational triumph that led to the "more advanced" European civilization's creation of the United State of America. The long view of history is one where, starting with tribes and evolving to today's nations, "cultures collide" as "the world got smaller." In this view, each time one culture or nation came in contact with another, one society was more advanced based on multiple possible attributes, such as literacy, military strength, technological advances, moral code, etc., but both societies learned something about themselves that led to change. That is the context of the Columbus story representing the Europeans coming into contact with the First Americans in the Caribbean. Like the prior clarification about "race," the term "First Americans" rather than "Native Americans" is more precise, since that population also migrated to the Americas: As evolutionary biologists have made clear, all humans began in Africa and migrated across the planet (Duplass & Cruz, 2009).

In a state's standards, a teacher will likely find standards related to the Columbus story such as these from Florida (FDOE, 2008):

Kindergarten

Recognize the importance of celebrations and national holidays as a way of remembering and honoring people, events, and our nation's ethnic heritage.

Grade 5

Describe technological developments that shaped European exploration.

Investigate (nationality, sponsoring country, motives, dates, and routes of travel, accomplishments) the European explorers.

Describe interactions among Native Americans, Africans, English, French, Dutch, and Spanish for control of North America.

Grade 8

Compare interpretations of key events and issues throughout American history.

View historic events through the eyes of those who were there as shown in their art, writings, music, and artifacts.

Discuss the impact of colonial settlement on Native American populations.

The substance of the content is ripe for the C3 Inquiry Arc approach and the opportunity for students to deploy the civic values of search for the truth, impartiality, open-mindedness, critical thinking, and engaged discourse. However, at each grade level, the investigations must be grade-appropriate. Elementary teachers should consider that the more complex version of the Columbus story is expected to be examined in later years. In lower grades, it would be grade-appropriate to focus on the great achievement of navigating the Atlantic; the irony of not finding India but a "new world;" learning the poem "In 1492" by Jean Marzollo (2020) and the strategies in a related downloadable internet lesson (see Bauer, 2012); or modifying a comprehensive seven-lesson unit plan about Columbus from the *Core Knowledge* website (see Collins, Gilbert, Kennedy, Larkin, & Pompa, n.d.). Making the judgment that limiting an elementary lesson plan to what is grade-appropriate should not be thought of as deceptive or indoctrinating because the elementary school teacher is preparing students for the next social studies teacher, who will revisit the Columbus story, adding in examinations that are more morally complex.

In middle and high school, the teacher's attention would turn to the violence, slavery, disease, and imposition of Christianity with questions of justice. For balance, however, there is also ample documented evidence of violence and slavery among the First Americans (see Mann, 2002). The concepts of clash of cultures, what makes cultures "advanced," and which of the Hazards of History should be considered are worthy objects of discussion. For teacher background information on the topic, a teacher might consider using *Examining Historical (Mis) Representations of Christopher Columbus within Children's Literature* by J.H. Bickford III (2013) and the comprehensive 95-page PDF lesson "Rethinking Columbus" by the American and Iberian Institute at the University of New Mexico (n.d.). A mock trial could also be held (see Graves, n. d.), allowing students to explore the multiple perspectives present in the Columbus story.

Resources

The following two books offer well-reasoned insights when teaching controversial issues and current events.
Hess, D. E. (2009). Controversy in the classroom: The democratic power of discussion. New York: Routledge.
Noddings, N. & Brooks, L. (2017). Teaching controversial issues: The case for critical thinking and moral communication in the classroom. New York: Teachers College Press.

Videos: *Learner.org*: Dealing with Controversial Issues | *TCH or YouTube:* Civic Knowledge Productive Discussions; Socratic Seminar Supporting Claims and Counter Claims; Socratic Seminar the "N-word;" Using Debate to Develop Thinking & Speaking Skills; Using the Argument Tool; Inquiry-based Teaching Building a Culture of Respect; Exploring Emigration Cultural Identity | *TED Talk*: Moral Issues | *YouTube:* Controversial Issues in Schools; Teaching Wellbeing; Helping Students Tackle Social Issues.

Documents: *Wiley Handbook of Social Studies Research*: Teaching and Learning About Controversial issues and Topics; A Critical Race Theory; Gender and Feminist Scholarship; Sexuality and Queer Theory | *Digital Civics* Toolkit | *Morningside Center:* Teachable Moments Time for Kids | *Pew Foundation* | *Public Agenda* | *ProCon*.org | *Smithsonian:* Tween Tribune | *ReadWriteThink*: From Friedan Forward – Considering a Feminist Perspective; Propaganda Techniques in Literature and Online Political Ads; Using Picture Books to Explore Identity, Stereotyping, and Discrimination.

References

American and Iberian Institute. (n.d.). *Rethinking Columbus.* Retrieved from http://thecolonial.org/wp-content/uploads/Best-Rethinking-Columbus-complete-guide.pdf
American Anthropological Association. (1998). *Statement on "race".* Retrieved from www.aaanet.org/stmts/racepp.htm.
Bauer, M. (2012). *Christopher Columbus: My first biography.* Scholasic.Com. Retrieved from. www.scholastic.com/content/dam/teachers/lesson-plans/migrated-featured-files/myfirstbio_christopher columbus.pdf.
Bickford, J. H., III. (2013). Examining historical (mis)representations of Christopher Columbus within children's literature. *Social Studies Research and Practice, 8*(2), 1–24.
Collins, M., Gilbert, A., Kennedy, S., Larkin, A., & Pompa, C. (n.d.). *Christopher Columbus: The man, the myth, the legend.* Core Knowledge. Retrieved from www.coreknowledge.org/wp-content/uploads/2016/11/Christopher-Columbus-The-Man-the-Myth-the-Legend.pdf.

Dewey, J. (1960). *The theory of the moral life.* Holt, Rinehart & Winston.

Duplass, J., & Cruz, B. (2009). Making sense of "race" in the history classroom: A literary approach. *The History Teacher, 42*(4), 426–440.

FDOE. (2008). *Florida social studies sunshine state standards.* Retrieved from www.google.com/search?q=next+generation+sunshine+state+standards+social+studies&rlz=1C1GCEU_enUS820US821&oq=sunshine+state+social+stuidesstandards&aqs=chrome.2.69i57j0l5.23499j0j4&sourceid=chrome¡UTF-8.

Goodreads. (2020). *James Baldwin.* Retrieved from www.goodreads.com/quotes/18154-children-have-never-been-very-good-at-listening-to-their.

Graves, M. (n.d.). *Mock trial of Christopher Columbus.* Retrieved from http://mrgravesamericanhistory.weebly.com/uploads/5/3/7/2/53720971/mock_trial_for_christopher_columbus_documents.pdf

Johnston, D. W., & Johnston, R. T. (1979). *Conflict in the classroom: Controversy and learning.* Review of Educational Research. Retrieved from www.researchgate.net/publication/240723519_Conflict_in_the_Classroom_Controversy_And_Learning.

Kelly, T. E. (1986). Discussing controversial issues: Four perspectives on the teacher's role. *Theory and Research in Social Education, 14*(2), 113–138.

Mann, C. C. (2002). 1491. *The Atlantic.* Retrieved from www.theatlantic.com/magazine/archive/2002/03/1491/302445/

Marzollo, J. (2020). *In 1492.* Retrieved from www.teachingheart.net/columbus.htm.

Noddings, N., & Brooks, L. (2017). *Teaching controversial issues: The case for critical thinking and moral communication in the classroom.* Teachers College Press.

Part 3

Best Practices in Social Studies Education

Genius is 99 percent perspiration and 1 percent inspiration.
Thomas Edison, Inventor Extraordinaire, 1847–1931 A(Wikiquote, 2020)

In pragmatic terms, new teachers often begin planning by opening the textbook to see what topics are included and to get a sense of what "**grade-appropriate**" reading content would cover. That conceptualization process to create daily lessons is iterative, requiring teachers to find state standards that can be meshed with a potential topic, decide on goals, objectives, and strategies, and find resources such ancillaries, other teachers' lesson plan ideas, and background resources. The standards recommended by learned societies and in Common Core are invaluable to understanding the basic critical thinking and procedural knowledge skills that should be used to shape the lesson.

How Do Students Like to Learn Social Studies?

Russell and Walters (2010) asked almost 500 middle school students what they disliked about social studies instruction and what they would prefer.

Dislikes	Likes
Lectures	Class discussions
Rote-memorization	Cooperative learning activities
Assignments from the textbooks	Graphic organizers
Worksheets	Student presentations
Note-taking	Use of technology
	Hands-on activities
	Field trips
	Review games

Three Key Considerations

1. **The thoughtful classroom** has become one of a few places where deliberative conversations about things that matter are cloistered from the often unbridled, unrelenting, harsh pontifications that are not grounded in the democratic ideals or due to political ideological clashes. Teachers of social studies need to create contemplative retreats where students feel free to think about who they are and test their beliefs about the democratic ideals and their identity with classmates and the teacher.

2. **Foundation of caring** is necessary to create the contemplative classroom. It can be achieved when teachers provide structure, exhibit a caring demeanor, and display their own commitment to a democratic ideology.

3. **Explicit teaching** is needed, more than ever, due to the impact social and mass media has on the culture and psyches of children and adolescents. Teachers find themselves competing for the hearts and minds of students in a world with so many other sources of unsifted information, misinformation, and misleading information that students are not sure who or what to believe or believe in. Explicit teaching of foundational knowledge and democratic ideals starts with planning so as to frame lessons that deliberately address civic and personal identity questions (refer to Figure 4.2, The Essential Identity Questions).

Resources

Documents: *Routledge Handbook of Research in Social Studies Education*: What Happens in Social Studies Classrooms.

References

Russell, W. B., & Walters, S. (Spring 2010). Instructional methods for teaching social studies: A survey of what middle school students like and dislike about social studies instruction. *Journal for the Liberal Arts and Sciences, 14*(2): pp. 7–14.

Wikiquote. (2020). *Thomas Edison*. Retrieved from https://en.wikiquote.org/wiki/Thomas_Edison

19 Classroom Culture, Communication, and Management

One looks back with appreciation to the brilliant teachers, but with gratitude to those who touched our human feelings. The curriculum is so much necessary raw material, but warmth is the vital element for the growing plant and for the soul of the child.
Carl Jung, Swiss Philosopher and Psychiatrist, 1875–1961 (Jung, 2003, p. 94)

Managing 25 students will take every intrinsic leadership and communication skill a teacher candidate has been able to develop. Preventing classroom management problems before they begin by having engaging lessons that move with a quick pace so that students don't have time to create problems is essential. When teacher candidates are hired, the assumption is they know the what and how to teach: The essential question of the school's administration is, can the teacher candidate manage the behaviors of students by commanding students' respect? Without the latter, teaching will be impossible. It is for this reason that what teacher candidates do during the orientation of students and parents to the class in the first few days is crucial – it sets the tone!

The classroom might best be thought of as a delicate, complex ecological setting of compliant, noncompliant, motivated, and unmotivated students with special needs, a history of high and low achievement, English as their second language, and of different economic statuses, "races," ethnicities, religious affiliations, and sexual orientations from stable and unstable home living situations. Coming to know and motivate each student begins with students coming to believe that the teacher cares about them. Merging the disparate students into a team working together toward a common goal is the great challenge of teaching.

The Stages of Classroom Evolution

The literature from group therapy describing the stages in which groups must evolve to be successful (Johnson & Johnson, 1991) is almost identical to the stages that a classroom of students must progress through to have a highly effective learning environment (Education Department of South Australia, 1980).

Stage 1: Dependence stage. Students start out relatively submissive, anxious, and fear of reprisal is high. Most of the communication comes from the teacher. There is little disruptive behavior, although some students will begin testing the teacher. Student motivations are mostly extrinsic.

Stage 2: Rebellion stage. Students begin to test the teacher for control of the class, noise levels tend to rise, students begin to evolve into camps, and "putdowns" and adversarial comments begin to rise between students. The more rebellious students or groups of students are driven by the need for peer acceptance and their unproductive behaviors are minimized by apprehension of teacher reprisal for unacceptable conduct. Teacher credibility is most vulnerable at this stage and can lead to loss of control if appropriate classroom management practices are not in place from the first day and responses to inappropriate behaviors are not immediate, appropriate, consistent, and equitable.

Stage 3: Cohesion stage. Trust develops between the teacher and students, and students and students. Peer and teacher acceptance becomes a priority. Disruptive behavior dissipates and the atmosphere becomes more cordial. Harmony becomes more important than adversarial interactions. Peer pressure based on students' norms tends to control for inappropriate behaviors, rather than direct teacher interventions.

Stage 4: Autonomy stage. When students take responsibility for their learning, statements reveal feelings as well as ideas and beliefs, disagreements are reconciled routinely by thoughtful, diplomatic responses, more flexibility in examining beliefs is exhibited, and the motivation is intrinsic because learning is seen as a source of agency, efficacy, authenticity, and autonomy.

The disposition of the teacher is the essential element in moving a class through these stages and requires the teacher to exhibit "trust, warmth, understanding, acceptance, kindness, and human wisdom" (Lambert & Ogles, 2004, pp. 180–181).

Classroom Communication

Verbal and nonverbal communications are equally important (Rolle, 2002). Whenever teachers communicate, they transmit: (A) knowledge; (B) who they are as an authentic person; and (C) how they perceive their relationship with the student(s). The persona projected by teachers communicates whether they are timid, unsure of themselves, arrogant, dispassionate, confident, poised, organized, caring, etc. At the same time and in "real time," teachers are metacognitively asking themselves, "Am I speaking loud enough? Did I say that correctly? What is she doing, she is not paying attention? Where is the next handout? Who should I call on next?" – all while trying to communicate foundational knowledge and democratic ideals. It is not what teachers know, but the way that teachers communicate what they know that contributes most to a productive relationship with students (Ferreira, 2000).

Best Practices for Classroom Communication

1. Over-prepare, create engaging lessons, and rehearse.
2. Act confidently, as if you know what you are doing, even though you will likely be anxious.
3. Be attentive to your attire, appearance, and posture – it speaks to your professionalism.
4. Be energetic, use eye contact and gestures, and move about the room to keep students' attention.
5. Change voice, intonation, rate, pitch, cadence, and emphasis to make your point.

Negative Speech	Positive Speech
Do not make so much noise	Please quiet down – you are getting too loud
Do not copy your neighbor's work	Try to work these out on your own without help
Do not just guess	Be ready to explain your answer – why you think it is correct
Do not yell out your answers	Raise your hand if you think you know the answer
Do not...	I think it would be best
Your homework is sloppy	Your homework could benefit by better proof reading and drafting
You are not paying attention	When you do not listen, you miss important information

6. Use positive speech (Good & Brophy, 1991).
7. Listen, do not just hear. Stop what you are doing and look at the student, make eye contact, show interest by nodding and facial expressions, and do not fold your arms – it is a "closed" position suggesting you are an unwilling listener.
8. Praise when its warranted: "You should be very pleased that you came up with that observation;" "You must have really thought that through;" "That must have taken a lot of time;" "You have been paying a lot more attention, good job;" etc.

Praise and Criticism

Because students are in the midst of developing autonomy and authenticity, praise is often necessary. The goal, however, is to have students be pleased with themselves, rather than to please a teacher. To encourage internal motivation, feedback is best phrased starting with, "You should be pleased with yourself..." rather than "I am pleased you..."

Praise

Research shows that overused praise for minor accomplishments, as opposed to positive feedback, can undermine intrinsic motivation (Black, 2000; Kohn, 1993). Whelan (2000) identifies three kinds of effective praise:

Recognition, which is a straightforward acknowledgement of the student's thinking, "That was very insightful."
Encouragement, "That was very insightful, keep up the good effort."
Coaching, "That was very insightful, did you also consider..."

The following suggestions are, in part, adapted from Good and Brophy (1991) and Kohn (1993) and Black (2000).

1. Praise the work effort (thinking or product), not the student: "That analysis must have taken a lot of thought" and "that essay was very well done."
2. Identify the specified behavior that is being praised: "You really thought that question through!"

3. Deliver praise naturally without gushing or over-dramatization: "That is a very good question."
4. Be genuine when praising, mean what you say by combining verbal praise with the nonverbal communications.
5. Do not praise when it is not warranted.
6. Praise students' behaviors over which they exercise personal control: "You have been paying a lot more attention in class lately."
7. Use a variety of praise statements, thumbs up, "great idea," "that was very helpful, did everyone hear that clarification to the assignment?" etc.

Criticism

The word "criticism" sounds harsh. In theatre rehearsals, directors do not criticize, they give "notes," and that is the same kinder, gentler tone that teachers should strive for. The goal is to redirect students' unproductive behavior.

1. Criticism directed to the whole class should be short and direct: "Please take your seats now." Never yell.
2. Whenever possible, admonitions should be delivered in close proximity to the individual students. Criticism of a student's behavior in front of the class should be avoided, but if necessary, low-key. It is better to walk over to the student and ask for his assistance.
3. Criticize the behavior – not the student: State the admonition in positive, behavioral terms, such as, "Please, it would be better if you raised your hand," and saying "thank you" will begin to earn the respect of all students, not just the misbehaving student(s), and they in turn will reinforce good behavior.
4. Body language and tone of the teacher should make it clear that the problem is not subject to debate or an opportunity for excuses. Do not correct students by phrasing the admonition as a question: "Do you really think that is appropriate?"
5. Responses by teachers to retorts ("answering back") by students should not include a response to the student's statement, but a restatement of the original criticism. Teachers should not debate or engage in lengthy discussion with students about misbehaviors: Get back to teaching the lesson as quickly as possible.
6. Appeal to a student(s)' sense of duty to the class because of the important work that needs to get done.
7. Use the **escalation approach**. Feedback must be consistent with increasing degrees of penalties. As an example, a student who continuously delays the class by not promptly taking his seat should result in a reminder to the class to be prompt, but with glances to the problem students. A second incident should be followed up as students exit the class with an appeal to the students' sense of what is the right thing to do could be a statement directed to the students. A third incident should result in the student being taken aside and talked to one-on-one with a warning that a continuation of the problem will result in a call to his parents, he will lose grade points, and be referred for disciplinary action by the school.

Not putting an end to unproductive behavior will result in the loss of respect from the other students and increase the number of students enacting unproductive behaviors.

Classroom Management

The management of individuals and groups begins with reinforcing the need for individuals to take responsibility for their own actions.

Choice Theory

William Glasser's (1998) **choice theory** offers a construct which maintains that it is a teacher's duty to help the student make good choices, which in turn results in greater student agency and efficacy and productive behaviors. If teachers start with this premise and the following principles, students will likely select strategies which produce positive results.

1. Behavior is a choice, students make choices, and unacceptable behavior is a bad choice.
2. Good choices produce good behavior and bad choices produce bad behavior.
3. Misbehavior should always be followed with appropriate consequences.
4. Teachers who care about their students accept no excuses for unacceptable behavior.
5. The teacher should establish rules and review classroom procedures.
6. The teacher should stress personal responsibility.
7. The teacher should emphasize the idea that students are in school to study and learn.
8. The teacher should have students make judgments about their misbehavior and require them to suggest suitable alternatives.
9. The teacher should stress the concept of "duty" to classmates as a reason to affirmatively work to make class a good experience for all.

The following best practices are gleamed from a number of sources.

Best Practices for Classroom Management

1. Do nothing if you do not know what to do until you have considered the situation – keep the goal in mind, i.e., redirect student(s)' behavior.
2. Never yell, always be calm, cool, and collected. Use a firm, deliberate tone of voice.
3. Focus on the behavior: "Please, I would like you to..." is better than "I want you to stop..."
4. Do not try to start class over chatter; wait for silence before you begin by your own silence. If it is the whole class being unruly, wait, stand quietly staring at the students who are being most disruptive and speak softly to draw their attention.
5. Never use group punishments.
6. Apply warnings and penalties equitably, making no exceptions.
7. Use **proximity control** by standing next to a noncompliant student's desk and teaching from that position.
8. Be deliberate: stop, look, listen, think, and act.
9. Your body language and verbal response should reflect disappointment.

10. Escalate to consequences only when verbal appeals to right action and nonverbal and verbal warnings have failed.
11. Do not deal with a student at length; correct the student and immediately return to teaching.
12. Do not get mad, overreact, make idle threats, threaten, taunt, or ridicule a student.
13. Do not insist on public apologies.
14. Do not physically handle students.
15. Do not show favoritism; be consistent.
16. Do not embarrass a student.
17. Praise students who change behavior favorably, saying, "I appreciate the changes you are making."
18. Stand at the door greeting each student as they enter and leave each day: Deliver a quick word to select students such as, "I really appreciate your question today," "Please only work on tasks for this class," or "It would be great if you could try to be a little more diplomatic, your response to … might have been phrased better."

Classroom Rules and Course Policies

The following scrolls would have different wording and alternatives depending on whether it is an elementary, middle, or high school classroom. Permanent classroom scrolls can be used as a reference when a student breaks a rule or to remind all students when the class becomes too unruly.

There is a distinction between classroom rules and policies. The **classroom rules** are intended to keep order so there is a productive classroom environment. **Classroom policies** would include expectations such as having parents sign homework, grading policies, etc. Figure 19.1 shows two examples of classroom scrolls that could be hung on classroom walls to support social studies instruction.

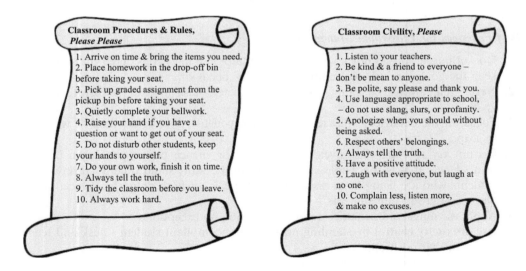

Figure 19.1 Classroom Scrolls of Rules and Civility

Best Practices for the First Weeks of Class

The following advice is gleamed from multiple researchers and practitioners

Two Weeks (Or Earlier) before the First Day of School

1. Contact three teachers in your new school. Ask each one to share their rules, policies, procedures, correspondence to parents, etc. Use these as a guide in constructing the rules and policies for your classroom, thus ensuring that your rules and practices "fit in" to the established culture of the school.
2. Spend an hour with three other teachers at the school and "pick their brains" about how they start the first day, their typical grade distribution, homework frequency and amount, how they handle late assignments, etc. By meeting with other teachers from the same school, you can more easily adjust your ideas to the school culture.
3. Prepare your "Year Long Instructional Plan" (see Chapter 20) and at least two weeks of lesson plans (see Chapter 21), a welcome letter to go home to parents about you, and a detailed list of policies that clarify your expectations for students and parents about homework, grading, etc. Include a copy of your version of the classroom scrolls.
4. Place the following scrolls on the classroom walls for:

Classroom Rules	Rights of the Individual
Classroom Civility	Responsibilities of the Individual
Discussion Etiquette	Freedoms of the Individual
Essential Identity Questions	Responsibilities of Government

The "First Week of Class Packet" includes the above along with the letter to parents and classroom policies

To establish a productive classroom, there should be a number of lessons about classroom expectations that should be prepared with the same rigor as any social studies lesson.

Day 1

1. Have tent name cards on each desk and create a bell work activity, perhaps a current events crossword puzzle for older students, something to color for younger students – a task that can be completed or partially completed in the first ten minutes of class.
2. Use the "**doorway entry**" (used every day) strategy as students enter the classroom. Stand in the doorway, greet each student, look them in the eye with a big grin, ask their names, welcome each one to the class, and ask them to take their assigned seat and quietly complete the bell work task on their desk.
3. Once all students have arrived, welcome them, give them a few minutes to complete the bell work.

4. Explain and discuss that students are expected to return the classroom to the way they found it each and every day or class period – make that their job, give them ownership of the classroom, and do not release the class until they tidy up the room.
5. Have a student(s) collect the bell work and put it in the assignments bin. Explain what each bin is for and how it is used: Homework drop-off, assignments drop-off, and pickup. Have a file folder with each student's name in the bins.
6. Share with the students a little information about yourself, discuss what *their* goals are for *their* class and interject your goals for the class as you list them on the board.
7. Build enthusiasm about what they will be learning. Hand out books and review the table of contents. Point out and explain the index, TOC, features, etc. Select the first chapter they will read and raise a question about a thing that matters. Explain the night's homework assignment is to select five words that they are unsure of what they mean from the first reading assignment. They are to write an explanation of the words to be turned in tomorrow in the homework bin as they enter the class.
8. Hand out a "First Week of Class Packet" and ask them to read the documents as homework, share the packet with their parents, and bring it to class the next day.
9. Use the **"doorway exit"** strategy (used every day) by standing in the doorway when the students depart, remind every student of the homework, and say something to each student. These small, quietly stated, quick "that-a-boys" and positively stated admonitions, create positive teacher–student bonds.

Days 2–5

1. **Debrief** the homework vocabulary assignment.
2. **Bell work assignment**, "I would like to get to know you." Have your timeline on the board with ten events from your life. A blank timeline should be on every desk. Have each student complete their timeline by adding day of birth and other items of importance, mimicking your timeline. When the bell work is complete, put students in groups of four to talk about themselves and then have one student stand and tell the story of one other student. **Debrief**, explaining how what they did was to choose important events like n historian and discuss "selectivity of items."
3. Explain and demonstrate your wait time questioning policy (see Chapter 25).
4. Begin going over each item in the First Week of Class Packet, saving the democratic beliefs to last. While walking around the room, begin a discussion of the bullet points by asking individual students (the ones paying least attention) why each statement within each scroll is important. Make sure every student is asked a question. Turn to a second student and ask if he agrees and why.
5. Have bell work for students to write and explain which classroom policies, rules, and discussion etiquette points they think are most important and most abused and why.
6. Point to the Essential Identity Questions, Rights of the Individual, Responsibilities of the Individual, Freedoms of the Individual, and Responsibilities of Government banners. While walking around the room, systematically lead a discussion of each with prepared analogies, questions, and examples to engage the students. Make a connection with each right, responsibility, and freedom to a topic you will cover in the upcoming year as a way to preview what they will be learning. This could take two days or more.

This systematic approach for the first week of class should increase the likelihood that a teacher will establish the right environment for a democratic classroom.

Resources

Videos: *ASCD*: Examples of Effective Classroom Management | *Edutopia:* Classroom Management; Power of Relationships in Schools; How to Keep Your Elementary Students Focused; Pom-Pom Jar (teaching kindness); Appreciation, Apology, Aha; Making Sure Each Child is Known; Snowball Toss; Developing Executive Function with Priority List; Turns at the Door; Demonstrating Self-regulation with Tone of Voice; Developing Agency with Student-led Conferences; Helping High Schoolers Manage Emotions; Developing Confidence Through Delayed Grading; Welcoming Students with a Smile; Professional Courtesy; Building a Belonging Classroom | *TCH* or *YouTube:* New Teacher Survival Guide; Parent-teacher Conference (10 videos) | *Teacher Toolkit*: Entry Ticket; Exit Ticket | *YouTube:* Classroom Management – Week 1, Day 1; Practical Classroom Management; Interventions for Classroom Disruption; How to Organize Your Classroom from *Instructor Magazine* [elementary] | An FBI Negotiator's Secret to Winning Any Exchange.

Documents: *Edutopia:* 30 Techniques to Quiet a Noisy Class; 12 Ways to Avoid Humiliation of Students (multiple short and to-the-point tips for teachers on classroom management); 8 Proactive Classroom Management Tips (with video) | *NEA:* Classroom Management (multiple short articles).

References

Black, S. (2000). The praise problem. *American School Board Journal*, v187 n8, August, 38–40.

Education Department of South Australia. (1980). *Developing the classroom group: A manual for the inservice trainer* (Report No. 4). Adelaide, South Australia: Government Printer of South Australia.

Ferreira, M. (2000). Defining caring teachers: Adolescents' perspectives. *Journal of Classroom Interaction*, 36, 24–30.

Glasser, W. (1998). *Choice theory.* Harper Collins.

Good, T. L., & Brophy, J. E. (1991). *Looking in classrooms* (5th ed.). Harper Collins Publishers Inc.

Johnson, D. W., & Johnson, H. (1991). *Learning together and alone: Cooperation, competition, and individualization* (3rd ed.). Prentice Hall.

Jung, C. (2003). *The wisdom of Carl Jung.* Philosophical Library: Kensington Publishing.

Kohn, A. (1993). *Punished by rewards: The trouble with gold stars, incentive plans, A's, praise and other bribes.* Houghton Mifflin Company.

Lambert, M. J., & Ogles, B. M. (2004). The efficacy and effectiveness of psychotherapy. In A. E. Bergin & S. L. Garfield (Eds.), *Handbook of psychotherapy and behavior change* (4th ed.) (pp. 139–193). Wiley.

Rolle, J. (2002). *The role of communication in effective leadership.* Retrieved from https://eric.ed.gov/?id=ED467282.

Yound, C. (2003). *The wisdom of Carl Young.* Philosophical Library: Kensington Publishing.

Whelan, M. S. (2000). *But they spit, scratch and swear! The do's and don'ts of behavior guidance for school aged children.* A-ha! Communication.

20 Textbooks and Planning Instruction

Plans are worthless, but planning is everything.
Dwight D. Eisenhower, President of the United States, 1953–1961 (Blair, 1957, p. 4)

Textbooks

Five textbook publishers in the US have about 80% of the market. Due to the economics of the industry, they create textbooks directed at the standards of the five most populated states because those states have over 50% of the students. The other states typically adopt the textbooks developed for those high-population states that most closely reflect their standards, curriculum sequence, and political ideological leanings. Textbook sales are about $2.2 billion a year (Institute for Progressive Education & Learning, 2020).

Textbooks are written to "readability standards," which means that students, on their own at the grade level for which the text was written, *should* be able to read and decipher the information. The impetus for the increased emphasis on reading instruction in the content areas at the elementary school level and by all teachers, not just language arts teachers, at the middle and high school levels, is a result of too many students not being able to independently read at their grade level (see Chapters 27, 28, and 31).

The impact on what students believe by reading their textbook cannot be overstated. As Pulitzer Prize-winner Frances Fitzgerald pointed out in her classic *America Revised* (1979):

> What sticks to the memory from those textbooks [referring to her K-12 social studies education experience] is not any particular series of facts but an atmosphere, an impression, a tone. And this impression may be all the more influential just because one cannot remember the facts and the arguments that were created.
>
> (p. 18)

Scope of Textbooks

There will be more topics in a textbook than could be "covered" in a school year, even if teachers mistakenly think their job is to teach the textbook with a few elaborations added as part of a survey type lecture. In Figure 17.1 there is an example of two elementary school textbook sequences. Figure 20.1 was fashioned using a typical national publisher's middle school American history textbook. This middle school textbook has almost 600 pages divided into 5 units, 17 chapters, and 67 sections, usually about 9 pages per section. Those sections represent topics, but each of those sections has multiple ("sub") topics embedded within it. As an example, the following chapter on the Civil War has 4 sections, 21 headings/topics, and multiple subtopics presented within 39 pages. The number of pages allocated to any topic often unduly influences teachers' decisions about the importance of the topic and the time that should be given to each topic (Wakefield, 2006). Figure 20.3 demonstrates how a textbook is used as part of a week-long plan.

Section 1: From Bull Run to Antietam,
    The First Battle of Bull Run
    Preparing for War
    War in the West
    War in the East
    The South Attacks
	Section 3: The Tide of War Turns
	    Politics of the South
	    Politics of the North
	    Emancipation and the War
	    African Americans Join the War

Section 2: Life Behind the Lines
    Victories for General Lee
    The Battle of Gettysburg
    Vicksburg
    The Importance of 1863
    The Gettysburg Address
    The Hardships of War
	Section 4: Devastation and New Freedom
	    Grant Takes Command
	    Sherman in Georgia
	    Election of 1864
	    A New Birth of Freedom
	    The End of the War
	    Lincoln is Assassinated

Figure 20.1 Typical Middle School Textbook Chapter

The Role of Textbooks

Explicit, declarative knowledge is the primary substance of textbooks. It is not likely that things that matter, such as the implied patriotism in "How Do We Celebrate Our Country?" in Figure 17.1, are overtly presented in a textbook beyond third or fourth grade. Consideration of democratic ideals must come primarily from teachers' imaginative development of a lesson plan. The topics in the textbook are not the outer boundary of what a teacher should consider teaching. Teachers need to go beyond the boundaries of the textbook (see "depth lessons" in later section). In other cases, because of limited class time, what students read about the topic as homework will need to suffice. Where a teacher decides that a topic will not be covered in class, students should be assessed on the explicit knowledge in the reading assignment from the textbook through an associated task (graphic organizer, worksheet, etc.) quiz, or bell work. Lessons on topics originating from the textbook should include reading of the textbook as homework as a prerequisite to the lesson. Some lessons might be constructed based on just a sentence from the textbook that spurs the teacher's imagination as the jumping-off point.

Textbooks and Political Ideological Stances

Because social studies cannot be divorced from ideology, the content in social studies textbooks can be controversial compared with other subject areas: "American history textbooks can differ across the country in ways that are shaded by partisan politics" (Goldstein, 2020). In his critique of 11th-grade history textbooks, Goldstein explains the process whereby publishers hire teams of experts to author textbooks that they hope to sell to multiple states with as little modification as possible. The most populated states are approached first, where review or "adoption" panels are created that can demand changes to the original text proposed by the publishers. He compares the results of the more left-leaning political ideological stance of California's panel and the more right-leaning stance of Texas's panel. Decisions about modifications are based on state standards and state laws and by the majority opinion of the panel. The differences in the two versions of the texts are reflected in what is left out, removed, changed, left in, and how the passages are phrased. Goldstein points out that the California panel consisted of educators who were appointed by the Democratic governor. They, as an example, did not want the word "massacre" used when referring to 19th-century First Americans' attacks on "white" settlers, and on immigration it preferred a feature about a family from the Dominican Republic. The Texas panel appointed by the Republican legislature consisted of educators, parents, business representatives, a pastor, and a politician. They preferred a feature about a border patrol agent rather than the Dominican Republic family narrative and required a passage on the Declaration of Independence to explicitly mention the number of signers who were clergy. Goldstein's analysis also concluded that California's version of the textbook dealing with capitalism is more likely to be "critical of wealth inequality and the impact of companies like Standard Oil on the environment": Whereas, Texas's version "is more likely to celebrate free enterprise and entrepreneurs like Andrew Carnegie."

Topics may be left out due to legitimate page limitations, grade-appropriateness, and/or political ideological preferences. As a hypothetical, the passage on Andrew Jackson might include the topics, in broad strokes, populism, the Battle of New Orleans, and the Trail of Tears. In a middle or high school history textbook there would likely be a whole chapter, "The Jacksonian Ear" which would include all three subtopics. In a fourth-grade textbook, there might be one or two paragraphs on Andrew Jackson, requiring a less developed explanation and a decision as to which of the three topics would not be included. Leaving out the Trail of Tears in favor of the Battle of New Orleans might be construed as ideologically biased. Some might believe the Trail of Tears is significant, but not necessary or grade-appropriate for fourth grade but absolutely necessary in a textbook for middle school. A teacher in New Orleans might have an in-depth lesson on the Battle of New Orleans and a teacher in Florida might go into depth about the Trail of Tears.

The Year-Long Plan

Although most school districts have an official calendar of about 180 school days, the reality is – due to holidays, weather, pep rallies, special events, emergency drills, school-wide testing, etc., – a teacher will likely have about 150 days in which to teach. States or schools will likely expect teachers to demonstrate that they have lessons that "cover" their standards. Figure 20.3 is a summary of one week of a year-long plan. It is based on Figure 20.1's Civil War chapters, the state of Florida standards, and the teacher's decisions as to what should be learned in class and out of class. The Monday lesson's standard includes both declarative and procedural knowledge, "S.8.A.5.5. Compare Union and Confederate strengths and weaknesses." The procedural knowledge is the critical thinking process to "compare" and the declarative knowledge is "strengths and weaknesses of the Confederacy and Union." The long-term goal of the Monday lesson, when most of the details of the declarative knowledge is forgotten, should be that students acquire the capacity to compare the strengths and weaknesses of any two countries in a military conflict and be able to apply that mode of reasoning of compare and contrast to concepts and facts on any topic in any of the social studies subject fields.

Breadth vs. Depth Lesson Plans

Breadth lessons are characterized by teacher-centered lectures that skim the surface knowledge in the textbook using the "sage on the stage" approach, with the teacher elaborating on selected facts or concepts found that go beyond what is in the textbook. This approach is typified by teachers dividing up what is presented in the textbook chapter, as an example, into five lectures for a week-long lesson plan that lightly covers all the content. This traditional survey approach is unnecessary if students have been required to read the textbook and is redundant because the teacher typically ends up wasting time re-teaching the book. Such lessons are rarely set up for critical thinking like those anticipated in the Arc of Inquiry and rarely can be structured to teach things that matter. In Figure 20.3, there are no breadth lessons presented but all the topics in the chapter are "covered" because the students are required to read the textbook as homework.

Depth lessons tend to take on two forms, both of which are intended to investigate selected topics that the teacher can use to develop critical thinking and procedural knowledge and consider things that matter. If starting with a textbook, a topic or a subsection, phrase, or word from a textbook is selected as a springboard to the creative endeavor of orchestrating a lesson plan.

A micro inquiry depth lesson, because students have read the assigned reading sections of the textbook, affords teachers the opportunity to lead examinations. Figure 20.3 comprises five daily depth plans. In the synopsis of the plan for Monday, the enduring idea involves the skills of how to interpret statistics, and on Tuesday, the time is spent examining the Emancipation Proclamation and other primary documents. Wednesday and Thursday are directed at things that matter.

A macro inquiry depth lesson expands to other subject fields or framing the topic in a broader context temporally, spatially, or conceptually. On Thursday, comparisons of fatalities are made with other wars, broadening the frame to periods closer to the age of the students. A sixth day could have been added to integrate civics by a lesson about the Constitution and that it is silent on a state's right to withdraw from the Union, thus – arguably – legally permitting the formation of the Confederacy.

Two examples not tied to the Civil War lesson would be the historical event of the Great Depression, where a teacher can integrate economics, sociology, and psychology. It is also a macro plan when teachers extend (or "integrate") a lesson into the humanities. The Era of Good Feeling is a period in the 1800s in American history that produced literature, music, and art that reflected and helped shape the American culture. A teacher might create a lesson on art from the Hudson River School and use classroom resources from a museum such as the Getty Museum to shape a lesson about Thomas Cole, the landscape artist.

Four Types of Lesson Plans

Lesson plans might be thought of as falling into four categories, but they should not be viewed as a choice between one or the other. Ambitious teachers are often able to combine the attributes of all four types when teaching one content topic.

A **declarative knowledge lesson plan** is where the teacher's primary goal is to transfer the information about the topic to the students – what Dewey (1916/2004) called a "Record of Knowledge." Such teachers tend to view students as "[a] piece of registering apparatus, which stores up information isolated from action and purpose" (p. 220) and create breadth lessons. The C3 Framework anticipates that teachers will move away from the record of knowledge approach. There are no exclusively declarative lessons described in the week-long plan in Figure 20.3, but all five daily lessons have an abundance of declarative knowledge.

A **skills lesson plan** (see Friday in Figure 20.3) is a plan where, regardless of the content, teachers have the specific intent to teach or model a skill. In the Friday daily lesson students are required to create a timeline. It assumes, however, that earlier in the year the teacher taught a skills lesson about how to create a timeline. Other examples of lessons that focus on skills could be how to identify the longitude and latitude of a location; annotate a primary source document; graph supply and demand; interpret a chart, etc.

A **procedural knowledge lesson plan** (every lesson in Figure 20.3) has an explicit goal to help students learn how to critically think and apply procedural knowledge about the declarative knowledge. On Monday students are taught to interpret statistics and on Wednesday how to source and contextualize. The skill of creating a timeline in the Friday daily lesson becomes a tool for students to help them reason about the importance of each battle. Based on that evidence, they are asked to make a reasoned judgment and argument as to the significance of each battle, rather than teachers starting the lesson telling the students the teacher's or an expert's opinions, as would be the case in a declarative knowledge lesson plan. It is in the interactive lecture, discussion, or debriefing, where the teacher solicits interpretations, that students reveal the modes of reasoning they used, and the teacher shares additional perspectives that further students' understanding. Teachers should elevate both skills and procedural knowledge lessons to also include consideration of compelling ideas and democratic ideals.

A **democratic ideals lesson plan** (see Tuesday, Wednesday, and Thursday in Figure 20.3) can stand alone or be part of skills and procedural knowledge lesson plans. Tuesday uses a civic values approach of searching for the truth and consideration of the virtue of courage as Lincoln moved to end slavery. Monday, Tuesday, and Wednesday each raise multiple democratic ideals.

Two examples unrelated to the Civil War would be a depth macro plan on rights across time that is crafted around the British Magna Carta, the United States Bill of Rights, the French Declaration of the Rights of Man and of the Citizen, and the Universal Declaration of Human Rights by the United Nations using compare and contrast strategy. At the elementary grades level, lessons focused directly on democratic ideals are frequently planned around a desired virtue or democratic ideal. A teacher could craft a lesson on civility using a children's book, such as *Words Are Not For Hurting* by Elizabeth Verdick (2004/2020). This typically lower elementary school approach does not require teasing out a democratic ideal from traditional social studies content, as is the case in discipline-based content organized by the academic disciplines. This elementary example starts with an idea that matters and requires teachers to make explicit connections to democratic ideals, identity capacities, and disciplines such as sociology and psychology.

Four Essential Planning Practices

Teachers, as they begin to envision their plans, would be prudent to keep the following in mind.

1. **The textbook is a launching pad.** The standards and textbook are good places to start lesson planning. Ambitious teachers understand their job is not to "teach the textbook." What reading activity will take place in the classroom and what reading can be accomplished at home is a key decision a teacher must make (refer to Figure 20.2).

   Modeling how to annotate, demonstrating how to analyze a broadside, or showing how to story-board requires a skills lesson. As a general rule, if teaching students how to read the social studies text (narrative, charts, cartoons, etc.), modeling and then practice takes place during class time.

2. **Baseline of information.** This strategy is necessary for planning and instructional efficiency. Assigning reading on an almost daily basis creates a baseline of uniform prior knowledge among all students so that the lesson can be planned on that assumption. As a result, the teacher creates more time in class for discussion of compelling propositions and enduring ideas. The teacher should plan the lesson with the assumption that students have completed the reading assignment and through an associated homework task, bell work, or assessment during questioning validates that each student has completed the reading. If teachers re-teach the book or do not hold students accountable for homework reading, students soon learn there is no benefit to completing the homework tasks and the teacher is forced into an inefficient instructional process. It should also be emphasized that students want consistency in their lives and school, and prescribing daily homework reading creates the kind of routine that increases student success.

   This baseline of information strategy entails three key elements: (A) **Pre-reading** in which the reading is assigned and the teacher "previews" the reading as a way to increase students' ability to extract the meaning out of the homework reading assignment (see Chapters 27 and 28); (B) reading is assigned almost daily as **homework**; and (C) **bell work** and/or an associated homework task is used daily along with the assigned reading as an assessment and is graded as an external motivator. Bell work, serves two purposes: It reduces classroom misbehavior at the start of class and affirms (assesses) that the students completed the homework reading assignment (Pearcy & Duplass, 2011).

3. **Teacher candidates do not have to re-invent the wheel.** Before the internet, comprehensive, detailed lesson plans created by other teachers were hard to come by. Today teachers can find wonderful, detailed lesson plans that include a complete set of supporting ancillaries that can be modified and used as the basis for a lesson plan for their students. Searching the internet for strategies and insights about content allows teachers to identify resources as they craft depth lesson plans.

4. **Assessment.** Teachers should envision how and what to teach in tandem with how they will assess the learning activity (see Chapter 31).

Planning creative, engaging lessons is a great source of satisfaction. The opportunity to be creative and pull together a lesson that will captivate and engage students can be a refuge from the disappointments that come with the everyday experience of a teacher. Seeing the planned lesson come to life becomes its own reward.

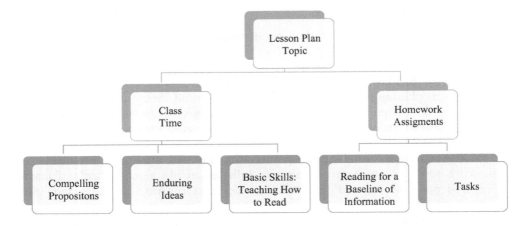

Figure 20.2 Class Time and Homework

Creating a Year-Long Plan

Figure 20.3 represents the kind of detailed thinking that should go into planning the weeks of a year-long plan. Elementary school teachers can apply the same principles in the broader context of their planning for mathematics, science, and language arts. These other subject fields also have standards that define basic skills, declarative knowledge, and procedural knowledge.

Well in advance of the beginning of the school year, teachers can start the planning by creating just the title of the week's lesson as in "The Civil War" and envision what will take place each day of that week with just the "TO" for "Topic" listed. This disciplines teachers into making a judgment about which of the hundreds of possible topics they will use to teach, and those they decide there is not sufficient time for. In this example, the plan is devised to complete the entire chapter of a textbook, the topic of the Civil War. Even after settling on this timeframe, it may well take more time than anticipated – it is better to plan too much than too little and to "do it right," even if it takes longer than planned. Once the chosen topics are spread across the school year, the teacher can turn to the details of each day of a week.

The following description of the abbreviations should be helpful to understanding Figure 20.3.

TO: The **topic** is a unique title given to the daily lessons.

EI|DI: The **enduring idea** and/or **democratic ideal** defines the goal of the lesson.

SS: This **state standard** is from the state of Florida. Documenting what standards a teacher plans to cover has become an important part of the national accountability movement.

C3S: These standards are taken from the **NCSS C3 Framework**. Depending on a teacher's state, they might prefer a Common Core standard.

CQ: This stands for the kind of **compelling question** called for in the Arc of Inquiry approach that sets up the lesson based on the EI|DI, SS, and C3S.

HD: Homework due defines the textbook reading assignment and/or task that is due.

BW: Bell work, in this example, includes five different kinds of bell work for variety.

RE: Briefly describes some of the essential **resources** that will be needed to be created and/or search words used to identify internet resources.

TSW and **TTW:** Popular abbreviations for what "**the student will**" do and "**the teacher will**" do.

OB: The **objective** describes the expected outcome and product that can be used for at least partial assessment.

ST: This briefly explains the variety of active learning **strategies** the teacher will be using.

AD|AS: These are the **assignments due**, usually at the end of class, that are typically used as the **assessment**.

PR|HA: A **pre-reading activity** takes place daily, since there is a daily textbook and/or other reading due the next day. It is a best practice to conduct a pre-reading (see Chapter 27 and 28). **Homework** assigned is in addition to the required reading that is due the next day.

Long-Range Plan: The Civil War			August 2020	
Monday	**Tuesday**	**Wednesday**	**Thursday**	**Friday**
24	25	26	27	28
TO: North and South before the Civil War. **EI|DI:** How to express & interpret statistical data. **SS:** *S.8.A.5.5.* Compare Union and Confederate strengths and weaknesses. **C3S:** *D2. His.14.6-8.* Explain multiple causes and effects of events and developments in the past. **CQ:** Which side had the best resources for War & why was the North loosing? **HD:** Pgs. 378-389	**TO:** *Emancipation Proclamation.* **EI|DI:** Importance of search for the truth, open mindedness, courage as epitomized by Lincoln, the right to liberty, responsibility to respect the rights of others, & government works for the common good. **SS:** *SS.8.A.5.3.* Explain major domestic and international economic, military, political, and socio-cultural events of Abraham Lincoln's presidency.	**TO:** *Gettysburg Address.* **EI|DI:** Right to dignity & responsibility to be compassionate. **SS:** *SS.8.A.1.5.* Identify, within both primary and secondary sources, the author, audience, format, and purpose of significant historical documents. **C3S:** *D2. His.3.6-8.* Use questions generated about individuals to analyze why they, and the developments they shaped, are seen as historically significant.	**TO:** Fatalities of War. **EI|DI:** Patriotism & respect for human life & sacrifice **SS:** *SS.8.A.1.2.* Analyze charts, graphs, maps, photographs and timelines; analyze political cartoons; determine cause and effect. **C3S:** *D2. His.1.6-8.* Analyze connections among events and developments in broader historical contexts. **CQ:** What is the "cost" of freedom and liberty? **HD:** Pgs. 410-417	**TO:** 10 Most significant Civil War Battles. **EI|DI:** How to interpret facts using a temporal mode of reasoning. **SS:** *SS.8.A.5.6.* Compare significant Civil War battles and events and their effects on civilian populations. **C3S:** *D2. His.15.6-8.* Evaluate the relative influence of various causes of events and developments in the past **CQ:** What makes one battle more significant than another?

Figure 20.3 Week-Long Lesson Plan

BW: TSW name & color code states in the Union and Confederacy on a map. **RE:** Chart on pg. 380 & packet of statistics **OB:** TSW describe the strengths & weaknesses of both the Union and the Confederacy before the Civil War by interpreting statistics, recording data on a map, & conceptualizing 5 questions about the data. **ST:** TTW use groups of 4 & debrief questions with Responsive Lecture. **AD|AS:** Class, map & handout with questions/ answers. **PR|HA:** Read handout & broadside of the *Emancipation Proclamation*, RE [gilderlehrman. org].	**C3S:** D2. His.16.6-8. Organize applicable evidence into a coherent argument about the past. **CQ:** Was Lincoln a racist? **HD:** Pgs. 390-401, *Eman. Proc.* & handout of excerpts from the Lincoln-Douglas debates, letters on repatriations to Africa & gradual emancipation with compensations to slave holders. **BW:** Crossword puzzle of vocabulary. **RE:** Teacher made handout - [Annenberg learner.org concerning emancipation, Gilder Lehrman History Now & LFL middle school lesson plan, loc.gov]. **OB:** TSW discuss & summarize Lincoln's changing views on slavery by completing a template. **ST:** TTW uses student pairs & debriefing. **AD|AS:** Handout. **PR|HA:** Read handout of hand-written Gettysburg Address, original form [US History.org]	**CQ:** Why is the Gettysburg Address so compelling? **HD:** Pgs. 402-409 **BW:** Venn diagram comparing battles of Gettysburg to Vicksburg. **RE: Gettysburg Address** reenactment [C-span reenactment video; PBS Gettysburg address; What so proudly we hail Gettysburg address] **OB:** TSW view the video reenactment & complete analysis handout [gilderlehrman. org Gettysburg analysis pdf. **ST:** TTW use pairs to complete handout & whole class discussion to debrief answers **AD|AS:** Exit slip. **PR|HA:** Strategy on how to read a chart.	**BW:** TSW will calculate percentages of Civil War fatalities to populations on chart handout. **RE:** Handout on desk for bellwork with WWI & II, Korean, Viet Nam, Iraq, and Civil Wars **OB:** TSW will compare fatalities in six wars including dates and populations & consider differences and why; at laptops replicate what the teacher demonstrates. **ST:** TTW use demonstration lecture using Excel to produce bar graph of fatalities to population with students & debriefing of the observations. **AD|AS:** Handout & print out of bar graph. **PR|HA:** Review chapter, use packet, & on template record the Who, What, When, Where, Why & How.	**HD:** Review of chapter & WWWWWH template. **BW:** Rank order the battles in terms of importance with written justification for rank order **OB:** TSW will complete the bellwork and create a timeline. **ST:** TTW use pairs for students to convert their homework /bellwork template to a timeline. Teacher will debrief justifications for reasons about the rankings. Teacher will demonstrate current timeline structure with first two battles. **AD|AS:** Homework template & timeline. **PR|HA:** Read "Reconstruction" 419-426.

Figure 20.3 (Cont.)

Two different teachers could have different numbers of days dedicated to a topic, select entirely different daily topics, develop different critical thinking and procedural knowledge skills, and consider different democratic ideals – and both could have created equally excellent lesson plans. Having to create multiple daily lesson plans during the first year of teaching is one of the major reasons that first-year teachers struggle. Wise first-year teachers adapt proven lesson plans from the internet, ask colleagues for their lesson plans, and team up with another first-year teacher and agree to divide up the labor, with one teacher taking one chapter/topic and another teacher taking another and sharing the daily lessons and the ancillaries.

Resources

Videos: *TCH or YouTube*: 10 Great Lesson Planning Templates and Resources.

Documents: *What I Have Learned:* Plan for Next Year – Organize the Year, Topics & Daily Lessons | Strategies for the efficient use of time in teaching.

References

Blair, W. M. (1957) President draws planning moral: Recalls army days to show value of preparedness in time of crisis. *New York Times*, Nov. 15.

Dewey, J. (1916/2004). *Democracy and education.* Dover.

Fitzgerald, F. (1979). *America revised.* Random House.

Goldstein, D. (2020). *Two states. Eight textbooks. Two American stories.* New York Times. Retrieved from www.nytimes.com/interactive/2020/01/12/us/texas-vs-california-history-textbooks. html?smid=nytcore-ios-share.

Institute for Progressive Education & Learning. (2020). *K12 textbooks and supplements.* Retrieved from http://institute-of-progressive-education-and-learning.org/k-12-education-part-ii/k-12-text books-and-suppliments/.

Pearcy & Duplass. (2011). Teaching history: Strategies for dealing with breadth and depth in a standards-based environment. *The Social Studies, 102*(3), 110–116.

Verdick, E. (2004/2020). *Words are not for hurting.* Free Spirit Publishing.

Wakefield, J. F. 2006. *Textbook usage in the United States*: *The case of U.S. history.* Paper presented at the International Seminar on Textbooks, Santiago, Chile. www.eric.ed.gov/ERICDocs/data/ ericdocs2sql/content storage../50.pdf. Retrieved, 2020.

21 Daily Lesson Plans

You got to be careful. If you don't know where you're going, you might not get there.
Yogi Berra, Major League All Star Baseball Player, 1925–2015 (Goodreads, 2020)

Choreography of Instruction

The transition from a weekly plan summarizing daily lesson plans to a detailed daily lesson is the next step in preparing to teach. Today, teachers are the authors, producers, and the primary actors of multimedia productions that rely heavily on "audience" participation. Detailed planning is important because it forces a teacher to think deeply about how and what is to be taught and what they will say. The plan itself then serves as a roadmap and script when teaching the lesson.

Teacher candidates may underestimate the need for the kind of detail proposed for class notes in this chapter. It is an accurate observation to make that experienced teachers typically have less need for such detail, but this is because of their experience. For a novice teacher, the importance and value of thinking deeply about the lesson plan that occurs during the authoring of the plan cannot be overstated.

The Daily Lesson Plan Components

Figure 21.1 depicts the components of a daily lesson plan. Envision a file folder that has class notes and ancillaries and that are also saved as digital files for future use.

Class notes would typically be what teachers have in their hands to refer to while teaching. Its purpose is to organize the lesson into a sequence of steps and to create a script, the "**teacher talk**," which is what the teacher will say. It includes the talking points, directions to students about tasks, and when and how ancillaries are to be implemented.

Tasks are the activities that are to take place, such as students completing a graphic organizer, organizing into groups, completing a simulation, etc.

Ancillaries are graphic organizers, worksheets, board work, visuals, didactic materials (a globe, etc.), etc., needed for the daily lesson plan. In most cases, such as for a graphic organizer, there is a completed ancillary that serves as the teacher's talking points when lecturing or debriefing and as an assessment key. The finished teacher's version includes annotations that serve as talking points along with the "answers" in the graphic organizer. The answers represent the expert level of thinking that is grade-appropriate and would be equivalent to an A grade on the assignment. If students are

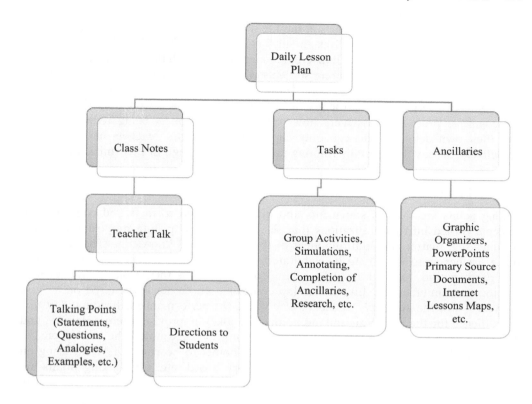

Figure 21.1 The Daily Lesson Plan Components

to complete the graphic organizer as the teacher lectures or if students are expected to complete the graphic organizer independently or in groups, copies of the blank version would be included to be handed out to students. As an example, if a professor were lecturing about daily lesson plans to teacher candidates, the professor could hand out a blank Figure 21.1. The professor would lecture from the finished version while students filled in the graphic organizer. The professor's finished version would look like Figure 21.1, but with annotations about each cell in the graphic organizer to serve as talking points.

Ancillaries also include lesson plans and background knowledge website pages. These ancillary resources should also be downloaded and saved. Even though a website's URL may be saved, prudent teachers create a PDF of the page or lesson plan because the URL address may change.

Teacher Talk

A lesson is not the activity or task, nor is it the text or resources we use ... or even the groups we arrange or the product of the activity. Clearly the partnership between teaching and learning and teacher and learner is forged by the talk of the classroom.

(Edwards-Groves, Anstey, & Bull, 2013, p. 15)

As John Henry Newman eloquently stated, "You may learn from books at home, but the detail, the colour, the tone, the air, the life which makes it live in us, you must catch all these from those in whom it lives already" (Newman, 1852/1902, p. 32).

Effective teachers use more nonverbal communication than average teachers and achievement levels are higher among students when their teachers use more movement, animation, and gestures (Beebe, 1980). Clark and Peterson (1986) found that the greatest amount of energy spent by the teacher when delivering the lesson is on the iterative, metacognitive process of assessing how well the instruction is being received, rather than their own delivery. This can only happen if, like actors, teachers have rehearsed the delivery, at least by mentally running the narrative through in their mind's eye.

Talking Points

Talking points are the key statements and questions linked to facts and concepts and concepts turned into generalizations that serve to raise compelling propositions linked to things that matter and enduring ideas of the foundational knowledge. They are notes to the teacher as to what is to be elaborated on. Because good teaching requires audience participation, teachers must be willing to improvise as they observe the students' reactions and interactions. Like a standup comedian whose act is premised on a "give and take" with the audience, teachers know where the performance is heading, "set up" the audience for the upcoming talking points (the joke), improvise where necessary, and are prepared to respond to hecklers. When planning the class notes, the teacher creates something akin to a script that lists the talking points to be covered. When using an ancillary such as a map, primary document, story board, etc., the talking points are listed on the ancillary as talking points. Unlike the standup comedian, the teacher can bring the class notes on stage.

Talking points are typically listed as statements, questions, or sometimes just a word on the class notes and serve as a reminder to the teacher of the key ideas to be conveyed. Talking points are most effective if they are converted to questions. Henry Youngman, the comedian, was the master of pace and making jokes by converting the joke to a question. So instead of saying, "The new Italian navy has glass bottom boats to see the old Italian navy," he asks, "Why does the new Italian navy have glass bottom boats? To see the old Italian navy."

Class Notes and the Instructional Sequence

The instructional sequence depicted in Figure 21.2 is based on the work of a number of psychologists and educators. The **direct instruction method** proposed by Madeline Hunter (1982) is a long-standing and widely used format. She identified key components of the instructional process that are intended to ensure mastery by students. Subsequently, educators converted the theories into a seven-step or ten-step process. The **nine events of instruction** (Gagne, Briggs, & Wagner, 1992); the **concept attainment method** (Bruner, 1996); and a **constructivist instruction model** (Gagnon & Collay, 2001) have components and a sequence very similar to the "**Madeline Hunter Method**," although the terminology is different.

Figure 21.2's class notes are based on the Wednesday Gettysburg Address daily lesson topic in the week-long plan (refer to Figure 20.3). Figure 21.2 mixes the terminology from the Hunter or Gagne approach. Many teachers prefer to include the

Steps & Time Estimate	Teacher Talk, Activities, Tasks, & Resources
Homework Due	Reading - pages 402-409 of the textbook & the *Gettysburg Address*
Bellwork (5 min.)	Handout 1. Open book - Venn diagram to compare the battles of Gettysburg to Vicksburg. https://www.eduplace.com/graphicorganizer/pdf/venn.pdf
Debriefing (5 min.)	Question: "What are 3 similarities and 3 differences from Handout 1?" List the responses on the board and elaborate. **Item A: Teacher Talk.** Teacher's completed version of Handout 1 would include the talking points to be elaborated on. [As an example, the talking points on Item A would be both battles around same time, July 1863 & considered turning points in the war. Vicksburg gave the Union control of the Mississippi River and split the Confederacy in half, Vicksburg was a siege as opposed to a "battle." If Lee had won at Gettysburg, he likely would have captured Washington D.C.!] Background: https://www.battlefields.org/learn/civil-war/battles/vicksburg https://www.battlefields.org/learn/educators/curriculum/elementary-school/gettysburg-address Collect Venn diagrams
Set Focus (5 min.) with Whole Class Discussion	What makes a great speech? Wait for students' answers, affirming possibilities. Video of Charlie Chaplain's "greatest speech" https://www.youtube.com/watch?v=uAd1WJ9gXo0. **Talking Points:** Explain what satire is using the above Hitler spoof. **Item B: Teacher Talk:** Use an annotated version of https://iedunote.com/top-10-qualities-good-speech to ask questions and list on board as students respond adding those qualities not thought of by students.
Review Discussion	**Teacher Talk:** What did you learn about the *Gettysburg Address* from your textbook or know about the speech? Who – Lincoln, What – Speech, When – November 1863, Where, Battlefield of Gettysburg (show map), How – from a makeshift stage, Why? – "lets wait on that."
Lesson Purpose	"We are going to figure out why the *Gettysburg Address* is considered one of the world's greatest speeches."
Content Presentation (25 min.) [There could be multiple content presentations in any lesson.] The following steps would be different and more or less in any lesson plan.	1. Distribute Handout 2. Typed copy of *Gettysburg Address* Handout 3. *Gettysburg Address*: Analysis of Literary and Rhetorical Devices. https://www.gilderlehrman.org/sites/default/files/inline-pdfs/Gettysburg%20Address%20Analysis.pdf **Talking Points:** Explain Handout 3 and clarify expectations.
Video	2. **Talking Points:** Preview the upcoming video using Item B. 3. Students watch video of performance by reenactor. https://www.c-span.org/video/?c4476933/gettysburg-address-reenactment

Figure 21.2 Class Notes – Gettysburg

Group in Pairs	4. Places students in pairs, play video again as students start to complete the <u>Handout 3</u>.
Group & Circulate	5. Circulate and work with low achieving and ELL students. 6. Students complete <u>Handout 3</u>.
Debriefing.	7. **Debriefing:** Solicit answers in whole class setting based on: **Item C: Teacher Talk** - The teacher's completed version of Handout 3 **Item D: Teacher Talk** - Marked-up copy of *The Gettysburg Address* identifying imagery and key words. **Talking Points:** Start with it is simple, short for its time, eloquent, it is a eulogy, but that to narrow, really about moving forward because dedicated to ALL soldiers?) Background: https://www.coursehero.com/lit/The-Gettysburg-Address/rhetorical-devices-used-in-the-gettysburg-address/ https://mannerofspeaking.org/2010/11/19/the-gettysburg-address-an-analysis/ .
Discussion	8. **Prompt:** Does Lincoln's speech make you think or feel differently about being an American? **Talking Points:** How might a Confederate soldier and Union soldier feel when reading the speech after the war? Patriotism, what is it? Pride that American democracy is capable of sacrificing to push the boundaries of liberty and equality. Does the speech create a kind of sadness, can you think of how a contemporary song includes an emotion? "Humble and Kind" by Tim McGraw
Guided Practice	Not used in this lesson
Independent Practice	Not used in this lesson
Assessment	Based on <u>Handouts 1 & 3</u>, and class participation
Prereading (5 min.)	Turn to book and preview the chart. Homework Pgs. 410-417

Figure 21.2 (Cont.)

standards in both the long-range and daily lesson plan: In this case, they are only in the long-range plan.

Description of Steps

Homework: Given limited class time, meaningful homework is an efficient way to create a baseline of foundational knowledge and have students practice independent learning (Robinson & Patall, 2006).

Bell work: Should be required at the beginning of class to authenticate homework completion and to bring the students to good order.

Debriefing: Is a dialogue that combines questioning and discussion following a specific task, such as student practice, discussion, or independent or group activity. The two primary purposes are to: (1) increase the likelihood that all students have the same understanding; and (2) engage students in a dialogue as practice for citizenship.

Review: Is used to assess students' current state of knowledge and understanding regarding the topic at hand.

Set focus (aka, hook, setup, anticipatory set, etc.): This is an attention-getter, something that captures the students' imagination, interest, engagement, etc. It could be a simulation, an image, music, video, question as per the C3 Framework, etc.

Lesson purpose: Students should be explicitly told what the objective or purpose of the lesson is.

Content presentation: Can be combinations of sequenced lectures, discussions, group activities, problem-solving tasks, to teach reading, simulations, etc. In the Gettysburg example, the examination is of a primary document. There is no "lecture," per se. The bulk of the detailed talking points would appear in four documents (Items). Talking points, in cases where the lesson does not have ancillaries, would be detailed in the content presentation of the class notes. An alternative is to include the talking points in the notes section of a PowerPoint slide (see Figure 21.3), or perhaps on a separate document using a format such as Cornell Notes.

Teacher talk: Should include detailed talking points. It is the driving force of the lesson plan because it uses students' anticipation as a motivating factor by choreographing the images, videos, ancillaries, and teacher talk into a sequential and tiered learning experience. The foundational knowledge is the basis for related evidence, analogies, examples, etc., used to illuminate democratic ideals, model modes of reasoning, and development of critical thinking skills.

Group and circulate: Group activities, to be successful, require teachers to circulate and work with individual students and groups. Putting students in pairs and groups within classes of 25 allows teachers to "tutor" students in groups such as those at the low end of the achievement range, while not disadvantaging students at the high end of the achievement range who work more independently.

Guided practice: Takes place in class. If students were taught how to annotate a document, as an example, guided practice would have been used for students to demonstrate, while in class, independently or in groups, that they can apply the skill.

Independent practice: Takes place in or out of class, but the students demonstrate the skill, independently.

Assessment: Students should be assessed based on the purpose of the lesson plan and the standards the lesson is planned to achieve (see Chapter 31). But a number of lessons can be assessed at one time.

Pre-reading: When there is an in-class or homework reading assignment, teachers should conduct a pre-reading (see Chapters 27 and 28).

If the lesson was a lecture-based lesson (see Chapter 22), the extensive talking points and points of emphasis would appear in the class notes, the PowerPoint presentation slides' notes section, or in something like the Cornell Notes format on a separate document. What is essential for novice teachers is to have detailed, well-thought-out talking points before the lesson begins.

Teacher Talk – Elementary Grades PowerPoint Example

Figure 21.3 is an illustration of the teacher talk in a PowerPoint format for a lower elementary lesson about Columbus's discovery of the new world. It assumes the students have to read a passage in the textbook about the "Exploration Period" and Columbus's voyages as homework to create a baseline of information. A textbook would provide a narrative of events, dates, people, and places, but would not likely explicitly explain the motivations. It is the teacher who must extract the consideration of enduring ideas and of things that matter out of the foundational knowledge. Figure 21.3 is structured as if it were a PowerPoint presentation and includes the talking points that would be crafted to accompany each slide. The slides would include images (suggested in italics) as well as statements or questions and answers. As an example, slide 1 includes an image of Columbus. The example reflects a decision by the teacher to make the question of motivations the thing that matters for the lesson and to focus on how students should organize their thoughts and think critically about the Columbus story.

Slide	*Image* & Statements Visible to the students [Images are in italics]	Talking Points/Points of Emphasis Not visible to students
1	*Columbus* Q. What are the names of Columbus' three ships?	A. *Nina, Pinta,* and *Santa Maria*
2	*Nina and the Columbia space shuttle* Q. How long is this classroom? [Note this could integrated with a mathematics lesson]	T. About 40 x 20 feet S. The Columbia space Shuttle was 122 ft. in length A. Nina 60 by 17 feet – use the desk to form the shape of the Nina and have students get inside. S. 27 men on the Nina Q. How would you feel about going into space? Q. How do you think the men felt on the Nina after 10 weeks at sea?
3	*Hispaniola & Map of Voyages* Q. Why do astronauts and deep-sea explorers want to explore today? Q. Why did Columbus and the other explorers want to "Explore?"	Hispaniola - Haiti and Dominican Republic A. To understand the universe, to find new things like minerals & new life forms. A. Sailed west to get to India hoping for a shorter route than land because that was where the valuable spices and silk fabric could be bought. – Use Map. T. Historians organize the motives into 5 categories that led Columbus and his crew to be brave enough to take on the challenge? This is called "multiple causation." Multiple causation means that for any event there are usually more than one reason.
4	*Group Cooperation & Discussion Etiquette Rules Scrolls*	T. Refers to scrolls S. Students get into preassigned groups.
5	What are 5 Primary Reasons?	S. Students in groups must come up with five reasons per group.

Figure 21.3 Content Presentation Talking Points – Columbus

	Why would you have wanted to risk your life to travel with Columbus?	Q. Solicit and list students' answers on board, then have students recommend how to group the answers based on similarities, and ask students what label should be used for each group. **Note:** Show following slides as students provide labels
6	Reason 1?	Wealth
7	Reason 1? Wealth *Treasure chest of gold coins*	T. Countries were competing to be the wealthiest so that more people could live better, to build more ships to become even wealthier, and to protect themselves from other countries who might want to go to war with them. The ships crews and captains would earn money from what they found.
8	Reason 2?	Religion
9	Reason 2 Religion *Notre Dame Cathedral*	T. Europeans believed their Christin religions were the "true" religions and wanted to "convert" the people in other countries to their religion because that would be the only way those people would get to heaven. In 1400, some people thought it was OK to make people follow their religion. Q. What do you Think
10	Reason 3?	Adventure
11	Reason 3? Adventure *Image of Conquistador in body armor.*	The explorers and their crews wanted the experience of going to the "new world," they were curious about what they would find.
12	Reason 4?	Fame
13	Reason 4? Fame *Images of Dakota Meyer (Afghan war hero)*	The explorers and their crews wanted to be famous and respected. They were seen as heroes. Q. Can you name some other heroes? Q. What do heroes have in common? A. Definition, a person who is admired or idealized for courage, outstanding achievements, or noble qualities.
14	Reason 5?	Nationalism
15	Reason 5? Nationalism *The American Flag*	Q. What is Nationalism? Pride in one's country? Is there nationalism today? Ex: First to walk on the Moon, winning the Olympics, helping other countries after natural disasters, that we put an end to slavery, that we are lucky to live in such a wonderful country etc.
16	History's Hazards, Present-mindedness In 1400, people did not think the way we think now.	Q. Does that make them bad people?

Figure 21.3 (Cont.)

17	Wealth *Bank, Home, Automobile, Cell Phone*	Connect to Scrolls Respect the Rights of Others Respect the Property of Others Right to Private Ownership of Property
18	Wealth Respect the Rights of Others Respect the Property of Others Right to Private Ownership of Property	Q. Can you give me an example of how things have changed? T. Explain the rise of the middle class, ownership of land possible today, etc.
19	Religion *Normal Rockwell – St. Thomas Church* *Synagogue* *Vandalized Mosque* *Native American Religious Ceremony*	Connect to Scrolls To be Tolerant Freedom of Worship
20	Religion To be Tolerant Freedom of Worship	Q. To be Tolerant, what does that mean? Q. How is Freedom of Worship guaranteed and respected in America? T. It would be wrong to force all Americans to have only one religion or for the U.S. to force a religion on the people of another country. It would be wrong to treat someone badly because they believed in another religion.
21	Adventure *Moon Walk, Underwater Diver, Mountain Climber*	Q. Have any of you been on an adventure or tried something that you were a little afraid to do?
22	Adventure	Going on an adventure require courage the same thing needed by heroes.
23	Fame *Zion Williamson, Lady Gaga*	Q. Just because you are famous, does it make you a hero? Q. What's the definition of a hero?
24	Fame vs. Infamous *Adolf Hitler*	Fame vs infamous, well known for some bad quality or deed.
25	Nationalism *Saluting the Flag*	Q. What is nationalism? A. Definition, identification with one's own nation and support for its interests Q. Can you think of other examples?
26	Nationalism "My country, right or wrong; if right, to be kept right; and if wrong, to be set right."-Carl Schurz.	T. Being proud of your country includes the obligation to keep it something you should be proud of.
	Writing a letter. Images of Letter Generator from http://www.readwritethink.org/classroom-resources/lesson-plans/dear-librarian-writing-persuasive-875.html	Write a letter to a person in another country and persuade the person to come to America by naming three things you like about your life in America that makes America special. Handout Persuasive map as a pre-writing requirement from http://www.readwritethink.org/classroom-resources/lesson-plans/dear-librarian-writing-persuasive-875.html Use the *letter generator* with computers from the laptop cart from the same website.

Figure 21.3 (Cont.)

Resources

Videos: The Cornell Note-taking System | How to Take Cornell Notes | *KIPP*: Cognitive Guided Instruction.

Documents: *ASCD:* Why Talk is Important in Classrooms | The Cornell Note-taking System.

References

Beebe, S. A. (1980). The role of nonverbal communication. Retrieved from https://files.eric.ed.gov/fulltext/ED196063.pdf

Bruner, J. (1996). *Toward a theory of instruction.* Harvard University Press.

Clark, C.M., & Peterson, P.L. (1986) Teachers' Thought Processes. In: Wittrock, M.C., Ed., Handbook of Research on Teaching, (3rd ed.). Macmillan. (pp. 255–296).

Edwards-Groves, C., Anstey, M., & Bull, G. (2013). *Classroom talk: Understanding dialogue, pedagogy and practice* (1st ed.). Newtown, NSW: Primary English Teaching Association.

Gagne, R. M., Briggs, L. J., & Wagner, W. W. (1992). *Principles of instruction design* (4th ed.). Harcourt Brace Jovanovich.

Gagnon, G. W., & Collay, M. (2001). *Designing for learning: Six elements in constructivist classrooms.* Corwin Press.

Goodreads. (2020). *Yogi Berra.* Retrieved from www.goodreads.com/quotes/266663-you-ve-got-to-be-very-careful-if-you-don-t-know.

Hunter, M. (1982). *Mastery Teaching.* Corwin Press.

Newman, J. H. (1852/1902). The idea of a university. Retrieved from. www.newmanreader.org/works/historical/volume3/universities/chapter2.html.

Robinson, J. C., & Patall, E. A. (2006). Does homework improve academic achievement? A synthesis of research, 1987-2003. *Review of Educational Research, 76,* 1–62.

22 Lecture

Professor Binns, their ghost teacher, had a wheezy, droning voice that was almost guaranteed to cause severe drowsiness within ten minutes, five in warm weather. He never varied the form of their lessons, but lectured them without pausing while they took notes, or rather, gazed sleepily into space.
From *Harry Potter and the Order of the Phoenix* (Rowling, 2003, pp. 228–229)

Lectures came into prominence in European universities as an efficient method of teaching known as scholasticism. The process had a rigid structure: first was the *lectio*, where the students were not permitted to speak and the teacher would read from a text and then comment on passages to illuminate their meaning; second, was the *meditation*, in which students reflected on what they heard; and third was the *quaestio*, where students could ask questions and interact with the teacher.

Influenced heavily by the mass production of textbooks in the 20th century, today's teachers have learned to choreograph the use of textbooks, books, chalkboard, copy machines, overhead projectors and, now, smartboards, handhelds, laptops, and the internet into effective lessons. Throughout the technological transitions, reading, lecture, memorization, and practice have been a constant, but recitation has all but disappeared. Note-taking became a mainstay of lectures once paper and pencil was introduced into the mix, if for no other reason than to compel students to pay attention. The still popular Cornell Notes System that was invented in the 1950s systematized note-taking by structuring the recording of facts, concepts, and generalizations. Lectures fall in the category of **"teacher-centered instruction."** Whereas **"student-centered learning"** typically relies on group or independent work (see Chapter 23 and 30).

Lectures, whether delivered traditionally by teachers talking or through videos, animations, PowerPoints, or a combination of all four, are efficient ways to communicate information, but bring to mind the limitation expressed in the age-old adage, "I didn't say he learned it, I only said I taught it." The internet and technology have made it possible to engage students' senses with multimedia experiences, but effective lectures are **interactive lectures** that engage students with questions and tasks that are laced throughout the presentation (see Jackson, 2009). **Engagement triggers**, such as planned questions, breakout groups, and tasks, are essential no matter how charming the teacher's personality or the visual effects. Classroom management problems that can come to plague new teachers are minimized when interactive lectures are astutely paced and frequent engagement triggers are used to accommodate limited attention spans.

Interactive Lectures

Interactive lectures are active learning experiences because the student is required to be an active participant in the lecture, even though it is teacher-centered. The following interactive lectures structures are adapted from multiple sources. Any one of the daily lessons from Chapter 20 could be constructed into one of the following interactive lecture frameworks. In many cases, these active lecture types are active experiences by the use of quick, "**breakout groups**," where students complete a task as part of the lecture with a "shoulder partner" (see Chapter 24, "turn and talk," "classroom mingle," and "find someone"). These lectures take advantage of the internet by including an array of rich images gleaned and organized into class notes.

LECTURE TYPE	DESCRIPTION
Socratic Lecture	*Pre-lecture*: Teacher prepares class notes with talking points staged as sequential questions. This changes the traditional lecture from one where students watch, listen and perhaps take notes, to one where students are thinking in anticipation of being called on and their answers are affirmed or refined by the teacher and followed up with more questions (see Chapters 24 & 25). *Lecture:* 40 minutes. *Debriefing*: 10 to 15 minutes. Students are asked to summarize with more teacher-directed questions. *Assessment:* Students' participation and quality of answers.

Feedback Lecture	*Pre-lecture*: Teacher prepares:
	 Handout 1 before the lecture begins.
	 Lecture: 10 to 15 minutes. The teacher lectures using Item A with students taking notes.
	 Handout 1: Outline of the lecture in the traditional
	 I.
	  A.
	   1).
	    a. (etc.) (see Thomas, 2020).
	 Item A: Class notes is Handout 1 annotated with teacher's talking points next to each outline item.
	 Handout 2: Four to five higher order discussion questions (see Chapter 25, "Bloom's Taxonomy-Based Questions"
	 Item B: Teacher's version of Handout 2 with preferred, expert answers to questions as talking points.
	 Breakout group: 15 to 20 minutes. Each student is given a copy of Handout 2. Based on the homework reading, lecture and their notes, students singularly, with partners, or in groups discuss and answer the questions in Handout 2. Every student records their answers to the questions while comparing their notes on their outline.
	 Debriefing: 10 to 15 minutes. The teacher leads the whole class discussion using Item B with students' reporting of their responses.
	 Assessment: Students turn in completed Handout 2.

Guided Lecture	*Pre-lecture:* Teacher prepares: **Handout 1**: Four Objectives, such as "The student will analyze and write down 4 causes of the American Revolution." **Item A**: Is Handout 1 with preferred expert answers to be used as talking points.

Figure 22.1 Interactive Lecture Types

	Lecture: 10 to 15 minutes. At the beginning of the lecture, students are given Handout 1 with space to write ideas under each objective. Students are asked to listen (no note-taking) to the lecture and are expected to be able to recall the information. The teacher lectures from class notes organized by the objectives. *Individual assignment*: 5 minutes. After each objective is lectured on, students are to write down all the information they can recall related to each objective. *Breakout group*: 10 to 15 minutes. At end of lecture, students work in pairs or groups to combine individual answers which would include the compelling ideas and democratic ideals based on the 4 objectives. *Debriefing:* 5 to 10 minutes. Students are asked questions about their answers to the objectives. The teacher calls on students to respond to other students and uses the class notes to elaborate on each objective with students filling in any missing information. *Assessment:* Students turn in completed Handout 1.
Responsive Lecture	*Pre-lecture:* The teacher, perhaps following a week of instruction, sets aside time for questions on the daily lessons covered during the week. **Item A:** Is a list of question that the teacher anticipates and will cover even if students do not ask the questions. *Homework/Bellwork:* Each student develops two higher-order, open-ended questions with preliminary answers based on the week's lesson. *Note*: This lecture assumes the teacher has modeled what higher-order and open-ended questions are. *Breakout group:* 10 to 15 minutes. Students are placed in groups of 5. Each student is asked to share her/his two questions/answers and the group is asked to rank order the questions for the teacher to answer, with at least one question from each student. *Debriefing:* 15 to 20 minutes. The teacher begins the dialogue by asking a student from one group for their top question, a 2nd student from the group on why it is important, and a 3rd student for an answer, before elaborating. Teacher follows the same process with all groups. *Assessment:* The teacher collects each student's two higher-order open-ended questions and answers for assessment. *Note*: This approach can also be used as a lecture based on an assigned reading or as a review.
Demonstration Lecture	*Pre-lecture:* [A timeline is used, as an example, of the 10 most important events associated with the American Revolution]. The teacher prepares **Handout 1:** A blank timeline **Item A:** The teacher's filled-in version of Handout 1 with points of emphasis to be used as class notes. Each student is given a blank timeline. The purpose is to: a) model a mode of reasoning (chronological cause and effect) and b) demonstrate the skill of how to properly construct a timeline. *Lecture:* 15 to 30 minutes. Part 1: The teacher explains the attributes of the blank timeline, such as equal increments of time, the span of time selected, how to enter a date and event with arrow to the precise location on the timeline, etc. Part 2: With the students' textbooks open, the teacher lectures from Item A while completing the timeline, giving students time to fill in dates, events, compelling ideas by asking questions as to how each event is connected to the next. The teacher models by the think-aloud approach about the rationale of the choices of events that are drawn from the textbook and their interrelatedness.

Figure 22.1 (Cont.)

	Assessment: Teacher collects each student's timeline for assessment. Note: This demonstration lecture is ideally suited for modeling many skills such as annotating a textbook passage, primary document, completing a specific kind of graphic organizer for the first time, etc.
Pause Procedure Lecture	*Note:* Assume the teacher has already used a demonstration lecture to model how students should construct notes using the Cornell Notes system (see *Resources*). *Pre-lecture:* Teacher prepares the following: **Handout 1**: Blank, 3 section Cornell notes pages(s). **Item A**: Class notes based on the Cornell Notes format. *Lecture:* 15 to 20 minutes. The teacher lectures from Item A while the students take notes. *Breakout pairs:* Every 5 to 7 minutes, the teacher pauses to allow pairs of students to share notes to correct, collect missing information, and discuss and compare the ideas presented. *Debriefing:* 5 to 10 minutes. The teacher calls on students to respond to prepared questions based on the Item A summary section in the Cornell Notes section to discuss and elaborate on compelling ideas and democratic ideals. *Assessment:* During debriefing, the teacher walks by students' desks to check and assist each with flaws in students' notes. Students turn in their Cornell Notes pages.
Think/Write/Discuss Lecture	*Pre-lecture:* Teacher Prepares **Item A**: Class notes with at least four key higher-order questions to be asked at pivotal points in the teacher talk. Students are told to take out a piece of paper to be handed in. *Lecture*: 15 to 20 minutes. The teacher lectures from the class notes that includes planned pauses where the teacher stops to ask one of the higher-order questions. Students write down the questions. *Student response:* 2 to 3 minutes. The teacher pauses after each question for each student to write answers to the questions. *Debriefing the questions:* 5 to 10 minutes. The teacher calls on students to share their written answers to the first question. The teacher repeats and summarizes compelling ideas and democratic ideals based on the first question and then continues the pattern until all four questions are addressed. *Assessment:* Students turn in their paper with responses to higher-order questions.
The Case Lecture	*Pre-lecture:* The teacher prepares a one paragraph case, such as this personal and civic identity case based on a compelling idea about civic duty: **Item A.** "You are a teenager and driving down the road and observe a car swerving slightly on to the siding and then across the line on a 4-lane road divided by a medium. You pull up to pass, and the person is texting and there is an infant in the back seat. What do you do?" The teacher prepares class notes of key questions based on likely responses that would come from the students. *Lecture:* The teacher reads the case to the students. *Debriefing:* A whole class discussion ensues by calling on multiple students. The teacher serves as an interlocutor and provocateur, never taking sides and primarily calling on other students to respond to the various scenarios and reasoning. *Assessment:* Students are asked to record a personal response of the what and why with a five-sentence explanation of their decision. Teacher collects students' personal responses. *Note:* In longer cases, the teacher would provide a handout of the case.

Figure 22.1 (Cont.)

Flipping the Classroom	*Note:* Flipping the classroom assumes all students have access to broadband internet at home because it anticipates that as homework prior to class they will view the equivalent of a teacher-made PowerPoint, lecture from the internet, or animation via the internet. The purpose is to make it possible for the teacher to allocate all classroom time to debriefing, practice, discussion, and/or modeling. If all students do not have such home access, such a strategy would not be appropriate and an in-class presentation would have to substitute. *Pre-lecture:* Teacher prepares a PowerPoint presentation or uses a grade-appropriate PowerPoint, video, or animation from the internet that meets a standard or a topic for students to watch as homework. **Item A:** Debriefing questions are prepared because the homework assignment serves as the "lecture." Note: As an example, the demonstration lecture on timelines could be converted into a mp4 video of a PowerPoint, uploaded to YouTube and assigned as homework or a preexisting video on the internet could be assigned. *Preview:* The teacher introduces the assignment for homework. *Homework:* Students complete the homework assignment. *Learning Activity:* Entails practice during class time. In groups or with single students the teacher becomes a tutor circulating around the room and the students produce a product based on what they watched. *Debriefing:* The teacher debriefs from a set of class notes to ensure all students have command of the skill or concept. *Assessment:* Teacher collects students' products.
Students Present as Experts	Note: This assumes the teacher used a demonstration lecture to teach how to research and create a presentation that is engaging and the teacher allows time in class to tutor individual students as they prepare their lectures. The idea is students will teach the topic to the class rather than the teacher. *Pre-lecture:* All students in the class are assigned or allowed to choose a topic from a list prepared by the teacher well in advance of the date the teacher would normally teach the topic. Teacher prepares: **Handout 1:** Directions and required elements for a great presentation **Handout 2:** Rubric for assessment **Handout 3**: List of topics to choose from. *Lecture:* Much like student-led discussions (see Chapter 24), a portion or all of the lecture is conducted by the students. The teacher takes notes from a seat in the back of the class and takes on the role of a student asking questions along with the other students. *Debriefing:* At the end of the student's presentation, the teacher reemphasizes the compelling ideas and democratic ideals. *Assessment:* The students' class notes, PowerPoint, etc.
Group Activity Setup Lecture	*Pre-lecture:* In advance of a planned group activity, the teacher creates: **Handout A:** Directions and rubric for the product to be created in the group activity. **Item 1**: Class notes on the topic. **Item 2**: Class notes of the directions on what the students are expected to do. *Lecture:* The teacher lectures from Items 1 and 2. The students begin the activity as soon as the lecture is completed. *Debriefing:* At the end of the group activity, the teacher reemphasizes compelling ideas and democratic ideals. *Assessment:* Group activities are best structured so that each student produces a product submitted at the end so teachers can give each student a grade, even if it was a group activity or product.

Figure 22.1 (Cont.)

LECTURE FORM (Modes of Reasoning)	DESCRIPTION	TOPIC EXAMPLE
Ascending-descending order	Topics are *arranged* according to quantifiable amount, importance, or significance.	*Arrange* the following states in order by population and by square miles.
Cause-and-effect	*Explain* cause-and-effect relationships.	The British persecution of Pilgrims in England led them to leave their homes and come to the New World. *Hypothesize* the reasons why people want to immigrate to America today?
Chronological	*Arrange* the order of events.	*Arrange* and *describe* the ten most important events leading up to the War Between the States.
Compare-and-contrast	*Compare* significant differences and similarities.	*Contrast* the advantages and disadvantages of electric cars and gas-powered cars.
Concept examples	A concept is presented and examples presented to *justify* the concept.	Right to justice examples are a trial by a jury of peers, Miranda warning, representation by a lawyer, etc.
Conflicting generalities	Pose one principle, then *critique* a counter principle.	Now that we *recognize* that freedom of speech is a right guaranteed in the Constitution, can you always say anything you want?
Parallel elements	Two events or ideas are *compared* based on a set of common elements.	*Reconstruct* the reasons for the American Revolution and the American Civil War into culture, economy, issues, and beliefs.
Part-to-whole	*Deconstruct* how an idea is composed of several concepts.	Before we can understand crime, we need to *evaluate* how economics, education, family environment, and culture contribute to criminal behavior.
Problem-solution	*Identify* a problem and then identifies solutions.	*Describe* what causes a recession and *explain* some of the solutions that have been tried.
Rule-example	State rule followed by examples then *analyze* the rule.	In the United States we have a right to privacy. Can you *select* and *justify* some examples and non-examples?
What-why	*Interpret* an effect in reverse order.	Now that we understand the differences between the Senate and the House, *support* the reasons the founders organized things this way?

Figure 22.2 Modes of Reasoning Lecture Types

Modes of Reasoning Lectures

The following lectures represent the most dominant modes of reasoning used by experts to examine social studies foundational knowledge and democratic ideals. Teachers should explicitly state to students the mode of reasoning type, define it, and then proceed through the topic so students acquire the expert vocabulary that represents the particular critical thinking process. These modes of reasoning are used in conjunction with the interactive lecture types. Note that each *italicized* word in the critical thinking lectures are from **Bloom's Taxonomy of Action Verbs** (Anderson & Krathwohl, 2001, and see Chapter 25). The taxonomy and the "action verbs" have been used extensively in teacher candidate training since the 1950s. The verbs are purposely used here as a tool to encourage teacher candidates to consider being precise in their communication.

Best Practices for Great Lectures

Lectures can be successful when the teacher:

1. Creates an interactive, multimedia experience by collecting and including ancillaries (images, video, handouts, graphic organizers, etc.);
2. Articulates the objectives for the lesson to the students at the beginning of the lecture;
3. Concentrates on modes of reasoning;
4. Focuses on just one or two compelling ideas and democratic ideals;
5. As part of planning, creates multiple questions, analogies, examples, and anecdotes that capture the students' imagination as part of the teacher talk;
6. Rehearses;
7. Presents the information in small, sequenced steps;
8. Sets a quick pace that keeps students engaged;
9. Starts the lectures with an intriguing question, image, a quote with one word missing for students to guess, a compelling story, a poll on an opinion about the lecture topic, etc.;
10. Talks with the students, not at them;
11. Gives motivational cues, "On Friday you will need to create a map and legend for a map of Florida, so let's pay close attention;"
12. Calls on multiple students, not just volunteers, and counts readiness to answer questions toward students' grade;
13. Infuses pop culture references to connect to students' lives;
14. Employs topic-related humor;
15. Uses breakout groups;
16. Constantly checks for student understanding;
17. Does not talk too fast;
18. Changes inflection, volume, and pitch;
19. Uses eye contact to keep every student engaged;
20. Moves about the room;
21. Uses "warm language" such as first names and "thank you," etc.;
22. Shows enthusiasm about the subject; and
23. Uses wait time (see Chapter 25).

Resources

Videos: *Teacher Toolkit*: Buddy Journal; Classroom Mingle; Turn & Talk; Find Someone | *TCH or YouTube:* Engaging Students in Direct Instruction | *YouTube:* How to Give a Lecture; How to Take Better Lecture Notes; *LBCC* Study Skills; *AVID* 2 Minute PD Cornell Notes.

Documents: Learning Taxonomy – Krathwohl's Affective Domain | Writing Objectives for Lesson Plans Using Bloom's Verbs | Bloom's Verbs | Cornell Notes.

References

Anderson, L. W., & Krathwohl, D. R. (2001). *A taxonomy for learning, teaching and assessing: A revision of Bloom's taxonomy of educational objectives.* Longman.

Jackson, S. (2009). The guide on the stage: In defense of good lecturing in the history classroom. *Social Education, 6*(4), 275–278.

Rowling, J. K. (2003). *Harry Potter and the order of the phoenix.* Scholastic.

Thomas, T. M. (2020). *Writing an outline.* Retrieved from www.austincc.edu/tmthomas/sample%20outline%201.htm

23 Group Learning

When three persons work together, each can be the teacher in some aspects.
Confucius, Philosopher, 551–479 BCE (Quotetab, 2020)

Group learning, **cooperative learning**, and **collaborative learning** are terms used interchangeably in the academic literature because they share one attribute – learning takes place in groups rather than instruction delivered in a teacher-centered whole class arrangement. Group learning started to become a mainstay of K-12 instruction in the 1970s, but had been a practice at the elementary school level since the initial theories of Maria Montessori were adopted in many American schools (Lillard, 2017).

It is particularly important in social studies education because it provides practice for the kind of collaboration needed for effective citizenship. Grouping strategies allow the teacher to change the class tempo, reduce teacher-centered instruction, provide more focused attention to sets of students with different skill levels, and increase student participation (Hendrix, 1999; Stalling, 1980). When compared with traditional whole-class or individualized learning, students who have participated in well-structured and meaningful group learning have been shown to develop increased higher-level reasoning; greater empathy for fellow students; enhanced social perspective-taking (the ability to understand how a situation appears to another person); and higher self-esteem (Johnson, Johnson, & Holubec, 1991; Kagan, 1993; Slavin, 1990; Stahl & VanSickle, 1992).

However, there are pitfalls, particularly when teachers are not vigilant and monitoring groups' activity. When teachers are not attentive to the groups, a few students in a group may dominate the discussion; do the majority of work on an assigned task; create classroom management problems; and cause the group to become unproductive. For these reasons, teachers should have a group cooperation scroll which details how students are to conduct themselves in groups.

Types of Grouping Tasks

Students should be put into groups to perform a task where additional, more intimate student-to-student interaction should produce a better result than whole-class instruction or a task done individually. Most of the interactive lecture types in Chapter 22 rely on breakout groups and tend to involve a specific task for individuals in pairs, threesomes, or foursomes. Tasks tend to fall into three categories and each should be followed by a debriefing in whole class format by the teacher:

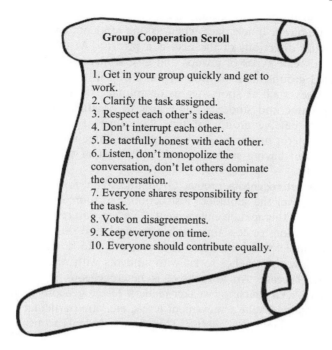

Figure 23.1 Group Cooperation Scroll

1. **Discussion tasks**, where students are expected to have a discussion that results in a more detailed analysis and dialogue by the group.
2. **Product tasks**, where a tangible product will be created by each individual or the group, which is facilitated by students collaborating. This would include simulations, skits, and presentations, as well as papers, charts, etc.
3. **Reading tasks**, where the teacher has planned a lesson to teach students how to read social studies, such as a chart, image, primary document, etc. (see Chapters 27 and 28).

Key Teacher Decisions about Groups

For the purposes of this textbook, group learning is segregated into two broad categories: The less formal **breakout groups** and more structured **cooperative learning groups**. Both share the following key attributes:

1. **Teacher- or student-appointed groups.** For efficiency teachers often allow students to form breakout groups quickly by students self-selecting a partner, threesome, or foursome based on their seating arrangement next to each other. However, this reduces the learning opportunity to have students work with all the students in the class and learn to adjust their interpersonal interactions to different learning styles and personalities of group members. Teachers should purposefully plan groups that mix all the students in the class over time.

2. **Transitions.** Transitions into groups can become chaotic and waste time. It is important to require a quick pace when asking students to transition into groups. Clarity in teacher directions of the task is a priority. At the beginning of the year the teacher can create types of groups and give students a handout indicating their names, assigned groups, and location of the group in the classroom. Teachers may give groups names, such as sports teams or animals, so the teacher only has to call out the group name and students know how to organize. As an example, for animals, there may be five groups of five, with tigers being homogeneous reading groups, hawks heterogeneous reading groups, and three more heterogeneous groups for the purposes of having students work with most of the students, such as bulls, sharks, and turtles.

3. **Homogeneous or heterogeneous groups.** Groupings allow for differentiated instruction between groups, "over the shoulder" instruction, and more of the kind of caring rapport necessary for a therapeutic engagement. Teachers can create differentiated assignments and spend more or less time with a group based on the group's abilities and needs. As an example, when the lesson is to teach how to read social studies, homogeneous groups allow the teacher to sit with students with reading deficits and coach them to greater success. An alternative is heterogeneous groups with one strong reader, who serves as a coach for weaker readers. Heterogeneous groups based on ethnicity, gender, income levels, achievement levels, etc., are particularly important when discussions involve things that matter. This allows students to hear and engage with students who bring perspectives based on their identities and unique experiences. Cooperative learning groups are typically heterogeneous.

4. **Teacher supervision.** While the groups are meeting, the teacher circulates among the groups to ensure that everyone is participating and the group is staying on task. The teacher intervenes when necessary to keep everyone on task.

5. **Evaluation.** For evaluation purposes, if a product like a graphic organizer is to be created, each student should create his or her own while working with the other students. Participation in the discussion or activity should be observed and graded as well. Students should be held accountable, so if questioning is used during a debriefing, the teacher must remember to call on different students on different days and to record their participation grades.

Group Types

The following are some of the most frequently used grouping methods compiled from multiple resources. It is a good idea to use several methods over time so as to vary the engagement. Almost every one of these group activities is preceded by a more teacher-centered lesson or "set-up" and they should be followed by a prepared debriefing by the teacher.

1. **Agreement circle:** Students stand in a circle and step in when they agree with the teacher's or student's statement.
2. **Co-op:** Students work in groups and each contributes to an assigned product by accepting responsibility for a part of the project. In a lower elementary class, students might create an ABC report on American history with the alphabet divided up between the members of the group.

3. **Corners:** Students form a team in each corner of the room, representing a teacher-determined idea, such as the critical attributes of rural, urban, and suburban communities. The team discusses its idea. Each corner shares its results and then the teams listen to and paraphrase ideas from the other three corners.
4. **Group graphic organizer:** A group designs a graphic organizer based on a teacher's lesson or reading assignment.
5. **Interview pairs:** After a content presentation or reading assignment, two students interview each other about the information to check for understanding.
6. **Jigsaw:** The number of members in a team is determined by the number of separate subtopics. As an example, the American Revolution could be divided into before the war, during the war, or the colonies could be divided into northern, middle, and southern. Each student on the team becomes an expert on one of the subtopics by working with the experts from the other teams. Upon returning to the primary team, the student teaches the other members about the subtopic.
7. **Learning together:** In addition to completing the assigned task, the group dynamics that lead to the success or failure of the teams and its members are explicitly analyzed during a debriefing as part of the process following completion of the task.
8. **Line opinion:** Students stand and form a line from strongly agree at one end to strongly disagree at the other, reflecting their opinions about a topic.
9. **Match mine:** One of the pairs must draw an image to reflect the lesson's content and the other must write a description.
10. **Numbered heads together:** Every team member is numbered, for example, in a team of four, students would take numbers 1 through 4. The teacher poses questions; team members consult to make sure that everyone knows the answer; the teacher calls a number and that student responds.
11. **Pairs check:** Students work in pairs. One coaches while the other solves a problem. Then they alternate. After every two problems, the pairs check their answers.
12. **Paired sequences:** Students write notes on small pieces of paper. Each pair of students compares notes and puts the notes in an order that reflects the organization of the new information.
13. **Pairs compare:** Members of pairs work independently but are allowed to check each other's work.
14. **Paraphrase pairs:** The teacher requires one student to paraphrase the other student's statement, verbally or in writing.
15. **Round robin:** Each team member takes a turn to share their idea.
16. **Round table:** Each team member writes one answer as a paper and pencil are passed around the group.
17. **STAD (student teams-achievement divisions):** Following a lesson, members help each other master the knowledge by sharing ideas. Students take individual quizzes, and the team's evaluation is based on the success of individuals.
18. **Student timeline:** Students write the date and event on a piece of paper and form a line based on the dates.
19. **TAI (team-assisted individualization):** TAI combines group and individualized learning. Students on a team work individually on a self-paced assignment and members check on each other and help solve problems that each of the members may encounter.
20. **Teach word webbing:** Teams create webs, with all group members contributing simultaneously on a piece of chart paper or at the chalkboard.

21. **TGT (team games tournament):** This is the same as STAD, but quizzes are replaced with a tournament in which teams compete with each other. Low-achievers from one team compete with low-achievers of other teams, and each member earns points.

22. **Think pair share:** Students think about a topic, pair with another student to discuss ideas, then share their revised thoughts.

Cooperative Learning

In breakout groups, typically, students are given a challenge that can be completed in a short period of time; they have short-term goals; and typically lack the formality and structure of cooperative learning. **Cooperative learning** is an effective group learning method that is very structured compared with breakout groups and can cover multiple days. To be successful in cooperative learning, students must master interpersonal skills, a crucial goal of social studies education. The cooperative learning structure helps students develop these skills by providing specific rules and roles during the group activity.

The Key Elements of Cooperative Learning

Following are some of the requirements for effective cooperative learning.

1. **Teacher supervision** is needed to establish the cooperative learning rules. The teacher should observe groups to ensure that all students are gaining from the experience. If a student is off task or misbehaving, the teacher should join the group to reinforce the rules or answer questions about the assignment.

2. **Heterogeneous groups** ensure that students of different abilities and backgrounds learn to work together to achieve a goal.

3. **Positive interdependence** is achieved through group goals, joint rewards, divided resources, and role assignments. Students are responsible for their own behavior in the group.

   a. Students are accountable for contributing to the assigned task.
   b. Students are expected to help any group member who wants, needs, or asks for help.
   c. Students will ask the teacher for help only when everyone in the group has the same need.

4. **Face-to-face interaction** encourages eye contact and verbal and nonverbal responses. Students explain, discuss, solve problems, and complete assignments as a team.

5. **Individual accountability** requires students to be held accountable for individual tasks that will help the group meet its overall goal. Some possible roles include:

   a. Leader   f. "Go-fer"
   b. Recorder   g. Artist
   c. Timer   h. Proofreader
   d. Encourager i. Researcher
   e. Reader   j. Author

6. **Social skills** are behaviors that enhance positive interaction and communication among group members. The social skills learned in cooperative learning are as important as acquiring knowledge. The teacher needs to establish expectations for

behaviors and rules through a content presentation as part of the lesson establishing the cooperative learning task.
7. **Group processing** is a discussion of how well the group has functioned and is part of the debriefing. Group processing allows for closure when a cooperative assignment is completed.
8. **Evaluation** should include both an individual performance assessment and a team assessment.

Cooperative learning focuses on the socialization and civility goals necessary for participation in a democracy. In addition, the interactive process supports multicultural education goals and identity capacity building.

Resources

Videos: *Teacher Toolkit:* Card Sort; Find Someone Who; Four Corners; Gallery Walk | *Learner.org*: Social Studies in Action a Teaching Practices Library Series (the following videos specifically include effective group activities) – Historical Change; China Through Mapping; Caring for the Community; California Missions; State Government and the Role of the Citizen; Using Primary Sources; Understanding Stereotypes; Public Opinion and the Vietnam War; Migration from Latin America | *TCH or YouTube:* Choosing Collaborative Groups; Collaborative Group Work with the 1-3-6 Protocol; Collaborative Learning Preparing for the Future; Structured Academic Controversy; Student Centered Civic Discussion & Deliberation; Peer Teaching Through Expert Groups | *YouTube*: 60 Second-Strategy: Cooperative Learning roles.

Documents: Cooperative Learning in the Thinking Classroom Research and Theoretical Perspectives | Cooperative Learning in the Social Studies Classroom: An Introduction to Social Studies, Bulletin no. 87.

References

Hendrix, J. C. (1999). Connecting cooperative learning and social studies. *The Clearing House, 73*(1), 57–60.
Johnson, D. W., Johnson, R. T., & Holubec, E. J. (1991). *Circles of learning: Cooperation in the classroom*. Interaction Book Company.
Kagan, S. (1993). The structural approach to cooperative learning. In D. D. Holt (Ed.), *Cooperative learning: A response to linguistic and cultural diversity*. (ERIC Document Reproduction Service No. ED355813). ERIC Clearinghouse for Social Studies/Social Science Education, pp. 9–16.
Lillard, A. (2017). *Montessori: The science behind the genius*. Oxford University Press.
Quotetab. (2020). *Confucius*. Retrieved from www.quotetab.com/quote/by-confucius/when-three-per sons-work-together-each-can-be-the-teacher-in-some-aspects.
Slavin, R. E. (1990). *Cooperative learning: Theory, research and practice*. Prentice-Hall.
Stahl, R., & VanSickle, R. (1992). *Cooperative learning in the social studies classroom: An introduction to social study*. Bulletin No. 87. Ed. ED361243.
Stalling, J. (1980). Allocated academic learning time revisited, or beyond time on task. *Educational Researcher, 9*(11), 11–16.

24 Discussions

Don't raise your voice, improve your argument.

Desmond Tutu, 1931–present (Tutu, 2004)

Discussion typically follows foundational knowledge acquired through reading or instruction but, as seen in some of the interactive lecture types, discussions can be woven into the fabric of a lecture. While there are important discussions about content and how to examine it, discussions are essential to examination of democratic ideals and identity formation. It is in these discussions, more than any other method of instruction, where students witness conceptions of democratic ideals different from their own; observe identity capacities in others that are more developed; practice the core civic values; and reflect on their own adherence to democratic beliefs and personal virtues. Participation in classroom discussions of things that matter is a significant predictor of an individual's commitment to democratic ideals and future participation in the civic life of a country (Torney-Purta, 2001).

Notwithstanding the benefits of discussions, Nystrand, Gamoran, and Carbonaro (1998) observed social studies classes in over 100 middle and high schools and found that 90% of the instruction involved no discussion at all! When there was discussion, it was brief, less than 42 seconds. Teachers have been shown to wait less than a second after a student's last syllable is voiced in a discussion before interjecting a proposition or opinion (Rowe, 1974). Students' responses are longer and more multifaceted when they are responses to statements by the teacher or students rather than to questions (Colby, 1961; Dillon, 1981; Mishler, 1978).

The reasons for not making more extensive use of discussion are many, but "Leading an effective discussion can be one of the most difficult tasks of teaching" (Barton, 1995, p. 346). It is in discussions where the ability of the teacher to manage teacher-to-student, student-to-teacher, and student-to-student interactions is tested the most because it is more unpredictable than the cozy, teacher-centered delivery of a lecture. Because discussions take longer than traditional lectures, they conflict with teachers' concerns about meeting increasingly rigid mandates. Planning for discussions is more mentally taxing for the teacher because they must consider and anticipate the multiple directions the conversation may take and how they can keep the discussion on the desirable considerations. Because of the unpredictability of discussions, planning requires even more thoughtfulness than lectures.

Whole-Class and Group Discussions

The following considerations should be part of planning whether the discussion is planned for an entire class period or laced through lectures, modeling, and questioning. Through the network of interchanges that crisscross the classroom, the teacher must manage the communication flow so that the lesson's goals are achieved and *all* students become participants. Discussions can be divided into either whole-class discussions or small group discussions.

Whole-class discussion is where, typically, the teacher serves as the interlocutor and provocateur ("devil's advocate") and leads the class in the discussion. A teacher can also have a student or student panels lead whole-class discussions or plan for students to lead discussions as part of a presentation.

Small-group discussions are where students are put into groups and the teacher circulates around the classroom, keeping the groups on task and joining in when beneficial. In group discussion, the students take on greater responsibility in the management of the dialogue and often the student who leads the discussion comes to the position organically, rather than appointed by the teacher.

Chandler (2013) recommends that both whole-class and small-group discussions should be concluded with a product, a task such as exit slips, reflection paragraphs, graphic organizers, etc., as a motivation to participation and for assessment. All discussions need debriefings to ensure continuity of understanding across all groups.

Reasons Why Discussions Fail

Researchers such as Hess (2004) who study discussions, suggest a number of reasons why discussions fail:

1. Students are not taught how to participate in discussions.
2. Students are not adequately prepared with the foundational knowledge needed for the discussion.
3. The prompt and questions before the students are not crafted to engage interest.
4. There is unequal participation by students because teachers do not set clear expectations, do not intervene to limit more vocal students' domination of discussion, and do not purposefully reach out to engage less vocal students.
5. Teachers monopolize what should be a discussion among the students.
6. Teachers do no not keep the discussion on point.
7. Discussion requires a commitment to a shared dialogue with students and restraint from the teacher.
8. Teachers do not realize discussion requires more preparation than lectures, not less.

Discussion Types

Like lecture types and types of groups, there are multiple discussion types, which are structured ways of having conversations that foster a trusting environment, critical thinking, and sharing of different perspectives in the classroom (McDonald, Mohr, Dichter, & McDonald, 2013; Teaching & Learning lab, 2020). In most cases, the terms below can be searched on the internet for a more detailed explanation.

Affinity mapping: Students, as part of a group activity, write ideas on sticky notes, place them on a wall or chalk board, then gather to organize the notes, grouping them as they discuss the merits and then label the categories.

Carousel brainstorm: The teacher posts prompts on five poster stations. Groups of students progress through the stations based on time limits, writing ideas on the poster paper.

Chalk talk: Students choose which poster stations to investigate and write responses to prompts posted around the room, including posing questions and comments and responding to questions from other students.

Final word: A student selects a quote from the text, reads it aloud, other students respond, the original student concludes the discussion with his idea.

Fishbowl: A small group of students in the fishbowl discusses a topic while the other students observe and take turns entering the fishbowl when asked to do so by the teacher.

Four As: Students discuss assumptions, what they agree with, what they argue with, and what they aspire to as a result of a prompt.

Four corners: The corners of the room are designated as strongly agree, agree, disagree, and strongly disagree, and based on a prompt, students join a corner and discuss the four options and then can switch corners after the students in each corner explain their reasoning.

Philosophical hot seat: The prompt requires agree or disagree, and students move to one or the other side of the room, discuss the evidence and logic of their arguments, and one student is selected by the opposite side to defend their position.

Inside/outside circles: One group of students forms an inside circle, facing the outside circle of students. Students pair off to discuss a prompt, and then rotate at timed intervals.

Socratic seminar: The prompt comes from the assigned reading and students are tasked to discuss the language from the text, building on each others' ideas, to analyze what the author is trying to say.

Student-led discussion: An alternative to whole-class teacher-centered discussion is to also systematically assign every student to lead a whole-class discussion. In preparation of student-led, whole-class discussions, the student should be informed well in advance and provided additional background resources.

Six thinking colors: Students in groups of six are assigned a color to represent their responsibility: White for neutrality and to ask questions; red for feelings and respond with a "gut" or intuitive response; black for negative and to report inaccuracies in the discussion; yellow for positive and to reports accuracies; green for creative and to ask questions for provocation and investigation; and blue for the facilitator, who keeps the group on task and summarizes.

Think-pair-share: Students, in pairs, individually reflect, and share their response to a prompt, and then share with the class their ideas.

TQE: Students are required to categorize their thoughts, questions, and epiphanies based on a prompt prior to whole-class discussion.

Whip around: Students write down an individual answer to a prompt, then each student briefly shares their thoughts with the class.

World café: White paper tablecloths are placed on tables and groups of students write responses on the tablecloths and then move to the next table.

When planning lessons with discussions, teachers need to plan a whole-class debriefing to ensure uniformity of knowledge from the experience.

Teacher Demeanor

When leading foundational knowledge discussions, the teacher can be more directive and use a faster pace because consideration of the subject matter does not initially engage identity and consideration of ideals. When leading discussions of democratic ideals, the communication style needs to be more informal and conversational because teachers take on the role of philosophical counselors. In such discussions, rearranging desks in a circle or semicircle with the teacher sitting among the students in a student desk conveys a message that the lesson is more about students grappling with beliefs than learning foundational knowledge or relying on the teacher as an authority. By design, discussions should have a slower pace. They require a high degree of self-control by teachers because they can become impatient and too quickly bring the dialogue to closure.

Student Participation

Some students are very deliberate and cognizant of their choice of speech and how they articulate their ideas. Others are not as self-aware as to how their demeanor and verbal interactions affect others' perceptions of them, how it affects their ability to persuade others to their ideas or beliefs, or how their interactions are affecting their classmates' feelings. Students choose to participate or not to participate in discussions based on a number of factors, including efficacy; perceptions about the teacher; prior success with the subject matter and in discussions; observations about the day's class environment, etc.

For the most quiet students, Hurt, Scot, and McCroskey (1981) found that their verbal communication participation rate was a result of a desire to be left alone; belief that peers do not value students who communicate with teachers; previous unsatisfactory feedback from the same or other teachers; and a fear of being thought of as "stupid" or "inept." The consequences for students who become non-communicators are significant. Such students can mistakenly be judged by teachers as less competent and end up being treated differently from more verbal students in terms of the attention, questions, and the individual assistance they receive (Motter, Beebe, Raffeld & Paulsel, 2009; Richmond & McGrosk, 1995). It is difficult to distinguish between naturally quiet students and students with high communication apprehension. However, in both cases the goal is to increase their comfort level so that they participate more in the class discussions because verbal communication is important to clarifying ideas, and the follow-up feedback from the teacher and peers prepares students for civic life. To increase participation rates, teachers can use small-group discussions because they often lower the apprehension threshold, give particular students a "heads up" that they will be called upon the next day so they should be prepared, and tactfully encourage students to share their ideas during classroom exit and entry routines. The simple act of saying to a student, "I would really like to hear what you think" can be a powerful motivator.

The overly verbal or overbearing students can be a distraction to all students and adversely impact other students' willingness to participate. The root causes can be low self-esteem leading to over-compensating, a desire to challenge the teacher, or unawareness of their behaviors because no one has given them thoughtful feedback adequate to produce a change in behavior. If a student is dominating a class, try to elicit responses from other students. If the behavior persists, a quiet word appealing to the student's sense of duty to the other students and encouraging greater attention to the ebb and flow of the class are best practices.

The Heated Conflict

In spite of a teacher's well-articulated expectations for civility, human nature will produce the kind of exchanges that range from a heated discussion to the disruptive and even mean-spirited interchange between students. Discussions of democratic ideals and application of virtues are given more to these kinds of episodes than foundational knowledge discussions due to the emotion-laden content of ideas that matter. Statements by students that do not meet teachers' expectations for civility can be spontaneous or purposeful. An offending student's comment should be viewed from a philosophical counseling perspective: that is, it is symptomatic of an inadequately formed identity and/or democratic ideal. The teachers should, through questioning and examples, lead the student to consider alternative ways of thinking that are based in a democratic ideology. Offensive statements, however, can place meaningful discussions in the future in jeopardy. As a result, the teacher must also make clear to all that such comments are not permissible and come to the defense of the offended student(s). The permutations of such situations are too abundant for a full analysis, but the following ideas should be helpful.

In the case of the offending student, it is unwise for a teacher to respond in a way that the student would perceive as being criticized. The teacher should set aside the offending statement or attitude of the student for the moment and ask the student if the statement could be rephrased, pointing out why others might consider the comment to be problematic or offending. The teacher needs to be tactful and exhibit a degree of caring for the student so that a lasting change might be considered by the students. Stay focused on the idea, not the person. Through questioning, use logic to unravel that student's ill-advised, undemocratic idea that is the basis for the offending statement. If the student becomes agitated or resistant, suggest the better language and plan to discretely talk with the student when the student exits the classroom. Should the original statement have the potential to have offended a particular student(s), discretely check with the offended student(s) to validate their unhappiness and express appreciation for not escalating the undesirable situation.

There is, however, a more problematic case, where a more direct response by the teacher is necessary. That is when a student uses what has come to be called "hate speech." Never demand a public apology, because a teacher cannot make a student apologize. A teacher should give the offending students the benefit of the doubt, but the teacher still needs to take a public stance against such undemocratic notions. All the students' feelings as well as the needs of the offending student to learn from the experience need to be taken into account. As an example, the teacher might say, empathetically, something like, "I really do not think you meant to say that, you might want to consider how you might rephrase that?" In a disappointed and calm tone, a teacher can follow up by speaking to the entire class that everyone will in the course of their lives state something in a way that they will regret. Then turn to the offended student(s) and say, "I want to apologize to you for that comment" and then move on with the lesson. As the offending student exits the class, have a quiet word asking him to consider a one-on-one apology in private to the other student(s), but in any case, the offending language should not happen again. When students use language of any kind that is less thoughtful than the teacher expects, the teacher must remember that the goal is for the teacher to model democratic ideals while responding. This is modeled by creating an environment that makes clear that a classroom is a better place to acknowledge mistakes in judgment or language because it is a place to learn.

Discussion Planning

Some teacher candidates might think that discussions are serendipitous undertakings, but discussions require even more preparation than lectures because of the multiple unanticipated directions they can take. Discussions are a form of content presentation that typically follow at least a brief content presentation which is used to summarize the baseline of information for the discussion and as a springboard to the discussion prompt. The discussion-based content presentation of the lesson plan would include the written talking points the teacher plans to use to steer the discussion should the students nor proffer the concepts and things that matter. The list of talking points that a teacher wants to make sure the students take away from the discussion would be crafted with foundational knowledge evidence, analogies, examples, etc. Integrated into the talking points would be references to the essential identity questions and the democratic beliefs. By preparing detailed notes just as if it were a lecture, the teacher is forced to think through the issues and mentally prepare for contingencies.

The **prompt** becomes the pivotal element because it sets the focus for the discussion (Johannessen, 1984). The prompt is how the discussion starts and can take many forms: a provocative statement, question, quote, picture, cartoon, short video, etc. But in all cases, it is the underlying question that gives the prompt its power. The topic of the prompt needs to have more than one possible perspective or answer worth discussing, such as "We have had genocide throughout history, Armenia, Nanjing, the European Holocaust, etc. What made the European Holocaust different?"

Best Practices for Discussions

There are a number of best practices to consider in planning and conducting discussions, some of which are drawn from Parker (2001), Johannessen (1984), Chandler and Ehrlich (2016) and others.

1. Create a classroom scroll of the Discussion Etiquette Rules. Figure 24.1 is a secondary education example that should be simplified for elementary students.
2. During the first week of class, arrange the desk in a circle and share and discuss the etiquette rules for discussions, asking students to give examples of each.
3. Use a combination of small-group and whole-class discussion types.
4. Use silence, a teacher's own! If a teacher is silent, the students will speak. Studies show that teachers dominate what are characterized as discussions almost as much as lectures (Bellack, Kliebord, Hyman, & Smith, 1966).
5. If a class discussion is not going well because of lack of momentum, energy, or enthusiasm, stop and discuss the reasons why with the students.
6. Purposely slow the pace so that students sense they have time to reflect.
7. Teachers are modeling for students how to listen while guardedly being involved in the *students'* class discussion (Borg, Kelley, Langer, & Gall, 1970).
8. At strategic moments relate a student's comment to talking points, the essential identity questions, and the democratic ideals.

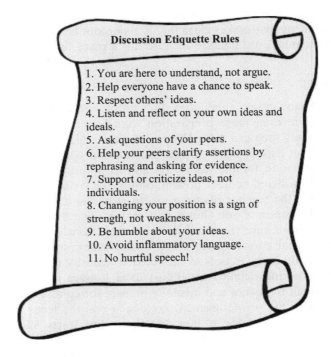

Figure 24.1 Scroll of Discussion Etiquette Rules

9. Guide participation by rephrasing a statement made by one student into a question for another.
10. Instead of responding to a question, ask another student what he or she thinks.
11. Encourage sharing of metacognition when a student makes a statement by asking a student for an elaboration, justification, or evidence.
12. Assist a student with imperfect statements, "Did you mean...?"
13. Student participation should be part of teachers' grading system.
14. After the prompt, call on a student to initiate the discussion.

Resources

Videos: *Learner.org*: Social Studies in Action a Teaching Practices Library Series (discussions are used in these videos); Leaders, Community and Citizens; Competing Ideologies; Economic Dilemmas and Solutions; Gender-Based Distinctions; The Individual & Society; Dealing with Controversial Issues | *TCH or YouTube:* Inquiry-Based Teaching Supporting Quieter Students; Four Ways to Create Equitable Discussions Using Socratic Seminar; Inquiry-Based Teaching the Inquiry Approach; Pinwheel Discussions; Student Centered Discussions; Student Centered Civic Discussion; Structured Academic Controversy; Teaching Through Silence; The Importance of High Quality Discussions.

Documents: *Routledge Handbook of Research in Social Studies Education*: Controversial Issues and Democratic Discourse | International Political Socialization Research | *ASCD:*

Effective Classroom Discussions | *Chronicle of Higher Education*: How to Hold a Better Class Discussion | *Indiana University:* Managing Difficult Classroom Discussions; The Dreaded Discussion | *NCSS:* Discussion in Social Studies: Is it Worth the Trouble.

References

Barton, J. (1995). Conducting effective classroom discussions. *Journal of Reading, 38*(5), 346–350.

Bellack, A. A., Kliebord, H. M., Hyman, R. T., & Smith, F. (1966). *The language of the classroom.* New York: Teachers College Press.

Borg, W. R., Kelley, M. L., Langer, P., & Gall, M. (1970). *The minicourse: A microteaching approach to teacher education.* London: Collier-MacMillan.

Chandler, P. (2013). We have seen the enemy and he is us: Using discussion to bring life to social studies. *Oregon Journal of the Social Studies, 1*(2), 39–45.

Chandler, P., & Ehrlich, S. (2016). The use of discussion protocols in social Studies. *The Councilor: A Journal of the Social Studies, 77*(1), 1–11. article 5.

Colby, K. M. (1961). On the greater amplifying power of causal-correlative over interrogative input on free association in an experimental psychoanalytic situation. *Journal of Nervous and Mental Disease, 1961*(133), 233–239.

Dillon, J. T. (1981). Duration of response to teacher question and statement. *Contemporary Educational Psychology, 6*, 1–11.

Hess, D. (2004). Discussion in the social studies: Is it worth the trouble? *Social Education, 68*(2), 151–155.

Hurt, T., Scot, M., & McCroskey, J. (1981). *Communication in the classroom.* Menlo Park, Calif.: Addison Wesley Publishing Co.

Johannessen, L. R. (1984). Making small groups work; Controversy is the key. *English Journal, 73*(2), 63–65.

McDonald, J. P., Mohr, N., Dichter, A., & McDonald, E. C. (2013). *The power of protocols: An educator's guide to better practice* (3rd ed.). New York, NY: Teachers College Press.

Mishler, E. G. (1978). Studies in dialogue and discourse: III. Utterance structure and utterance function in interrogative sequences. *Journal of Psycholinguistic Research, 7*, 279–305.

Motter, T. P., Beebe, S. A., Raffeld, P. C., & Paulsel, M. L. (2009). The effects of student verbal and nonverbal responsiveness on teachers' liking of students and willingness to comply with student requests. Communication Quarterly.

Nystrand, M., Gamoran, A., & Carbonaro, W. (1998). *Towards an ecology of learning: The case of classroom discourse and its effects on writing in high school English and social studies.* Albany, NY: Center on English Learning & Achievement.

Parker, W. (2001). Classroom discussion: Models for leading seminars and deliberations. *Social Education, 65*(2), 111–114.

Richmond, V. P., & McGrosk, J. C. (1995). *Communication apprehension, avoidance, and effectiveness.* Scottsdale, AZ: Gorsuch Scarisbrick.

Rowe, M. B. (1974). Pausing phenomena: Influence on quality of instruction. *Journal of Psycholinguistic Research, 3*, 203–233.

Teaching & Learning lab. (2020). *Discussion protocols.* Harvard University. Retrieved from labewww.google.com/url?sa=t&rct=j&q=&esrc=s&source=web&cd=1&ved=2ahUKEwjKgZ6c5PPkAhVFRqwKHT0sD1IQFjAAegQIABAC&url=https%3A%2F%2Fwww.gse.harvard.edu%2Fsites%2Fdefault%2Ffiles%2FProtocols_Handout.pdf&usg=AOvVaw2R63Gg7uS2acO2hEQYYdjj

Torney-Purta, J. (2001). *Citizenship and education in twenty-eight countries: Civic knowledge and engagement at age fourteen.* Amsterdam: International Association for the Evaluation of Educational Achievement.

Tutu, D. (2004). *Nelson Mandela Foundation address.* Retrieved from www.nelsonmandela.org/.

25 Questioning and Debriefings

Judge a man by his questions rather than by his answers.
Voltaire (Pierre-Marc-Gaston, duc de Lévis, 2012/1808, maxim xviii)

Socrates, in the *Meno* and *Crito*, as examples, is depicted teaching his students in the streets of Athens where he typically began responding to a student's question – not by answering the question – but by asking a series of compelling questions – thus the "**Socratic method**." Through questions and propositions, Socrates avoids telling students what to think, but skillfully models how to think critically and reach elegant conclusions. This oral tradition continues today in the form of questioning in lectures, discussions, and debriefings.

Questioning is integral to all great lectures, discussions, and debriefings because the teacher, effectively, shifts the burden of critical thinking to the students who learn to refine their questions and answers. Questioning, as a strategy, entails both the questions themselves and the process of questioning. Questions take much more skill and planning than a "one-way" lecture from a teacher and it should not be forgotten that the quality of the teacher's questions serve as a model for students in developing their questioning skills. There are two broad categories of questions: precipitating questions and responsive questions.

Debriefings, in contrast to lectures with questions, are created as a follow-up to a lecture or a task such as homework, bell work, group discussions, students completing a handout in class, students' presentations, simulations, a video, etc. Like lectures that include extensive questions, debriefings create the continuous interactive engagement that motivates students to pay attention in anticipation of being called on to answer a question or respond to a proposition. Its purpose is not to summarize but to analyze the foundational knowledge or democratic ideals from the prior lecture or task and insure a uniformity of understanding.

Precipitating Questions

Precipitating questioning is an essential aspect of turning what could be a boring, passive, teacher-centered lecture or debriefing into an active learning engagement. Precipitating or triggering questions cannot be left to serendipity; they need to be planned and structured into class notes. It starts during lesson planning, when teachers, after thinking traditionally and planning what they will say, convert statements to precipitating questions with follow-up questions and statements. The goal is to create a scaffold of sequential questions. It takes more time to rethink the teacher talk planned as statements and to envision the statements as answers to carefully crafted questions. Well-formed questions are essential to students developing their critical thinking skills and learning the modes of reasoning of social studies because they also indirectly reflect teachers' metacognition (Brogan & Brogan, 1995).

Responsive Questions

In *Critical Thinking in a World of Accelerating Change and Complexity*, Elder and Paul (2008) focus on social studies and the kinds of follow-up, **responsive questions** teachers can ask to develop critical thinking skills in their students. The responsive questions are the second, third, or fourth questions that follow the initial precipitating question. These kinds of questions require students to re-analyze their conceptualizations and reasoning. The students who are not responding to the questions learn from the interaction of the student and teacher. Responsive questions should also be included in the talking points of a teacher's class notes. Figure 25.1 provides examples of responsive questions.

Targeting the Analysis of Thought	Questions
1. Questioning Goals and Purposes	What was your purpose when you made that comment?
2. Questioning Questions	I am not sure exactly what question you are raising. Could you explain it?
3. Questioning Information, Data, and Experience	On what information are you basing that comment?
4. Questioning Inferences and Conclusions	How did you reach that conclusion?
5. Questioning Concepts and Ideas	What is the main idea you are using in your reasoning? Could you explain that idea?
6. Questioning Assumptions	What exactly are you taking for granted here?
7. Questioning Implications and Consequences	What are you implying when you say...?
8. Questioning Viewpoints and Perspectives	From what point of view are you looking at this?
Targeting the Quality of Reasoning	**Questions**
9. Questioning Clarity	Could you give me an example or illustration of your point?
10. Questioning Precision	Could you give me more details about that?
11. Questioning Accuracy	How could we check that to see if it is true?
12. Questioning Relevance	I don't see how what you said bears on the question. Could you show me how it is relevant?
13. Questioning Depth	What makes this a complex question?
14. Questioning Breadth	What points of view are relevant to this issue?
15. Questioning Logic	Does what you say follow from the evidence?
16. Questioning Fairness	Does one group have some vested interest in this issue that causes them to distort other relevant viewpoints?

Figure 25.1 Types of Responsive Question

Grounded vs. Ungrounded Questions Strategy

Distinguishing between grounded and ungrounded questions can help to motivate students to be prepared for class discussions and for teachers to diagnose misunderstandings of students.

Grounded questions are questions grounded in the baseline of information students should know by a task such as a reading assignment, group activity, or lecture. Using the same example from Chapter 21, if the Nina, Pinta, and Santa Maria ships of Columbus's voyage are part of the baseline of information, students should be able to report out the information because the question, "What are the names of Columbus's ships?" is "grounded" in the foundational knowledge. The grounded questions typically require students only to recall. Grounded questions are a starting point for a scaffold of questions leading to higher-order questions requiring critical thinking and application of procedural knowledge.

Students should be held accountable for answers to grounded questions by including answering questions in a teacher's grading scheme. If not, students will soon learn they do not have to pay attention or complete assigned tasks and the teacher will waste time re-teaching what the students could have learned on their own – leaving less time to examine compelling ideas and democratic ideals. Problems of inattention and incomplete tasks will be minimized when questioning becomes a systematic part of assessment. The external motivator of grades will dissipate as students reap the intrapersonal benefits of sharing what they know and learning from others.

Ungrounded questions, as opposed to grounded questions which only require recall, require some level of critical thinking. As an example, the Columbus sequencing of questions might include the analogy, "I want everyone to think about why we explore space," followed by "What could be some of the motives that led Columbus and his crew to sail across the Atlantic?" This requires students to form a hypothesis, find the critical attributes shared by a current event and event in the 1400s, to infer from the foundation knowledge of the text, draw on their common sense, and use intuition.

Both grounded and ungrounded questions and expected answers would appear in the talking points of the class notes. Students should be held accountable for a good-faith response in ungrounded questions, but not an incorrect answer because it is not grounded.

Equal Distribution of Questions Strategy

The grounded/ungrounded strategy requires a commitment to call on all students an equal number of times, as an example, over a two-week period. It is not uncommon to observe classrooms where teachers appear to call on the same relatively small group of students almost all the time and impatiently "shop" questions around the classroom until someone, anyone has any answer. These are counterproductive practices because it communicates a teacher's greater interest in finishing the lesson than engaging with every student so every student has the opportunity to demonstrate their foundational knowledge and thinking about democratic ideals. Ensuring an equal distribution of questions to all students communicates that teachers care about each and every one of their students. Teachers should use a checklist (or other means) to track questions to students. The equal distribution protocol changes the dynamics of classroom questioning and motivates students to come to class ready to at least answer grounded questions. It uses the intrinsic motivation of self-interest because they do not want to be called on in front of their peers and not be prepared.

During the first week of classes, the teacher's approach to questioning should be explained. It starts with putting an end to volunteering and hand-raising for precipitating questions.

1. During grounded questioning, there is no volunteering. Students need not raise their hand because "you care about each one of them." All students will be called on an equal number of times during the course of any two-week period or sooner and it will count as part of their grade.
2. The question will be announced before calling on a student, so that students will have plenty of time to think about the answer.
3. Students are required to respond with their best answer; the teacher will wait in silence for as long as it takes for the selected student to answer. Correct, thoughtful answers result in better grades.
4. Another student will not be called on until the student initially called on has given an answer or has said that he or she does not know the answer.
5. The next question would typically be an ungrounded question, a responsive question, to the same or another student that the teacher selects.
6. Students who wish to comment or expand upon another student's or the teacher's answer may volunteer.

Wait-Time Strategy

The wait-time approach is based in part on the research and principles of **wait time** (Rowe, 1972) and **think time** (Stahl, 1980), among others, and applies to grounded and ungrounded questions. The most basic principles are:

1. The teacher always asks the question before calling on a student.
2. A question is followed by a minimum of three seconds of silence (Wait Time 1) so that every student has time to collect his or her thoughts and devise an answer.
3. Then a student is selected.
4. A second wait time (Wait Time 2) is used for the student to collect his or her thoughts prior to answering.
5. The student answers.

It is essential to this strategy that the teacher maintain a patient demeanor and silence during wait time, so students see that the teacher is willing to wait "forever" for an answer. As a consequence of knowing they will be called on and the teacher will wait for a response, individual students become motivated to avoid the uncomfortable experience of the teacher and students waiting in silence for an answer. The strategy of equal distribution of questions and unlimited wait time is based on the principle that learning to participate in class is essential to their success in a democratic society.

Some of the positive aspects of this combined strategy of grounded questions, equal distribution, scaffold questions, and wait time are:

1. All students are motivated to pay attention and complete tasks so they can be ready to answer questions.
2. The length and correctness of students' responses increase.
3. Silence and the number of "I don't know" responses diminish.

4. The number of volunteered and correct answers to ungrounded questions increases.
5. Scores on academic achievement tests increase.
6. Teachers tend to increase the number of higher-level, ungraded questions.
7. The classroom becomes a quieter and more civil community of learners.
8. Students become more active agents in their own learning.
9. More students become prepared participants.

Five General Types of Social Studies Questions

Engle and Ochoa (1988) identified five types of questions used frequently in social studies education.

1. **Definitional questions:** The teacher is only asking for a coherent definition, such as, "Can you define a rural community?" or "a law?" Definition questions are intended to create an objective, shared starting point. This entails helping students overcome their biases or prejudices by differentiating between the **critical attributes** and **non-critical attributes** of a term. A question like, "Can you define illegal immigrant?" requires a teacher and students to construct a definition based on critical attributes by examining what the meaning of "illegal" vs. "legal" and political ideologically-based nuanced differences between "illegal immigrant" vs. "undocumented resident." This process with a controversial topic requires students to account for their feelings while using the civic values of search for the truth, open-mindedness, and critical thinking.
2. **Evidential questions:** What evidence can students cite to support their answers? "Can you give some examples of what would constitute a legal and illegal immigrant?"
3. **Policy questions:** What should be done about societal problems? "What do you think would be the best policy for handling people who want to permanently move from one nation to another nation?" "Do nations have a right to have geographic borders?" and "What are the implications for a country and the world if there were no geographic borders?"
4. **Value questions:** What values underlie suggested solutions to policy questions? "Why do you think it is wrong or right for immigrants not to be able to move to a new country unless the laws allow it?" and "Why do you think it is wrong or right for a country to restrict immigration?"
5. **Speculative questions:** What might have happened if things developed or were done differently? "Why are people willing to come to America, even if illegally?" "What kind of law would you write to solve all or part of this problem?"

Bloom's Taxonomy-Based Questions

Bloom's *Taxonomy of Educational Objectives* (Bloom, Englehart, Furst, Hill & Krathwohl, 1956) and its revision (Anderson et al., 2001) has become the education standard for writing learning objectives and creating precise questions based on different levels of cognition. The taxonomy has six increasingly sophisticated levels of cognitive processing (Figure 25.2).

Included below are "verbs" from each level that are frequently used when preparing questions for a lesson. The questions in the following examples represent what would be the first of multiple, sequenced questions aimed at moving students to the higher level of cognition.

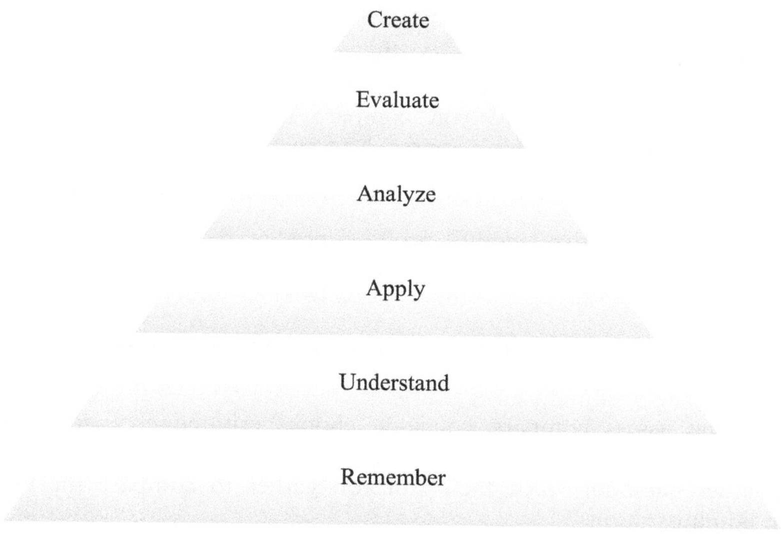

Create

Evaluate

Analyze

Apply

Understand

Remember

Figure 25.2 Bloom's 2001 Taxonomy

Remembering questions require the student to retrieve relevant knowledge from memory. A remembering question should have a follow-up question using a higher-order cognitive process.

> **Verbs:** Define, identify, label, list, match, name, recall, what, when, where, which, who, why, etc.
> **Base question:** Who is the president?
> **Follow-up higher-order question:** Would you tell us some of the changes you would make if you were president?

Understanding questions require the student to demonstrate comprehension beyond a restatement of factual knowledge. Understanding questions usually require the student to explain the answer in his or her own words.

> **Verbs:** Classify, compare, contrast, differentiate, explain, infer, interpret, rephrase, etc.
> **Base question:** Would you explain the duties of the president based on the Constitution?
> **Follow-up higher-order question:** Can you compare this with the duties of a senator?

Applying questions require the student to use their knowledge and comprehension by applying it to a situation.

> **Verbs:** Apply, connect, construct, interpret, demonstrate, develop, restructure, relate, utilize, etc.
> **Higher-order question:** Would you interpret the chart to explain the number of votes needed in the Electoral College to be elected president?

Analyzing questions require the student to dissect information and make inferences based on motives or causes.

> **Verbs:** Analyze, argue, categorize, classify, compare, contrast, deduce, differentiate, dissect, examine, hypothesize, scrutinize, separate, etc.
>
> **Higher-order question:** Would you compare and contrast President Obama's approach and President Trump's approach to legal and illegal immigration?

Evaluating questions require the student to use a set of criteria to make a reasoned judgment.

> **Verbs:** Critique, generalize, modify, propose, predict, recommend, etc.
>
> **Higher-order question:** Based on what the president said he would do and did, can you rank his success?

Creating questions require the student to combine knowledge to form a new idea based on relationships.

> **Verbs:** Argue, assess, compare, conclude, choose, critique, criticize, decide, evaluate, estimate, select, etc.
>
> **Higher-order question:** What facts can you gather to compare the Obama and Trump administrations?

Best Practices for Questioning

Based on the work of Newmann (1988) and others, when questioning is used, teachers should:

1. Praise correct answers, and ask a follow-up question that is of a higher order.
2. Call on other students to repeat a particularly well-thought-out answer.
3. Encourage students to answer to the entire class.
4. Form questions that are precise and definite, not ambiguous; avoid fill-in-the-blank questions.
5. Encourage students to ask qualifying questions.
6. Keep questions short and to the point.
7. Do not ask for trivial information.
8. Focus on sustained examination of a few topics rather than superficial, surface coverage of many.
9. Give students sufficient time to think before being required to answer questions.
10. Press students to clarify or justify their assertions with follow-up questions.
11. Rephrase an answer to model a more sophisticated use of language or terminology from the terms of the social studies.
12. Encourage original and unconventional ideas in the course of the interaction.
13. Use only open-ended questions.
14. Distribute questions to all students on an equal basis.
15. Always announce the question, then call on the student.
16. Use Bloom's verbs to construct questions.
17. Use the responsive questions strategy.
18. Use wait time.
19. Include questioning and answers as part of assessment and grading.

Resources

Videos: Bloom's Taxonomy | *TCH or YouTube*: Asking Open-Ended Questions; Checking in With Questions; Closed or Open: That is the Question; Designing Leveled Questions; Get Back to Me (wait time); Higher Order Questions; Inquiry-Based Teaching: Asking Effective Questions; Open-Ended Question to Encourage Conversation; Say No to No; Structure Learning with Essential Questions; The Art of Questioning; Using Questions to Develop Understanding; Questions are More Important than Answers | *YouTube:* 60 Second Strategy Equity Sticks.

Documents: *ASCD*: Questioning for Learning | Illinois State University Bloom's Question Starters | Bloom's Taxonomy Verbs and Questions | Questions Stems for Each Level of Bloom's Taxonomy.

References

Anderson, L. W., & Krathwohl, D. R. (Eds.). Airasian, P. W., Cruikshank, K. A., Mayer, R. E., Pintrich, P. R., Raths, J., & Wittrock, M. C. (2001). *A taxonomy for learning, teaching, and assessing: A revision of Bloom's Taxonomy of Educational Objectives* (Complete edition). Longman.

Bloom, B., Englehart, M., Furst, E., Hill, W., & Krathwohl, D. (1956). *Taxonomy of Educational Objectives: The classification of educational goals. Handbook I: Cognitive domain.* New Longmans, Green.

Brogan, R. R., & Brogan, W. A. (1995). The Socratic questioner: Teaching and learning in the dialogue classroom. *Educational Forum, 59*(3), 288–296.

Elder, L., & Paul, R. (2008). Critical thinking in a world of accelerating change and complexity. *Social Education, 72*(7), 388–391. Retrieved from www.socialstudies.org/publications/socialeducation/november-december2008/linda-elder-and-richard-paul

Engle, S., & Ochoa, A. (1988). *Education for democratic citizenship: Decision making in the social studies.* Teachers College Press.

Newmann, F. (ed). (1988). *Higher order thinking in high school social studies: An analysis of classrooms, teachers, students, and leadership.* University of Wisconsin, National Center on Effective Secondary Schools.

Pierre-Marc-Gaston, duc de Lévis. (2012/1808). *Maxims and reflections on different moral and political subjects.* Nuba Press.

Rowe, M. B. (1972). *Wait-time and rewards as instructional variables, their influence in language, logic, and fate control.* ERIC Document Reproduction Service No. ED 061 103. Paper presented at the National Association for Research in Science Teaching, Chicago, IL.

Stahl, R. J. (1980). *Improving the effectiveness of your questions: Some A, B, C's of questioning.* Eric Document Reproduction Service No. ED 198052. Paper presented at Annual Meeting of the National Council for Social Studies, New Orleans, LA.

26 Modeling, Practice, and Homework

Nothing is free. You got to pay to be in society. First you start with homework.
Mel Brooks, Filmmaker, Actor, and Comedian, 1926–present (Quotefancy, 2020)

Modeling is one of the most powerful ways to transmit democratic ideals, modes of reasoning, and basic skills because students learn by observing and emulating teachers (Bandura, 1979; Nauta & Kokaly, 2001).

Metacognitive Modeling

The **think-aloud approach** is a pedagogical strategy for teachers to share their **metacognition**, their "inner thoughts." It is where teachers plan and then explicitly articulate their underlying thinking process about their critical thinking, procedural knowledge, a democratic ideal, or foundational knowledge. The intent is to have students hear and understand the more sophisticated mental gymnastics of the expert teacher and adopt the disposition of thinking about their own thinking. Metacognition is one of the critical elements that distinguished successful from unsuccessful students (Puntambekar & duBoulay, 1997).

For some students, teachers may be the first models of how to systematically, objectively examine foundational knowledge and democratic ideals. As a well-versed social studies educator, it is all too easy to make assumptions about what students know and their critical thinking skills. Overlooking how little students know hinders teachers from restructuring the knowledge to be grade-appropriate and communicating it in a way that allows students to reconstruct the knowledge. It is particularly necessary when the lesson focuses on a process of deciphering information, interpreting data, analyzing assertions, or drawing conclusions about ideas that matter.

For the think-aloud approach, the planned teacher talk must deliberately include the teacher's metacognition that reveals the teacher's more sophisticated use of modes of reasoning. While the teacher comes to class with a lesson in mind using, as an example, a cause-and-effect mode of reasoning to discuss the Great Depression, failure to articulate the inner speech leaves the students without an understanding of the thought process of the expert teacher. The think-aloud approach flows from the teacher talk planned in the class notes of the lesson. Teachers' metacognition often starts with a planned prompt. The following are some examples of prompts of what a teacher might say during metacognitive modeling:

That passage made me think of. . .

I wonder why. . .

That did not make sense, I need to reread that. . .

As I look at that chronology, I wonder how. . . impacted . . .

I am focused on the terrain in the map and want to know. . .

In decision-making, problem-solving and **values formation**, unless the teacher models how to think during the process of working through the sequence of steps (refer to Chapters 8, 9, 10), students will not have learned the metacognitive process of applying the steps. As an example (refer to Chapter 8), in the problem-solving process, the teacher might say, "Now that we know it is, on average, warmer in Juneau, Alaska than Chicago in December, I am going to hypothesize about the determinates that cause the difference. I am thinking the first might be elevation?"

During the shared reading strategy with students, as an example, the teacher asks rhetorical questions or makes comments to demonstrate the kinds of questions and thoughts that students should be processing while reading (see Chapters 27 and 28). For example, while reading about the Lincoln assassination, the teacher might say, "I am wondering what impact this will have on how the North and South might reconcile?" The teacher would then ask a student what he or she is thinking. This metacognitive process can be used not only with declarative knowledge, but also with procedures. As an example, if modeling how to create a data retrieval chart out of text on the strengths and weakness of the Confederacy and Union, the teacher might say, "What categories do I want to use to label these rows [of a data retrieval chart] that might be useful to know? I think I will start with number of soldiers."

In questioning, the teacher asks a question and then explains how he or she would think about answering it. The teacher shares not the answer but the thinking process. As an example, in the case of a lesson on *Plessy v. Ferguson*, for students not to commit the mistake of historical projection (the shortcoming of judging historical events by today's standards), the teacher might muse, "I wonder what was so different about America in 1896 from now that led the Supreme Court to conclude that separate could be equal?" and then the teacher engages the students in the discussion by sharing more metacognitive insights.

Tasks Modeling

The **gradual release method** systematically shifts the responsibility to students for tasks that they are to master. The comprehensive approach starts with the teacher, "I do it," next "we do it," then "students do it together," and finally "the students do it alone" (Fisher & Frey, 2013). It requires that teachers share their thinking during the process during the first two stages.

Tasks modeling is usually directed toward procedural knowledge. It takes place when the teacher demonstrates a task as the centerpiece of a content presentation followed by guided and/or independent practice in which the students perform the same tasks but with different content. The teacher models, as examples, how to create a map and legend, a timeline, annotate a primary document, etc., so the students can observe the process or, in the alternative, the teacher can provide a sample of an end product and describe the process that led to its creation. Once demonstrated and practiced, the teacher can then assign the same tasks on multiple occasions during the year without having to remodel or have students practice again. This modeling can be less teacher-centered by working with different students who present and explain their work as a way of modeling the task for other students. One of the ways of assessing if students have acquired the metacognitive process of a task is if the students can teach the task to others.

Disposition Modeling

Because the intent of social studies education is more than just the transmission of knowledge, but to have students adopt democratic ideals and develop the capacities of a holistic civic and personal identity, **disposition modeling** is a paramount consideration for social studies teachers.

Teacher Modeling

Students are constantly making judgments about a teacher's character. A teacher's integrity, empathy for students, high expectations, and personal affirmation of the democratic ideals are communicated to students through their personal and civic identity, whether planned or not, "you cannot *not* teach values." Also, teachers who are creative, diligent, well prepared, and organized model the disposition needed to succeed in any career in a democratic society. This personal modeling is not limited to formal instruction, but includes the transitions in a classroom, hallway encounters, school events, etc., where there are more informal interactions. A teacher cannot stop being a model of a good citizen, even in those informal moments.

Student Modeling

While the teacher must be thoughtful and strive to model an identity that conforms to a democratic ideology, students' modeling can exhibit both productive and unproductive thinking and behaviors. Teachers promote productive modeling beyond themselves by publicly recognizing students who model democratic ideals and conceptualizations of foundational knowledge so that other students might choose to adopt similar behaviors and beliefs. However, a student who states an undemocratic idea in a discussion on poverty, such as, "all poor people are lazy," should be viewed as having articulated a conclusion that is based on an inadequate analysis or understanding of the democratic ideals. The teacher should view such a statement as an indication that the student is in need of philosophical counseling. When something like this happens, the teacher's approach should be to focus on the thought process rather than the conclusion, saying something like, "Let's take a moment to analyze that argument." Through a dialogue about the concept with the class as a whole, the student who made the statement can practice reconsideration of his statement, be exposed to a better quality of analysis, and reflect on his belief in light of the democratic ideals. Teachers should recognize that their response is for the benefit of all the students and the dialogue is most effective if conducted with questions to the student who made the assertion and others, rather than "correcting" statements.

Practice

The idea of practice as an essential component of instruction was introduced in Figure 21.1. Practice, in this book's framework, is conducted in class under the teacher's supervision, as opposed to homework, where students practice by completing an assignment independently. Teacher candidates may associate practice with basics skills such as writing and mathematics rather than with social studies. Teaching a mathematics procedure like adding two-digit numbers and carrying over the remainder is followed by student practice with new problems. Social studies also has to be practiced. For example, after a teacher has modeled the procedural knowledge about gathering facts using a graphic organizer such as the Who, What, When, Where, Why, and How Organizer with an example of an event in history, students could be given individual information packets about historical figures or events and they would be expected to apply the method to the new set of events as a practice activity.

Automaticity (also see Chapters 27 and 28) refers to the importance of students mastering a process so that critical thinking occurs rapidly with little conscious effort. As an example, adults have had so much practice that adding 2 plus 2 requires little thought. By repeated practice, individuals do not have to commit substantial memory to the process and thus free up memory for reconstructing and making meaning of knowledge that is more complex (Willingham, 2003a, 2003b). **Overlearning** is the way thinking processes become automatic. It means learning something to a point of mastery so that it can be replicated repeatedly, with little thought, and over extended years. Overlearning requires practice – not just an explanation or exposure to the concept underlying the task by the teacher. Sustained practice over the time period of a course, a semester, a year, or several years is the overlearning strategy that allows students to develop automaticity in using critical thinking and procedural knowledge skills.

Guided Practice

Guided practice takes place in the classroom. The teacher actively interacts with students, providing "over-the-shoulder" coaching. Students can be expected to apply the procedure as individuals, or they can be allowed to complete their individual assignments in groups. They are permitted to consult with other students while working, but not to copy results. Students are responsible for their product of the assigned class task or, in the case of cooperative learning, their contribution to the group project. The task is usually graded to ensure that students take it seriously, but it would typically be given a lower value than a test since it is the students' first practice of the task. In group guided practice, the teacher may give both group and individual grades, but it is not a wise practice to give only group grades.

Independent Practice

Independent practice can take place in the classroom or as homework and would typically follow guided practice. The student is expected to complete the task a second time with new content without assistance from the teacher, other students, or anyone else. For example, using the gradual release method in a lesson on longitude and latitude, the teacher might model how to locate the city of New Orleans by longitude and latitude. The guided practice would require groups or pairs to apply the knowledge to New York City, and the independent practice would require each student to find a different city's longitude and latitude. Time constraints may only allow using guided practice or independent practice rather than both. Independent practice is graded to ensure that students take the assignment seriously. It would typically be given a lower value than a test and a higher value than guided practice.

Teacher Supervision of Practice

To facilitate the gradual release model, the teacher could use the Socratic method to draw the analysis and conclusion (answers) out of the students. A teacher who too quickly responds to students' questions during practice will have taught students that they do not have to pay attention to the teacher when modeling and will have begun a potentially unending process of answering questions. At the end of the modeling, teachers should ask for questions to minimize the problem of inattentiveness or lack of forethought. If, however, such questions are asked, respond with a question such as, "what do you think is the best way to proceed?" Redirect the question, "perhaps you can ask one of your fellow students." This encourages listening skills. If a student persists in asking questions over weeks of practice, the teacher might ask the student if he understands before the group activity begins and provide more over-the-shoulder supervision. The teacher should counsel the student privately about attentiveness because the goal is to motivate the student to act independently.

Homework

Time outside of school is used to ensure that all the learning that needs to take place during a school year is completed. **Homework** has two strategic uses. As stated in previous chapters, it is used to create a baseline of information through reading assignments or other kinds of assignments upon which a teacher will draw for instruction. It is also a form of independent practice that comes after instruction or modeling of what is to be practiced. Parents often see homework as an indicator of a productive classroom and their child's development.

The Value of Homework

Often overlooked in discussion of homework is that, like a consistent entry and exit procedure (refer to Chapter 19), questioning approach (see Chapter 25), and lesson plan sequence (see Chapter 21), homework required on a daily basis creates the kind of routine that children and teenagers need in their lives: Such routines provide a sense of comfort and confidence as the cosmos take twists and turns.

There are, however, both advocates and opponents of homework. Disagreements about the value of homework stem in large measure from what individuals identify as its purpose as well as from the complexity of measuring its academic effects. However, the results of a review of research over 25 years indicates that there is a positive correlation between homework and academic achievement (Cooper, Robinson, & Patall, 2006).

Advocates see homework not only as improving academic performance but also as improving study habits, developing autonomy and self-discipline, promoting efficiency by effectively using both the classroom and the home for learning, and facilitating parental involvement in children's education. Such results lead advocates to conclude that time beyond the classroom by assigning thoughtfully conceived and meaningful homework is too valuable not to be used. Objections to homework often stem from poorly thought-out homework assignments and policies, homework viewed as "busy work" by parents, and cultural changes that have resulted in parents not seeing homework as a priority. When homework is well conceived and required in moderation, it can be an effective strategy in the development of the child's potential.

Teachers have the challenge of persuading parents that homework is crucial to their children's future and that the parent, teacher, and child make up a team that needs to use homework to maximize learning. The best way to do that is to require homework that is easily judged by parents as meaningful. Because homework is completed outside of the classroom and requires integration into family life, teachers should consider releasing on a Friday or Sunday the homework for the upcoming week so parents can plan with their children so that homework is completed on time or in advance.

The Goals of Homework

The goals and advantages of well-conceived homework are:

Goals	Advantages
1. To practice skills learned in class.	1. Makes efficient use of home and class time.
2. To learn a baseline of information in advance of a lesson.	2. Improves academic performance.
3. To complete projects explained and/or started in the class.	3. Promotes valuable independent study habits.
4. To develop self-discipline and time management.	4. Increases parents' awareness of the productivity of the classroom and what their children are learning.

Parents' Duties

Teachers are expected to provide a consistent learning environment in their classrooms, but each home is unique. Successful homework assignments start with teachers soliciting parents' cooperation and explaining reasonable expectations. Parents should not be viewed as having the capacity to substitute expertise for the teacher's expertise because not all parents have the training to assist with homework. Parents can be called upon and should be expected to monitor their children and teenagers so that their children complete their homework as prescribed and on time.

While teachers express frustration with students who do not do homework, parents express frustration when their children have too many seemingly trivial assignments and when assignments are not clearly explained. The following list includes examples of what teachers might communicate to parents regarding homework.

1. Provide a specific and consistent time each day for homework so that it becomes a routine part of the home's daily routine.
2. Designate a specific place where homework is to be completed.
3. Limit distractions by eliminating TV, phones, etc., during homework.
4. Check the child's understanding of the assignment prior to starting.
5. Parents should not provide answers, but help the child figure out the answer.
6. Children should not do homework with their friends; homework is independent practice.
7. Expect the work to be neat and orderly.
8. Check the work for accuracy, if the parent has the expertise.
9. Parents should sign each homework assignment.

Teachers' Duties

Teachers should have policies that assure parents that homework is necessary, reasonable, and as accommodating as possible. Such policies might include:

1. Only homework that students should know how to do if they were paying attention in class will be assigned.
2. Reading assignments will follow a pre-reading activity and/or be followed by bell work or a post-reading activity. Students will be held accountable for reasonable factual information prior to instruction.
3. The assignment directions will be clear and definite, and the student will be able to do it at home, even if they do not have computers, access to a library, or other specialized materials.
4. The amount of time students will be expected to spend on homework will be limited.
5. Students will have homework every day. Where possible, all the homework for the week will be announced/posted a week in advance so parents can plan around other activities.
6. Homework will be collected, read, and graded and feedback given within two days of receipt. Marking will include positive comments as well as notes about errors.
7. Students will be required to use a homework planner.
8. Daily check-in and checkout of homework will be required.

CMSs for K-12 education is rapidly automating many of the ways to communicate test results, feedback, homework assignments, and due dates. Teachers should take full advantage of the technology.

Resources

Videos: *ACPS*: Gradual Release Model Videos | *TCH or YouTube:* Efficient & Meaningful Homework | *YouTube:* Think Aloud; Think About Thinking – It's Metacognition!

Documents: *ASCD*: Rethinking Homework Best Practices; Gradual Release of Responsibility Instructional Framework.

References

Bandura, A. (1979). *Social learning theory.* Prentice-Hall.
Cooper, H., Robinson, J., & Patall, E. (2006). Does homework improve academic achievement? A synthesis of research, 1987–2003. *Review of Educational Research, 76*(1), 1–62.
Fisher, D., & Frey, N. (2013). *Better learning through structured teaching: A framework for the gradual release of responsibility.* Alexandria, VA: ASCD.
Nauta, M., & Kokaly, M. (2001). Assessing role model influences on students' academic and vocational decisions. *Journal of Career Assessment, 9*(1), 81–99.
Puntambekar, S., & duBoulay, B. (1997). Design and development of MIST – A system to help students develop metacognition. *Journal of Education Computing Research, 16*(109), 1–35.
Quotefancy. (2020). *Mel Brooks.* Retrieved from https://quotefancy.com/quote/1108517/Mel-Brooks-Nothing-is-free-You-got-to-pay-to-be-in-society-First-you-start-with-homework.
Willingham, D. T. (2003a). *Cognition: The thinking animal.* Prentice-Hall.
Willingham, D. T. (2003b). Students remember what they think. *American Educator, 27*(3), 37–41.

27 Literacy and Reading

It is a wise man who only believes half of what he reads and hears: It is a genius who knows which half.

Benny Hill, British comic, 1924–1992 (BrainyQuote, 2020)

Children and teenagers bring diverse reading and writing skills to their school, even though they are clustered by age into grades or tracks. Every teacher, regardless of teaching field, needs to teach reading and writing skills for their subject field.

The term "literacy" can be confusing because it is used in so many different ways. Literacy and basic skills are frequently used interchangeably. **Traditional literacy** is defined as the ability to read and write; whereas **basic skills** is the broader term and usually includes the ability to use mathematics and is frequently expanded to include such things as oral communication, study skills, computer skills, etc. "**Thoughtful literacy**" was defined by Allington and Johnston (2000, p. 1) as the "ability to read, write and think in the complex and critical ways needed in a post-industrial democratic society." It is thoughtful literacy that is the particular interest of social studies education and the Common Core movement.

Text Materials

"**Text**" **materials** can be subdivided into two broad categories: **Text** includes words, sentences, and paragraphs, and **graphics** would include maps, charts, pictures, drawings, reproductions of narratives such as an image of the Constitution, etc. The internet has revolutionized social studies education by making available text materials beyond the traditional mainstay of textbooks. However, textbooks continue to play a central role in social studies education.

The field of social studies has been criticized for too much reliance on book-based instruction in which students absorb and reproduce "surface" and trivial information (Scheurman & Newman, 1998). There is concern that the textbook remains the driving force in instruction because teachers may view it as the "outer boundary" of the foundational knowledge – rather than one of many assets that should be part of choreographed instruction. In addition, there are widespread and long-standing criticisms of textbooks based on concerns of lack of rigor, selectivity, if not biased content and interpretations, superficiality, too little narrative and too many images, etc. (Ravitch, 2003; Zhao & Hoge, 2005).

Informational and Narrative Text

At its core, reading involves knowledge of (a) letters and sound correspondences, (b) words and word forms, and (c) syntax (the grammatical structure of sentences). Text falls into two broad genres:

- **Information (or expository) text**, which is typical of textbooks starting in middle and secondary grades, and ancillary materials (primary sources documents, etc.), and is typically focused on foundational knowledge in the social studies; and
- **Narrative text**, which dominates elementary school reading instruction. It is "story-based" text found in fiction and non-fiction stories (Flood & Lapp, 1986; Yopp & Yopp, 2000). With narrative texts, students are able to develop generic reading skills and a general vocabulary. It sets the stage for concurrent or future reading skills development of expository text in the content areas, such as social studies.

As a consequence of the need to emphasize general reading literacy in elementary schools, students do not necessarily develop the vocabulary or the expert reading skills in a domain such as social studies that they will encounter in middle and high school textbooks or as part of their civic life. There is all the difference in the world between reading the quaint story of George Washington and the cherry tree and a historical account of George Washington's role in American history. The former is often used in direct teaching of democratic ideals and is written in a conversational tone that encourages the pleasure of reading. The latter is intended to relay foundational knowledge and it is used to teach how to interpret a historical text. The same principle applies to all the social studies, such as the first grade topic "Why do People Work?" (see Chapter 17), as compared with the technical language of an economics chapter on the concept of work found at the middle or high school level.

Vocabulary

A vocabulary word serves as a trigger to a concept. Children learn their first words in the home and these words become resources for reading. Research (Hart & Risley, 2003) has exposed what is known as the "30-million-word gap." They have extrapolated that by four years of age, there is a 30-million-word gap between children from professional families and low socioeconomic status families, with working-class family's children falling roughly in the middle. This gap becomes most evident in fourth grade, where the more sophisticated demands of the curriculum require **comprehension** of foundational knowledge, rather than the basic skills of **decoding** used in lower elementary grades (Chall, Jacobs & Baldwin, 1990).

Text's vocabulary is static and devoid of a conversational context (Nagy & Scott, 2000). Expository text is more complex than narrative text because it requires skill in both decoding and comprehending which is dependent on a rich working vocabulary in the subject area.

Reading expository text requires:

- **Fluency** – the momentum and speed with which one reads; and
- **Automaticity** – the quick and accurate recognition of words and phrases.

Without these two acquired capabilities, the student becomes so bogged down in deciphering words and phrases that by the end of the sentence, paragraph, or page, the student has lost sight of the facts, concepts, and generalizations portrayed by the text in the earliest parts of the passage. Fluency and automaticity rely on a strong vocabulary that enables students to perform the feats of analysis and synthesis needed to make meaning out of foundational knowledge and consider democratic ideals.

The Gradual Release Model

The **gradual release model** is used for modeling in general and in particular in reading (see Fisher & Frey, 2013). Often referred to as the "I do, We do, You do" approach, the goal is to position the student to become independent in performing tasks. In reading it is intended to develop confident readers of expository text materials in social studies. CRISS (creating independence through student-owned strategies), a well-established approach to achieve gradual release, involves three concepts upon which the three phases of reading progress. Students: (a) monitor their learning to assess what they are learning while reading; (b) integrate new knowledge with prior knowledge; and (c) are actively engaged about what was read by discussion, writing, or analyzing through a task based on the knowledge they have acquired (U.S. Department of Education, 2010).

Reading in Class

Reading during class to simply gain declarative knowledge is a questionable use of valuable class time. Teacher modeling how to read social studies' unique text materials is an easily overlooked type of lesson and an excellent use of class time. Developing lesson plans focused on different types of social studies reading materials is just as important as developing lesson plans around traditional topics such as the Reformation or the geography of the Southern Hemisphere. The teacher must model reading techniques with different kinds of text materials so students can then be expected to read new material at home – on their own – in anticipation of upcoming classroom instruction and in their future lives as citizens. Rather than "jumping" into content at the beginning of the year, teachers should plan lessons that teach how to annotate, close read by metacognitive questions, decipher charts, analyze the meaning in cartoons, interpret maps, etc., and then rely on that instruction as they create future lesson plans.

Reading as Homework

The practice of assigning social studies textbook passages as homework fulfills three primary goals: (1) It creates a baseline of foundational knowledge to build upon so a teacher can focus classroom instruction on examination of democratic ideals and procedural knowledge; (2) It allows classroom instruction to be efficient with a strategic allocation of learning tasks to home and school; and (3) It requires self-discipline of the students. Requiring students to read as homework entirely new material is a reasonable task if the teacher uses an effective pre-reading strategy. The pre-reading options explained in the following section should come at the end of one lesson in preparation for a reading homework task for the next lesson.

The Three Phases of Reading

The sequence of teaching students how to read social studies content comes in a number of forms, but most typically it is depicted as either: **PRP**, for pre-reading, reading, and post-reading, or **BDA**, for before reading, during reading, and after reading (adapted from Avery & Graves, 1997). The sequences are the same and should be used as part of reading instruction. In the *Resources* at the end of the chapter, there are multiple examples with videos and documents that provide an array of reading strategies beyond what is cited in this chapter.

Pre-reading Options

The main goal of pre-reading is to prepare students for the reading assignment. The "Okay, kids, open your books to page 73 and start reading" approach is not an acceptable practice. Each of these pre-reading strategies can be enhanced by teachers using graphic organizers. The examples in Figure 27.1 represent just four approaches, others are readily available on the internet (see *Resources*).

Pre-reading Options	
Strategy	**Considerations:**
Pre-teach Vocabulary	*Previews key vocabulary so as to position students for better automaticity and fluency*
Examples: **Create a Wordsplash** and have students make predictions about the words' meanings and connections. **Word maps**, the Frayer model (see IRIS Center, 2020) uses a graphic organizer to define vocabulary and its characteristics with examples and non-examples with illustrations or definitions. **Context clues** has the teacher select 4 or 5 sentences from the assigned reading and leads students in guessing the meaning of a word based on context. **Semantic map,** the teacher chooses one term and writes it in the center of the white board. Students create a list of related words from the textbook, categorize by commonalities, add labels to the groups, and add the categories and words to the whiteboard. **I spy** has students play in teams or pairs to find vocabulary in the text from a teacher-prepared list and then participate in defining the terms. **Traditional list** is when vocabulary and definitions are placed on the board or distributed as a handout and discussed with students	
Pre-teach Concepts	*The teacher previews compelling principles or enduring ideas using the talk-aloud approach revealing the teacher's metacognition about the concepts.*
Examples: **Graphic Organizers** with teacher-centered instruction is particularly effective by converting the concepts to visual representations. **Knowledge Rating** is where students rate their understanding of terms provided by the teacher.	
Promote Objectives	*The focus is on the foundational knowledge the teacher wants students to understand from the reading.*
Example: **KWL chart** has students state what they know and want to know and following the reading, what they learned. **Anticipation Guide** has students respond to multiple statements about the foundational knowledge of the upcoming reading assignment prepared by the teacher based on what the teacher thinks the students may believe. Students make notes as to what they believe is correct or incorrect and discuss in pairs or groups. Students read the passage and write down changes in their opinions about the statement. The teacher follows with a whole-class debriefing **Predict** and **Proof** is a two-column chart where students predict based on the heading (s) of the passage what the passage will "tell them" and after the reading they indicate if there is proof to support their prediction.	
Promote Reading Strategies	*Involves the teacher pointing out and explaining strategies for students to use.*
Examples: **Graphics:** Explain how to interpret images, charts, inserts, pictures, etc. and explain the relationship to the text passages. **Model metacognition:** Teachers "think aloud" asking questions to demonstrate the art of close reading. **Text Features**: Highlight text features such as headings and callouts in a passage. **Retelling**: Demonstrate how students can rephrase what they read after each paragraph. **Story Mapping:** Model how to create a story map. **Annotating**: Provide an example and explain the thinking when it was created. **Questioning the Author**: Share a couple of questions students might ask themselves.	

Figure 27.1 Pre-reading Options

Reading Options

The reading strategies listed in Figure 27.2 have relative advantages and disadvantages. Teachers should vary their approaches by using different approaches. Although rotational or "round-robin" and choral reading are listed, they are not considered a best practice due to their inefficiency, lack of sustained practice that can be assessed, and potential adverse impact on weaker readers forced to display their limited reading skills before the entire class.

Reading Options	
Strategy	**Considerations**
Reading as Homework	*Students are assigned text material to read at home prior to the lesson.*
Develops independent reading skills. Creates a baseline of information knowledge upon which the teacher can use to move directly to compelling principles and ideas that matter. Is effective if the teacher has previously taught how to close read the text and different kinds of graphics. There is an assessment such as a graphic organizer or worksheet to be completed at home or bell-work before the lesson begins. Teachers often add graphic organizers, dialectical journals, etc. as part of the homework reading assignment. The teacher debriefs prior to the lesson.	
Reading Aloud by the Teacher	*Teacher reads the text material.*
The most straightforward approach to modeling metacognition/reading skills is for the teacher to articulate his or her own thinking while reading a passage of text. This think-aloud approach explicitly teaches the underlying thinking process that students should use when reading (refer to Chapter 26). Provides a model of correct pronunciation and how "expert" reading sounds. Students listen and periodically respond to teacher's thoughts as the teacher calls on students to keep them engaged.	
SQ3R Method	*Teacher can have students work independently or in groups for the different phases.*
Survey – Have students preview the title, pictures, graphs, and captions, then read the first and last paragraph of the text and make a list of their perceptions of main points or objectives. **Question** Have students write questions based on their survey of the text. **Read** – Have students read the text and answer the questions they wrote down when they surveyed the text. **Recite** – Have students look over their questions and be able to recite the answers without looking them up. **Review** – Have students summarize what they wrote Teacher debriefs.	
Marking up Strategy (i.e. "annotating").	*Students are required to annotate a reading.*

Teacher having taught how to annotate and provided a list of annotation marks to use such as the following; Students:
    Survey the reading
    Number paragraphs,	

Figure 27.2 Reading Options

Bracket unfamiliar words,
Circle key words,
Underline author's claims,
Writes main idea of each paragraph in the right margin, and writes a question that the student has in the left margin.
Teacher debriefs comparing it to the projected teacher's annotated example.

Independent Silent Reading	*Students reading of a passage in silence has a number of shortcomings, unless paired with annotating or SQ3R Method.*

Reading takes place in class and the teacher can circulate to provide individual assistance to students with weaker reading skills.
Students finish at different times creating potential classroom management problems.
The teacher does not know who is actually reading the material or what students' level of comprehension is, so this strategy should be paired with a strategy that can be assessed.

Reading Out Loud in Groups	*Students take turns reading. Is preferable to rotational and round-robin because each student reads more times.*

Heterogeneous groups of four allow every student to read multiple paragraphs.
Strong readers can be coached to assist weaker readers.
Weak readers feel less embarrassed in supportive smaller groups. Students can reflect and share ideas for reinforcement and uniformity of understanding.
Teacher must circulate among groups.
Homogeneous groups can be used so the teacher can work with weaker readers.
Teachers often incorporate guided notes, a handout that mimics the sequence of text material but with blanks for students to fill in.

Rotational or Round-Robin	*Each student reads a paragraph aloud.* *These have a number of shortcomings, reading in groups a better practice*

Inefficient compared to group reading.
Weaker readers often feel embarrassed; when their turns come up, other students may become irritated because they have to wait for weaker readers and they don't benefit from the experience.

Student-Teacher Shared Reading	*Teacher begins to read and asks individual students to read. The teacher then asks questions to ensure comprehension or the teacher assigns short sections to be read independently and guides the discussion.*

Questions can be interspersed to keep everyone attentive and to ensure a baseline of content knowledge.
Has similar shortcomings to rotational or round-robin reading, if not carefully choreographed.
Teacher can model techniques typical of pre-reading and close reading.

Choral Reading	*All students read in unison* *This has a number of shortcomings.*

Allows weaker readers to follow along in a large group with anonymity and little apprehension, but the teacher cannot assess individual reading ability and whether the student is reading along with the others.
Often students do not participate and their minds wander.

Dramatic Reading	*Teacher reads document that appeals to the emotions and exalted aims.*

This is a powerful approach often used with passages from history or literature when there is tension in the storyline or compelling ideals.
Students learn the joy of reading and the powerful images that words create.
Not usually possible with textbooks.

Figure 27.2 (Cont.)

Post-reading Options

Reading should be followed by a post-reading activity in which the teacher reinforces the foundational ideas found in the reading and/or to elevate the reading to consideration of the things that matter. What takes place in the post-reading can take on a number of forms (Figure 27.3).

Post-reading Options	
Strategy	**Considerations**
Lesson plan	Based on the reading, selected parts are developed by the teacher into a comprehensive depth lesson (refer to Chapter 21) that uses the foundational knowledge to explore procedural knowledge and/or things that matter.
Debriefing	The teacher prepares, in advance, questions and propositions drawn from the reading and in a whole-class setting reinforces the foundational knowledge and explores procedural knowledge and/or things that matter. Teacher-centered probing of students allows them to summarize, synthesize, and report their construction of the information. The teacher can engage students with additional concepts beyond those within the text.
Discussion	The teacher creates provocative propositions to stimulate consideration of democratic ideals gleamed from the foundational knowledge of the passage. Students in whole-class or heterogeneous groups should focus on the propositions that require predicting, synthesis, or analyzing. If groups are used, the teacher should circulate among the groups and then debriefs in whole-class setting after groups are finished.
Simulation/Role Playing	Students create a simulation or role-playing activity to demonstrate their understanding of the reading. Requires a debriefing by the teacher after each skit.
Summarizing	Students are asked to summarize the reading in a whole-class setting or in groups. A debriefing by the teacher should follow. Summarizing is not as effective as debriefing and discussion because some students may not close read because they anticipate that the teacher or other students are going to summarize.
Debate	Students are organized to debate issues based on the reading and then the teacher or students are asked to summarize conclusions in a debriefing
Handout Task	The handout may be distributed before, during or after the reading and requires a debriefing by the teacher. The task is used for students to demonstrate their understanding. **Graphic Organizers** such as timelines, webs, KWL charts, hierarchies, etc. **Reading Organizers** such as story maps, anticipation guides, PLAN (predict, locate, add and note), QAR (question, answer, relationships), list, group and label, etc. (also see Chapter 28). **Basal Worksheets** tend to be fact-based and evaluate only lower-level learning. It is better to use graphic or reading organizers. **Exit Tickets** are a quick assessment students complete and hand in to the teacher who is standing at the doorway as the students exit.
Writing	Writing is thinking! After reading, writing activities based on the reading require higher-order thinking skills. Examples are RAFT (role, audience, format, topic), QTA (question the author), 5 paragraph essays, etc. (see Chapter 29 Writing)

Figure 27.3 Post-reading Options

The availability of multiple types of downloadable graphic organizers on the internet makes it possible for teachers and students to use a variety formats to restructure text into graphic images that help students better comprehend the content (see document resources below and Chapter 32).

Resources

Videos: *ReadingRockets.org Strategies* (over 50 how-to videos and downloadable ancillaries on writing and reading directed at elementary education) | *TCH or YouTube*: Interactive Read Aloud; Informational Texts; Reading for Inquiry; Vocabulary Paint Chips; Seven Step Vocabulary; Gradual Release Model | College Talk Improving Students' Vocabulary; Total Physical Response Vocabulary; Learning Difficult Vocabulary; Extending Understanding Vocabulary Development (Gettysburg Address); Kick Me Making Vocabulary Interactive; Writing, Inquiry, Collaboration & Reading, Interacting with Complex Texts; Scaffolding Reading; Read, Discuss, Debate: Evaluating Arguments | *Teacher Toolkit:* KWL; Frayer Model; Pictionary; Anticipation Guide; My Other Half; Guided Notes | *AVID:* 2 Minute PD; Dialectical Journal; Marking the Text; Charting the Text | *YouTube:* Word Splash; Word Map; SQ3R; Annotate It!; Charting the Text; Guided Reading; Reading Groups; Exit Tickets: Checking for Understanding.

Documents: *Wiley Handbook of Social Studies Research*: Leveraging literacy – Research on Critical Reading; Emergent Bilinguals | *IRS Center:* Literacy in Content Area Instruction | Beyond the Yellow Highlighter by Porter-O'Donnell | *ReadingRocket:s* Classroom Strategies (over 50 reading and writing strategies with downloadable ancillaries) | Notable NCSS Trade Books for Young People | *History Tech:* Book Bits (prereading strategy) | *What Works Clearinghouse*: Literacy.

References

Allington, R. L., & Johnston, P. H. (2000). *What do we know about effective fourth grade teachers and their classrooms?* Albany, NY: The National Research Center for English Learning & Achievement. Retrieved from http://cela.albany.edu/4thgrade/index.html

Avery, P., & Graves, M. (1997). Young learners: Reading of social studies text. *Social Studies for the Young Learner,* March/ April, 10–14.

BrainyQuote. (2020). *Jeff Cooper.* Retrieved from www.brainyquote.com/quotes/jeff_cooper_384695.

Chall, J. S., Jacobs, V. A., & Baldwin, L. E. (1990). *The reading crisis: Why poor children fall behind.* Harvard University Press.

Fisher, D., & Frey, N. (2013). *Better learning through structured teaching: A framework for the gradual release of responsibility.* ASCD.

Flood, J., & Lapp, D. (1986). Types of text: The match between what students read in basal and what they encounter in tests. *Reading Research Quarterly, 121,* 284–297.

Hart, B., & Risley, T. R. (2003). The early catastrophe: The 30 million word gap by age 3. *American Educator, 27*(1), 4–9.

Iris Center. (2020). *Literacy in content area instruction.* Retrieved from https://iris.peabody.vanderbilt.edu/module/sec-rdng/cresource/q2/p07/sec_rdng_07_link_frayer_types_04/#content.

Nagy, W., & Scott, J. (2000). Vocabulary processes. In M. Kamil, P. Mosenthal, P. Pearson, & R. Barr (Eds.), *Handbook of reading research* (pp. 269–284). Erlbaum Associates.

Ravitch, D. (2003). *The language police: How pressure groups restrict what students learn.* New York: Knopf.

Scheurman, G., & Newman, F. M. (1998). Authentic intellectual work in social studies: Putting performance before pedagogy. *Social Education, 62*(1), 23–25.

U.S. Department of Education. (2010). Project CRISS (Creating independence through student-owned strategies). *What Works Clearinghouse.*

Yopp, R. H., & Yopp, H. K. (2000). Sharing informational text with young children. *The Reading Teacher, 53*, 410–423.

Zhao, Y., & Hoge, J. (2005). What elementary students and teachers say about social studies. *Social Studies, 96*(5), 216–221.

28 Reading Social Studies and Vocabulary

Don't just teach your kids to read; teach them to question what they read. Teach them to question everything!

George Carlin, Comedian and Social Critic, 1937–2008 (Goodreads, 2020)

Reading in the Digital Age

There is wide consensus among scholars that digital technology is fundamentally changing the culture and the way people access and interact with information. Expository text is less dense due to inexpensive graphics. The low cost of creating websites has created an abundance of information and opinions in dynamic formats integrating videos, stills, etc. Students have unsupervised, easy access to the internet and are accustomed to reading text and graphics on phones and tablets or by asking Siri a question. Websites that carry social science, historical, and current events topics have no "establishment" oversight as in days past. Hate groups and more subtly biased online venues appear to students and the public to have the same credibility as established organizations, such as CNN, FOX, the Heritage Foundation, the *Guardian*, which have a journalistic mission.

Teachers now find themselves competing with political ideological claims that are unfiltered. Teaching students to "**close read**" text in any form is the anecdote: To close read means to systematically analyze, synthesize, and evaluate text and graphics *and* the subtext that is inherent in both. The good news is teachers, through the internet, now have multiple examples of texts that can be used to model close reading. The prevalence of video adds the additional burden of "**close viewing**," which also needs to be explicitly taught. For students to be adult participants in a democratic society, teachers of social studies must model how to assess video and text sources.

The NCSS Acquiring Information Skills

The Essential Skills of Social Studies Education (NCSS, 1989) that was introduced in Chapter 12 also provides the following short list of reading skills that students should acquire during social studies instruction. These skills for "acquiring information," although centered on reading and study skills, are best considered in conjunction with Chapter 12's list of NCSS (1989) "Thinking Skills" (see Figure 12.2).

Reading Skills and Vocabulary	Study Skills

1. Comprehension
 	
 • Read to get literal meaning
 • Use topic and section headings, topic sentences, and summary sentences to select main ideas
 • Differentiate main and subordinate ideas
 • Select passages that are pertinent to the topic studied
 • Interpret what is read by drawing inferences
 • Detect cause-and-effect relationships
 • Distinguish between fact and opinion; recognize propaganda
 • Recognize author bias
 • Use picture clues and picture captions to aid comprehension
 • Read for a variety of purposes: critically, analytically, to predict outcomes, to answer questions, to form an opinion, to skim for facts
 • Read various forms of printed material: books, magazines, newspapers, directories, schedules, and journals
 • Use context clues to gain meaning
 • Recognize and understand an increasing number of social studies terms
	1. Find Information
	
	 • Use various parts of a book (index, table of contents, etc.)
	 • Use key words, letters on volumes, index, and cross references to find information
	 • Evaluate sources of information–print, visual, electronic, etc.
	 • Use appropriate sources of information, internet, etc.
	 • Use the community as a resource
	
	 2. Arrange Information in Usable Forms
	
	 • Make outline of topic
	 • Prepare summaries
	 • Make timelines
	 • Take notes
	 • Keep records
	 • Use italics, marginal notes, and footnotes
	 • Write reports and research papers
	 • Prepare a bibliography
	
	 3. Maps, Globes, and Graphics
	
	 • Use map- and globe-reading skills:
	
	   • Orient a map and note directions
	   • Locate places on map and globe
	   • Use scale and compute distances
	   • Interpret map symbols and visualize what they mean
	   • Compare maps and make inferences
	   • Express relative location
	
	 • Interpret graphs
	 • Detect bias in visual material
	 • Interpret social and political messages of cartoons
	 • Interpret history through artifacts
	
	 4. Community Resources
	
	 • Use sources of information in the community
	 • Conduct interviews of individuals in the community
	 • Use community newspapers

Figure 28.1 NCSS Essential Skills for Acquiring Information

Common Core

An explanation about the Common Core Standards for reading informational text and writing were provided in Chapter 10. Traditionally, elementary school teachers have received much more training in generic reading and writing theory and methods than middle and high school teachers. Neither have necessarily received training in strategies for how to close read maps, cartoons, primary documents, etc., or the kind of historical or conceptual rendering in expository text that are unique to the social studies. Chapters 27, 28, and 29 are intended to assist the teacher candidates create grade-appropriate, basic skills, social studies lessons.

Types of Social Studies Vocabulary

Parker (2001) has identified various types of vocabulary that students encounter in social studies and for which teachers must unpack a commonsense meaning.

Technical terms: *plateau, century, longitude, polls, legislature*
Figurative terms: *political platform, Cold War, Sun Belt, pork barrel*
Words with multiple meanings: *cabinet, mouth, bank, revolution*
Locality-specific terms: *grits* (southern breakfast dish), *bayou* (predominantly used in Louisiana to refer to a body of water), *coulee* (a Chinese immigrant working on the transcontinental railroad), and *Oklahoma Sooner*
Alike words: *peasant* for *pheasant, principle* for *principal, alien* for *allies*
Acronyms: *NATO, NASA, OPEC, NAFTA, NCAA, MADD*
Quantitative terms: *century, decade, GNP, acre*
Names: *Lewis and Clark, the American Revolution, 1776, Gettysburg*

Best Practices for Teaching Vocabulary

There does not appear to be a single best way for students to learn vocabulary. Following are some basic principles that can serve as a guide. They are based on the findings of Brett, Rothlein, and Hurley (1996), Beck, McKeown, and Omanson (1987), and others.

1. Teach the concept while presenting the unknown word.
2. During reading instruction, students learn significantly more vocabulary if teachers explain new vocabulary when the word is first encountered during the reading, rather than waiting until the end of the reading activity.
3. Students should be encouraged to determine the meaning of new words they encounter by inferring the meaning from the context, using a dictionary, etc.
4. Teachers should explain the implicit and explicit meaning of words.
5. Students should be required to explain or otherwise demonstrate their use of new vocabulary.
6. Create and display a word web, matrix, etc., or use assignments such as crossword puzzles to preview new vocabulary as an alternative to just listing words and definitions.

7. When students are reading silently in class or during a homework reading assignment, have students record the new words in a journal that they think they understand in a left-hand column and in the right column, words they don't understand. Debrief both by calling on students to provide explanations prior to instruction.
8. Debrief homework reading assignments and in-class readings referring to and using the new vocabulary.
9. Provide opportunities to decipher a word's structure (morphological knowledge), such as roots of words like trespass, overpass, impasse, etc.
10. Require a vocabulary notebook.

Expository Texts, Literal Information, and Subtext

Expository text appears in paper-based and electronic mediums. An author's goal in creating such documents is, fundamentally, to create a treatise to synthesize information or ideas, make an argument, and adapt it into usable knowledge for an audience. In one sense, textbooks are a **treatise**, a written work formally and systematically explicating a subject, such as this textbook or a textbook on economics. They are, typically, a **secondary source document** authored by an expert who may or may not draw on primary sources. But the *Communist Manifesto*, as an example, is also a treatise and a **primary source document**, just as a graphic of broadside of an announcement of a slave auction from the early 1800s or a document such as *The Declaration of the Rights of Man and of the Citizen* during the French Revolution. Primary source documents are documents, graphics, or artifacts that provide first-hand testimony or direct evidence concerning a historical topic.

Most textbooks are formatted with features such as chapters, headings, subheadings, bold words, etc. Textbooks on sociology, psychology, and civics topics tend be organized around concepts. Economics is also organized around concepts, but because of its quantitative underpinnings, makes greater use of graphics such as charts and graphs. Geography is organized by regions in many textbooks, with concepts and examples lodged within the regions and with an abundance of images such as maps. History texts are almost always chronologically ordered, but make extensive use of primary sources and concepts are embedded within the text.

Because of students' trust in authority figures such as teachers, they tend to think the text materials provided by schools, particularly textbooks, as the only set of facts that should be used to draw a conclusion. Students too easily fail to recognize the basic assumption used by historians, in particular, that textbooks or other secondary sources and primary documents are the product of an author's idea, interpretation, summarization, and/or point of view (Stahl, Hynd, Britton, McNish, & Bosquet, 1996). For both primary and secondary sources, students must learn to process both the transparent, surface **literal information** *and* extract the subjective, oblique **subtext information**, the ideas the author is trying to convey (Lesh, 2011). The teacher of social studies must model and have students practice the process of extracting the subtext from the surface knowledge of text and graphic materials. As one example, a textbook section on the battle of Gettysburg will often have an annotated map and chronological development of the events in narrative form. The literal information is providing an explanation of the logistics, characters involved, geographic features, etc. But the subtext, which is typically not explicitly stated, is left to be gleaned from the surface information, such as the horror of the battlefield, the bravery of the soldiers, and significance of the battle to the fate of the Confederacy. A second example was provided in Chapter 14, where the author's subtext revealed a potential bias in constructing a narrative about the Founders' efforts on behalf of women. In both of these cases, teachers would create close reading depth lessons that begin with the surface knowledge of the text and proceed to unpacking the subtext. The purpose of teaching how to close read social studies is to assist students to become insightful readers so once their formal education has come to an end, they can independently and astutely sift through the political issues of their time that appear in texts and graphics.

Close Reading

Close reading means reading to understand the literal information and uncover the layers of subtext that lead to deep comprehension. Close reading, unlike reading for leisure, is intense and purposeful. It requires critical analysis of expository texts that focuses on significant details or patterns in order to develop a deep, precise understanding of foundational knowledge or the democratic ideals being explained and/or proposed by the author. Close reading begins with **skimming** to quickly get a general idea of what will be read. Close reading consists of five levels (adapted from Boyles, 2014; Paul & Elder, 2008).

Level 1: Paraphrasing consists of restating the text – sentence by sentence, paragraph by paragraph, passage by passage.
Level 2: Explication includes stating the main point, elaborating, drawing analogies, and citing additional examples.
Level 3: Analyzing the logic includes:
    What is the author's purpose?
    What is the key question the author is trying to answer?
    What is the author's point of view?
    What are the author's assumptions?
    What are the implications?
    What information is the author using and is it accurate?
    What are the inferences and subtext?
    What are the concepts and generalizations?
Level 4: Assessing the logic of the author requires a judgment about the text clarity, logic, significance, bias, and relevance.
Level 5: Speaking in the author's voice involves having students be able to dialogue as if they were the author. Could you explain it to others with the clarity of the author?

There are multiple strategies to achieve these goals, some of which were explained in the previous chapter and others that will appear in the following sections and resources.

Corroboration, Sourcing, Contextualization, and Close Reading

The concept of teaching close reading is embedded in the C3 Framework (refer to Chapter 12), which promotes an inquiry approach based on applying disciplinary knowledge, evaluating sources, and using evidence. The field of history has taken a leadership position among the social studies communities of practice in creating a rich framework and resources for the close reading approach: It should serve as a model for teaching how to read expository texts in all the social studies subject fields (see Stanford History Education Group, 2020, and *Resources*). By using the following approaches with multiple primary and secondary source documents, students can not only come to think like historians, but experts in other social studies fields of study. The Stanford History Education Group identifies four processes used by historians that should be learned by students. Students should become familiar with the terms and the questions to ask when reading text or examining graphics.

Corroboration, or comparing and contrasting documents with one another. The technique, which historians call "intertextual reading," involves reading each document with the others as backdrop, weaving them together to bring to life the world of the past.

- What do other documents say?
- Do the documents agree? If not, why?
- What are other possible documents?
- What documents are most reliable?

Because the goal of corroboration is to build a strong argument, it also involves sourcing.

Sourcing is looking first at the source of the document before reading the text itself to consider how the bias of the source might have affected the content of the document.

- Who wrote this?
- What is the author's perspective?
- Why was it written?
- When was it written?
- Where was it written?
- Is this source reliable? Why? Why not?

Contextualization is situating a text in a temporal and spatial context to consider how the time or place in which the document was written might have affected its content or the perspective taken. Contextualization is the act of placing an event within the web of personalities, circumstances, locals, and occurrences that surrounds it.

- When and where was the document created?
- What was different then? What was the same?
- How might the circumstances in which the document was created affect its content?

Close reading means to analyze, synthesize, and evaluate text and the subtext inherent in text.

- What claims does the author make?
- What evidence does the author use?
- What language (words, phrases, images, symbols) does the author use to persuade the document's audience?
- How does the document's language indicate the author's perspective?

Graphics and Interpretation

Graphics in social studies take many forms, such as maps, broadsides, charts, cartoons, etc. Each requires its own nuanced reading strategy and there are multiple ancillary documents by national organizations that facilitate the examination (close reading) of most images and primary source documents (see *Resources* and Chapter 32).

Graphics in textbooks, however, "are often ignored by students and teachers" (Gillespie, 1993, p. 350). Graphics pose a number of unique challenges. The very simplicity that makes some graphics appealing to many is a source of confusion to others, who prefer the "message" in expository text form (Monk, 1988). Graphics appeal more to visual as opposed to less visual learners. Graphics appear in so many different forms, the reader must adjust to each, as compared with the comfortable, linear, sentence structure of expository text. Graphics, like text, have surface knowledge and also convey a subtext that an author is trying to communicate. The same principles found in close reading described previously for text must also be systematically used in close reading graphics (Duplass, 1996).

The following description of how to read (interpret) a chart and cartoon would be modified for maps, pictures, videos, diagrams, broadsides, etc. – but the systematic nature of the process would be preserved. Teachers would model the process early in the school year where they – through sharing their metacognition – would emphasize the examination of literal and subtext information contained in the graphic. The process would proceed as follows and would be best presented as a series of questions by the teacher, although presented here as statements.

Charts

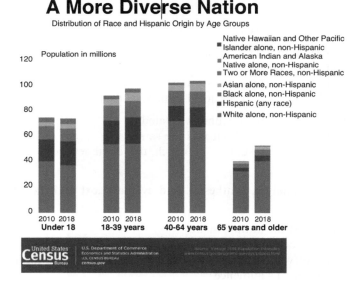

Figure 28.2 Example Chart: "A More Diverse Nation"

The teacher will:

1. Present and skim the chart.

   a. Explain the type of chart (line chart, figure, pie chart, etc.) and what makes it this kind of chart by comparing with other kinds of charts.

    b. Identify the title and make connections to the social studies topic.

    c. Evaluate the reliability of the source and date.

2. Examine the categories of the literal information from left to right, top to bottom, line by line to ensure a baseline of understanding of the axis titles, headings, scale, and data labels.

3. Share conclusions based on the literal information.

4. Determine the subtext

    a. What argument is the author making?

    b. What other data would affect the argument, pro or con?

    c. What change in the presentation might affect the argument?

5. Extend learning by predicting how the information in the chart might affect decision-making or problem-solving.

6. Assess the effectiveness of the chart in terms of communicating the authors' position and expose possible bias by the choice of categories and chart format.

(adapted from Duplass, 1996).

Cartoons

Figure 28.3 Example Cartoon: "Literacy Test"

Cartoons such as "Literacy Test" (Evans, 1916) and information about their history are readily available on the internet. From the National Archives (2020), one can find a downloadable PDF ancillary document, "Cartoon Analysis Worksheet," that can be used with students. The teacher would complete the worksheet with anticipated answers in advance to serve as the class notes. Upon or during the deconstruction of the cartoon, the teacher would debrief students, tying the cartoon to the time period, current events, and democratic ideals. The methodical sequence in its simplest form would be as follows:

1. Present and skim the cartoon

    a. Examine the cartoon information, the who, when, where, etc.
    b. Identify the title and make connection to the events of the time period.

2. Visuals

    a. List the objects/people you see in the cartoon.
    b. Which objects/people are symbolic?
    c. Hypothesize what each object/person symbolizes?

3. Words

    a. List the key words or phrases used by the cartoonist.
    b. Hypothesize which words or phrases in the cartoon appear to be the most significant and why.
    c. List any adjectives that describe the emotions portrayed in the cartoon.

4. Discuss the subtext and its relationship to democratic ideals.

Resources

Videos: *EngageNY*: MLK Letter from Birmingham Jail | *PBS*: Common Core Video Series: Close Reading of a Text | Teaching Reading K-12 A Library of Classroom Practices; Teaching Reading 3–5 Workshop; Reading and Writing in the Discipline | *TCH or YouTube*: Seven Step Vocabulary; Analyzing Texts: "Text Talk Time"; Using Debate to Teach Academic Language; Preparing Students to Read Word & Inference; Silent Tea Party Pre-reading for Challenging Texts; Evidence & Arguments: Ways of Experiencing a Text; Text Graffiti: Previewing Challenging Topics; Document-Based Questions: Warm & Cool Feedback; Reading Formal and Informal Texts; Interpreting Ancient Art in Social Studies; Reading Formal and Informal Texts; Fact or Opinion; An Integrated ELD Lesson Keep it or Junk it; A Student-Run Lesson; Selective Highlighting with a Purpose; Jigsaws: A Strategy for Understanding Texts; Organize Your Thinking to Analyze Text; Reading like a historian – Sourcing, Re-assessing Reliability, Contextualization, Corroboration, Primary Source Documents, Philosopher Chairs, Focus Questions, Turn to Your Partner, Repetition, Historian in Training, R | *YouTube*: Close Reading – Grade 6 Social Studies.

Documents: *Readwritethink:* Where Are We? Learning to Read Maps; ABC Bookmaking Builds Vocabulary in the Content Areas; Analyzing Famous Speeches as Arguments; Analyzing the Purpose and Meaning of Political Cartoons; Argument, Persuasion, or Propaganda? Analyzing World War II Posters; Beyond History Books: Researching with Twin Texts and Technology; Biographies Creating Timelines of a Life; Breaking Barriers, Building Bridges; Critical Discussion of Social Issues (picture books); Comparing Electronic and Print Texts About the Civil War Soldier; Developing Searching, Skimming, and Scanning Skills with Internet Bingo; Diagram It! Identifying,

Comparing, and Writing About Nonfiction Texts; Engaging Students in a Collaborative Exploration of the Gettysburg Address; Guided Comprehension; Self-Questioning Using Question-Answer Relationships; Timelines and Texts; Motivating Students to Read Non-fiction; Using Pictures to Build Schema for Social Studies Content; Analyzing the Stylistic Choices of Political Cartoonists; Guided Comprehension: Making Connections Using a Double-Entry Journal | *Stanford History Education Group*: History Lessons; Historical Thinking Chart; U.S. History (102 lessons); World History (47 lessons); Reading Like an Historian | *Teachinghistory.org:* Crop It.

References

Beck, I. L., McKeown, M. G., & Omanson, R. C. (1987). The effects and uses of diverse vocabulary instructional techniques. In M. C. McKeown & M. E. Curtis (Eds.), *The nature of vocabulary acquisition*. Lawrence Erlbaum Associates.

Boyles, N. (2014). *Closing in on close reading*. Retrieved from www.ascd.org/publications/educational-leadership/dec12/vol70/num04/Closing-in-on-Close-Reading.aspx.

Brett, A., Rothlein, R., & Hurley, M. (1996). Vocabulary acquisition from listening to stories and explanations of target words. *The Elementary School Journal, 96*(4), 415–418.

Duplass, J. (1996). Charts, tables, graphs, and diagrams: An approach for social studies teachers. *The Social Studies, 87*(1), Jan/Feb, 32–38.

Evans, R. (1916). *Literacy test*. Library of Congress. Retrieved from www.loc.gov/pictures/item/2006681433/.

Gillespie, C. S. (1993). Reading graphic displays: What teacher need to know. *Journal of Reading, 36*(5), 350–354.

Goodreads. (2020). *George Carlin*. Retrieved from www.goodreads.com/quotes/569565-don-t-just-teach-your-children-to-read-teach-them-to.

Lesh, B. (2011). *"Why won't you just tell us the answer?": Teaching historical thinking in grades 7-12*. Stenhouse.

Monk, G. S. (1988). Students' understanding of functions in calculus. *Humanistic Mathematics Network Newsletter, 2*, 236–241.

National Archives. (2020). *Cartoon analysis worksheet*. Retrieved from www.archives.gov/education/lessons/worksheets/cartoon.html.

NCSS. (1989). In search of a scope and sequence for social studies. *Social Education, 53*(6), 376–385.

Parker, W. C. (2001). *Social studies in elementary education*. Prentice-Hall.

Paul, R., & Elder, L. (2008). *How to read a paragraph: The art of close reading*. Foundation for Critical Thinking Press.

Stahl, S., Hynd, C., Britton, B., McNish, M., & Bosquet, D. (1996). What happens when students read multiple source documents in history? *Reading Research Quarterly, 31*(4), 430–456.

Stanford History Education Group. (2020). *Read like a historian*. Retrieved from https://sheg.stanford.edu/.

29 Writing

Writing is thinking. To write well is to think clearly. That's why it's so hard.
David McCullough, Pulitzer Prize-Winning Historian, 1933–present (Cole, 2002)

The Value of Writing Assignments

Social studies, because students experience it in their daily lives, is uniquely positioned to fulfill John Dewey's observations when he said, it is "all the difference in the world between having something to say and having to say something" (Dewey, 1899/1980, p. 35). Social studies writing assignments should be integrated into investigations about foundational knowledge and consideration of things that matter. The act of writing requires:

1. **Comprehension** – by organizing, comparing, translating, interpreting, giving descriptions, and stating the main ideas;
2. **Analysis** – by examining and dividing information into parts, identifying motives or causes, making inferences, and finding evidence to support generalizations;
3. **Evaluation** – by presenting and defending opinions by making judgments about information or the validity of ideas based on a set of criteria; and
4. **Synthesis** – by compiling information together in a different way, combining elements in a new pattern, and proposing alternative solutions.

Writing Feedback

Because writing is a process, teachers need to structure writing assignments so that students receive feedback during the writing stages. Langer and Applebee (1986) point out that one of the keys to success in teaching students to write is for the teacher to be more of a collaborator and coach than an evaluator during the process of writing. The following collaborative strategies are intended to increase the likelihood of students developing the writing skills that will allow them to express their ideas.
Strategies include:

Teacher verbal feedback is crucial. To facilitate individual, verbal feedback, teachers must create time and learning activities to keep students busy as the teacher coaches individual students. It is particularly important at the beginning of the process, following the teacher's modeling and explanation of expectations, so students can articulate their thinking about how they plan to proceed.

Writing workshops place students in groups, often heterogeneous, so that students can confer about their ideas to incorporate into their individual products and compare their progress with other students.

Mimicry is where students use a textbook, manuscript, or other form of treatise as an example of style and format of the assigned writing task.

Student collaborations in pairs allow each student to confer on topics, thesis, components, sequence, formatting, selection of illustrations, etc., and deletions, additions, and corrections during drafting.

Peer review should be incorporated into the process for proofreading and peer-to-peer feedback. Teachers should teach and model for students how to proofread and give feedback.

Writing Tasks

Almost any topic or lesson in social studies education can be paired with a writing activity. Social studies teachers should not limit their thinking to the more traditional approaches of just short and long essays. The following list of selected writing products could be incorporated into lessons and are intended to offer variety. Many are suited for elementary education teachers because their students are beginner writers. But they can also be used for differentiated instruction at higher grade levels. In almost all cases, the task requires modeling by the teacher the first time it is required.

ABC report – The ABC report is 27 pages long, with a cover page followed by one page for each letter of the alphabet. The author of the report identifies content that can be associated with a letter. For example, if the topic is the American Revolution, *A* could be arms used in the Revolution, *B* could be the Boston Massacre, and so on. The author writes multiple paragraphs for each page on each letter combining facts, conclusions, and opinions. Students could also be given the option of creating or including images. Students can be divided into three-person groups, with two group members responsible for nine letters each and one for eight letters and the cover.

Brochure – Students can write travel brochures after doing research on select countries, the 50 states, cities, historical sites, etc.

Cornell Notes – The Cornell note-taking system provides a systematic format for condensing and organizing ideas while attempting to answer key questions.

Double-entry note-taking – Requires students to take notes from the text in the left-hand column (usually in required notebooks), and in the right-hand column they must write questions about the material.

Editorials – Students write editorials for a newspaper or a TV news broadcast from the perspective of a historical figure about a historical event or about a current event.

Entrance/exit ticket – The teacher poses a question – students write the answer. The entrance tickets are assigned for homework and are due as the students enter the classroom the next day.

Exit tickets are completed in class during the last 3–5 minutes and turned in as students exit the classroom. These allow the teacher to monitor student understanding of the subject matter being taught.

Essay ("the five-paragraph essay" or "hamburger paragraph") – The five-paragraph essay follows a specific format.

1. The first paragraph introduces the thesis of the essay and leads to the three main supporting subtopics.
2. The second through fourth paragraphs are all similar in format. They individually restate the subtopics, and are developed by giving supporting information of the thesis.
3. The fifth paragraph restates the main thesis idea and reminds the reader of the three main supporting ideas that were developed.

Feature story – Each student reads a biography of a historical figure and takes on the significant person's persona. One student interviews the other classmate, who stays in character, and writes a feature story about the historical figure.

Gallery walk – This is used for presentation of poster board sessions, where posters are created by students with student-authored documents and graphics. Half the class displays their researched topic and explains it as the other half of the students circulate around the room listening to the presentations and asking questions. The next day the other students display their posters.

Image prompts – A photograph, painting, advertisement, broadside, etc., is used as an attention-getter, requiring students to write a description of what they see, what their analysis of the information is, and how it makes them feel.

Journals – Encourage reflection, writing, and a dialogue with the teacher about what students are thinking, feeling, and learning on a daily or weekly basis as an end-of-class task or homework. There are multiple types of journals.

> **Teacher prompt** – The teacher has students respond to a prompt, an idea, provocative thought, etc. drawn from the lesson.
>
> **Lifted line response** – Students select a line from the text and write a response to it.
>
> **Brainstorming** – This can be a pre-reading activity, where the teacher asks students to write down everything they know about a topic, or a post-reading activity, where they summarize the topic.
>
> **Dual-entry format** – A line is drawn down the center of the journal page. The student writes a factual statement from the text on the left, and on the right, their thoughts and feelings about the statement.
>
> **Freewriting** – Students can write whatever thoughts they have about what was learned.
>
> **Vocabulary** – Students can use their journal to record vocabulary and definitions.

Lists, group, and label – Students brainstorm ideas about a selected topic, such as the causes of the Civil War, and the students divide the list into categories, such as economic, social, and political causes.

Microthemes – The microtheme is a short 100–500-word essay in which a great deal of thinking precedes a rather small amount of writing. There are four main formats:

> **The summary-writing microtheme** – Based on an assigned reading, the students are required to condense the knowledge learned to its most important arguments and conclusions.
>
> **The thesis-support microtheme** – The student must take a stand and defend a hypothesis or position on a topic from a lesson or reading assignment.
>
> **The data-provided microtheme** – Data is provided in the form of tables or factual statements to the class and the students must comment on its significance and make assertions by selecting, arranging, connecting, and generalizing about the information.
>
> **The quandary-posing microtheme** – Based on a conflict of competing ideological stances, the student must explain the underlying arguments and pose a solution.

One of the main advantages of microthemes is that they are relatively easy to evaluate, score, and provide feedback.

Newspaper/magazine article – Students write a newspaper or magazine article on a contemporary or historical event, person, or place. This activity allows students to write for an audience.

Outlining – The students outline based on the textbook or a newspaper, webpage, magazine article, etc. The classic outline form is the Roman numeral I, A, 1, a, etc. When it is applied to text narrative, the task emphasizes the importance of the sequence, hierarchy, and organization of ideas.

Personal letter/diary/journal – Students step into the time period of a specific person in history and write a historical letter, diary, or journal entry.

PowerPoint/webpage – Students design a PowerPoint presentation or a webpage on a historical event or current person, place, or public policy.

Quick writes – Students aggregate factual information to make an evidence-based argument, to rank the evidence by importance and usefulness, and to demonstrate specific historical thinking concepts such as periodization, interpretation, causation, comparison, and synthesis. Students are given choices and in five to seven sentences must use examples from the lesson's discussion and evidence. An example of a prompt might be, "The two most important pieces of evidence were _____ because..."

Rap – Students write song lyrics using historical content and present their lyrics in front of the class. The teacher can use a song from the musical *Hamilton* as an example.

RAFT – This type of tasks requires a student to write from the position of a historical figure. Students decide and list the elements of RAFT, then use them when writing an essay. Students can use or create illustrations and graphics. The student decides:
Role: Which role from the historical past will you play?
Audience: Who will you be writing to? The student has many choices based on the format selected.
Format: What type of format or writing style will you use? You could write to yourself in a diary entry, the public in a speech, letter to an editor, a loved one in a letter or poem, etc.
Topic: What significant event will prompt you to write about it?

Résumé – Students are taught about résumés, create one for themselves, and then research and craft a résumé of a historical figure.

Role-playing – Students research a historical figure and write a script. Students role-play as the historical figure while presenting to the class individually or as a group of the personalities in a historical setting.

Sentence passage spring board – Ask students to select a specific sentence or short passage from their reading that has captured their attention and to write it across the top of the page. They should then be given time (in class or at home) to express in writing their thoughts about the sentence or passage.

Short summary – This is a homework assignment that requires students to come to class with a no more than 50-word summary of the reading assignment from the night before.

Speech – Students write a speech from the perspective of a historical or contemporary public figure. Students may present their speech to the class to practice public speaking skills.

Student-generated test questions – Students write test questions and answers from the topic being studied.

Take turns paper – This kind of paper requires students to work in pairs or foursomes and to take turns adding the next sentence to respond to a compelling issue taught by the teacher.

Term papers – Term papers should have the full scope of the writing activity in social studies, from a thesis to proper citation of sources. The teacher should provide an example of an end product, teach the components, and coach students in authoring their papers.

Write around – Students, in small groups, are given a question to write on the top of their papers. Each student answers the question. After one minute students trade papers to the right and now must respond to the previous student's answer. They trade again after one minute until the students receive their own papers back. The group discusses their answers and how they were alike/different.

Written interview – Students write out a list of questions that could be used to interview a contemporary or historical figure. Another student in the class answers the questions as the historical person being interviewed.

Most of these writing strategies can be researched further on the internet, so most will not be included in *Resources* at the end of the chapter and each can be modified for different subject fields.

The Social Studies Essay Lesson

Social studies teachers should not assume that students know how to write an essay that has the hallmarks of the modes of reasoning and writing craft of the disciplines of social studies – whether it is just a paragraph, essay, or a comprehensive term paper. By teaching how to write an essay in the first weeks of class and setting in motion a collaboration during each assigned essay or writing assignment, the teacher uses the gradual release model so that by the end of the year, students have developed the skills to write more confidently with less support.

At the beginning of the year teachers should plan a lesson where they model for students how to write an essay explaining in detail the types of writing, attributes of social studies narratives, and steps in writing using a concrete example from a topic the teacher has already covered. Envision a teacher creating a PowerPoint presentation that covers the elements of an essay. The teacher then distributes an example of a five paragraph essay that the teacher wrote. It is then referenced in the PowerPoint slides so students have a concrete example. Using the think-aloud approach, the teacher demonstrates how the essay fulfills the elements and the decisions the teacher made in crafting the essay. The following are some ideas that would be included in the PowerPoint presentation. It could start with the four types of writing in social studies and the teacher would explain which type the essay is, etc.

Four Types of Writing

Risinger (1987) identified four types of writing that are often used in social studies.

1. **Reporting:** Students are directed to compile information with a minimum of critical or original thinking – Write about four major events of the American Revolution.
2. **Exposition:** Students are asked to explain an idea, conduct a critical investigation, synthesize issues, or bring a fresh point of view to a problem – Comparing British and colonists' reasons for the American Revolution.
3. **Narration:** Students are asked to write a story, an anecdote, a tall tale, a legend, a short story, a drama, or a vignette – Pretend you are a spectator at the Boston Tea Party and write a fictitious, firsthand account that includes some facts known about the event.
4. **Argumentation:** Students are asked to evaluate and defend or oppose an idea or belief – Write a letter to your fellow colonists detailing the reasons why they should not declare independence.

The Components of a Social Studies Essay

The following components and attributes of an essay are drawn from multiple sources. Teachers would add into the PowerPoint specific examples from their model essay. Once taught, teachers can create a guide for the students to follow. Coaching is particularly important at the selection of a topic, development of the question, thesis, and initial claims.

Topic

The **topic** is the starting point and is either assigned by the teacher or selected by the students from the subject matter to be investigated.

Thesis

The **thesis** requires the teacher to teach students to ask, "Why do I think this about the topic?" and "What in particular leads me to this conclusion?" Depending on the kind of essay and grade level, the essay may require finding and evaluating resources. After examples and explanation, students should be coached to at least a "working thesis" that will help them map out the outline of the essay. Having students think about the how and why of the topic to be investigated and/or considered often leads the student to a thoughtful and enlightening thesis for the teacher to confirm and provide more coaching.

Introduction

The most common introductions are:

The **anecdote approach** is where the author relates an example which exemplifies the thesis.

The **funnel approach** is where the writer identifies the general subject area in the opening sentence, making some generalization aimed at arousing interest and, perhaps, establishing a bond of common awareness and knowledge with the reader, and then narrows the subject down sentence by sentence, to the specific viewpoint towards it that forms the thesis.

The **question approach** has a rhetorical question that is proactive based on the thesis or antithesis that captures (shocks) the reader.

The **quote approach** uses a famous quote to lead the reader into the thesis.

Organizing Schemes

The most common organizing schemes are:

Chronological order
Cause and effect order
Order of importance
Spatial order, and
Comparison-contrast order (refer to Chapter 21's "Modes of Reasoning" for additional organizing schemes).

The Body of the Essay

The **topic sentence** is the introduction to the thesis that begins the essay in the first paragraph.

Paragraphs require that the students order their analysis, both within and between paragraphs, and by weaving together original narrative, facts, concepts, generalizations, quotes, and paraphrasing to make an argument that proves or supports the thesis.

Connecting words – Teachers should provide a list of "connecting words": such as *although, moreover, as a result, meanwhile, to begin with, as a consequence*, etc.

Facts – Information known to be true (dates, places, people, events, etc.).

Concepts and generalizations that logically follow a set of facts and examples.

Examples – Illustrations for comparison or contrast and typically follow phrases like "such as," "for example," etc.

Reasons and conclusions – drawn from the facts, examples, concepts and generalizations.

Conclusions

The most common types of conclusion are:

Challenging the reader – Rephrases the thesis argument to have it apply to the reader.

Echoing the introduction – Restate the thesis found in the opening paragraphs with a new insight.

Looking to the future – Repeat the thesis in terms of its implications for the future.

Posing a question – Calls on the reader to reflect on the topic and take a position.

The Writing Process

Constructing the essay should follow a staged, scaffolded process. The "**process writing**" approach that follows is adapted from the Five Step +1 writing process of Leu and Kinzer (1999) and others.

Pre-writing: It is the planning phase of the writing process. The pre-writing stage helps students expand or narrow their focus and identify and/or organize ideas. The student narrows the broad topics into manageable subtopics for which evidence (documents, images, etc.) is likely available.

Drafting: This stage involves the students organizing ideas into a coherent structure without being constrained by word choice, sentence structure, conventions, and presentation. Models of exemplary writing help students build a visual map in order to draft their ideas according to specifications. Conferences with teachers or peers can occur during this phase to provide feedback to the writer

Revising: This stage focuses on improving student writing by examining ideas, organization, voice, word choice, and sentence fluency. Students rethink, rework, and refine their writing. Students apply their knowledge of language skills and sentence structure in order to become better writers.

Editing: This stage involves the beautification of the piece and should be undertaken when all revisions to the content are complete. The writing is revisited to correct errors in grammar, mechanics, and usage and may be done independently or by engaging in peer editing.

Publishing: This stage involves sharing the writing with an intended audience and may involve preparing a neatly handwritten or word-processed copy of the final draft and the addition of illustrations or other graphic elements. The writer works to polish the essay to make the piece appealing and inviting to the audience. Publication may extend to a multimedia presentation or lead to a public presentation. In most cases, the teacher is a member of the audience.

Revisiting: This post-publication stage occurs after the essay is published and graded. Based on teacher direction, the students may return to the composition to "rework" language of the text.

Resources

Videos: *Learner.org*: Developing Writers; Write in the Middle: A Workshop for Middle School Teachers; Reading and Writing in the Discipline | *TCH or YouTube:* Cross-discipline Socratic Seminar Refining Essays (role of religion); Getting Ready to Write: Citing Textual Evidence; Evidence & Arguments: Lesson Planning Using Personal Anecdotes; Analyzing Test Brainstorm Before Writing; Writing to Learn; The Writing Recipe Essay Structure for ELLs; Evidence & Arguments: Passing Notes to Exchange Ideas; Performance as a Culminating Activity; Gallery Walk; Spark Your Persuasive Writing 3 Simple Prompts; Art of Persuasion and Craft of Argument; Making Punctuation Engaging; Cross-Discipline Socratic Seminar: Moving Beyond Brainstorming; Detective Work: Using Evidence to Form Theories; Refining Essays; Writing Commentaries: The Power of Youth Voice; Writing, Inquiry, Collaboration & Reading; Developing Persuasive Arguments Through Ethical Inquiry – Two Prewriting Strategies; Film Review; Equipping Students for Writing; UK Guided Writing Workshop; Writing Sentence Frames to Jumpstart Writing; Small Group Writing | *ReadWriteThink*: Has multiple videos demonstrating best reading and writing practices | *YouTube:* Gradual Release – Modeled Guided Independent Practice; How to Teach the Writing Process | *Doing Social Studies*: Argumentative Writing Prompts, Scaffolded Tasks, and Using Evidence | *KU:* The Writing Process.

Documents: *ReadWriteThink*: has over 150 of the best writing and reading strategies sorted by grade level and social studies | *What Works Clearinghouse*: Literacy; Teaching Secondary Students to Write Effectively | *NEA* 6 + 1 Trait Writing Rubric |

ReadingRockets Classroom Strategies (over 50 reading and writing strategies with downloadable ancillaries) | Teaching Secondary Students to Write Effectively.

References

Cole, B. (2002). Interview with David McCullough. *Humanities, 23*, 4. Retrieved from www.good reads.com/quotes/320581-writing-is-thinking-to-write-well-is-to-think-clearly

Dewey, J. (1899/1980). *School and society.* Carbondale: southern Illinois University Press.

Langer, J. A., & Applebee, A. N. (1986). Reading and writing instruction: Toward a theory of teaching and learning. In E. Z. Rothkoph (Ed.), *Review of research in education* (Vol. 13, pp. 171–194). American Educational Research Association.

Leu, D., & Kinzer, C. K. (1999). *Effective literacy instruction, K-8* (4th ed.). Prentice-Hall.

Risinger, C. F. (1987). *Improving writing skills through social studies.* ERIC Document Reproduction Service No. ED285829.

30 Six Activities-Based Strategies

It usually takes me more than three weeks to prepare a good impromptu speech.
Mark Twain, Author and Humorist, 1835–1910 (BrainyQuote, 2020)

The following six activities are part of a social studies teacher's repertoire to engage students in a variety of ways.

Presentations and Self-Directed Learning

The Common Core Standards (2020) includes teaching students public speaking. Presentations should reflect comprehension of content knowledge and be preceeded with modeling by the teacher and coaching of students through the process. By tying presentations to self-directed learning products, students have something that is of interest to them to make a presentation about. Teachers need to prepare lessons on the process of researching, writing, and presenting just as they would for writing an essay so students can gain confidence in public speaking.

Presentations and Product Ideas

The following ideas are drawn from multiple sources. All the presentations and products require a variety of skills and can be assigned on an individual basis with preparation completed in pairs or groups.

Book reports – These can take on many topics such as historical events, individuals, inventions, cultures in various geographic locations, etc. A major source of books that may serve as the basis for book reports is the *Notable Social Studies Trade Books for Young People* (NCSS, 2020).

Three-minute poster board displays – Students create three-panel poster board displays with half of the students presenting on one day, the others on the second day. Students set up around the classroom and make three-minute presentations as other students visit and ask questions timed for five- to ten-minute intervals for students to visit multiple presentations. This can be further enhanced by multiple teachers participating and having, as an example, a "4th grade poster board day."

Introduce your neighbor – Two students interview each other about their family and family's ethnicity, history, culture, habits, etc., and write a biographical paper to be edited by each other, and then both present to the class about their partner. This can be very effective in creating a positive classroom environment at the beginning of the year and as a lesson on how history is constructed by historians.

Monologues – Students research a historical figure, author a monologue based on the events surrounding the figure which made him or her notable and, with an introduction by the teacher, take on the person's persona and act out the character for the class.

News broadcast – Students work in pairs to create the "evening news" broadcast where they create a script of a newscast and report on events from a historical period as if television was in existence at the time, or they can report on a current event.

Replace the teacher – While the goal is for the students to learn the techniques of pre-paring a presentation and the skill of presenting, presentations by students can be structured to partially replace the teacher-centered classroom. After modeling how to research, prepare, and make a presentation at the beginning of the year, the teacher assigns or lets students pick a "depth" topic, meaning a narrow, focused topic appropriate to the grade level. This would include topics the teacher expects to cover during the year. The topics might be major figures, historic sites, major events or documents, geographic locations, elements of the Constitution, economics con-cepts, etc. On the planned week of the lesson by the teacher, students deliver their presentation on the lesson day and then are followed by a debriefing by the teacher to make up for any missed foundational knowledge or democratic ideals.

Podcast – Introduce students to podcast technology as a substitute for the live presentation.

Skits – These are group presentations where a team of students author and act out a fictionalized dramatization of a historical event, a simulation, or reenactment.

Talk show host – Students plan an interview of historical figures based on talk show formats, with one student as the host and the other students as historical figures.

Best Practices for Self-Directed Learning and Presentations

The teacher:

1. Models how to create the product using examples and rubrics.
2. Sets aside "practice" days for all the students to research, write, and prepare the products and rehearse presentations. This is often a group activity, although the content topic for each student is different.
3. Divides the process up into increments with scheduled deadlines and a check-off sheet to ensure progress by each student.
4. Serves as a consultant at scheduled times for coaching students.
5. Incorporates peer review into the process.

Role-Playing, Reenactments, and Simulations

Role-playing, reenactments, and simulations have evolved into important active learning strategies in social studies, particularly for elementary students, because they combine the cognitive and affective domains and thus are active learning, not just an activity (Chilcoat, 1996). **Reenactments** are a form of role-playing that focus on people and events in history, recent history included. Students are expected to reflect and project emotions appropriate to the skit as well as develop an appreciation of the people involved and of the time period. **Simulations**, another form of role-playing, are different from reenactments. Rather than depicting a person or an event, simulations provide a simplified representation of a real experience. The following are examples of role-playing activities.

Reenactments	Simulations
Classroom or schoolyard battle field	Archeological digs in the schoolyard
Ellis Island immigrant arrival	City Hall hearings
Impeachment trial of Andrew Johnston	Assembly line
Napoleon's coronation	Legislation being passed
Olympic Games	Mock trials
Peace treaty signing	Preparing a household budget
Pilgrims' Thanksgiving	Planning a trip across the United States

Role-playing should be integral to a comprehensive lesson rather than a gimmick or an afterthought. Based on ideas from Morris (2001) and McDaniel (2000), the following approach can be used to heighten the role-playing experiences. For an event such as Napoleon's coronation, the teacher creates a transparency of the painting by Jacques-Louis David. The overhead projector with the transparency of the painting is placed on the floor pointing at a white wall and to keep the image at ground level. Have students stand in front of the images projected on the wall to begin the reenactment. This creates a theater-like backdrop.

Best Practices for Role-Playing and Reenactments

1. Model for students how to prepare a script and act out a skit.
2. Allow students to select from a menu of topics (events) and then roles to give them ownership.
3. Explain the limitations of role-playing to the students: The audience must suspend disbelief and accept the limits of the scenario.
4. Coach each group through the process of preparing to ensure the content is accurate.
5. Preview the skit by providing the audience (the other students) with ideas about what to look for or questions to ask if there are not roles for all students.
6. Keep all students focused while the role-playing is taking place.
7. Guard against trivialization.
8. Debrief the role-playing by pointing out or having students point out motives and actions.
9. Allow students to share ideas and relate the situation to their own lives.
10. Ensure that all students have an opportunity to role-play over a period of time.

Games

Games can add enthusiasm and energy to learning experiences and offer a change of pace from the daily routine. There are multiple game-like activities on the internet (see *Resources*). Some traditional games that may be adapted for integration into a meaningful social studies learning experience are:

Bees (geography bee, history bee, etc.)	Detectives (finding a missing person by making educated guesses to name a person, place, or thing based on clues from the teacher)
Bingo	Stump the teacher (the reverse of detectives, with the students giving the clues and the teacher making the educated guesses).
Trivia games	
Map puzzles	
Charades	
Tic-tac-toe	
Commercial board games	

Guest Speakers

Guest speakers can provide powerful learning experience: However, they can also be disasters. Many potential speakers are experts on very particularized areas and are unable to adapt their knowledge and presentation to the elementary, middle, or high school classroom. Presenters who want to come to a teacher's classroom may have biased or particular ideological agendas and do not understand the difference between indoctrination vs. enculturation and preaching vs. education. Some guest speakers are performers, "reenactors" with no substantive background in the content they propose to represent. Teachers need to investigate and decide if a guest speaker is the best source of information for the students.

Examples of Guest Speakers

Experts on population, ecology, local history, etc.	Representatives of different cultures
Military personnel and first responders	Storytellers
Politicians	Reenactors
Representatives of civic organizations and charities	Researchers
	Judges, attorneys, etc.

Best Practices for Guest Speakers

To ensure an excellent outcome, teachers should set expectations for guest speakers.

1. If at all possible, observe the speakers before extending the invitation. If that is not possible, meet with them, interview them by phone or Skype, or call a reference who has had them in their classroom. Deciding to invite the speaker based solely on a brief phone conversation is risky.
2. Obtain the school principal's approval.
3. The teacher should clearly state the focus of the presentation and expectations. If an agreement cannot be reached, it would be better to withdraw the invitation. Remember, it is the teacher's credibility that is on the line.
4. Communicate all the arrangements (arrival time, parking, length of presentation, number of students) verbally and confirm in writing. Send the speaker a map; alert the front desk; and have someone meet the presenter at the entrance to the school.
5. Limit the time for the presentation and questions.

6. Encourage the presenter to have an active presentation based on active learning strategies, to use realia, music, artwork, primary documents, pictures, apparatus, manipulatives, handouts, and visual aids, if appropriate.
7. Suggest the value of storytelling and anecdotal stories, and advise the speaker to avoid preaching.
8. Provide instruction about the topic as part of a comprehensive lesson before and after the presentation.
9. Prepare students by reviewing etiquette and questioning skills.
10. Require students to prepare questions in advance for the visitor.
11. Give students specific assignments to be completed as a result of the presentation.
12. Send a thank-you note from the class.

Field Trips

The field trip can be used as a motivating device and would have both a lesson preparing students for the field trip and the venue itself. There should also be a debriefing after the visit that is part of the lesson plan. Virtual field trips can be very effective and efficient (see *Resources*). Some teachers use field trips as rewards that students must earn. This practice implies that the field trip is not an essential part of an important planned learning experience. When a trip is used as a reward for students who are achieving or those who do not have behavior problems, the students who might be motivated to improve their behavior or performance by the field trip experience are deprived of the opportunity to do so.

Field Trip Venues

The following are some local venues that have educational value and should be considered.

Archeological dig	Military base
Art Museum	Municipal building
Factory	Newspaper or TV station
History museums	Police or fire station
Farm	Reenactment site
Historic site	State parks

Best Practices for Field Trips

Field trips require a significant commitment of time to plan and organize. The following are useful guidelines.

1. Make a pre-trip visit before deciding to take the students.
2. Take the time to meet with the administration and explain the educational goals.
3. Decide if a venue's docent will conduct the tour.
4. Verify and confirm all arrangements in writing, such as transportation, meals, departure and return information, additional supervision, etc.
5. Make arrangements for students with special needs.

6. Create clear rules about conduct for the students.
7. Review appropriate conduct and attire with the students.
8. Invite parents to serve as additional supervisors.
9. Create a permission slip that includes a statement of the educational goals.
10. Take roll before, during, and after the trip to keep track of students.
11. Preview the trip with students as part of the lesson plan.
12. Provide each student with a "guide sheet" or questions to ask while on the trip.
13. Provide a debriefing after the trip.

Service-Learning

Service-learning is directly tied to democratic ideals. The NCSS position paper states:

> Service-learning connects meaningful service in the school or community with academic learning and civic responsibility. Service-learning is distinguished from community service in two ways. First, the service activity is integrated with academic skills and content. Second, students engage in structured reflection activities on their service experiences.

(NCSS, 2000)

There are different types of service-learning activities that teachers can consider:

One-time or an ongoing service project;
Individual or group service project;
Optional self-directed experience where the students may replace another assignment with a service-learning assignment;
Required of all students or an alternative to another assignment and students are given options;
School-wide service project.

The following examples would be highly dependent on the grade level of the students.

Examples of Service-Learning

Action research project that results in an authored report to a community agency.	Create an anti-bullying campaign or other type of awareness campaign with posters.
Adopt a food pantry, retirement community, animal rescue center, etc.	Develop a school or community beautification project.
Assist voter registration efforts.	A lunch room "yard" sale.
Classroom or school cleanup day.	Organizing a food drive in the classroom or
Collection for a food drive or items for overseas' soldiers.	school.
	Tutoring.
Organizing a crowdfunding initiative for a worthy cause.	Reading buddies from an older class to a younger class

Best Practices for Service-Learning

A. Consult the school administration.
B. Let the students come up with possible service-learning activities.
C. Use the following five components:

1. **Investigation:** Teachers and students investigate the community problems that they might potentially address.
2. **Planning and preparation:** Teachers, students, and/or community members plan the learning and service activities, and address the administrative issues needed for a successful project.
3. **Action** (implementing the service activity): The "heart" of the project: engaging in the meaningful service experience that will help students develop important knowledge, skills, and attitudes, and will benefit the community.
4. **Reflection:** Activities that help students understand the service-learning experience and to think about its meaning and connection to them, their society, and what they have learned in school; and
5. **Demonstration/celebration:** The final experience when students, community participants and others publicly share what they have learned, celebrate the results of the service project, and look ahead to the future (RMC, 2006/2009, p. 7).

D. Let students take the lead in components 1, 2, and 3.
E. Ensure all students contribute equally to the experience.

Resources

Videos (also search "online educational games"): *Discovery Education:* Virtual Field Trips | *Edtechteacher*: Games and Animations | *TCH or YouTube:* Inspirational Speeches; Sophomore Speeches; What It Means to be a Learner; Persuasive Speeches; Planning a Lesson Series; Examining Elements of Persuasive Speeches; Historical Detective Work; Delivering and Evaluating Persuasive Speeches | *ICivics:* Games | *IXL:* Social studies (membership required but over 500 interactive games) | *National Geographic:* Virtual Field Trips | *Social Studies Central:* Interactive Simulations | *YouTube*: Rotation Differentiating Instruction | *Smithsonian*: Learning Lab Resources.

Documents: *Routledge Handbook of Research in Social Studies Education*: Service learning research) | *ReadWriteThink:* Creating a Persuasive Podcast; Giving Voice to Child Laborers Through Monologues; Book Report Alternative: Getting Acquainted with Facebook; Storytelling in the Social Studies Classroom; My Life/Your Life: A Look at Your Parents' Past; Connecting Past and Present – A Local Research Project; Getting to Know You – Developing Short Biographies to Build Community; Oral Presentation Rubric; Biography Project: Research and Class Presentation | Building Vietnam War Scavenger Hunts Through Web-Based Inquiry; Glogging about Natural Disasters; Learning about Research and Writing Using the American Revolution; Searching for Gold – A Collaborative Inquiry Project; The Year I Was Born – An Autobiographical Research Project; Persuasive Essay – Environmental Issues | *TCH:* Differentiating with Learning Menus | Social Studies Projects Handbook St Charles' Parish | Florida Learn and Serve | The Texas Center for Service-Learning | Service-Learning and Assessment: A Field Guide for Teachers.

References

BrainyQuote. (2020). Mark Twain. Retrieved from www.brainyquote.com/quotes/mark_twain_100433.

Chilcoat, G. W. (1996). Drama in the social studies classroom: A review of the literature. *Journal of Social Studies Research, 20*(2), 3–17.

Core, C. (2020). *Speaking*. Retrieved from www.corestandards.org/ELA-Literacy/SL/1/.

McDaniel, K. N. (2000). Four elements of successful historical role-playing in the classroom. *The History Teacher, 33*(3), 357–362.

Morris, R. V. (2001). Using first-person presentation to encourage student interest in social history. *Gifted Child Today Magazine, 24*(1), 46–53.

NCSS. (2000). Service-learning: An essential component of citizenship education. *Social Education, 65*(4), 240–241.

NCSS. (2020). *Notable social studies trade books for young people*. Retrieved from www.socialstudies.org/publications/notables.

RMC Research Corporation. (2006/2009). K-12 service-learning project planning toolkit. National Service-Learning Clearinghouse, Retrieved from www.servicelearning.org/library/resource/8542.

31 Accommodations, Differentiated Instruction, and Assessment

But there are advantages to being elected President. The day after I was elected, I had my high school grades classified top secret.

Ronald Reagan, 40th President of the United States, 1911–2004
(Reagan Foundation, 2020)

Teachers should enter the year expecting that every student will succeed at a high level, even though the statistical reality suggests otherwise. Teaching would be easy if every student came to school motivated and with the academic and emotional capacities to learn; every teacher was as gifted as Socrates; and every parent was attentive to their student's education and needs. One of the great challenges and dilemmas for teachers is how to have a class of students achieve the uniform expectations dictated by standards, when the individuals who enter the classroom door bring with them a range of skills, academic acumen, family circumstances, and dispositions. Virtually every reform movement of the past 75 years, from Head Start to charter schools, has attempted to resolve the fundamental challenge that humans do not all begin their lives at the same starting line due to the serendipity of birth into one family as opposed to another or with the same innate abilities. The research is unequivocal: The one unchanging variable is that 60–80% of American schools' "failure" is the product of non-school factors (Muijs, 2020). Schools serving predominantly low socioeconomic status families have the highest rates of student failures and students from low socioeconomic families interspersed in classrooms that reflect the broader US social economic statuses have a greater likelihood of academic failure. The public's expectations that teachers and schools can mitigate the ills found in society have never been higher. This is not to say that there are not schools and students that overcome the disadvantages or teachers cannot make a difference (see *Conclusion*). KIPP schools' graduates have a higher rate of college completion than the national average for all students and do so by emphasizing character education, no excuses, high expectations, parent commitment, and teacher professional development (KIPP, 2020). Saint Benedict's Prep in New Jersey is an all-boys school of about 500 students, almost all Hispanic and African American students from broken, poverty-level families. It graduates almost 100% of its students and integrates the theory of philosophical counseling into its mission and curriculum (St. Benedict's, 2020).

The often-repeated macro analysis of the sociology of families and communities' impact on schools shows its face to teachers in the day-to-day challenge of teaching 25 "mixed abilities" students (Tomlinson, 2001). The idea of grouping students by age was based on the assumption that students of like age would reduce the range of abilities so teachers and students could be more successful. The personal moral quandary and heart-breaking experience of seeing students fail due to circumstances beyond the student's control and a teacher's best efforts takes an emotional toll on teachers, not just students and parents.

Accommodations and Differentiated Instruction

Accommodations are thought of as adjustments to methods for an individual student based on unique circumstances, such as those required by the Disabilities Education Improvement Act of 2004 that requires Individualized Education Plans (**IEPs**). A less technical use of the term calls for teachers to accommodate, as an example, English language learners (**ELLs**) due to their unfamiliarity with the nuances of the English language (see Cruz & Thornton, 2013 for strategies).

The **differentiated instruction** approach typically entails use of a variety of strategies so as to appeal to different learning preferences of individual students so as to increase their likelihood of success. This would include using a variety of approaches such as those in this book. In addition, it extends to allowing choices by individual students. As an example, allowing students to choose between authoring an essay or creating a PowerPoint presentation differentiates instruction, but the expectation of excellence stays the same. The following are frequently used forms of differentiated instructions and accommodations.

Stations are a particularly effective strategy at the elementary school level where one teacher has the students all day. Four third-grade teachers, as an example, agree to create a week-long social studies lesson on Mexico. Each teacher agrees to create one station with enough tasks and materials for all four classes of 25 students each. There should be more task options than students could complete in a week. One station might be culture (with music, beginning Spanish, etc.) and the other stations of geography, history, and government of Mexico. All students in each classroom are required to complete a minimum number of tasks in each station, but they have the choice to spend more time in one station than another. While students are completing stations, the teacher is available for consultation, but more important during the time period of the stations lesson, teachers "pull out" students for individualized coaching in basic skills.

Packets require teachers to create learning packets of tasks and materials for individualized, self-paced (within limits) learning. It converts the learning centers approach by placing all the tasks and materials into a learning packet given to each student. Each task has a pre-assessment and students who demonstrate competency in tasks do not have to complete that task in the packet, but can spend more time on other tasks, and when all tasks are completed, the students have free time to work on other subject areas. The packets approach also allows the time for teachers to work with students individually or in groups for extra coaching while other students are busy working on the packets. This packet strategy works equally well at the elementary, middle, or high school level.

Tiered assignments allow students, based on a rubric, to decide which tier level they want to perform at.

Assessment

Assessment options include take-home tests, oral vs. written tests, "second chance" tests, quantitative vs. qualitative tests, participation check sheets, etc., plus "**assessment tools**" such as rubrics, directions, and checklists, which are prepared during the lesson planning process and help teachers structure their own thinking about the lesson plan. If there is one "truism," it is that teachers should use multiple forms of assessment. In addition, teachers should not lose sight of assessment results as an important indicator of the effectiveness of a teacher's lesson planning and implementation of the lesson.

Assessment, feedback, and grading can be time-consuming, tedious work and gives rise to unpleasant encounters with students and parents. The primary goal of assessment is to give students feedback on how much they are learning and include advice on how they can improve going forward. The grade should be thought of as a shorthand statement of what is communicated in more depth in the assessment feedback. Great care should be taken in crafting written feedback as well as the words chosen during verbal feedback. Establishing and clearly communicating a teacher's assessment and grading practices to students and parents should be a top priority during the first week of school.

The foundational knowledge (declarative knowledge and application of procedural knowledge), whether in social studies or another subject field, is relatively easy to assess through traditional tests and assignments. The core civic values can be assessed during discussions and questioning based on participation. However, as stated throughout this book, social studies is unique because, unlike other subject areas, social studies education has an exalted aim. While students can be tested on the knowledge of the concepts of and the right to freedom of religion, the degree to which students value and act on a set of virtues and democratic beliefs is difficult, if not impossible, to measure while they are in school or during their lifetime. The ultimate measure of the success of social studies education is the student's long-term commitment to democratic ideals.

When students exhibit or state undemocratic notions in class, it should be subject to philosophical counseling, not assessment. It should be perceived as a flaw in logic or an ill-formed belief that a teacher should attempt to counsel the student out of. In the final analysis, social studies teachers, like counselors in group therapy, must hope what questions are considered and what is said leads to reflection and a commitment to a democratic ideology.

Because participation in civic life is essential to a democratic way of life, participation in a civic dialogue via questioning and discussions about things that matter needs to be assessed as part of the grading scheme. Tracking participation can include a checklist where a teacher's observations are recorded to reflects students' engagement in discussions and responses to questions. Students who are consistently inactive or inattentive participants should be given feedback during entry and exit of the classroom and called on more frequently to increase their participation.

The National Council for Social Studies (NCSS, 1990) urges frequent, challenging, and consistent assessment of social studies instruction; assessment of progress in knowledge, thinking skills, valuing, and social participation; and a variety of methods of assessment. The NCSS calls for evaluation instruments to:

1. Focus on stated curriculum goals and objectives.
2. Be used to improve curriculum and instruction.
3. Measure both content and process.
4. Be chosen for instructional, diagnostic, and prescriptive purposes.
5. Reflect a high degree of fairness to all people and groups.
6. Involve a variety of instruments and approaches to measure students' knowledge, skills, and attitudes.
7. Measure long-term effects of social studies instruction.

Bias Considerations and Documentation

Teachers have to guard against the subtle problem of the **halo effect**, which occurs when teachers – often unknowingly – tend to grade some students' qualitative work product more favorably than is warranted because of their positive perceptions of the student. The opposite **Golem effect** works against students who have traditionally done poorly or have behavior problems (Rowe & O'Brien, 2002). To mitigate the possibility, at a minimum, teachers should avoid looking at students' names when grading products and tests until the scores are finalized. It would be wise to communicate this practice to parents and students the first week of classes.

In addition, because parents and school districts demand "proof" beyond teachers' assertions about students' performance, there is a greater emphasis on documentation. This has led to what is sometimes referred to as "defensive assessments," in which teachers assess to document students' failures rather than as a basis to remedy them. Product examples, rubrics, and checklists become part of the detailed record keeping required of teachers. Providing rubrics, checklists, and examples clarify the expected outcomes and places more responsibility on the learner. These tools are intended to eliminate most confusion for students as to what is expected; be used to accurately and consistently assess the products or tests; and create a record for teachers to demonstrate to parents and administrators what standards the students were expected to attain. Extensive feedback on products that is demonstrably consistent can insulate a teacher from accusations of incompetence, favoritism, or prejudice.

Quantitative Assessments

If one thinks back to the one-room school house, teacher assessments were ongoing as part of the intimate personal interactions during instruction, making it possible for teachers to make judgments and give verbal feedback contemporaneously and continuously as students participated in class tasks. Quantitative paper/pencil, point-in-time assessments became a preferred mode of testing due to new technology, the ease of administering and scoring, and relative objectivity. With online technology, they have become even more popular because the scoring is completed by the technology. The following are some considerations about quantitative tests.

Fill-in-the-Blank and Completion Test Items

Fill-in-the-blank and completion items typically require simple recall.

Advantages: They are usually easy to construct; eliminate guessing; require recall of knowledge; support spelling skills.
Disadvantages: They take more time to administer and to score than true-false tests.
Advice:

1. Create an answer sheet in advance.
2. When testing for definitions, put the term in the question, and require students to supply the definition.
3. There should be no more than two blanks per question.

4. Take points off for spelling and grammatical errors, and give positive points for correct content.
5. Do not take sentences directly from the textbook.

True-False Tests Items

True-false tests may be the most widely used tests in schools because they are so easy to construct and score.

Advantages: They can cover a lot of material in a short period of time; are easy to score; provide quantitative comparative scores for students.

Disadvantages: They encourage guessing; can be poorly phrased and confusing; tend to focus on facts, although care can be taken to create higher-level true-false questions; there is little recall because key terms must be used in the item.

Advice:

1. Have no more than one concept in a question.
2. For some questions, also require additional written elaboration (this is a modified true-false item).
3. Since most students guess "true," more than half the questions should be false.
4. Avoid clues like "all," "never," and "only."
5. Avoid double negatives.
6. Avoid complex and compound sentences.
7. Avoid giving clues in the choice of grammar.
8. Avoid trivial knowledge.
9. Do not take wording directly from the text.
10. Make the test an application of critical thinking skills by providing a reading, diagram, graph, or image, and having students answer true or false.

Multiple-Choice Test Items

Multiple-choice tests have a distinct advantage over true-false tests because they require judgments among multiple answers.

Advantages: Same as true-false; work well for concepts with closely related potentially correct answers; reduce guessing possibilities and can be constructed to require the choice of the "best" answer as well as the only correct answer.

Disadvantages: Require little recall because key terms are included as options; time and skill are needed for the teacher to construct plausible wrong answers; tend to focus on facts, although higher-order test items can be created.

Advice:

1. Stems (the phrases before the possible answers) should be either questions or incomplete statements.
2. Make sure there is only one correct answer.
3. All options should be plausible.
4. Do not use "all of the above" or "none of the above."

5. An approximately equal number of correct answers should appear in each position (a test of twenty stems with four answers each should have five correct answers in the first position, and so on).
6. Four possible answers per question is a good amount. They should consist of parts of speech such as nouns and verb phrases.
7. Make the test an application by providing a reading, graph, diagram, or image, and having students make choices.

Matching Tests

Matching tests have a problem column and a response column. They can consist of terms and definitions, causes and effects, dates or people and events, and problems and solutions.

Advantages: Same as true-false; focus students on key ideas; reduce guessing possibilities; can be constructed to require choice of "best" answer as well as the only correct answer; require less paper.

Disadvantages: Require no recall; developing homogeneous columns (columns with all like items, such as names on the left and what the people did on the right) takes time and skill.

Advice:

1. Place like items in one column (like terms or people) and their matching definitions or events in the other column.
2. Number the left column and use letters for the right column.
3. Make sure there is only one correct answer.
4. Provide more items in the response column than in the problem column.
5. Keep the test to one page, with fifteen or fewer items.
6. Disperse responses throughout the list.
7. Arrange responses in alphabetical or some other logical order.
8. Keep responses short.
9. Make the test an application by providing a reading, graph, diagram, or image.

Qualitative Assessments

Qualitative assignments such as graphic organizers, the variety of writing tasks described in Chapter 29, etc., are subject to greater subjectivity during assessment than quantitative tests. The open-ended nature of such assignments requires considerably more time to score and assess. Rubrics, detailed directions, and checklists (and sometimes examples of the intended end product, refer to Chapter 29) are intended to at least partially overcome the subjectivity of students' interpretations of what is expected and teachers' assessments.

Essays and Short-Answer Responses

Essays and short essay answer assessments, arguably, provide the most insight into students' grasp of the knowledge learned.

Advantages: They eliminate guessing; reveal recall of knowledge as well as construction of knowledge; and support writing across the curriculum.

Disadvantages: They take more time to score; are more subjective; usually take more time to administer than traditional tests which can be automated with most course management systems.

Advice:

1. Create a rubric for essays for students and use the same rubric to put in the expected correct answers or components to reduce subjectivity when scoring.
2. Score one question at a time for all the students, rather than all questions for one student.
3. Take off points for errors in spelling, handwriting, and grammar, etc.; give positive points for correct content.
4. Have some questions that are required of all students and some from which students can select; but do not use optional or bonus questions.
5. One way to approach short-answer questions is to provide a "lead phrase" for students to complete. A teacher may provide leads that are based on Bloom's Taxonomy. Evaluation leads would be phrased such as "I think the most important event was ... because ..." Synthesis leads would be words such as "what if" and "I wonder." Analysis leads would use words like "it's like," "compared to," and "why would." Application leads would use words like "based on," "if ... then," and "another example of."

Rubrics

A rubric usually includes a description of a task; the components; the standards; and the point scale of the components. They should be given to students along with the directions at the time the task is assigned. Figure 31.1 provides a partially developed rubric as an example. The language in each cell would be tailored to the specific kind of assignment. There are multiple examples of rubrics on the internet that teachers can adapt to their planned assignments (see *Resources*).

When adapting or creating a rubric, assign a number and letter such as 1A, 2A, etc., in the example in Figure 31.1 for each criterion/descriptor so that it can be referred to in the teacher's comments on the assignment. The levels of performance are defined by **descriptors** (A through E in the example), which define the expectations for the quality of the student's product and the teacher's assessment. The most important part of the assessment, however, is the additional teacher feedback, verbal or written, based on the submission as compared with the assessment tools given to the student.

Checklists

A checklist of each item to be included in a project should be included with the directions and rubric. As an example, if students were to prepare a PowerPoint presentation, the directions would state the expected number of slides, number of pictures, etc. A numbered checklist should be required to be turned in with the assignment with check marks indicating the student has done a self-assessment because that promotes diligence. The checklist would be used by the teacher to score a product with a greater degree of consistency. Some detailed checklists can be used in lieu of a rubric.

Criterion	A. Superior 90-100	B. Above Average 80-90	C. Sufficient 70-80	D. Needs Improvement 60-70	E. Insufficient 0-60
1. Clarity of thesis supported by relevant information and ideas	1A The thesis is clear, supporting ideas are accurate and relevant, and accurate details support the ideas and thesis.	1B The thesis is clear and most supporting ideas and details are relevant.	1C The thesis is clear, some supporting ideas and details need to be more connected or are not relevant or too few.	1D The thesis purpose is not well-defined, ideas and details are too few or irrelevant and appear disconnected.	1F The thesis is poorly defined, lacks sufficient ideas and details.
2. Content Knowledge	2A The explicit and implicit CK is fully covered and accurately stated.	2B The explicit and implicit CK is substantially and accurately stated.	2C The explicit and implicit CK is minimally covered and accurately stated.	2D The explicit and implicit CK is incomplete and/or lacks accuracy.	2F The explicit and implicit CK is inadequate and/or lacks accuracy.
3. Quality of Argument					
4. Quality of Written Arguments					
5. Spelling and Grammar					
6. Checklist Directions					

Figure 31.1 Sample Rubric

Directions

Directions can be just verbal, but are best given in writing and explained verbally. They should include step-by-step statements that students can follow and students should be given the opportunity to ask questions before they begin working on the product.

The Wise Feedback Approach

Feedback given to students is more likely to be constructively internalized if the feedback points to the information in the assessment tools. This directs the student back to expectations and encourages greater thoughtfulness for the next assignment on the part of the student.

Positive feedback is important to encourage students to sustain excellence but rarely causes consternation for the teacher, student, or parent. The purpose of **negative feedback** is to produce a change in the student and the desired performance going forward. Tension over unwelcomed feedback can often be eased by sharing with the class the high, low, and average scores on tests and products. When giving verbal feedback, teachers should keep in mind the demeanor of a philosophical counselor (refer to Chapter 10).

Quantitative assessments provide numeric feedback, but it is also good practice when returning such assessments to make comments on the back of the paper. Patterns can be detected in the answers that can result in comments ranging from, "This is disappointing. From your answers it appears you were not able to prepare for the quiz. See me at the end of class so we can talk. I know you can do better than this," to "Well done!" Qualitative assessments typically require more feedback than just the recording of a score because the products involve writing and organizing.

Teachers should set aside time after returning tests to review them with the class if a pattern arises out of the answers of a number of students. For product assessments, teachers should plan a task that will keep students busy who do not need feedback, so the teacher can meet individually with students to reinforce negative feedback. If patterns arise in the assessment of a product across multiple students, that is an indication that there is a problem with the assessment tools or the modeling of the tasks was not well articulated. That kind of a problem should be resolved prior to final scoring to the benefit of all the students. When approached by a student unhappy with the written feedback, often it is best not to respond to a student immediately, but to ask the student to review the rubric, checklist, and directions, write the questions down about the feedback, or annotate the assessment feedback and return it and indicate that it will be given consideration. The student's annotations would allow a more focused conversation once the teacher has considered them. Cohen, Steele, and Ross (1999) and Yeager et al. (2013) urge teachers, in addition to specific feedback comments within the product where warranted, to use the three-part "**wise feedback**" statement as an overarching statement. The three parts would appear on the back of the last page of the product along with the grade:

1. **Feedback description** – The teacher describes the nature of the feedback being offered.

   Examples: "Please review my comments and the checklist," or "Please review my comments and revise by Monday after reviewing the rubric, checklist, and directions."

2. **High standards** – The teacher emphasizes and explains the high standards used to evaluate the student's work and generate the instructional feedback.

   Examples: "You will see my detailed feedback, but the submission is missing important elements of the assignment, see the checklist," or "The PowerPoint is adequate, remember the goal is to show your knowledge of the subject matter and creativity, see the rubric," or "It is a challenge to write your first essay, please review the handout on how to write an essay."

3. **Assurance of student ability** – The teacher states explicitly that the student has the skills necessary to successfully meet the criteria.

   Examples: "Your past assignments have shown that you have the skills and motivation to use my feedback to improve your PowerPoint," or "Based on your participation in class, I know you have a better understanding of this than it shows," or "I hope you can find the time to excel in the next assignment," or "I can see you put in some effort on this assignment, but you left out some key components, see comments."

Best Practices for Grading and Reporting

The following are ideas on the practicalities of how to mark up, score, and report grades. Some of the practices fit only tests while others fit products.

Grading Policies for the School Year

1. Establish a grading scale, such as A = 90–100, etc. Typically, it would be prescribed by the school or school district.
2. Establish categories and their weights: For example, 100 total points for participation; 100 points for correct answers from questioning; 200 points for tests; 200 points for products; 100 points for conduct and following directions, etc.
3. Provide for dropping the lowest grade or two in tests and products during a grading period as an alternative to make-up tests or late submission due to absences.
4. Consider whether to provide for extra tasks and points to help students make up for poor grades (this is not the same thing as giving all students the opportunity to redo or resubmit an assignment). However, extra credit can be argued to be contrary to the most basic accountability principle, i.e., that the teacher knows what every student needs to know, defines what they need to know, and assesses the student based on what they can report they learned.
5. Consider the inequity, based on an appeal, of one student being allowed more time or to resubmit an assignment due to misunderstanding of expectations, due dates, or negligence. The policy a teacher establishes at the beginning of the year for all students to request a late submission or resubmission with revisions should be applied uniformly to avoid accusations of favoritism or bias. If a teacher makes an exception to the rules for one student, the teacher needs to make it for all or run the risk of losing credibility.

Assessment Planning

6. Create the assessment during lesson planning.
7. For traditional tests, vary the value of questions based on Bloom's Taxonomy, with greatest weight to higher-level abilities.
8. For product assessments, create a rubric, checklist, example and/or detailed written directions. As stated in prior chapters, teacher coaching should be built into the process at intervals based on stages of the development of the product.

Peer Review

9. Consider having students self-assess using a rubric or check sheet to be turned in with the paper.
10. After checking that each student has created a product that meets minimum standard, consider having students peer review and edit each other's work and then revise for final submission.
11. Students should never be asked to grade other students' tests or products.

Scoring Initial Evaluation

12. Products and paper-based tests are placed in random order: Do not look at the students' names.
13. Make a cursory, initial assessment without marking and sort the papers into five stacks based on initial rating, A, B, C, D, F, for between-grade consistency.
14. Make another initial assessment of each stack for within-stack consistency.

Marking-Up

15. Start by marking and commenting on the correct answers.
16. For products, consider circling problems and assign the number and letter from the rubric, checklist, or directions where there is a problem and having students as homework re-write or explain what they think is the problem. By doing so, students learn it is more beneficial to excel the first time to avoid additional work.
17. For tests, use the same strategy requiring students to find the correct answers in their book or notes.
18. In the alternative, write comments in the form of questions, suggestions, alternative phrases, and/or referrals to assessment tools, the text, or notes that should have been taken during the lesson.
19. Assess each stack and, while doing so, move the product to another stack when warranted.
20. Record points lost or earned in pencil next to comments based on a rubric, checklist, point scale, etc., and record the overall score in pencil on the back of the paper.
21. Put the papers in point order within each stack and review to ensure in-stack consistency.
22. Modify grades should a pattern become evident that indicates the lesson was inadequate, and plan to reteach and modify the final scores accordingly.

Grading and Recording

23. Grade all papers within two days of receipt, and return them on the third day.
24. Assign the final grade by writing it in ink on the back of the last page (so students do not see other students' grades) with a final overall comment, using the wise feedback approach.
25. Put papers in alphabetical order to be returned or placed in the students' "pick-up" bin.
26. Consider a policy requiring students to have their parents sign all assessments below an average grade.
27. Have students maintain a file folder at home with all of their returned assessments.
28. Have a conference with a student who has done poorly in two consecutive assessments. If the student does poorly on the next test or assignment, call the parent: Do not wait until the school's scheduled parent-teacher conferences.

Post-Grading

29. If a student points out or the teacher recognizes a mistake in scoring across the board based on an inaccurate test item or confusion about the assessment tools' expectations, change the grades and explain why to the class. Otherwise, do not

change individual grades based on individual student appeals, unless there is a convincing argument.

30. Share with the class the high, average, and low grade on the assignment, so students can reflect on their relative success on the assignment.
31. After returning products or tests, go over items on which all students generally did less well than expected, and answer students' questions about other items. Share the consistent problems with the class as a debriefing, offering new examples and non-examples.

Resources

Videos: *TCH or YouTube:* Sharing Formative Assessment Notes; Growing from Peer Feedback; Using Tech Tools for Formative Assessment; Meeting the Needs of Diverse Learners; Making Learning Personalized and Customized; Making Feedback Meaningful; Highlighting Mistakes a Grading Strategy | *Thomas Fordham Institute*: What Teens Want from Their Schools | *USDE*: Nation Survey of High School Strategies for At-Risk Students (14 PDFs) |*YouTube:* Accommodation and Modifications for Students with Disabilities.

Documents: *Routledge Handbook of Research in Social Studies Education*: Assessment and accountability in the social studies | Differentiated Instruction | Glossary of Differentiated Instructional Strategies | *Intervention Central*: Wise Feedback; Growth Mindset Statements | K-12 Rubrics Common Core | *NEA:* 6 + 1 Trait Writing Rubric | *RCampus*: Rubric Gallery | *ReadWrtieThink:* Assessment Gallery | Common Classroom Accommodation and Modifications | *Teacher Toolkit*: Exit Ticket; Teacher; 5-3-1 Assessment; Peer Evaluations | *USDE*: Nation Survey of High School Strategies for At-Risk Students (14 PDFs).

References

Cohen, G. L., Steele, C. M., & Ross, L. D. (1999). The mentor's dilemma: Providing critical feedback across the racial divide. *Personality and Social Psychology Bulletin*, *25*(10), 1302–1318.

Cruz, B., & Thornton, S. J. (2013). *Teaching social studies to English language learners*. Routledge.

KIPP. (2020). Kipp Schools. Retrieved from https://www.kipp.org/

Muijs, D. (2020). Improving failing schools: Towards a research-based model-Stating the problem – What are failing schools. *International Congress of Effectives and Improvement*. Retrieved from www.fm-kp.si/zalozba/ISBN/978-961-6573-65-8/077-090.pdf.

NCSS. (1990). *Social studies curriculum planning resources*. Kendal/Hunt.

Reagan Foundation. (2020). Ronald Reagan. Retrieved from www.reaganfoundation.org/ronald-reagan/reagan-quotes-speeches/remarks-at-the-high-school-commencement-exercises-in-glass boro-new-jersey/.

Rowe, W. G., & O'Brien, J. (2002). The role of Golem, Pygmalion, and Galatea effects on opportunistic behavior in the classroom. *Journal of Management Education*, *26*(6), 612–628.

Benedicts S. (2020). Sant Benedicts. Retrieved from https://www.sbp.org/

Tomlinson, C. A. (2001). *How to differentiate instruction in a mixed ability classroom*. ASCD.

Yeager, D. S., Purdie-Vaughns, V., Garcia, J., Apfel, N., Brzustoski, P., Master, A., & Williams, M. (Eds.). (2013). Breaking the cycle of mistrust. Wise interventions to provide critical feedback across the racial divide. *Journal of Experimental Psychology General*, *143*, 804–824.

32 Technology, Video, and Ancillaries

Technology is just a tool. In terms of getting the kids working together and motivating them, the teacher is most important.

Bill Gates, Founder of Microsoft, 1965–present (Oxford Reference, 2020)

Digital Technology and Lesson Planning

Digital technologies' exponential pace of innovation creates significant challenges and opportunities that students and teachers will adapt to just as their predecessors have since the creation of the laptop in 1982 and the World Wide Web in 1991. Amazon's efforts in artificial intelligence through Alexa will drive demand to have one in every classroom to be consulted by teachers and students.

In its 2018 report, the National Center for Education Statistics reports that 94% of children ages 3 to 18 have access to a computer at home and 61% have internet access through either a mobile internet service or broadband land lines. Low socioeconomic status is the most significant limitation of digital technology in homes, which in turn affects schools with high levels of low socioeconomic status (SES) students. Without 100% access to the internet at home by a teacher's students, tasks to be completed as homework that require such access cannot ethically be required of students. The alternative is, for some kinds of assignment, teachers can provide the equivalent in paper form. While many students have cell phones while at school, unless all students in the class have cell phones, classroom tasks that require handheld devices cannot ethically be incorporated into lessons.

There are schools with broadband access that provide "1:1" laptops assigned to each student and digital textbooks placed on the school's laptops that are lent to every student and that are taken home on a daily basis. Other schools have computer carts or labs so that teachers can plan classroom lessons that integrate technology. Regrettably, some schools have not yet reached even this standard. However, one can envision a day in the not too distant future where all schools will not only have the 1:1 laptop model and will subsidize internet access at home for every student through contracts with cable providers using the free lunch model now used for low SES students. Such a model would dramatically open up opportunities for students to take even more responsibility for their learning outside of class and for teachers to plan investigations knowing all students have equal access to technology. Such a uniform platform would allow the focus in classrooms to be on democratic discussions of things that matter and the practice of modes of reasoning and basic skills rather than the initial transmission of knowledge – because the baseline of information could be consistently learned at home. As an example, the use of video on demand about content by expert teachers, if available to all students, would make it possible for the "Flipping the Classroom" model (see Vanderbilt Center for Teaching, 2020) to be a consistent practice. The hallmark of this kind of instructional choreography is the teacher, as the "sage on the stage," is replaced by an expert on video that is required to be watched at home as the content presentation. The classroom time is then dedicated to practice with coaching by the teacher to individuals and groups, peer-to-peer coaching and, most important for social studies, the discussion of things that matter. Without 100% access to a computer and the internet at home, teachers must use the technology of expert-prepared videos, games, simulations, etc., from the internet in class.

The following three examples describe integration of technology into lesson plans where there is not 100% access.

Lower elementary civics – During a lesson on the American Revolution, students would take a virtual field trip to the Betsy Ross House (search Betsy Ross House) with the teacher moderating using a large TV screen in whole-class instruction or students in a computer lab or with laptops completing a list of pages to be read and activities to be completed. The teacher would debrief the field trip and website and lead a discussion of the differences between folklore and history. The lesson would be integrated with art by completing the art project of a five-pointed star described at the website and also be integrated with music by learning the history of the national anthem through the Smithsonian's Star-Spangled Banner website or one of the 63 million hits when searched for in Google.

Upper elementary history/anthropology – Like the example above, students would watch *Crash Course World History* "Rethinking Civilization" on YouTube and be debriefed by the teacher. "The Emergence of Civilization" lesson plan and "Odyssey" online from the Michael C. Carlos Museum of Emory University (2020) would have been modified by the teacher as the lesson. At the computer lab or on laptops, students would complete two online activities to explore the emergence of civilization. The first is an introduction to analyzing objects and what they can tell us about a culture. The second asks the students to organize ancient objects into an "exhibition" about the elements of a civilization. The teacher would debrief the activities, and lead a discussion about objects the students might suggest for a time capsule.

Middle school geography – Students watch the YouTube video "Maps and Compass Navigation Part 1" as the first part of the lesson to learn the basic geography skill of navigation. This would be followed by a second activity-based content presentation based on the CPALMS website lesson plan, "Mapping my way around school."

High school economics – The teacher creates a lesson based on the PBS lesson and the included videos, "How the deck is stacked" as a template. Students also watch the YouTube video by *Crunch*, "Is the inequality gap really widening?" *Crunch* videos emphasize data-driven decision-making. The class period could be dedicated to what the data says and a discussion of its relevance to consideration of democratic ideals related to poverty and wealth.

Videos

Videos appeal to multiple senses with sound and images. Videos as well as podcasts, sound recordings, etc., are so familiar to students that it is almost a given that teachers will use this technology in the classroom. Since 2015, the percentage of young people who watch online videos every day and the amount of time they spend doing so has risen sharply. For 8–12-year-old students the number has doubled to 56% and for 13–18-year-old students it is now 69%. The amount of time spent watching online videos has increased to almost an hour a day (NCES, 2018, 2019). Students with the financial resources to afford handheld devices with unlimited plans have an undisputable advantage over students without such resources in finding videos to help with school work to be completed outside of class.

Radio, then television, and now the internet's extensive portfolio of professionally developed, targeted videos on skills such as how to change the oil in a car to the kind of social studies educational topics in the resources in this book is still in the early stages of changing how humans gather information and learn skills. Digital technology has already put in place the possibility that anything that can be read in a book can be replaced with audio books or a video with voiceover, diminishing the traditional role of reading in formal learning. And it costs less. The transition from a culture based on reading since Guttenberg to the digital technology created in the late 1950s will certainly require changes to the way we, even currently, use technology in learning. Alexa, by Amazon, is in its infancy, and such artificial intelligence will place an even greater emphasis on listening skills. No doubt the NCSS will soon find a need to update the essential skills (see Figure 12.2 and 28.1) to give much stronger weight as to how to "close" listen and watch videos as an educational enterprise.

Viewing videos in the classroom should not be the same experience as the passive experience of consumers viewing feature films in theaters, at home on the television, or on handheld devices. In using a video, the teacher should follow the same kinds of close reading protocols used with documents and images. The video should be previewed by the teacher during planning, integrated into the lesson, played for or watched by the students on digital devices, and then debriefed. As part of the lesson, students should be guided as to what to look for and to record their observations on a rubric or in a prescribed note-taking or narrative form as the video is being played (see *Resources, National Achieves*).

Feature films can give students a sense of a period in history, can graphically depict characters from history, and can dramatize historical events. Videos of news broadcasts can serve as a basis for case studies, depictions of current social issues, and declarative information. Documentaries from sources such as National Geographic and the History Channel provide vivid details, rich visual images, and background information of history, other countries, cultures, and geographic regions. Animated features often provide ideas that matter for values analysis.

In spite of the merits just listed, video is arguably the most misused technology in the classroom. A growing number of teachers show videos of animated features and shorts and other films as rewards or as entertainment while they perform other duties. This is a questionable use of valuable instructional time.

Best Practice for Video

1. The **key clips approach** is the best practice for use of films, newscasts, and documentaries because it is effective, efficient, and appropriate to students' attention spans, and it ensures that the video is grounded in a lesson (Duplass, 2010). In this approach, the teacher shows only about a 10-minute clip of the video to make

a very specific point related to the lesson. For example, the movie *Glory* is a compelling dramatization of the Civil War. It would not be a good practice to show the entire movie, either in segments over a number of days or at one sitting because it would use up too much valuable class time and the movie provides too much information that is not relevant to a lesson plan on slavery and the Civil War. With the key clips strategy, the following three approaches to using *Glory* in a lesson plan could be legitimately used. One or more clips could be chosen to depict:

A.   The period dress (hoop skirts, soldiers' uniforms, slaves' ragged clothing) and transportation (carriages, trains), so the students better understand the time period;

B.   The bravery of the African American soldiers related to a democratic ideal of duty to a principle;

C.   The democratic ideal of sacrifice of the character played by Matthew Broderick, who chose to lead the former slaves at risk to his own career and whose loyalty compelled him to lead his men into a situation that meant his own almost-certain death.

2.   Video must be integrated into a comprehensive lesson plan and include a preview and debriefing.

A.   Video quick clips can be used as an attention-getter to stimulate students' interest. For example, a recording of the Gettysburg Address or a clip of a movie showing an actor portraying Lincoln delivering the Gettysburg Address could be used to gain students' attention and interest in learning about one of America's notable figures and speeches.

B.   Video can be used as a content presentation or part of a content presentation. For example, a National Geographic video clip of the Amazon rainforest could be integrated into a lesson on the environment.

Ancillaries

Ancillaries cover all those kinds of resources for teaching that are mostly found by an internet search and at a book publisher's restricted website. They include "**consumables**" that serve as handouts such as downloadable PDFs and MSWord documents of graphic organizers, maps, tests, worksheets, primary documents, images, etc.; online games, interactive maps, virtual tours, etc.; and comprehensive lesson plans with consumables, WebQuest, background knowledge webpages, and documents for the teacher, etc., to adapt to their lesson plans. Consumables such as handouts of graphic organizers (excluding most "hunt and find" worksheets) are effective because they require the application of critical thinking or procedural knowledge and the demonstration of that knowledge with a skill. As an example, creating a timeline is a skill that reflects critical thinking about what events to include by a judgment about their importance to the purpose of the story to be told by an analysis of the timeline, all of which is an application of history procedural knowledge. Some of the following websites are cited in earlier chapters, but are included in Figure 32.1 as part of a short list of recommended websites for new teachers so that they do not feel they have to "reinvent the wheel."

Website	Description
American Heritage Education Foundation	Free membership and can download two over 200-page books of lesson plans, content and ideas for civics.
Annenberg Classroom	Includes 65 videos on the Constitution's' concepts and Supreme Court cases as well as games, lesson plans, timelines, etc.
The Avalon Project	Includes all the major documents of history, law and diplomacy since 400 BCE.
CIA World Factbook	The World Factbook provides information on the history, people and society, government, economy, energy, geography, communications, transportation, military, and transnational issues for 267 world entities.
Civics Renewal Network	Over 1300 lesson plans, videos, and resources for Civics and American History.
Common Core Resources for History and Social Studies	This website is a compendium of resources for middle school history and social studies teachers endeavoring to meet the Common Core State Standards with creative, student-centered activities and lessons
Core Knowledge	Has extensive, detailed lesson plans with full sets of disposables for history, civics, and geography focused on grades K-6 and typically integrated with extensive reading and writing.
Crash Course YouTube Channel	Hundreds of colorful, fast-paced videos designed more for elementary and middle school and organized into World and US History, Economics, U.S. Government and Politics, and psychology.
Digital History	Has lesson plans, handouts, quizzes, primary sources, maps, digital stories, historical music, etc.
Econedlink	The most extensive collection of lesson plans, games, and simulations on personal finance and economics, tied to standards, and can be sorted by grade level.
EDSITEment	Over 500 lesson plans and activities from the National Endowment from the Humanities.
EuroDocs	A gateway website to significant documents by country.
EdTechTeacher	A gateway website organized by lesson plans, maps, games and animations and historical periods and categories.
Fordham Internet Modern History Sourcebook	A gateway website of information from Reformation to present (includes section on history in movies).
ICivics	Lesson plans and games to teach Civics.
IUE Gateway to History United States	A gateway website of information on U.S. History.
IUE World History	A gateway website of information on World History.
Google Graphic Images	Over 100 graphic images
HistoryTech	25 brief lesson strategies explain in evidence and analysis from cartoons to films
Holt Rinehart and Winston Reading Strategies for the Social Studies Classroom	10 comprehensive strategies.
Kahn Academy humanities	

Figure 32.1 Key Websites

	Hundreds of lesson plan ideas and videos for students on history, geography, government, economics, sociology, philosophy, anthropology, and psychology.
Library of Congress Printable Worksheets	Over 2000 printable worksheets for every grade level.
Library of Congress Digital Collections	Photographs, music, motion pictures, manuscripts.
Library of Congress classroom materials lessons	Among the most comprehensive lessons working with primary source documents.
Library of Congress World Digital Library	Thousands of primary document images organized chronologically by historical periods.
National Archives Document Analysis Worksheets	24 high-quality worksheets to analyze videos, photographs, artwork, posters, etc.
National Geographic Resource Library	Thousands of lesson plans, maps, activities, and videos can be sorted by grade level and geography, social studies, anthropology, and conservation.
NCSS Notable Trade Books	From 2000 to 2019, the best trade books for elementary and middle school social studies.
Perry-Castañeda Library Map Collection	Historical maps by time periods and geographic areas.
PBS	Has 100s of videos, lesson plans, and consumables that can be sorted by subject and grade level.
Public Agenda	Nonpartisan research on current issues.
ReadWriteThink	43 reading and writing strategies. Over 100 social studies reading and writing strategies.
Scholastic Social Studies Graphic Organizers and Mini-Lessons Robeson	15 lesson strategies with completed examples of the downloadables.
Smithsonian	Has online games and activities for K-12 students and lesson plan ideas and resources for teacher.
Social Studies Central	A gateway to social studies resources such as primary source documents, audio files of eyewitness accounts, map machines, etc.
Stanford History Group Reading Like an Historian	Over 150 lesson plans and printables.
Teaching History.Org	A gateway to multiple resources and history content, as well as best practices.
WebQuest Garden	WebQuest is a structured approach to self-directed learning and there are over 20,000 WebQuest lesson plans available at this site.
World History Matters	A gateway to history content for use in the classroom.
World History Timeline	This clickable online timeline is organized by people, history, politics, science, culture, religion, events, and maps by time periods with summary captions.

Figure 32.1 (Cont.)

Resources

Videos: *EdTechReview*: Assistive Technologies in the Classroom | *Learner.org:* Essential Lens – Analyzing Photographs Across the Curriculum | *YouTube*: PBS What a Flipped Classroom Looks Like.

Documents: *Routledge Handbook of Research in Social Studies Education*: Technology and Social Studies | *Wiley Handbook of Social Studies Research*: The Diffusion of Technology | *National Achieves*: Document Analysis Worksheets (26 different worksheets to use) | *NCSS:* Technology Position Statement and Guidelines | *TCH:* Teaching Email Etiquette; Taking a Leap into Blogging; Using Tablets for Teaching Sensitive Subjects; Preparing Youth for Civics & Politics in the Digital Age; Creating Digital Stories; Tweet to Share Your Learning; Podcasting to Personalize Feedback.

References

Duplass, J. (2010). *Teaching elementary social studies: Strategies, standards, and internet resources* (3rd ed.). Wadsworth Cengage Learning.

Michael, C. & Carlos Museum of Emory University. (2020). *Teacher resources.* Retrieved from https://carlos.emory.edu/htdocs/ODYSSEY/Teachers/ll/Lesson_Plans/Civilization/CivOverview.html & https://carlos.emory.edu/teacher-resources

National Center for Education Statistics (NCES). (2018). *Digital access to digital learning resources outside of the classroom.* Retrieved from https://nces.ed.gov/pubs2017/2017098/index.asp.

National Center for Education Statistics (NCES). (2019). *Common sense media.* Retrieved from www.commonsensemedia.org/about-us/news/press-releases/the-common-sense-census-media-use-by-tweens-and-teens-new-research).

Oxford Reference. (2020). *Interview with Bill Gates.* Independent on Sunday. 1997 Oct. 12. Retrieved from www.oxfordreference.com/view/10.1093/acref/9780191826719.001.0001/q-oro-ed4-00012282.

Vanderbilt Center for Teaching. (2020). *Flipping the classroom.* Retrieved from https://cft.vanderbilt.edu/guides-sub-pages/flipping-the-classroom/

Conclusion

In the University of South Florida application process for the Master of Arts in Teaching (MAT) initial certification degree in social studies education, students must submit an essay indicating what influenced their decision to consider becoming a teacher. Eric H. Hollaway II authorized me to share his statement with you. It is included in the book with the hope that it will inspire you to be an ambitious teacher of social studies and a philosophical counselor.

> Mr. Murphy [pseudonym] was not a typical teacher. It was 2005 and he couldn't have been older than a quarter of a century. He was tall with an athletic build. He had jet black hair that he would spike up with gel and a New York accent that was thicker than molasses. He was never cleanly shaven, maintaining a perpetual 5 o'clock shadow. He was unusual. Aside from the way Mr. Murphy looked or carried himself as a teacher, there was something else that set him apart. From day one he always saw me. When I say that he saw me – I don't mean it in a literal sense; he was not blind. I had felt patronized many times by teachers I interacted with. It was almost as if I was wearing a sign on my forehead that only they could read. That sign said "FAILURE." I have always been perceptive and I never missed a thing. He always saw me and believed in my potential and he wasn't shy in telling me when he felt I was squandering it. He would tell me that it didn't matter what color I was or what economic situation I was born into. He preached that if I wanted to succeed then I could not give in to the temptation of viewing myself as a victim who was owed something by this unfair and cruel world. In my entire K-12 experience, he is the only person that I felt had ever treated me as if I was a unique person and not a black boy. He never had expectations of failure for me even though popular statistics at the time might have justified having them. I have never forgotten how it felt to have a teacher who cared about me. He was invested in my success and unabashedly held me accountable when I messed up.
>
> I want to be Mr. Murphy, a social science expert who chose to judge others by the content of their character. I would care and be invested in the success of my students who might be invisible to others. I want them to know that I see them.
>
> Eric H. Hollaway II

The Student Is the Subject

Index